BIBLICAL AFFIRMATIONS
OF WOMAN

Published by The Westminster Press

LEONARD SWIDLER
Biblical Affirmations of Woman

LEONARD SWIDLER
ARLENE SWIDLER
Ed. and Tr.
Bishops and People

Biblical Affirmations of Woman

by
LEONARD SWIDLER

THE WESTMINSTER PRESS
Philadelphia

Excerpts from *The Jerusalem Bible* are copyright © 1966 by Darton, Longman & Todd, Ltd., and Doubleday & Company, Inc. Used by permission of Doubleday & Company, Inc.

BOOK DESIGN BY DOROTHY ALDEN SMITH

First edition

Published by The Westminster Press ®
Philadelphia, Pennsylvania

PRINTED IN THE UNITED STATES OF AMERICA

9 8 7 6 5 4 3 2 1

Library of Congress Cataloging in Publication Data

Swidler, Leonard J
   Biblical affirmations of woman

   Includes index.
   1. Women (Theology)—Biblical teaching.
2. Women in the Bible. 3. Woman (Theology)—History of doctrines. I. Title.
BS680.W7S97   261.8'34'12   79–18886
ISBN 0–664–21377–4
ISBN 0–664–24285–5 pbk.

Contents

PART TWO

WOMAN IN HEBREW-JEWISH TRADITION

PART THREE

WOMAN IN CHRISTIAN TRADITION

Introduction

In the past there have been a number of discussions of women in the Bible. At times they have been flawed by an apologetic approach that assumed, unconsciously or consciously, a male chauvinist perspective. In any case, they did not have the advantage of the raised collective consciousness and new insights resulting from the recent women's liberation movement and its interaction with religion and theology. Usually the first result of this interaction has been the leveling of criticism at portions of the Judeo-Christian tradition for its sexism. This was not difficult to do as far as having sufficient subject matter was concerned; the Jewish and Christian traditions— as the traditions of every other world religion and parareligion—are extremely sexist. The cultures from which these religions sprang were strongly patriarchal, and the religions reflected those cultures. This sexism was also true of the Bible.

All Jewish and Christian biblical scholars, save the most fundamentalistic, insist on the humanness of the Scriptures, that they are human words spoken in a particular time, place, and culture, all of which limiting factors must be understood if the inspired revelation of God's self is to be perceived through them. Gone from modern religious scholarship is the precritical notion that each word of the Bible was whispered in the inner ear of the inspired writer by God; the Bible is no longer perceived as inerrantly true word by word— only the inner religious message is, whatever it may be. Consequently the way is clear to point out critically the sexist patriarchal assumptions, structures, stories, sayings, etc., bountifully to be found in the Bible. This negative, critical task was surely the first that needed to be done—as in all creative reform efforts. And it has been done significantly, though of course the critical task needs to continue: *Traditio religiosa semper reformanda!*

However, in creative reform, an emphasis on the positive elements is also necessary as an early second task, even as the negative critical task proceeds. This positive reform task is by no means the same as the old defensive apologetic. Rather, it accepts, presumes, the proven negative criticisms and moves on to discern the true positive values in the tradition that can be used as building blocks in re-forming the inherited religious structures, adding on to them, or indeed, building new ones from the heritage of the old.

This book is an attempt to search out the positive elements of the biblical tradition as far as women are concerned (which of course immediately means that men are concerned too); to bring them together in one place; to quote them in full (unfortunately most hurried modern persons will not reach for a Bible and look up the chapter and verse references); and to provide a context and brief commentary that will lift up their significance and implications as far as woman, her relationship to herself, to man, and to God are concerned.

The book is thought of primarily as a sort of "companion," a vade mecum, which can be read in snippets as time and inclination allow, as one way for modern people to get into the riches of the biblical tradition and profit by its deeply human, and at times even surprisingly "feminist," insights and values. However, this book is so designed that it can likewise be read in longer sittings so that an overview of developments can also be gained. Alternatively the book can also serve as a reference tool for those wanting to look up a "feminist" perception of certain passages or books.

Though the main purpose of this book is to present and exegete those passages of the Bible and kindred material which are judged by the author to be of positive orientation as far as women are concerned, it was felt that to do only that would project a dangerous distortion. To those readers not familiar with the negative critical work done on the Bible mentioned above, an unreal impression, an unwarrantedly positive image of the attitudes toward and status of women in the Bible would be given. To avoid that disservice to many readers, a very brief survey of the negative aspects of the Jewish and Christian biblical traditions will also be provided, as well as a discussion of ambivalent portions of the biblical traditions.

Bible is meant here in a somewhat extended sense. It includes the Hebrew Bible, or Old Testament, and the Apostolic Writings, or

New Testament. But just as the Apostolic Writings are in many ways a commentary on or interpretation of the Hebrew Bible, so also are the Rabbinic writings (Mishnah and Talmud). Hence, they will also be dealt with here. That will bring us to around the year 500 C.E. (of the Common Era). But just as the Rabbinic writings are to the Hebrew Bible, so also the writings of the early Christian fathers (of roughly the same time period as the Mishnah and Talmud) are to the Apostolic Writings (New Testament). Hence, they also will be treated, but in a briefer fashion since they do not carry anything like the weight of authority in Christianity that the Mishnah and Talmud carry in Judaism. The Jewish religious writings composed in the period between Old and New Testaments, namely, the Apocrypha and Pseudepigrapha, will also be covered, as well as the documents of fifth-century B.C.E. Elephantine Judaism. In parallel fashion the apocryphal New Testament and Gnostic Christian writings will likewise be investigated.

The translation of the Bible basically used throughout is usually that of the Jerusalem Bible. However, on numerous occasions its translators (and those of all other available translations as well) have, slightly or badly, missed meanings that are very important for an accurate understanding of some passages in relationship to women—and men. The author himself, therefore, has not hesitated to translate many words or whole passages from the original Hebrew or Greek.

A word should be said here about the term "feminist," which to some extent has become sloganized, positively and negatively. The term is used in this book purely in its descriptive sense. That is, a feminist is understood to be a person who is in favor of and promotes the equality of women with men, a person who advocates and practices treating women primarily as human persons—as men are so treated. Obviously men who claim to favor justice should be feminists as well as the women. This book, then, is written to help all feminists, potential and actual, female and male. To the extent that it does so, it will serve all humanity.

Prologue: Women in the Ancient World

The land of Palestine lies in the center of the fertile crescent of the ancient Near East. The fertile crescent extended from the lower end of the Tigris and Euphrates rivers in the east (Sumer, in present-day Iraq), up through present-day Syria and Lebanon, and down through Palestine, with Egypt and the Nile valley at its western tip. Civilization developed about the same time at the two extremities, Sumer in the east and Egypt in the west, and the status of women in both civilizations was relatively high in their early periods. Before 2400 B.C.E. in Sumer, polyandry (more than one husband to a wife) was at times practiced; some women also owned and controlled vast amounts of property, enjoyed some laws that in effect prescribed something like equal pay for equal work, and were able to hold top rank among the literati of the land, and to be spiritual leaders of paramount importance. In Egypt, during the third and fourth, and into the fifth dynasties (2778–2423 B.C.E.), when the highest level of culture of the Old Kingdom was reached, daughters had the same inheritance rights as sons, marriages were strictly monogamous (with the exception of royalty) and tended to be love matches; in fact, it can be said that in the Old Kingdom the wife was the equal of the husband in rights, although her place in society was not identical with that of her husband.

However, in the east, in the land of Mesopotamia, "Between the Rivers," the Sumerian civilizations gave way gradually during the last quarter of the third millennium B.C.E., bowing to successive conquerors—Akkadia, Babylon, and Assyria. Here the lot of women declined drastically. For example, the Babylonian Code of Hammurabi (1728–1636 B.C.E.) and similar codes permitted men to repudiate their wives for any or no reason, though the woman was able to divorce the

13

husband only for very serious cause; indeed, even if in such a case a wife were a "gadabout," her life was forfeit: "If she was not careful, but was a gadabout, thus neglecting her house [and] humiliating her husband, they shall throw that woman into the water" (Codex Hammurabi, 143). For complete documentation on the above paragraphs, see Leonard Swidler, *Women in Judaism: The Status of Women in Formative Judaism,* pp. 4f.; Scarecrow Press, 1976). This general trend is confirmed by the reports on the analyses of the excavations of the ancient Mesopotamian city of Mari, where for a short period in the first half of the eighteenth century B.C.E. some women enjoyed a relatively high status.

There can be no doubt that men were culturally dominant. . . . A cultural bias against women is revealed by incidental disparaging remarks sprinkled throughout these texts about the weak, unheroic character of women. . . . In the matter of male dominance, Mari was in accord with the general Mesopotamian culture. The surprising fact, then, is not that women were regarded as inferior but that they were able to attain the great prominence that they did.

This political prominence of women in Mari and upper Mesopotamia stands in contrast both to their role in succeeding periods in Mesopotamian history and to the role of their contemporaries in lower Mesopotamia. . . . Lamentably, the cultural standing of women deteriorated in succeeding periods of Mesopotamian history. (Bernard Frank Batto, *Studies on Women at Mari,* pp. 136–138; Johns Hopkins University Press, 1974)

The status of women also declined at the western tip of the fertile crescent, in Egypt, with the disintegration of the Old Kingdom in 2270 B.C.E. Eventually, however, it rose again, so that in Egypt, over the almost three-thousand-year history before the coming of Alexander the Great in 330 B.C.E., the status of women was quite high for about fifteen hundred years, corresponding with strong central governments. The periods of high status were, broadly speaking, 3000–2270 B.C.E., 1580–1085 B.C.E., and from 663 B.C.E. into the Greco-Roman period until the dominance of Christianity around 375 C.E. Thus, Jacques Pirenne could write: "We have arrived at the epoch of total legal emancipation of the woman. That absolute legal equality between the woman and the man continued to the arrival of the Ptolemies [Hellenistic successors to Alexander the Great] in Egypt" (Jacques Pirenne, "Le Statut de la femme dans l'ancienne Egypte," *La Femme. Recueil de la Société Jean Bodin,* XI, 1, p. 76; Brussels, 1959). Though taking a somewhat more pessimistic view, Jean Vercoutter is in large agreement when after his extensive history of women in ancient Egypt he concludes:

If all the sources are in agreement that, everything considered, the woman in Egypt was subordinate to the man, that her duty was to please him, give him children and care for his house, it also appears that in turn custom allowed women a large freedom: they could go out freely and if perchance they owned some goods they would become the equal of the man in order to assure its management. In this sense the condition of the female Egyptian was superior to that of the Greek, for example, and when with the Macedonian conquest Hellenistic customs and then Roman penetrated the Nile valley the female Egyptian lost many of the privileges which she had acquired little by little. It would indeed take centuries for that relative liberty which Egyptian women enjoyed to again be their lot. (Jean Vercoutter, "La Femme en Egypt ancienne," in Pierre Grimal, ed., *Histoire mondiale de la femme,* Vol. 1, p. 152; Paris: Nouvelle Librairie de France, 1965)

When we shift our focus to the world of Hellas, we also find women enjoying a relatively high status in the early period of Greek civilization, as in the Minoan culture of Crete (3000–1100 B.C.E.) and the Greece of the time of the Homeric poems (before 900 B.C.E.). But there too women's status declined, reaching a low point during the Golden Age of Greece, in the fourth and fifth centuries B.C.E. —though a distinction would have to be made between Athens, where women had a very inferior status, and Sparta, where they had great freedom.

But after the spread of Greek culture by Alexander the Great around 330 B.C.E. from Egypt to the Indus River, the lot of women gradually improved. We can trace a growing movement for women's liberation with the passage of time in this Hellenistic world, so that in general women were more nearly equal to men in rights by the time of the New Testament than they had been in 300 B.C.E. Likewise, in general, greater freedom for women could be found the farther west one traveled. Naturally these are overall descriptions which admit of variations in details, but they are basically valid.

Let us look at least at some of the most important indicators of this women's liberation movement in Hellenistic culture. In fifth-century Greece marriage was monogamous, but the husband was allowed sex with *hetaerae* (courtesans) and concubines. By 311 B.C.E. we find a marriage contract from the Greek island of Cos:

Contract of Heracleides and Demetria. . . . He is free, She is free. . . . It is not permitted to Heracleides to take another woman, for that would be an injury to Demetria, nor may he have children by another woman, nor do anything injurious to Demetria under any pretext. If Heracleides be found performing any such deed, Demetria shall denounce him. . . . Heracleides will return to Demetria the dowry of 1000 drachmas, which she contributed, and he will pay an additional 1000 drachmas in Alexandrian silver as an additional fine. (O. Rubensohn, *Elephantine-Papyri*, No. 1; Berlin, 1907)

Women in Hellenistic times also exercised extensive rights in the economic sphere. A woman could inherit a personal patrimony— equally with her sons—buy, own, and sell property and goods, and will them to others. Indeed, in Hellenistic times there were wealthy Greek women, some of whom were greatly honored for their philanthropy. Klaus Thraede summed the matter up when he wrote: "The emancipation of the woman in private law was decisive for the development which began already in the classical period: the equalization in inheritance and property rights as well as the de facto independence in marriage and divorce" ("Frau," *Reallexikon für Antike und Christentum,* col. 199; 1973).

Unlike the Greek (Athenian) wives of the classical period, who did not even eat with male guests when they were in their own homes, let alone go out in mixed gatherings, the wives of the Hellenistic period were quite likely to turn up at social gatherings *(symposia),* and women went on long journeys. Whereas earlier it was customary for only Spartan women to participate in sports, including the Olympics, women's involvement in this area advanced in later Hellenistic times to the point where there were women professional athletes, as, for example, the three daughters—Tryphosa, Hedea, and Dionysia—of Hermesianax of Tralles, who engaged in foot and chariot races in the years 47 to 41 B.C.E. Many women pursued music as a profession. Asia Minor was known for its women physicians, though according to Pliny the Elder much of the information about these women physicians was deliberately suppressed. On the level of skilled artisans, a woman often pursued a craft similar to her husband's, e.g., a woman goldsmith and a man armorer—or think of Priscilla, who with her husband Aquila was a tentmaker (Acts 18:3).

In an advanced civilization the key to advanced status is education; by itself it will not accomplish everything, but without it usually little will be possible. Whereas in classical Athens among women usually only the *hetaerae* had any kind of education, education for young girls became ever broader and more widespread throughout the Hellenistic period, and one result was that more and more wives as well as husbands were educated. In fact, in Hellenistic Egypt there were more women who could sign their names than men, and thus Hellenistic literature, particularly the novel, was written for a feminine public. Another result of the broader Hellenistic education of women was the appearance of a flood of Hellenistic women poets.

It is perhaps most of all in that discipline of the spirit for which the Greeks are most renowned, philosophy, that one can see the striving for women's liberation. In the seventh century many women were students of Pythagoras. But by the fourth century Plato and Aristotle paid only lip service to equality for women. However, in the Hellenistic period women again took up the study of philosophy. For example, we know that one of Aristotle's followers, Theophrastus (d. 287 B.C.E.), had both a woman disciple, Pamphile (some of whose writing is extant), and a woman opponent, unfortunately anonymous. Thereafter to some extent the Cynics also spoke out in favor of equal rights for women, and women played a prominent role in the school of Epicurus (343–270 B.C.E.), not only as disciples but even as favorite teachers.

But the philosophical school which did most to promote the improved status of women was that of the Stoics. These grassroots philosophers stressed the worth of the individual woman, the need for her education (consequently there were many women followers of Stoicism), strict monogamy, and a notion of marriage as a spiritual community of two equals. The Roman knight C. Musonius Rufus, a contemporary of Philo the Jew and the apostle Paul, discussed at length whether women should also pursue philosophy and whether daughters should be brought up the same as sons; he answered yes to both questions.

In religion and cult, women in classical Greece, i.e., during the fifth century B.C.E., experienced restrictions that were broad, but by no means absolute. There were a number of religious activities or places that they could not enter upon, as, for example, the very important oracle of Delphi or the cult of Hercules; and usually only maidens, not married women, could watch the sacred games at Olympia. Women were also almost entirely absent from, or were kept in the background of, the activities of state religion. Still, in some cults, such as those of Artemis and Dionysus, women did play a significant role.

In the Hellenistic period, however, the extraordinary popularity of the eastern cults and mystery religions and the burgeoning women's liberation movement dramatically changed the situation. Women not only took part in these religious cults, they often did so in great numbers and often in leading and even priestly roles, as, for example, in the Eleusinian, the Dionysian, and the Andanian mysteries. The cult of the goddess Isis, which came from Egypt but spread all over the Hellenistic and Roman world, was at the beginning of its popularity exclusively a women's cult, and even after men were admitted it still provided women with leading religious roles and justly had the reputation of being a vigorous promoter of women's equality and liberation.

The Hellenistic world was largely conquered by the Romans a century or so before the birth of Jesus. Although it was the Hellenistic cultural world that exercised the greatest outside influence on Judaism and Christianity, the influence of Rome was also present in its own way, i.e., mostly political, legal, and military, from the time of Pompey's conquest of Palestine in 63 B.C.E. Hence, it is proper to note briefly the condition of women among the Romans.

Behind the culture of Rome there stood the extraordinarily developed culture of the Etruscans, stretching in space from Rome up to Pisa, and in time from before the seventh into the third century B.C.E. We find in Italy, as in Minoan Crete, a civilization characterized by a preeminence of women. Everywhere women were at the forefront of the scene, playing a considerable role and never blushing from shame, as Livy says of one of them, when exposing themselves to masculine company. In Etruria it was a recognized privilege for ladies of the most respectable kind, and not just for *hetaerae* as in Greece of the contemporary classical period, to take part with men in banquets, where they reclined as the men did. They attended dances, concerts, and sports events and even presided, as a painting in Orvieto shows, perched on a platform, over boxing matches, chariot races, and acrobatic displays.

Women, of course, did not enjoy such a high status in contemporary Greece, nor did they in early Rome. But by the third century B.C.E., Rome moved to improve the property rights of women. Somewhat later in the republic, doubtless because of the influence of the Etruscan culture and the growing pressure of the women's liberation movement in Hellenism, the condition of women improved to the point where a woman could in general marry and divorce on her own initiative and even choose her own name. During the same period the image of leading women appeared on coins—for the first time. The Roman Cornelius Nepos (d. 32 B.C.E.) even felt that the advanced status of Roman women was something to boast about: "What Roman would find it annoying to be accompanied by his wife to a banquet? Or what housewife does not take the first place in her house or go about in public?"

The status of women continued to improve dramatically under the empire. Indeed, the political activity of women of the senatorial class developed so vigorously that we find on the walls of Pompeii the names of women running for office, a definite advance over Egyptian and Greek women, who had few political rights; women were sent on imperial missions to proconsuls; the possibility of a woman consul was even discussed. Nevertheless, it is basically true to say that "only the men exercised the political rights of citizens: military service, voting at the assemblies of the people, access to magistratures" (Jacques-Henri Michel, "L'Infériorité de la condition féminine en droit romain," *Ludus Magistralis,* No. 46, 1974, p. 7).

Women were everywhere involved in business and in social life— i.e., theaters, sports events, concerts, parties, traveling—with or without their husbands. They took part in a whole range of athletics and even bore arms and went into battle.

In family affairs one would have to speak of a certain equality of the sexes in daily life. The woman's consent was necessary for marriage; in an increasing number of marriages *(non in manu)* she had no obligation to obey, nor did the husband have any legal power over his wife. Speaking of this kind of marriage, one scholar noted that "the married woman without *manus* was without doubt the most emancipated wife in the history of law!" (Michel, "L'Infériorité de la condition féminine," p. 6). From the point of view of money the pattern increasingly was one of equality and of separation. The equality of the spouses was in effect total, whether concerning the full liberty of divorce in classical law, the limiting causes of that liberty in the late empire, or the sanctions of an unjustified divorce.

Republican Rome, acting originally under the influence of Etruscan culture, took up the impulse of women's liberation from Hellenism and carried it forward to where the empire (30 B.C.E. onward) also made it its own and continued to promote it ever further throughout the first several centuries of the Common Era. This evolving liberation of women in Roman society was expressed in the legal forum by that extremely influential Roman jurist in the second century of the Common Era, Gaius:

It would appear that there is scarcely any very persuasive reason for women of adult age to be in tutelage. For the common notion that because of the levity of their minds they are often deceived and that therefore it is fitting that they be placed under the authority of tutors would appear to be more specious than true. In fact women of adult age conduct their own business for themselves, and in certain cases, for the sake of form only the tutor gives his authorization. Indeed, even if he refuses it he is often forced to grant it

by the praetor. (Gaius, *Institutes* 1.190)
[Quoted in Latin and French by Michel, in "L'Infériorité de la condition
féminine," p. 13, who remarked, "Perhaps this text, which deserves to be
better known, . . . should figure one day in some feminist pantheon." For
an excellent overview of the history of women in Greco-Roman society, see
Sarah B. Pomeroy, *Goddesses, Whores, Wives, and Slaves: Women in Classical Antiquity;* Schocken Books, 1975.]

In sum: The status of women in the ancient world of the fertile
crescent after the early Sumerian period was almost uniformly low
except in Egypt, where it was early and often quite high. In the
classical Greco-Roman world (after the Minoan and pre-Homerian
Greek periods) the condition of women was varied, but often quite
restricted, with the clear exception of Etruscan culture. It nevertheless improved, particularly during the Hellenistic period, so vigorously
and continually that one must speak of a women's liberation movement which had a massive and manifold liberating impact on the lot
of women—not everywhere and in every class and at every period
equally effective, of course. This improving impulse was picked up
and carried forward by Rome. In fact, the general rule in this matter
is that the farther west one goes, the greater is the freedom of women
—though in detail there are the greatest possible variations—and
that also in general there is a progression in the freedom for women
according to time. Thus, as the women of Rome tended to be freer
than those of Greece, who were more liberated than women of the
oriental world, so also the women of the time of the Roman empire
had greater freedom than those of the time of the Roman republic,
and their sisters in the Hellenistic world and period were less restricted than those of Greece at the time of the Athenian empire.
Due account must be taken, of course, of the unsympathetic vagaries
of all human history, and the fact that in so many ways the liberation
of women was long since anticipated in ancient Sumer, Egypt, Minoan Crete, and later also in Etruria.

It is in this context and under this surrounding and pervading
influence that the biblical traditions, Jewish and Christian, developed.

I. Feminine Imagery of God–
Biblical Period

A. A FEMININE GOD

Although the Hebraic tradition early perceived God to be transcendent, beyond limitations, including sex, it nevertheless persisted in referring to God in terms and images that included sexuality. It is inevitable that this would happen, for so many things which humans value highest are found in other human beings (who normally are female or male)—such as being a knowing, loving person—that to speak of God as "It" would denigrate God. Thus the tradition often speaks of God in masculine—and feminine—images, although it also continues to affirm God's transcendence of sexuality and all else, following the apophatic way, the *via negativa,* what the Hindus call the path of *neti neti* (not this, not that). The masculine images of God in the Hebrew Bible are well known (e.g., God as father, jealous husband, warrior). They are far more pervasive throughout the Bible than feminine imagery of God, reflecting that patriarchal, male-oriented society. But the feminine divine imagery is there too, albeit in a much lesser degree. A selection of it will be given below. In order to appreciate better the trajectory which some of the female imagery of God followed, examples of how this imagery developed into the early Christian as well as the early Jewish era will be presented below in their chronological places.

But first it would be helpful to spell out in a little detail something of the Goddess-worshiping culture that lay behind, around, and within the biblical religion.

§1. Goddess Worship

The earliest evidence we have of human religious activity in the Old World points to the worship of the Goddess—the divine would seem to have first been worshiped as female. The archaeological excavations at the upper paleolithic levels (25,000–8,000 B.C.E.) have produced innumerable female statuettes that appear to be either figurines of the Goddess or perhaps at least attempts at sympathetic magic, endeavoring to induce the fertility that all life depended on (see Edwin O. James, *Prehistoric Religion,* pp. 147, 153; Barnes & Noble, 1961; J. Edgar Bruns, *God as Woman, Woman as God,* pp. 8–10; Paulist /Newman Press, 1973). There would appear to have been *no male God* at this early period (see Edwin O. James, *The Cult of the Mother Goddess,* pp. 21f.; Frederick A. Praeger, 1959). As the paleolithic period gave way to the mesolithic (8,000–4,000 B.C.E.) and the neolithic (4,000–2,500 B.C.E.), the worship of the Goddess became even more vigorous and explicit. All of the Old World areas that cradled major civilizations (i.e., complex societies in which towns and cities, and the differentiation of culture that accompanies them, developed) show strong evidence of having initially been Goddess-worshiping. That includes the Indus Valley, the Near East, Old Europe (i.e., the Balkans, Asia Minor, and the Eastern Mediterranean islands), and Egypt.

The gradual shift away from total dominance of the Goddess (except perhaps with Egypt, whose history is even more complex than the others) to the participation of a clearly subordinate male God seems to have been connected with the development of animal husbandry, whence the role of paternity became apparent. There never was any question about the female's essential role in bringing new life into the world; but the role of the male and sex was not always so obvious. Still, even at this stage the male God played a vastly subordinate role vis-à-vis the Goddess.

The role of the God, however, in a number of instances advanced to that of an equal and even that of a superior of the Goddess, apparently under the impact of waves of attacks of patriarchal, male-God worshiping, animal-herding Indo-Europeans who came down out of the northern mountains, perhaps originally from around the Caspian Sea (see James, *Cult of the Mother Goddess,* pp. 47, 99, 138). They appear, e.g., as Hittite conquerors of Anatolia, sometime before 2,000 B.C.E., ranging eventually down into Palestine. In the second millennium B.C.E. the patriarchal father-God worshipers swept into almost all the Goddess-worshiping civilizations, from the Indus Valley on the east through Mesopotamia and Asia Minor to Old Europe on the west (see H. R. Hays, *In the Beginnings,* pp. 209f.; G. P. Putnam's Sons, 1963). Perhaps only Egypt was unconquered by the patriarchal Indo-Europeans, though even it was dominated at times by Asian nations that were probably "carriers" of Indo-European patriarchal ideas, e.g., the Hyksos in the seventeenth and sixteenth centuries B.C.E. Marija Gimbutas describes in detail the world of the early Goddess worshipers in Old Europe and notes that "it is then replaced by the patriarchal world with its different symbolism and its different values. This masculine world is that of the Indo-Europeans, which did not develop in Old Europe but was superimposed upon it. Two entirely different sets of mythical images met. . . . The earliest European civilization was savagely destroyed by the patriarchal element and it never recovered, but its legacy lingered in the substratum" (Marija Gimbutas, *The Gods and Goddesses of Old Europe,* p. 238; University of California Press, 1974).

§2. Male-God Invaders

A little should be noted about the characteristics of the God of those Indo-European tribes who over a period of centuries, perhaps starting in earnest in the latter half of the third millennium B.C.E., invaded in waves all of the existing civilizations. He was a father God, a warrior God, a supreme God, a God who dwelt in light and fire, on a mountaintop (the Indo-Europeans came from a mountainous area and perhaps originally worshiped volcanoes). He took the Goddess of the conquered nation as his heavenly consort and soon (usually) totally dominated her, as the Indo-Europeans dominated the conquered peoples. The Indo-European dead were said to dwell in "realms of eternal light," in "glowing light, light primeval." Their God was described as "he whose form is light." The Sanskrit word for God, *dev,* literally means "shining" or "bright." And in Iran, God—Ahura Mazda—was a great father who was referred to as the Lord of Light, dwelling on the top of a mountain, glowing in golden light; this mountain is supposedly Mount Hara, the first mountain ever created. In Greece there was the Indo-European Zeus with his fiery lightning and thunderbolts on top of Mount Olympus; the Indo-European Hittites and Indo-European-ruled Hurrians had storm Gods with lightning bolts in their hands standing on a mountain; Indra of India, glowing in gold, holding a lightning bolt, was called Lord of the Mountains. Almost none of this was characteristic of the Goddess (see, e.g., Merlin Stone, *When God Was a Woman*, pp. 72, 114; Dial Press, 1976).

§3. Yahweh, a God of Mountain and Light

Much of the imagery connected with the Hebrew God Yahweh is startlingly similar to the Father of Lightning, dwelling on a mountaintop, of the Indo-European patriarchal people. Consider the following:

> [And Moses said to the people of Israel:] "Do not forget the things your eyes have seen; . . . rather, tell them to your children. . . . The day you stood at Mount Horeb in the presence of Yahweh your God, . . . you came and stood at the foot of the mountain, and the mountains flamed to the very sky, a sky darkened by cloud, murky and thunderous. Then Yahweh spoke to you from the midst of the fire; you heard the sounds of words but saw no shape, there was only a voice. . . . Since you saw no shape on that day at Mount Horeb when Yahweh spoke to you from the midst of the fire, see that you do not act perversely, making yourselves a carved image in the shape of anything at all, whether it be in the likeness of man or of woman* . . . for Yahweh your God is a consuming fire. . . . Did ever a people hear the voice of the living God speaking from the heart of the fire, as you heard it, and remain alive? . . . He let you see his great fire, and from the heart of the fire you heard his word. . . . These are the words Yahweh spoke to you when you were all assembled on the mountain. With a great voice he spoke to you from the heart of the fire, in cloud and thick darkness . . . while the mountain was all on fire." (Deut 4:9–12, 15–16, 24, 33, 36; 5:22–23)
>
> *[In fact the Israelites did later make an image, a golden calf, a widespread image in Egypt of the Goddess.]

There are of course many, many other references to Yahweh as a pillar of fire (Ex 13:21), Father of lights (Jas 1:17), as "wrapped in a robe of light" (Ps 104:2), as one asked to "touch the mountains, make them smoke, flash your lightning" (Ps 144:5), and as a rock (Ps 18; 19; 28; 31; 42; 62; 71; 89; 92; 94); and it is on Mount Zion that he is to be worshiped, though the northern tribes of Israel argued for Mount Gerizim. Yahweh is very often imaged as a father, a warrior God who slays his enemies in battle, the supreme creator of all; and in Elephantine Judaism the goddess Anath was the consort of Yahweh (see §5).

Exactly what connection there might be between the patriarchal Hebrews and their God Yahweh and the patriarchal Indo-Europeans and their Gods remains unclear. But whatever the direct connections may or may not be, it is clear that the stance of both patriarchal peoples and their theologies vis-à-vis the religion of the Goddess would be, and was, very similar—hostile.

§4. Hebrews Worship the Goddess

The Yahwists struggled for hundreds of years to suppress the worship of the Goddess among the Hebrews. In tracing the history of this struggle, it should be noted first that in the Land of Canaan the Goddess worship was quite diversified by biblical times, so that there were at least three names of the Goddess: Anath, Astarte, and Asherah, who were subordinate to the male god Baal. (These three were probably originally one; Asherah is the Canaanite name for the earlier Sumerian goddess Ashratum, the consort of the god Anu, who closely corresponded to the Canaanite god El—a name for God also used by the Hebrews in many forms, e.g., El, Elohim—see §22—as they were both the God of Heaven; see William F. Albright, *Archaeology and the Religion of Israel,* p. 78; Johns Hopkins Press, 1942. Astarte is related to the Babylonian goddess Ishtar, and she in turn to the Sumerian Inanna.)

There have been thousands of female figurines, many of which represent the Goddess, dug up all over Palestine at pre-, early, and middle biblical levels, though little in the way of male-God figurines (see Raphael Patai, *The Hebrew Goddess,* pp. 58–61; KTAV Publishing House, 1967).

Kathleen M. Kenyon *(Archaeology in the Holy Land,* p. 214; Frederick A. Praeger, 1960) in writing of the Late Bronze Age states that "the Astarte plaques . . . are the most common cult object on almost all sites of the period. . . . Tell Beit Mirsim [in Palestine] itself provides clear evidence for the occurrence of such plaques or similar figurines right down to the 7th century B.C. The denunciations by the prophets are enough to show that Yahwehism had continuously to struggle with the ancient religion of the land." Although biblical texts give us only a glimpse of the pervasiveness of the Goddess worship among all the Hebrews, mostly by way of condemnations of it by Yahwist prophets and destruction of Goddess images, etc., by reforming Yahwist kings, it is worth outlining this history briefly to gain some sense of the implacable fury vented by the Yahwists on the Goddess worshipers.

In the time of the Judges (before 1000 B.C.E.) the people of Israel stopped worshiping Yahweh and served the Baals and Astartes (Judg 2:13). Later Solomon (961–922) "worshiped Astarte, the goddess of Sidon" (1 Kings 11:5). Then the prophet Ahijah said: "Yahweh the God of Israel says to you, 'I am going to take the kingdom away from Solomon. . . . I am going to do this because they have rejected me and have worshiped Astarte, the goddess of Sidon' " (1 Kings 11: 31–33). In the next generation Ahijah said to the wife of Jeroboam, king of Israel (922–901), that "Yahweh will punish Israel . . . because they have aroused his anger by making idols of the goddess Asherah" (1 Kings 14:15). Meanwhile in Judah the people "put up stone pillars and symbols of Asherah to worship on the hills and under shady trees. Worst of all there were cult prostitutes (sing. *qadesh*) in the land. And they imitated all the abominations of the people Yahweh had thrown out before the Israelites came" (1 Kings 14:23f.). Then in Judah the next king, Asa (913–873), "expelled from the country all Temple prostitutes *(qedeshim)* from the land and removed all the idols his fathers had made. He removed his grandmother Maacah from her position as queen mother, because she had made an obscene idol of the goddess Asherah. Asa cut down the idol and burned it in the Kidron valley" (1 Kings 15:12f.). In the next generation King Ahab (869–850) of Israel "put up an image of the goddess Asherah" (1 Kings 16:33). "At that time there were at least four hundred prophets of Asherah" (1 Kings 18:19) in Israel. Under King Jehoahaz (815–801) the people of Israel "still did not give up the sins into which King Jeroboam had led Israel, but kept on committing them; and the image of the goddess Asherah remained in Samaria" (2 Kings 13:6). The Goddess cult in the Northern Kingdom apparently continued, for in 721 when Israel fell to the Assyrians it was recorded that it fell "because the Israelites sinned against Yahweh their God. . . . They worshiped other gods. . . . On all the hills they put up stone pillars and images of the goddess Asherah" (2 Kings 17:7-10).

The Bible redactors report somewhat more favorably on the attempts at reform led by some of the kings of Judah, but in the process indicate the pervasiveness and persistence of the Goddess worship among the Hebrews. After early reforms under King Joash (837–800) of Judah it was said that the "people stopped worshiping in the Temple of Yahweh, the God of their ancestors, and began to worship idols and the images of the goddess Asherah" (2 Chron 24:18). Goddess worship obviously continued until King Hezekiah (715–687) of Judah "broke the stone pillars and cut down the image of the goddess Asherah" (2 Kings 18:4). But his own son Manasseh followed as king and "made an image of the goddess Asherah" (2 Kings 21:3). Then came the last great reform efforts before the exile, under King Josiah (640–609) of Judah, who "removed from the Temple the symbol of the goddess Asherah, took it out of the city to the Kidron valley, burned it, pounded its ashes to dust. . . . He destroyed the living quarters in the Temple occupied by the Temple prostitutes. It was there that women wove robes for the Asherah" (2 Kings 23:6–7).

All three of the greater prophets mention the worship of the Goddess. The oldest, Isaiah, predicts around 735 B.C.E. that when Yahweh punishes Israel the people "will no longer rely on altars they made with their own hands, or trust in their own handiwork—symbols of the goddess Asherah" (Is 17:8). At another place he adds that "Israel's sins will be forgiven only when the stones of pagan altars are ground up like chalk, and no more symbols of the goddess Asherah or incense altars are left" (Is 27:9). Ezekiel, who traditionally is said to have been active around the time of the fall of Jerusalem a generation after King Josiah in 586, reported being shown "at the inner entrance of the north gate of the Temple an idol that was an outrage to God" (Ezek 8:3). In line with most scholarship the New American Bible notes here that "this was probably the statue of the goddess Asherah erected by the wicked King Manasseh—cf. 2 Kgs 21:7; 2 Chr 33:7, 15. Though it had been removed by King Josiah—2 Kgs 23:6—it had no doubt been set up again." In the same vision Ezekiel reported on a sight three times more abominable, namely, at the north gate of the Temple were "women weeping over the death of the god Tammuz" (Ezek 8:14; a part of a seasonal ritual in which the death of plants in fall was likened to the descent into the nether world by the subordinate male god Tammuz, to be triumphantly restored to life in spring by the source of life, the goddess Astarte—or Ishtar in Babylonian or Inanna in Sumerian traditions).

Some years before, Jeremiah complained that the people of Judah "worship at the altars and symbols that have been set up for the goddess Asherah by every green tree and on the hill tops and on the mountains in the open country" (Jer 17:2–3). Later the same prophet Jeremiah was taken with the remnant of Judeans, after the Babylonian destruction of Jerusalem in 586, into Egypt. He berated the people for having brought on the disaster by worshiping other Gods. Who the "other God" was is made clear by the people's response:

Then all the men who knew that their wives offered sacrifices to other gods and all the women in the crowd . . . said to me, "We refuse to listen to what you have told us in the name of Yahweh. We will do everything that we said we would. We will offer sacrifices to our goddess, the Queen of Heaven*, and we will pour out wine offerings to her, just as we and our ancestors, our king and our leaders, used to do in the towns of Judah and in the streets of Jerusalem. Then we had plenty of food, we were prosperous, and had no troubles. But ever since we stopped sacrificing to the Queen of Heaven and stopped pouring out wine offerings to her, we have had nothing, and our people have died in war and starvation." And the women added, "When we baked cakes shaped like the Queen of Heaven, offered sacrifices to her, and poured our wine offerings to her, our husbands approved of what we were doing." (Jer 44:15–19)

*[Anath-Astarte was addressed as Queen of Heaven in Egypt—Patai, *Hebrew Goddess*, p. 55.]

The Oxford Annotated Bible also links this Queen of Heaven with the Babylonian Ishtar and the Canaanite Astarte (likewise with the Greek Aphrodite and Roman Venus), and states that "the cult was especially popular among women, who had an inferior role in the cult of the LORD [Yahweh]. . . . The cult persisted into the Christian centuries, and features of it were incorporated by the early Syrian church in the adoration of the Virgin." It is clear from the Jeremiah text that the women too were "priests" in the ancient Hebrew cult of the Queen of Heaven.

§5. Hebrew Goddess at Elephantine

Probably from around this time onward a colony of Jews lived at Elephantine, Egypt, an island in the Nile river, opposite Aswan, about four hundred miles south of Cairo. From their papyrus letters and documents of the late fifth century B.C.E. we know not only that the Jewish women as well as men contributed money to the Temple, and that the women could divorce their spouses as well as the men could, but also that in the Temple along with Yahu (as Yahweh was addressed there) the goddess Anathbethel was also worshiped (Arthur E. Cowley, *Aramaic Papyri of the Fifth Century* B.C., p. 72; Oxford: Clarendon Press, 1923).

The name Anath-Bethel literally means "Anath the House of El [the God of Heaven]"—cf. Cowley, *Aramaic Papyri*, p. 72. Since in Hebraic culture a wife is referred to as the husband's "house," this name suggests that the goddess Anath was understood as the "God of Heaven's" consort. This is further confirmed by the fact that Yahu (derived from a variant of an older spelling of Yahweh) is called the "God of Heaven" in the same Elephantine papyri (ibid., p. 114) and that Anath is often referred to as the "Lady of Heaven," especially in Egyptian culture (see Patai, *Hebrew Goddess*, p. 55). Still further, the Jewish writings of Elephantine also include an oath to Yahu and to Anath, "consort of Yahu": "He swore to Meshullam b. Nathan by Yahu the God, by the temple and by Anathyahu" (Cowley, *Aramaic*

Papyri, p. 148). (Alternatively, Kraeling suggests that Bethel in Anath-Bethel is simply an alternative name for Yahu, and offers reasons—Emil G. Kraeling, ed., *The Brooklyn Museum Aramaic Papyri,* pp. 88–90; Yale University Press, 1953.)

Moreover, it is likely that refugees from Bethel, some fourteen miles north of Jerusalem, played an important part in the development of this syncretistic worship in Elephantine Judaism, for Bethel was known not only as a place where Yahweh was early worshiped; Bethel was a place where later the Goddess was also worshiped, as indicated by the calf image there (cf. e.g., Hos 10:5—the cow, the calf, was a symbol of the Goddess, the source of life, fertility; see James, *Cult of the Mother Goddess,* p. 81). After describing temples of the Goddess and of Yahweh alongside each other at Tell-en-Nasbeh in Palestine, Edwin O. James goes on to state:

> This equipment suggests that it was a centre of the Goddess cult where Astarte was worshipped, probably in later times alongside of Yahweh at the neighbouring shrine, possibly as his consort. If this were so, the goddesses under Canaanite names (e.g., Anath-Yahu comparable to Yo-Elat in Ugaritic texts) assigned to Yahweh in the Jewish community at Elephantine after the Exile can hardly have been an innovation. (James, *Cult of the Mother Goddess,* p. 80)

§6. Goddess Worship "Suppressed"

After the return of the Jewish people to Jerusalem from the Babylonian exile the public worship of the Goddess seems to have been successfully suppressed, being relegated largely to feminine manifestations of God as in the postexilic Wisdom books' praise of the feminine Hokmah (Hebrew) or Sophia (Greek), "Wisdom," and the growing reference to God's feminine Presence, Shekinah, an Aramaic term first found after the beginning of the Christian Era in Rabbinic and Targumic writings. One of the high-cost ways this was accomplished was by the banning of intermarriage. By this time Jewish women in any case normally could not marry non-Jews; Jewish men also were not supposed to marry non-Jewish women, though in fact they did. The reason foreign wives were not to be taken is that they were seen as the source of corrupting Goddess worship, e.g., Jezebel and her worship of Asherah and Baal. This enforcement of the Deuteronomic prohibition (Deut 7:1–4) took the drastic form of the divorce and driving out by the Jewish men of their non-Jewish wives and children (Ezra 9 and 10; cf. Neh 13:23–28). Despite all the efforts, however, to eliminate the feminine dimension of the deity, it persisted in biblical writers perhaps far more than is often realized. Some examples follow.

§7. God a Seamstress

Already in the most ancient part of the Bible, the Yahwist's story of the Fall, one finds Yahweh performing a customarily female task in Hebrew society (cf. Prov 31:10–31): Yahweh God acts as a seamstress:

> And Yahweh God made tunics of skins for the man and his wife and clothed them. (Gen 3:21)

§8. God Mother and Nurse

When the Israelites in the desert complained of their problems to Moses, he in turn complained to Yahweh with rhetorical questions that by negative implication project onto Yahweh the images of a mother and a wet nurse—and this also in the ancient Elohist-Yahwist portion of the Bible.

> Was it I who conceived all this people, was it I who gave them birth, that you should say to me, "Carry them in your bosom, like a beloved little mother with a baby at the breast?" (Num 11:12)

§9. God a Loving Mother

While the eighth-century prophet Hosea makes heavy use of the image of Yahweh as the husband of a faithless Israel, he also projects Yahweh in the image of a parent teaching a child to walk, healing its hurts, feeding it—all tasks a mother, not a father, normally performed in that society. Yahweh further frets and agonizes over the wayward child, but in the end declares in favor of mercy instead of deserved punishment by clearly rejecting any identification with the male—*ish*, meaning male, is the term used.

> When Israel was a child I loved him, and I called my son out of Egypt. ... I myself taught Ephraim to walk, I took them in my arms; yet they have not understood that I was the one looking after them. I led them with reins of kindness, with leading-strings of love. I was like someone who lifts an infant close against his cheek; stooping down to him I gave him his food. ... I will not give rein to my fierce anger, I will not destroy Ephraim again, for I am God, not man *(ish)*. (Hos 11:1, 3, 4, 9)

§10. God Who Gave Birth to Humanity

In the last book of the Pentateuch, Deuteronomy (possibly seventh century), in the Song of Moses, God describes herself in clearly feminine, motherly imagery (if the first verb is understood in the less likely paternal sense, then an androgynous parental image of God is projected):

> You were unmindful of the Rock that bore you *(yiladeka)* and you forgot the God who writhed in labor pains with you *(meholeleka)*. (Deut 32:18) [Note: *yiladeka* almost always means "that bore you," and only rarely can mean "begot," as it is almost always translated—see P. A. H. DeBoer, *Fatherhood and Motherhood in Israelite and Judean Piety*, p. 52; Leiden: E. J. Brill, 1974.]

§11. Humanity in Yahweh's Womb — I

In Hebrew, *rechem* means womb. The plural form, *rachamim*, extends this concrete meaning to signify compassion, love, mercy. The verb form, *rchm*, means to show mercy, and the adjective, *rachum*, means merciful. Thus to speak of compassion or mercy automatically calls forth maternal overtones. This motherly compassion is attributed to God in a number of places; it is especially striking in a passage from Jeremiah, a seventh-century prophet. After a careful, penetrating analysis, Phyllis Trible *(God and the Rhetoric of Sexuality*, p. 45; Fortress Press, 1978) provides a translation of the passage that is much more accurate and sensitive to the Hebrew poetry in general and the words related to *rechem* in particular. In the last line Yahweh speaks of herself with the doubly uterine words *rachem, arachamennu*, "motherly womb-love."

> Is Ephraim my dear Son? my darling child?
> For the more I speak of him,
>   the more do I remember him.
> Therefore, my womb trembles for him;
>   I will truly show motherly-compassion
> *(rachem arachamennu)* upon him.
>   Oracle of Yahweh (Jer 31:20)

§12. Humanity in Yahweh's Womb — II

The above passage of Jeremiah is a key one in a larger poetic structure where the very form expresses a superiority of the female over the male in that the male came forth from the female's womb, is "surrounded by" the female, therefore. The passage Jer 31:15–22 reaches its climax with the statement: "For Yahweh has created a new thing in the land: female surrounds [*tesobeb*] man." (v.22) This "female surrounding man" has manifold referents: Rachel the mother embracing her sons (v.15), Yahweh consoling Rachel about Ephraim (vs.16–17), Yahweh proclaiming motherly compassion for

Ephraim (v. 20), the *daughter* Israel superseding the son Ephraim
(v. 21).

[Words of a *woman*]
  A voice is heard in Ramah,
  lamenting and weeping bitterly:
  it is Rachel weeping for her children
  because they are no more.
[Words to a *woman*]
  Yahweh says this:
  Stop your weeping,
  dry your eyes,
  your hardships will be redressed:
  they shall come back from the enemy country.
  There is hope for your descendants:
  your sons will come home to their own lands.
[Words of a *man*]
  I plainly hear the grieving of Ephraim,
  "You have disciplined me, I accepted the discipline
  like a young bull untamed.
  Bring me back, let me come back,
  for you are Yahweh my God!
  Yes, I turned away, but have since repented;
  I understood, I beat my breast.
  I was deeply ashamed, covered with confusion;
  Yes, I still bore the disgrace of my youth."
[Words of a *woman*—Yahweh]
  Is Ephraim my dear son? my darling child?
  For the more I speak of him,
  the more do I remember him.
  Therefore, my womb trembles for him;
  I will truly show motherly-compassion upon him.
[Words to a *woman*—Jeremiah's commands]
  Set up signposts,
  raise landmarks;
  mark the road well,
  the way by which you went.
  Come home, virgin of Israel,
  come home to these towns of yours.
  How long will you hesitate, disloyal daughter?
  For Yahweh has created a new thing in the land:
  female surrounds man. (Jer 31:15–22)

As Phyllis Trible notes (*God and the Rhetoric of Sexuality*, p.
50): "The very form and content of the poem embodies a womb:
woman encloses man. The female organ nourishes, sustains, and
redeems the male child Ephraim. Thus our metaphor is surrounded
by a cloud of witnesses."

§13. God in Birth Pangs

This feminine divine imagery is, if possible, intensified in the middle of the sixth century by Second Isaiah through whom Yahweh God speaks of herself as crying out with labor pains—a *ne plus ultra* in feminine divine imagery.

Yahweh God goes forth. . . . "But now, I cry out as a woman in labor, gasping and panting." (Is 42:13, 14)

§14. Israel in the Womb of God the Mother

Yahweh continues, in the mouth of Second Isaiah, to liken herself to a mother, describing her concern for exiled Israel as that of a mother for her own baby:

Listen to me, house of Jacob and all the remnant of the house of Israel who have been borne by me from the belly *(beten)*, carried from the womb *(racham)*, even until old age I am the one, and to gray hairs am I carrying you. Since I have made, I will bear, carry and save. (Is 46:3–4)

§15. God a Nursing Mother

Yahweh goes on, through Second Isaiah, to liken her loving memory of Zion to that of an affectionate mother with a child at the breast.

For Zion was saying, "Yahweh has abandoned me, the Lord has forgotten me." Does a woman forget her baby at the breast, or fail to cherish the son of her womb? Yet even if these forget, I will never forget you. (Is 49:14–15)

§16. God a Comforting Mother

Third Isaiah expresses the words of Yahweh wherein she again likens herself to a mother consoling her son. As Phyllis Trible notes (*God and the Rhetoric of Sexuality*, p. 67): " 'So I *('anoki)* will comfort you.' The use of the first-person pronoun, *'anoki*, stresses the divine agent. Although the comparison stops just short of calling God mother, it does not stop short of this meaning. Yahweh is a consoling mother to the children of Jerusalem."

For thus says Yahweh: . . . Like a son comforted by his mother, so will I comfort you. (Is 66:12–13)

§17. God a Mother and a Father

Elsewhere Third Isaiah projects Yahweh with both maternal and paternal imagery. This androgynous balance is lost in most translations, but Phyllis Trible's analysis and translation makes the alternation between the God of the womb and God the Father clear (*God and the Rhetoric of Sexuality*, p. 53):

> Yahweh, . . . where is your ardor and your might,
> the trembling of your womb and your compassion?
> Restrain not yourself, for you are our Father. (Is 63:14–15)

§18. Yahweh the Midwife

In Ps 22:9, Yahweh is depicted in an intimate female role, that of a midwife:

> Yet you drew me out of the womb,
> you entrusted me to my mother's breasts. (Ps 22:9)

§19. Mistress Yahweh

The psalmist projects an image that by association likens Yahweh to both a master and a mistress.

> I lift my eyes to you,
>   to you who have your home in heaven,
> eyes like the eyes of slaves
>   fixed on their master's hand;
> like the eyes of a slave-girl
>   fixed on the hand of her mistress,
> so our eyes are fixed on Yahweh our God. (Ps 123:2)

§20. God Motherlike

In The Psalms there is also an image of a motherly Yahweh who comforts her weaned child, the psalmist, on her divine motherly lap:

> O Yahweh, . . . I have calmed and quieted my soul like a weaned child,
> like a weaned child on its mother's lap. (Ps 131:1, 2)

§21. God a Mother and a Father Even in Irony

In the early fifth-century Book of Job an ironic rhetorical question is put to Job. He is asked whether the dew and frost have a father and a mother. The answer is both, "no, for they come from God," and "yes, they both come from God": it is through human imagery that we come to a knowledge of the transcendence of God (see Trible, *God and the Rhetoric of Sexuality*, pp. 67f.).

> Has the rain a father?
> Who begets the dewdrops?

What womb brings forth the ice,
    and gives birth to the frost of heaven? (Job 38:28–29)

§22. "Androgynous" God

Throughout much of the Hebrew Bible the word used for the notion "God" is *'elohim.* This is one of the three Hebrew variants, *'el, 'eloah, 'elohim* (*'elah* in Aramaic portions of the Bible), which usually are used interchangeably (similar words are used in the rest of the ancient Semitic world for the deity, e.g., Akkadian *ilu*, Arabic *'ilah*). Of special interest is that Elohim is plural (which is reflected in the occasional plural verb forms used, e.g., Gen 1:26), probably coming from the singular feminine form of the word for God, Eloah (*ah* is a singular feminine suffix; *im* is a plural suffix that can be feminine or masculine). There is likely a residue of a very ancient Semitic female God, Eloah, a male God, El, and a court of female and male Gods, Elohim, reflected in this Hebrew biblical usage. This intermixing of masculine and feminine forms for God by the biblical writers indicates both a combining of sexual images in God, and a transcending of all sexuality. The combining of feminine and masculine forms seems to be the first phase, and the transcending of sexual forms the second phase.

The first, combining, phase in God is reflected by God's image, humanity, and is underscored by the Priestly writer when he writes: "and God (Elohim) said, 'Let *us* make humanity *(adam)* in *our* own image, in the likeness of *ourselves.*'. . . And God (Elohim) created humanity *(ha adam)* in the image of himself, in the image of God (Elohim) he created it, male and female he created *them*" (Gen 1:26–27). Then, just as humanity is sometimes spoken of in a sexually undifferentiated, or androgynous, sense, sometimes in reference to the female portion, and sometimes in reference to the male portion, so too the God of the Bible is sometimes spoken of as female (Eloah), as male (El), and as "androgynous" (Elohim, in Gen 1:26–28).

All these reasons point at a God and a Goddess as subject of "We shall make people." God, pictured as a king with a court, making heaven and earth through royal strength, makes man. The ancient believer recognised man's fertility and power as a gift of his God who himself is male and female. Only if man is conscious of holiness in his being man and woman might he be able to understand that a conception of God: Father and Mother, guarantee of life and existence, is no blasphemy but expression of true faith. . . .
Praying to God, "Our Father who art in heaven" and forgetting the Mother of all living, is inadequate. Praying to "Our Mother who art in earth" [recall the ancient references discussed above to Mother-earth, source of life]

and forgetting the fatherly authority, is likewise inadequate. Due to what became visible of divine Fatherhood and Motherhood in ancient Israelite and Judean piety we ought, I think, to pray to God's totality, respectfully desiring to belong to his family. (DeBoer, *Fatherhood and Motherhood in Israelite and Judean Piety*, pp. 46–53)

B. DIVINE LADY WISDOM

The ancient biblical literature about Wisdom was written in Hebrew (Proverbs; Job 28); some of it, however, we know largely through its early Greek translation (Ben Sira—also called Sirach or Ecclesiasticus; Baruch); some later Wisdom literature, however, was composed originally in Greek (the Book of Wisdom—also called the Wisdom of Solomon). Baruch, Ben Sira, and Wisdom are accepted by Catholicism and Orthodoxy as part of the Bible; Judaism and Protestantism place them outside the canonical Bible, in the so-called Apocrypha.

It is in these five books that the feminine divine Wisdom is presented. Wisdom is feminine not only grammatically (*hokmah* in Hebrew and *sophia* in Greek) but also in the way she is depicted in this literature, i.e., as a woman (for example, in Proverbs she is Lady Wisdom in contrast to Dame Folly—Prov 9:13). It should also be remembered that in Hebrew both the adjectives and verb forms reflect the feminine gender of the subject—this in addition to the *ah* feminine ending of the noun *hokmah*. All of this makes the Hebrew reader of the following passages constantly aware of the feminine quality of divine Wisdom, Hokmah. Lady Wisdom, Hokmah, is also doubtless the Hebrew expression of the ancient Goddess that has been biblically canonized, for the Goddess was widely worshiped as the source of all knowledge and wisdom, particularly in the symbol of the Serpent Goddess, as mentioned below in §76. The highly respected scholar Hans Conzelmann, after careful analysis, concluded similarly: "Personified Wisdom's . . . predecessor is the syncretistic goddess which is most widely known under the name of Isis." (Hans Conzelmann, "The Mother of Wisdom," in James M. Robinson, ed., *The Future of Our Religious Past*, p. 243; London: SCM Press, 1971.)

§23. Feminine Wisdom—Quasi-Divine

In the oldest book of the biblical Wisdom literature by far, Proverbs, this feminine Wisdom, Hokmah, at times has a quasi-divine quality; she is like an attribute of God.

I, Wisdom (Hokmah), am mistress of discretion,
    the inventor of lucidity of thought.
Good advice and sound judgment belong to me,
    perception to me, strength to me.
. . . .
Yahweh possessed me when his purpose first unfolded
    before the oldest of his works.
From everlasting I was firmly set,
    from the beginning, before earth came into being.
. . . .
I was by his side, a beloved little mother*
    delighting with him day after day. (Prov 8:12, 14, 22, 23, 30)

§24. A Feminine Personification of God

In Proverbs, Wisdom, Hokmah, is also personified, a feminine
dimension of God that literally takes on a separate existence. It is
clearly a feminine image of the divine, just as fatherhood is a masculine image. In the beginning of the book of Proverbs, Hokmah issues
her warning to the ignorant.

Wisdom calls aloud in the streets,
    she raises her voice in the public squares;
she calls out at the street corners,
    she delivers her message at the city gates,
"You ignorant people, how much longer will you cling
        to your ignorance?
    How much longer will mockers revel in their mocking
    and fools hold knowledge contemptible?
Pay attention to my warning:
    now I will pour out my heart to you,
    and tell you what I have to say.
Since I have called and you have refused me,
    since I have beckoned and no one has taken notice,
since you have ignored all my advice
    and rejected all my warnings,
I, for my part, will laugh at your distress,
    I will jeer at you when calamity comes,
when calamity bears down on you like a storm
    and your distress like a whirlwind,
    when disaster and anguish bear down on you.
Then they shall call to me, but I will not answer,

*This difficult word is so translated by P. A. H. DeBoer: " 'Beloved little mother'
is a rendering of the Hebrew *'mwn*, read as *'immôn*, a hypocoristicon for *'ēm*, mother,
possibly a love-name for the beloved and inspiring consort. Wisdom, merry, making
sport before the Lord, is a remarkable line of this wonderful poem of which is said,
there is here 'a fleeting suggestion of marital joys' " (DeBoer, *Fatherhood and Motherhood in Israelite and Judean Piety*, p. 5).

they shall seek me eagerly and shall not find me.
They despised knowledge,
    they had no love for the fear of Yahweh,
they would take no advice from me,
    and spurned all my warnings:
so they must eat the fruits of their own courses,
    and choke themselves with their own scheming.
For the errors of the ignorant lead to their death,
    and the complacency of fools works their own ruin;
but whoever listens to me may live secure,
    he will have quiet, fearing no mischance." (Prov 1:20–33)

§25. Lady Wisdom Praised

The ancient sage sings of the joy, the transcending value, of follow-ing Lady Wisdom, Hokmah.

Happy the person *(adam)* who discovers Wisdom (Hokmah),
    the person *(adam)* who gains discernment:
gaining her is more rewarding than silver,
    more profitable than gold.
She is beyond the price of pearls,
    nothing you could covet is her equal.
In her right hand is length of days;
    in her left hand, riches and honour.
Her ways are delightful ways,
    her paths all lead to contentment.
She is a tree of life for those who hold her fast,
    those who cling to her live happy lives. (Prov 3:13–18)

§26. God's Feminine Lovableness Sought After

Lady Wisdom, the divine Hokmah, is like one's beloved, to be sought after and held fast—God in her lovableness to humanity.

Acquire Wisdom, acquire Perception,
    never forget her, never deviate from my words.
Do not desert her, she will keep you safe,
    love her, she will watch over you.
The beginning of Wisdom? The acquisition of Wisdom;
    at the cost of all you have, acquire Perception.
Hold her close, and she will make you great;
    embrace her, and she will be your pride;
she will set a crown of grace on your head,
    present you with a glorious diadem.
. . . .
I have educated you in the ways of Wisdom,
    I have guided you along the paths of Honesty.
As you walk, your going will be unhindered,
    as you run, you will not stumble.

Hold fast to Discipline, never let her go,
   keep your eyes on her, she is your life. (Prov 4:5–9, 11–13)

§27. Feminine Wisdom Loved

The sage again addresses the divine Hokmah with a term of endearment, sister, as men did to their beloved in that culture (cf. Song of Songs 4:12; 5:1–2).

To Hokmah say, "My sister!" (Prov 7:4)

§28. Humanity Is Masculine: Divinity Is Feminine

The paean of feminine divine Wisdom reaches its height in Proverbs, chapters 8 and 9. Hokmah is still personified, the feminine side of the divine that can be perceived and is to be sought for by humans. The masculine (human)–feminine (divine) relationship is accentuated here in the Hebrew by the use of the term "O men" (males, *ishim*).

Does Wisdom not call meanwhile?
   Does Discernment not lift up her voice?
On the hilltop, on the road,
   at the crossways, she takes her stand;
beside the gates of the city,
   at the approaches to the gates she cries aloud,
"O men! *(ishim)* I am calling to you;
   my cry goes out to the sons *(bnei)* of humanity *(adam)*.
You ignorant ones! Study discretion;
   and you fools, come to your senses!
Listen, I have serious things to tell you,
   from my lips come honest words.
My mouth proclaims the truth,
   wickedness is hateful to my lips.
All the words I say are right,
   nothing twisted in them, nothing false,
all straightforward to him who understands,
   honest to those who know what knowledge means.
Accept my discipline rather than silver,
   knowledge in preference to pure gold.
For Wisdom is more precious than pearls,
   and nothing else is so worthy of desire. (Prov 8:1–11)

§29. In Praise of Feminine Divine Wisdom

The feminine divine Wisdom sings her own praises:

"I, Wisdom, am mistress of discretion,
   the inventor of lucidity of thought.
Good advice and sound judgment belong to me,

perception to me, strength to me.
(To fear Yahweh is to hate evil.)
   I hate pride and arrogance,
   wicked behaviour and a lying mouth.
I love those who love me;
   those who seek me eagerly shall find me.
By me monarchs rule
· · · · · · · · ·
   and the great impose justice on the world.
With me are riches and honour,
   lasting wealth and justice.
The fruit I give is better than gold, even the finest,
   The return I make is better than pure silver.
I walk in the way of virtue,
   in the paths of justice,
enriching those who love me,
   filling their treasuries." (Prov 8:12–21)

§30. Eternal Feminine Wisdom

According to the sage of Proverbs the feminine Hokmah is, like
Yahweh, eternal, being present even before creation. As noted above,
Hokmah here is quasi divine, the eternally present feminine aspect
of the divine vis-à-vis the nondivine. (The Hebrew verb *qanani* was
translated as "acquired" or "possessed" in three Greek translations
(Aquila, Symmachus, and Theodotion) and Jerome's Latin; as
"created" by the Targum's Aramaic and the Septuagint's Greek.)

"Yahweh possessed *(qanani)* me when his purpose first unfolded,
   before the oldest of his works.
From everlasting I was firmly set,
   from the beginning, before earth came into being.
The deep was not, when I was born,
   there were no springs to gush with water.
Before the mountains were settled,
   before the hills, I came to birth;
before he made the earth, the countryside,
   or the first grains of the world's dust.
When he fixed the heavens firm, I was there,
   when he drew a ring on the surface of the deep,
when he thickened the clouds above,
   when he fixed fast the springs of the deep,
when he assigned the sea its boundaries
   —and the waters will not invade the shore—
   when he laid down the foundations of the earth,
I was by his side, a beloved little mother,
   delighting him day after day,
   ever at play in his presence,

at play everywhere in his world,
   delighting to be with the sons of humanity." (Prov 8:22–31)

§31. Lady Wisdom Extends an Invitation

Wisdom now issues an invitation (despite the feminine quality of
Wisdom, or perhaps because of it, this advice is addressed mainly to
men, here, sons—*banim*) to hearken to her.

"And now, my sons *(banim)*, listen to me;
listen to instruction and learn to be wise,
   do not ignore it.
Happy those who keep my ways!
Happy is the one who listens to me,
   who day after day watches at my gates
   to guard the portals.
For the one who finds me finds life,
   will win favor from Yahweh;
but they who do injury to me do hurt to their own souls,
   all who hate me are in love with death." (Prov 8:32–36)

§32. A Divine Hostess

Hokmah prepares a divine banquet for all, acting as hostess, sending out her *maid*servants.

Wisdom has built herself a house,
   she has erected her seven pillars,
she has slaughtered her beasts, prepared her wine,
   she has laid her table.
She has despatched her maidservants
   and proclaimed from the city's heights:
"Who is ignorant? Let him step this way."
   To the fool she says,
"Come and eat my bread,
   drink the wine I have prepared!
Leave your folly and you will live,
   walk in the ways of perception." (Prov 9:1–6)

§33. Dame Folly

The feminine divine Hokmah is contrasted to another "hostess,"
Dame Folly.

Dame Folly acts on impulse,
   is childish and knows nothing.
She sits at the door of her house,
   on a throne commanding the city,
inviting the passers-by

as they pass on their lawful occasions,
"Who is ignorant? Let him step this way."
To the fool she says,
"Stolen waters are sweet,
    and bread tastes better when eaten in secret."
The fellow does not realise that here the Shades are gathered,
    that her guests are heading for the valleys of Sheol. (Prov 9:13–18)

§34. Lady Wisdom, Mistress of the Cosmos

In the early fifth century B.C.E. Book of Job, the hymn of praise to the feminine Hokmah is continued. She is not subject to the laws of the cosmos but is its mistress. She is inaccessible to humanity, being known only by God. The feminine Hokmah is again both personified and an attribute of God. For human beings the only access to Wisdom is through fear of the Lord (cf. Prov 1:7).

But tell me, where does Wisdom come from?
    Where is understanding to be found?
The road to her is still unknown to humanity,
    not to be found in the land of the living.
"She is not in me" says the Abyss;
    "Nor here" replies the Sea.
She cannot be bought with solid gold,
    not paid for with any weight of silver,
nor be priced by the standard of the gold of Ophir,
    or of precious onyx or sapphire.
No gold, no glass can match her in value,
    nor for a fine gold vase can she be bartered.
Nor is there need to mention coral, nor crystal;
    beside Wisdom pearls are not worth the fishing.
Topaz from Cush is worthless in comparison,
    and gold, even refined, is valueless.
But tell me, where does Wisdom come from?
    Where is understanding to be found?
She is outside the knowledge of every living thing,
    hidden from the birds in the sky.
Perdition and Death can only say,
    "We have heard reports of her."
God alone has traced her path
    and found out where she lives.
(For he sees to the ends of the earth,
    and observes all that lies under heaven.)
When he willed to give weight to the wind
    and measured out the waters with a gauge,
when he made the laws and rules for the rain
    and mapped a route for thunderclaps to follow,
then he had her in sight, and cast her worth,
    assessed her, fathomed her,

And he said to humanity,
   "Wisdom?—the fear of the Lord.
   Understanding?—the avoidance of evil." (Job 28:12–28)

§35. Lady Wisdom: God Facing Humanity

Baruch was the companion of the prophet Jeremiah. One "canonical" book of the Bible is attributed to him, although he did not in fact write it; two further pseudepigraphical books are also, falsely, attributed to him. The "canonical" book is not found in the Hebrew Bible, but in the Greek Septuagint Bible, and is hence called "deuterocanonical" (however, there probably was an original Hebrew text). Catholic and Orthodox Christianity accept the deuterocanonical books as an inspired part of the Bible, whereas Judaism and Protestantism place them in the so-called Apocrypha.

In this biblical Book of Baruch the references to Wisdom are to the Greek Sophia, also feminine in gender, like Hokmah in Hebrew. Baruch here also sings the praises of Lady Wisdom, who is again personified in feminine form. She is inaccessible to humanity, known only to God, the creator of all. The song intimates that only the creator of the universe can know Sophia, implying that she is coeval with creation (cf. Prov 8:23), making her an attribute of the divine Being. But in the song of praise to Lady Wisdom she is made known to humanity through Israel; she is God as known by humanity, the feminine divine face turned toward creation.

Listen, Israel, to commands that bring life;
hear, and learn what knowledge means.
Why, Israel, why are you in the country of your enemies,
growing older and older in an alien land,
sharing defilement with the dead,
reckoned with those who go to Sheol?
Because you have forsaken the fountain of Wisdom.
Had you walked in the way of God,
you would have lived in peace for ever.
Learn where knowledge is, where strength,
where understanding, and so learn
where length of days is, where life,
where the light of the eyes and where peace.
But who has found out where she lives,
who has entered her treasure house?
. . . .
Nothing has been heard of her in Canaan,
nothing has been seen of her in Teman;
the sons of Hagar in search of worldly wisdom,

the merchants of Midian and Tema,
the tale-spinners and the philosophers
have none of them found the way to Wisdom,
or discovered the paths she treads.
How great, Israel, is the house of God,
how wide his domain,
immeasurably wide,
infinitely lofty!
In it were born the giants, famous to us from antiquity,
immensely tall, expert in war;
God's choice did not fall on these,
he did not reveal the way to knowledge to them;
they perished for lack of Wisdom,
perished in their own folly.
Who has ever climbed the sky and caught her
to bring her down from the clouds?
Who has ever crossed the ocean and found her
to bring her back in exchange for the finest gold?
No one knows the way to her,
no one can discover the path she treads.
But the One who knows all knows her,
he has grasped her with his own intellect,
he has set the earth firm for ever
and filled it with four-footed beasts,
he sends the light—and it goes,
he recalls it—and trembling it obeys;
the stars shine joyfully at their set times:
when he calls them, they answer, "Here we are";
they gladly shine for their creator.
It is he who is our God,
no other can compare with him.
He has grasped the whole way of knowledge [Wisdom],
and confided her to his servant Jacob,
to Israel his well-beloved;
so causing her to appear on earth
and move among humanity.
This is the book of the commandments of God,
the Law that stands for ever;
those who keep her live,
those who desert her die.
Turn back, Jacob, seize her,
in her radiance make your way to light:
do not yield your glory to another,
your privilege to a people not your own.
Israel, blessed are we:
what pleases God has been revealed to us. (Baruch 3:9–15, 22–38; 4:
    1–4)

§36. Lady Wisdom Praised in Poetry

The deuterocanonical biblical book Ben Sira, or Ecclesiasticus, was written in Hebrew around 190 B.C.E. Only about two thirds of the text is available in Hebrew; the whole of it is in the Greek Septuagint.

As in Proverbs, Job, and Baruch, the sage Ben Sira sings the praises of the feminine Sophia, or Hokmah, who is personified, being created by God before all the rest of creation. Only to God is Lady Wisdom known, and to those he favors. Here she is everlasting, but created, separate from God.

> All Wisdom is from the Lord,
>   and . . . is his own for ever.
> The sand of the sea and the raindrops,
>   and the days of eternity, who can assess them?
> The height of the sky and the breadth of the earth,
>   and the depth of the abyss, and Wisdom, who can probe them?
> Before all other things Wisdom was created,
>   shrewd understanding is everlasting.
> Wisdom's source is the word of God in the heavens;
>   her ways are the eternal laws.
> For whom has the root of Wisdom ever been uncovered?
>   Her resourceful ways, who knows them?
> To whom has the knowledge of Wisdom been manifested?
>   And who has understood the abundance of her ways?
> One only is wise, terrible indeed,
>   seated on his throne, the Lord.
> The Lord himself has created her, looked on her and assessed her,
>   and poured her out on all his works
> to be with all humanity as his gift,
>   and he conveyed her to those who love him. (Ben Sira 1:1–10)

§37. Lady Wisdom Is God in Creation

Here Ben Sira surpasses his earlier praise of divine Lady Wisdom, making her not only created from eternity, a feminine person separate from God, but also the very presence of God to creation. In one instance Lady Wisdom identifies herself with the spirit (*ruach,* also of feminine gender in Hebrew; see §41) of God hovering over creation in Gen 1:2. The image here, and elsewhere, of the spirit or breath of God coming forth from God's mouth was picked up in later Jewish and Christian writing. In Christianity the development went partially to the Word of God, thence to Jesus as the Word incarnate, and partially to the Holy Spirit. The image of the pillar of cloud here is one of God's presence among men and women (cf. Ex 13:21–22);

Hokmah, Sophia, places herself therein. Feminine Wisdom again is God's presence in creation from eternity to eternity. She partakes of the divine; this and her separate personhood led later to divine trinities and quaternities in Judaism (see Patai, *Hebrew Goddess*) and a divine trinity in Christianity (see pp. 57ff.).

> Wisdom speaks her own praises,
>   in the midst of her people she glories in herself.
> She opens her mouth in the assembly of the Most High,
>   she glories in herself in the presence of the Mighty One;
> "I came forth from the mouth of the Most High,
>   and I covered the earth like mist.
> I had my tent in the heights,
>   and my throne in a pillar of cloud.
> Alone I encircled the vault of the sky,
>   and I walked on the bottom of the deeps.
> Over the waves of the sea and over the whole earth,
>   and over every people and nation I have held sway.
> Among all these I searched for rest,
>   and looked to see in whose territory I might pitch camp.
> Then the creator of all things instructed me,
>   and he who created me fixed a place for my tent.
> He said, 'Pitch your tent in Jacob,
>   make Israel your inheritance.'
> From eternity, in the beginning, he created me,
>   and for eternity I shall remain.
> I ministered before him in the holy tabernacle,
>   and thus was I established on Zion." (Ben Sira 24:1–10. Cf. also 1: 11–28; 4:11–19; 6:18–37; 14:20–27; 15:1–10; and 51:13–30, where Sophia is praised and sought after by humanity as a virtue.)

§38. Lady Wisdom the Feminine Divinity

The author of the deuterocanonical Book of Wisdom (also called "The Wisdom of Solomon") was a Jew of the first century B.C.E. from Alexandria; he wrote in Greek. The divinization of the feminine Wisdom in the Jewish biblical tradition here reaches its high point. There is no talk of Sophia being created by God. The closest thing to that notion is in Wisdom 7:15, where God is said to be the guide "of" Sophia (the ancient Arabic translation renders this as the guide "to" Sophia, however), but that does not really limit the powerful divinizing statements. Sophia is said to possess omnipotence (7:23, 27), omnipresence (7:24), immutability (7:27), sanctity (7:22)—all clearly exclusive divine characteristics. Moreover, she participated in creation (7:12, 21), and is at present the sustainer and ruler of the world (8:1). Still further, Sophia is described as a breath of the power of God, a pure emanation of the glory of the Almighty (7:25). Sophia here is clearly the ancient Goddess rediviva!

All that is hidden, all that is plain, I have come to know,
instructed by Wisdom who designed them all.
For within her is a spirit intelligent, holy,
unique, manifold, subtle,
active, incisive, unsullied,
lucid, invulnerable, benevolent, sharp,
irresistible, beneficent, loving to humanity,
steadfast, dependable, unperturbed,
almighty, all-surveying,
penetrating all intelligent, pure
and most subtle spirits;
for Wisdom is quicker to move than any motion;
she is so pure, she pervades and permeates all things.
She is a breath of the power of God,
pure emanation of the glory of the Almighty;
hence nothing impure can find a way into her.
She is a reflection of the eternal light,
untarnished mirror of God's active power,
image of his goodness.
Although alone, she can do all;
herself unchanging, she makes all things new.
In each generation she passes into holy souls,
she makes them friends of God and prophets;
for God loves only those who live with Wisdom.
She is indeed more splendid than the sun,
she outshines all the constellations;
compared with light, she takes first place,
for light must yield to night,
but over Wisdom evil can never triumph.
She deploys her strength from one end of the earth to the other,
ordering all things for good. (Wisdom 7:21–8:1)

§39. Lady Wisdom a Divine Consort

Although, as we have seen, in the ancient world there were many theologies that spoke of consort Goddesses and Gods, wife and husband divinities, such notions were vigorously opposed and eventually normally excluded in the Hebraic tradition, at least after the Babylonian exile in the sixth century B.C.E. Here, however, in this Jewish deuterocanonical biblical Book of Wisdom, the sacred writer speaks of Sophia "living with *(symbiōsin)* God and the Lord of All has loved her" (Wisdom 8:3), using the same word, *symbiōsis*, for living together as he does elsewhere in the same chapter in the sense of marital connubium: "Therefore I determined to take her to live with *(symbiōsin)* me" (8:9). "It is therefore clear that Wisdom here was regarded as God's wife" (Patai, *Hebrew Goddess,* p. 139). The renowned first-century Jewish thinker Philo stated straight out that God is the husband of Sophia (Philo, *On the Cherubim* XIV.49; Loeb Classical Library, *Philo,* Vol. 2, p. 39). As a reinforcement of this clear statement in Wisdom 8:3, the sage adds the prayer, "Grant me Sophia, consort [*paredron;* literally, "the one sitting beside"] of your throne; . . . send her forth from your throne of glory to help me" (9:4, 10). If more were needed, the Wisdom writer adds that Sophia was "an initiate in the mysteries of God's knowledge, making choice of the works he is to do; . . . where is there a greater than Sophia; . . . she who knows your works, she who was present when you made the world; . . . she knows and understands everything" (8:4, 6; 9:9, 11).

> Her (Sophia's) living with God *(symbiōsin)* lends
>   lustre to her noble birth,
> since the Lord of All has loved her.
> Yes, she is an initiate in the mysteries of God's knowledge,
> making choice of the works he is to do.
> If in this life wealth be a desirable possession,
> what is more wealthy than Wisdom whose work is everywhere?
> Or if it be the intellect that is at work,
> where is there a greater than Wisdom, designer of all?
> . . . .
> "God of our ancestors,
> . . . .
> grant me Wisdom, consort of your throne.
> . . . .
> With you is Wisdom, she who knows your works,
> she who was present when you made the world;
> she understands what is pleasing in your eyes
> and what agrees with your commandments.
> Despatch her from the holy heavens,
> send her forth from your throne of glory
> to help me and to toil with me
> and teach me what is pleasing to you,
> since she knows and understands everything." (Wisdom 8:3–6; 9:1, 4,
>   9–10)

§40. Feminine Divine Wisdom in the New Testament

Twice it is recorded in the Gospels that Jesus spoke of feminine divine Wisdom.

"For John came, neither eating nor drinking, and they say . . . The Son of Man came, eating and drinking, and they say . . . Yet Wisdom (Sophia) has been proved right by her actions." (Mt 11:18–19)

"And that is why the Wisdom (Sophia) of God said, 'I will send them prophets and apostles.'" (Lk 11:49)

C. THE FEMININE DIVINE SPIRIT

It should be apparent that the religion of the ancient Hebrews depicted the divine in feminine as well as masculine imagery. Two pressures were exerted on this androgynous imagery with the passage of the centuries: one was to transcend all sexual and other material descriptions in favor of God as spirit; the other was to suppress the feminine imagery in favor of a totally masculine one. As long as the first tendency was kept in balance, that is, did not make the human perception of God anemic and ineffective, it was in the direction of "progress," i.e., it further "humanized" and "divinized" humanity. The second tendency, however, was simply reactionary, dehumanizing and dedivinizing humanity by splitting it into oppressor and oppressed groups. Still, the oppressive pressure did not entirely submerge the feminine image of the divine in the Hebrew Bible; the above material traces the outline of its persistence.

There are two other terms of the Hebrew Bible which are feminine in grammatical gender and which ought also to be noted here. They are *ruach*, spirit; and *torah*, teaching, Law, or commandment (the latter will be treated below in §45 with the postbiblical Jewish material). Of course not every Hebrew word with a feminine gender reflected feminine thought imagery. But both of these terms are very closely connected with the biblical talk about God; they do in fact at times become personifications of aspects of God; as such, in later biblical texts they take on some of the qualities of a feminine divine or quasi-divine personification; and, finally, both provide a source for feminine divine or quasi-divine personifications in post-Hebrew Bible Jewish and Christian traditions.

§41. The (Feminine) Spirit of God Hypostatized

In many instances the spirit of God is described as separate from God, a distinct substance or hypostasis; at times the term "holy spirit" of God is used thus. A few examples spread over the whole biblical period will suffice here:

In the beginning God created the heavens and the earth. . . . And God's spirit hovered over the water. (Gen 1:1–2)

Yahweh said, "My spirit must not for ever be disgraced in humanity." (Gen 6:3)

Raising his eyes Balaam saw Israel, encamped by tribes; the spirit of God came on him. (Num 24:2)

The spirit of God has made me. (Job 33:4)

Do not deprive me of your holy spirit. (Ps 51:11)

When you send forth your spirit, they are created. (Ps 104:30)

Where could I go to escape your spirit? (Ps 139:7)

Since you are my God may your good spirit guide me. (Ps 143:10)

[Yahweh] said, "Truly they are my people." . . . But they rebelled, they grieved his holy spirit. . . . Where is he who endowed him with his holy spirit? (Is 63:8, 10, 11)

The spirit of Yahweh then entered me, and made me stand up, and spoke to me. (Ezek 3:24)

Elisha was filled with his holy spirit. (Ben Sira 48:12, following the fifth-century A.D. Alexandrinus manuscript, which adds the word "holy," *hagiou.*)

Clearly the term "spirit" is used with a variety of meanings in these several sample passages. The spirit is that aspect of God which relates to creation, particularly humanity, by which God enters into a human being, and through which a human being comes into contact with God—becomes holy through God's holy spirit. Of course, all through this Hebrew writing the divine spirit, Ruach, is feminine in gender, with the adjectives and verbs following in form.

§42. Feminine Divine Spirit and Wisdom Identified

While the spirit of God is hypostatized in these and other passages, this originally probably was only a literary device to focus on the divine relationship to creation, especially humanity. However, with the Book of Wisdom the Spirit comes close to being something more than a mere metaphor, just as does Wisdom, with which it is at times likened and even identified.

No, Wisdom will never make its way into a crafty soul; . . . the holy spirit of Wisdom [some versions say: instruction] shuns deceit. . . . For Wisdom is Spirit, loving to humanity *(philanthrōpon gar pneuma sophia).* . . . The Spirit of the Lord, indeed, fills the whole world, holds all things together and knows every sound uttered. (Wisdom 1:4–7)

All that is hidden, all that is plain, I have come to know, instructed by Wisdom who designed them all. For in her is Spirit, intelligent, holy, unique *(Estin gar en autē pneuma noeron hagion).* . . . (Wisdom 7:21–22)

As for your intention, who could have learnt it, had you not granted Wisdom and sent your Holy Spirit from above? (Wisdom 9:17)

II. Feminine Imagery of God—
Postbiblical Period

A. JEWISH FEMININE IMAGERY OF THE DIVINE

§43. Even Qumran

At about the same time as the Book of Wisdom, that is, the first century B.C.E., one of the members of the Jewish sect at Qumran near the Dead Sea (which tended to be very negative toward women and sex) wrote a prayer that addressed God both as father and as mother, thus continuing the same ancient tradition discussed above in §17; it is also a natural concomitant of the imagery of Wisdom as a divine consort as expressed in the Wisdom literature:

> My father does not concern himself with me
> and in comparison with you my mother has left me,
> but you are father of all thy faithful
> and you rejoiced at those like a loving mother at her infant
> and like a nurse you cherish in your bosom all your creatures.
> (1QH ix. 35f.)

§44. Yahweh and Sophia: Divine Consorts

Philo was an extraordinary Jewish thinker from Alexandria in Egypt. He lived before and during the first half of the first century of the Common Era, which made him a contemporary of Hillel, Jesus of Nazareth, Paul of Tarsus, and Johanan Ben Zachai. Alexandria of Philo's day contained an extremely prosperous Jewish community, quite possibly the largest in the world, for the city was very large and was perhaps 40 percent Jewish. Philo had been to Jerusalem and knew the biblical tradition well, but wrote in Greek. Hence when he wrote of the Hebrew *Elohim* he used the Greek word for God, *Theos*.

In Philo the tradition of Lady Wisdom, Hokmah, Sophia in Greek,

51

very much continues the ancient Goddess line that was reflected in the Hebrew Bible and reached an acme in the Book of Wisdom, analyzed just above. Philo clearly speaks of Sophia (sometimes with synonyms like Knowledge, Gnosis) as God's wife. The process of creation is represented in the following passage symbolically but quite unequivocally as procreation.

> The Architect who made this universe was at the same time the Father of what was thus born, whilst its mother was the Knowledge possessed by its Maker. With His Knowledge *(gnōsis)* God *(theos)* had union, not as humans have it, and begot created things. And Knowledge, having received the divine seed, when her travail was consummated, bore the only beloved son who is apprehended by the senses, the world which we see. Thus in the pages of one of the inspired company, Wisdom *(sophia)* is represented as speaking of herself after this manner: "God obtained me first of all his works and founded me before the ages." [Prov 8:22] True, for it was necessary that all that came to the birth of creation should be younger than the Mother and Nurse of the All. . . . I suggest then, that the Father of the schools, with its regular course or round of instruction . . .   The Husband of Wisdom drops the seed of happiness for the race of mortals into good and virgin soil. (Philo, *On Drunkenness,* VIII.80 and IX.33; Loeb Classical Library, *Philo,* Vol. 3, pp. 333–335; *On the Cherubim,* XIV.49; Loeb Classical Library, *Philo,* Vol. 2, p. 39)

§45. Torah, Daughter of Yahweh

a. Feminine Wisdom and Torah Identified

Torah, Hebrew for "teaching," or "Law," as it is most often translated, is not only feminine in gender, but as it takes on the character in the Jewish tradition of a quasi-divine personification it also projects a feminine personality into the divine family. Particularly after the sixth-century B.C.E. return of the Jewish remnant from exile the study and living of the Torah became ever more prominent in Jewish life. The longest psalm in the Bible, Ps 119, is devoted entirely to the praise of the Torah, which is identified with God's Word *(dabar).* Perhaps the earliest personification of the feminine Torah occurred in Ben Sira, or Ecclesiasticus (190 B.C.E.), who sang at length the praises of feminine divine Wisdom, Hokmah, and then expressly identified her with Torah.

> Wisdom speaks her own praises,
>   in the midst of her people she glories in herself.
> She opens her mouth in the assembly of the Most High,
>   she glories in herself in the presence of the Mighty One;
> "I came forth from the mouth of the Most High, . . .

From eternity, in the beginning, he created me." . . .
All this is no other than the book of the covenant of the Most
  High God,
the Law [Torah] that Moses enjoined on us."
(Ben Sira 24:1-3, 9, 23)

b. Feminine Wisdom and Torah Identified by Rabbis

The rabbis continued and intensified this identification of the feminine quasi-divine Torah with the feminine divine Hokmah.

R. Hoseia the Elder [c. 225 c.e.] began his lecture with Proverbs 8: 30: "I (Hokmah equals Torah) was with him, a skilled worker [female], a delight day by day. The Torah says: I am the instrument of God. . . . Likewise God looked at the Torah [as a blueprint] and thus made the world. And the Torah spoke Genesis 1:1: "Through the First One [the rabbi here understands the first word of Genesis, *bereshit,* to mean "through the First One," rather than the usual "in the beginning"] God created the heavens and the earth," and the "First One" is none other than the Torah, as it says in Proverbs 8:22: "Yahweh made me (Hokmah equals Torah) as the First One of his works." (Genesis Rabbah 1)

R. Simeon b. Laquish [c. 250 c.e.] said: "By 200 years the Torah preceeded the creation of the world; that is the meaning of Proverbs 8:30: I (Hokmah equals Torah) was with him a skilled worker [female], a delight day by day." (Genesis Rabbah 8(6a); for other citations, see Hermann L. Strack and Paul Billerbeck, *Kommentar zum Neuen Testament aus Talmud und Midrasch,* Vol. 2, pp. 353ff.; Munich: 1922–1928)

c. Feminine Torah Pre-Existent

It was not only in identifying the feminine Torah with Hokmah that the rabbis spoke of Torah's numinous pre-creation character. The following are a few other such examples.

Seven things were made before the world was made, namely, the Torah, repentance, the garden of Eden, Gehenna, the throne of glory, the Holy, and the name of the Messiah. (Talmud bPesachim 54a)

She [Torah] lay on God's lap while God sat on the throne of glory. (Midrash Psalm 90, 3, 12 [Buber 196a])

God said to Israel: "Before I made this world I prepared the Torah." (Exodus Rabbah 30 [89d]; for further citations, see Strack and Billerbeck, Vol. 2, pp. 335ff., and Vol. 3, pp. 435ff.)

d. Torah God's Daughter

The rabbis developed the feminine personification of Torah further than by identifying her with the feminine divine Hokmah and combining the feminine gender of the word with the literary hypostatization of it. They also had God speak of Torah as his daughter, again giving her a divine character.

> Whoever recites a verse of the Song of Songs and (thereby) makes it into a sort of (secular) song . . . brings illness into the world: then the Torah puts on sackcloth and goes before God and says before him: "Lord of the world, your children have made me a zither like the pagans play on!" He answers her: "My daughter, if they only eat and drink with what shall they concern themselves?" (Talmud bSanhedrin 101a)

> "God said, . . . My daughter, that is, the Torah." (Leviticus Rabbah 20[120a])

> They said to him, "Perhaps tomorrow you will allow your Shekinah [see below for a discussion of this feminine divine "personification"] to dwell with those below!" God answered them [his angels]: "My Torah I grant to those below but I dwell here with those above. I send my daughter for her marriage contract into another land so she along with her spouse may be honored on account of her beauty and charm, for she is the daughter of a king and she will be honored; but I will dwell with you, with those above." (Midrash Song of Songs 8, 11[133b]; for further citations, see Strack and Billerbeck, Vol. 2, pp. 355ff.)

Thus, beginning at least two hundred years before the Common Era, there was a movement in the Hebraic-Judaic tradition to personify the feminine Torah and give her a quasi-divine or divine character, which movement intensified on into the rabbinic period during the Common, or Christian, Era.

§46. The Shekinah, Rabbis, and a Feminine Divinity
Shekinah is a feminine Hebrew word for "dwelling," and refers to God's dwelling or presence in the world. It was first used in the Targums (translations or paraphrases of the Bible from around the first century C.E.) to avoid referring to God directly, out of reverence. It also appeared frequently in the early rabbinic writings, but did not take on the quality of the feminine dimension of God until the Middle Ages in the writings of the Jewish mystics, the Kabbalists. The foremost scholar of Jewish mysticism, Gershom Scholem, writes:

> In all the numerous references to the Shekhinah in the Talmud and Midrashim . . . there is no hint that it represents a feminine element in God. . . . Nowhere is there a dualism with the Shekhinah, as the feminine, opposed to the "Holy One, praise be to Him," as the masculine element in God. (Gershom Scholem, *Major Trends in Jewish Mysticism,* p. 225; Schocken Books, 1941)

Nevertheless, there were some rabbinic references to the mother-like qualities of God in the early rabbinic materials. For example, Shemuel bar Nahman, a rabbi of the late third and early fourth century C.E., quoted Ps 103:13 and Is 66:13 (see above), and then went beyond them with a statement he put in God's mouth.

> It is the wont of the father to have mercy, "Like as a father has compassion upon them that fear Him"; and it is the wont of the mother to comfort, "as one whom his mother comforts, so will I comfort you." God said: "I shall do as both father and mother." (Midrash Pesiqta Rabbah 139a)

§47. The Feminine God in Jewish Mysticism

Although the feminine dimension of God does not become pronounced in Jewish mysticism until the Middle Ages, and hence is beyond the chronological scope of this book, because the trajectory of the feminine in the divine began before the Hebrew tradition, continued through the Hebrew Bible, the Apocrypha, and Philo, and then faded from view, only to reappear in the medieval Kabbala, a very few examples from the Kabbala will be provided. But first a word about the importance of the Shekinah as the feminine element in God from Gershom Scholem.

> The introduction of this idea was one of the most important and lasting innovations of Kabbalism. The fact that it obtained recognition in spite of the obvious difficulty of reconciling it with the conception of the absolute Unity of God, and that no other element of Kabbalism won such a deep degree of popular approval, is proof that it responded to a deep-seated religious need. (Scholem, *Major Trends in Jewish Mysticism*, p. 225)

a. God the Mother and Father

There are many passages in kabbalistic writings, particularly the most celebrated of them, the thirteenth-century Zohar, in which the feminine and masculine dimensions of God are expressed most explicitly. The language sounds very much like that of the ancient Gods and Goddesses, of Proverbs, Hokmah, the developed Sophia language of the Book of Wisdom and Philo, and that of the Christian Gnostics, to be discussed below. However, doubtless, as with the Christian belief in a Trinity, the Jewish kabbalistic teachings about the Mother (other terms are also used) and the Father in God also presumes monotheism. What is of note here is that the female and the male dimensions are both seen as essential elements in divinity.

> Never does the inclination of the Father and the Mother toward each other cease. They always go out together and dwell together. They never

separate and never leave each other. They are together in complete union.
. . . The Father and the Mother, since they are found in union all the time
are never hidden or separated from each other, are called "Companions."
. . . And they find complete satisfaction in complete union. (*Zohar* I.162a–b;
III.77b–78a)

b. A Jewish Divine Quaternity: Female and Male

Also, many are the kabbalistic passages that speak not only of the
Mother and Father God, but also the Son and Daughter (sometimes
called *Matronit*) God. Let one suffice here; it is connected with the
Tetragrammaton, the four consonants in God's Hebrew name:
YHWH.

The Supernal H [i.e., the Mother] became pregnant as a result of all the
love and fondling—since the Y never leaves her—and she brought forth the
W [the Son], whereupon she stood up and suckled him. And when the W
emerged, his female mate [the Daughter, represented by the second H in the
Tetragrammaton] emerged with him. (*Zohar* III.77b)

c. Union with the Feminine Divinity

The goal of mysticism is the union of the human with the divine.
Since in the Jewish mystical tradition the Divinity, insofar as it relates
to creation, is known as the female Shekinah, it is with her that the
Jewish mystic strives for union. This of course simply continues the
ancient Hebrew tradition of Hokmah being God vis-à-vis creation,
with whom union was avidly sought by human beings. In one instance in the Zohar this union of a human being (Moses—he was the
only case) with the Shekinah was described as having taken place in
terms of sexual intercourse (analogous to the "coming upon" Mary
the mother of Jesus by the Holy Spirit in Lk 1:35 and Mt 1:20).

The Matronit* . . . became mated *(isdavga)* with Moses. Moses had
intercourse *(shimesh)* while he was in the body of the moon.* (*Zohar* I.21b–
22a)
*[The Matronit is here a synonym for Shekinah; the moon is a symbol of
the Shekinah.]

d. The Shekinah and a Female Messiah

In the seventeenth century one offshoot of Jewish mysticism, Sab-
batianism, developed a trinitarian notion of God, including the
Shekinah, who had a corresponding female Messiah.

The object of religion, the goal of our prayers, can only be "the God of
Israel" and its unity or union with his Shekhinah. From this original dualism

some Sabbatians developed a Trinity of the unknown God, the God of Israel and the Shekhinah, and it did not take long for the idea to develop that the completion of Salvation is dependent upon the appearance of a Messiah for each of these three aspects of Trinity, with a female Messiah for the last! (Scholem, *Major Trends in Jewish Mysticism,* p. 320)

e. Kabbala Nevertheless Fundamentally Masculine

Despite the projection of a feminine dimension in the Divinity by Jewish mysticism, two counterpuntal elements should be noted: one, the female represents not the tender but the stern; two, like most of the rest of Judaism, Kabbalism is by and for men.

It is of the essence of Kabbalistic symbolism that woman represents not, as one might be tempted to expect, the quality of tenderness but that of stern judgment. . . . Both historically and metaphysically it is a masculine doctrine, made for men and by men. The long history of Jewish mysticism shows no trace of feminine influence. There have been no women Kabbalists; Rabia of early Islamic mysticism, Mechthild of Magdeburg, Juliana of Norwich, Theresa de Jesus, and the many other feminine representatives of Christian mysticism have no counterparts in the history of Kabbalism. (Scholem, *Major Trends in Jewish Mysticism,* p. 36)

B. FEMININE HOLY SPIRIT IN CHRISTIAN TRADITION

Because the Book of Wisdom was written originally in Greek (most likely by a Jew of Alexandria in the first century B.C.E.), the word used for Wisdom is *sophia,* which, like the Hebrew *hokmah,* is feminine in gender and imagery. As noted above, the Hebrew word for Spirit of God, *ruach,* is also feminine. However, the Greek word for Spirit, *pneuma,* is not feminine, but neuter. Nevertheless, in the Book of Wisdom the two, Wisdom and Spirit, are identified. Because the tradition of Wisdom as feminine was so strong, plus the fact that Spirit is also feminine in Hebrew, though neuter in Greek, the identification of the Spirit of God with Lady Wisdom has at times in the Christian tradition led to the imaging of the Holy Spirit as feminine. A few examples follow.

§48. Holy Spirit the Mother of Jesus — I

In the second-century Coptic-language apocryphal Epistle of James (see below, pp. 66f., for a brief discussion of apocryphal and Gnostic Christian writings), the Holy Spirit is cast in the image of the parent of Jesus; since elsewhere in the epistle God the Father is referred to as Jesus' father, presumably the Holy Spirit is meant to be Jesus' mother. The risen Christ says to James and the other disciples:

You are chosen, you are like the Son of the Holy Spirit. (*Vigiliae Christianae*, Vol. 8, 1954, p. 12)

§49. Holy Spirit the Mother of Jesus — II

Another motherly image of the Holy Spirit is found in the apocryphal Gospel to the Hebrews, written around A.D. 150.

And it came to pass when the Lord [Jesus at his baptism in the Jordan River] came up out of the water, the whole fount of the Holy Spirit descended upon him and rested on him and said to him: My son . . . thou art my first-begotten Son that reignest for ever. (Edgar Hennecke and Wilhelm Schneemelcher, eds., *New Testament Apocrypha*, Vol. 1, pp. 163–164; Westminster Press, 1963)

§50. Holy Spirit the Mother of Jesus — III

If there be any doubt that the Holy Spirit was depicted in the Gospel to the Hebrews as Jesus' mother, the following quotation will lay it to rest.

Even so did my mother, the Holy Spirit, take me by one of my hairs and carry me away onto the great mountain Thabor. (Ibid., p. 164)

§51. The Holy Spirit Is a Woman — I

In the third-century Gnostic Christian apocryphal Gospel of Philip the Holy Spirit of God is at one place assumed to be a woman, as is clear from the quotation below referring to the Matthean and Lukan claims of the virginal conception of Jesus.

Some said, "Mary conceived by the Holy Spirit." They are in error. They do not know what they are saying. When did a woman ever conceive by a woman? Mary is the virgin. . . . (Gospel of Philip, *The Nag Hammadi Library*, tr. by James M. Robinson et al., p. 134; Harper & Row, 1977)

§52. The Holy Spirit Is a Woman — II

The Acts of Thomas, an early third-century Gnostic Christian apocryphal writing, contains several lengthy prayers and one brief one, which address or refer to the Holy Spirit in feminine imagery. The three lengthy prayers are all epicleses, that is, prayers calling on the Holy Spirit to descend upon the liturgical matter, usually the bread and wine used in the celebration of the Eucharist. The first orthodox text of one is from Hippolytus in the early third century, contemporaneous with the Acts of Thomas. In the latter, two of the epicleses are invocations of the Holy Spirit at a Eucharist, but one is connected with Confirmation, which is also customary in orthodox Catholic Christianity. The connections between the feminine Wisdom, the Mother (Mater Magna, the Goddess), love, the Eucharist, the dove (symbol of the Goddess, and of the Holy Spirit, discussed in §55), and the Holy Spirit are all obvious.

"O Jesus Christ, . . . we glorify and praise thee and thine invisible Father and thy Holy Spirit and the Mother of all creation." (Acts of Thomas, Edgar Hennecke and Wilhelm Schneemelcher, eds., *New Testament Apocrypha,* Vol. 2, p. 465; Westminster Press, 1966)

And the apostle took the oil and pouring it on their heads anointed and chrismed them, and began to say:
Come, holy name of Christ *that is above every name;*
Come, power of the Most High and perfect compassion;
Come, thou highest gift;
Come, compassionate mother;
Come, fellowship of the male;
Come, thou (fem.) that dost reveal the hidden mysteries;
Come, mother of the seven houses, that thy rest may be in the eighth house;
Come, elder of the five members, understanding, thought, prudence, consideration, reasoning,
Communicate with these young men!
Come, Holy Spirit, and purify their reins and their heart
And give them the added seal in the name of the Father and Son and Holy Spirit. (Ibid., pp. 456–457)

And spreading a linen cloth, he set upon it the bread of blessing. And the apostle stood beside it and said: "Jesus, who hast made us worthy to partake of the Eucharist of thy holy body and blood, behold we make bold to approach thy Eucharist, and to call upon thy holy name; come thou and have fellowship with us!" And he began to say:
Come, gift of the Most High;
Come, perfect compassion;
Come, fellowship of the male;
Come, Holy Spirit;
Come, thou that dost know the mysteries of the Chosen;
Come, thou that hast part in all the combats of the noble Athlete;
Come, treasure of glory;
Come, darling of the compassion of the Most High;
Come, silence
That dost reveal the great deeds of the whole greatness;
And make the ineffable manifest;
Holy Dove
That bearest the twin young;
Come, hidden Mother;

Come, thou that art manifest in thy deeds and dost furnish joy
And rest for all that are joined with thee;
Come and partake with us in this Eucharist
Which we celebrate in thy name,
And in the love-feast
In which we are gathered together at thy call.

And when he had said this, he marked the Cross upon the bread and broke it, and began to distribute it. And first he gave to the woman, saying: "Let this be to thee for forgiveness of sins and eternal transgressions!" And after her he gave also to all the others who had received the seal. (Ibid., pp. 470–471)

And when they were baptized and clothed, he set bread upon the table and blessed it and said: "Bread of life, those who eat of which remain incorruptible; bread which fills hungry souls with its blessing . . . we name over thee the name of the mother of the ineffable mystery of the hidden dominions and powers, we name over thee the name of Jesus." (Ibid., p. 512)

§53. The Deaconess a Type of the Holy Spirit

In the third-century A.D. orthodox Christian document written in Syriac (a Semitic language, derived from the earlier Aramaic), the Didascalia, the imagery moves in the other direction. There a woman, a deaconess, is likened to the Holy Spirit.

And the deaconess shall be honored by you as a type of the Holy Spirit. (Didascalia II.26.4)

§54. The Holy Spirit, Mother of Humanity

The tradition continued in the Syriac-speaking area ("spirit" also has the feminine gender in Syriac, as in Hebrew), as in the writings of the fourth-century orthodox Christian father Aphraates.

A man who is yet unmarried loves and honors God his father and the Holy Spirit his mother. (Aphraates, Homily XVIII.10—on Genesis 2:24)

§55. The Dove, Symbol of the Holy Spirit
and the "Great Mother"

The dove appears many times in the Hebrew Bible, but its most pervasive symbolic meaning is "love," as is amply exemplified, especially in the Song of Songs. In Christian tradition it is also immediately connected with the Holy Spirit, for all four Gospels, in speaking of the baptism of Jesus, say that "the Holy Spirit descended on him in bodily shape, like a dove" (Lk 3:22; cf. Mt 3:16; Mk 1:10; Jn 1:33). Of course, in Christian tradition the Holy Spirit is also said to be the spirit of love, so that the two currents of meaning flow together. But it is also particularly interesting to note that the dove is also a very ancient symbol for the Goddess of Love, which of course fits perfectly well with the Hebrew Bible symbol of love and the Christian carry-over of the feminine Wisdom traditions to the Holy Spirit, who is also the Spirit of Love, and thus also the Christian continuance of the Goddess of Love, the Mater Magna, the "Great Mother."

However, since the most ancient times the dove is the holy animal not only of the Cyprian Aphrodite, but also of almost all the Goddesses of Fertility and Love of the Near East. Already in neolithic times the "Great Mother" who was venerated in Crete was represented with dove and lily. The Greek word for dove, *peristera,* means "bird of Istar," the Assyrian-Babylonian Goddess of Love, but also of the Underworld and Death. Istar had many names: Astarte (Ashtoreth) and Hathor, Inanna and Nut, Cybele and Isis, and many others. However, as also with the Greek Aphrodite and the Roman Venus, the dove was always holy to them. Often they themselves appeared winged, like a great dove brooding over the world, as in Knossos and Mycenae, in Sicily and Carthage, on the Euphrates and on Cyprus, and even in India. Doves were culticly protected; great towers were built for them in which they could nest; they were called *columbaria* (*columba* is the Latin word for dove). *Columbaria,* dove houses, were also known in ancient Rome, however, as grave chambers with niches for urns.

The dove is the only symbol for the Holy Spirit that is permitted by the Church. Thus the figure of the dove in the cupolas or over the high altars of Diessen, Dietramszell, Ettal, Ottobeuren, Vierzehnheiligen, Weingarten, and the Wieskirche also point to the "Great Mother" just as much as do the fact that the cathedrals of Hagia Sophia in Constantinople, Kiev, and many other Orthodox cities are consecrated to heavenly Wisdom, which is presented in feminine form. (Gerd-Klaus Kaltenbrunner, "Ist der Heilige Geist weiblich?" *Una Sancta,* 1977, pp. 275ff.)

§56. Feminine Holy Spirit in Church Art

Let a single visible example indicate that this Christian tradition of depicting the Holy Spirit as feminine continued on into the Middle Ages even in the West. There is a small twelfth-century Catholic church in the tiny village of Urschalling near Prien am Chiemsee, southeast of Munich, which has a fourteenth-century fresco depicting the Holy Trinity. It has three human forms for the upper half of the body and the lower half wrapped in a single cloak so that there would appear to be one body below. One of the upper figures is an old man with a white beard, one is a young man with a dark beard, and in the middle is a woman— Father, Son, and Holy Spirit.

§57. The Gifts of the Holy Spirit

In Christian theology the identification of the feminine Hebraic spirit, *ruach*, with the third person of the Trinity, the Holy Spirit, is reflected in the association of the words of Is 11:1–2 with the seven gifts of the Holy Spirit: counsel, piety, fortitude, fear of the Lord, knowledge, understanding, wisdom (see Thomas Aquinas, *Summa Theologiae*, I.II.69).

> But a shoot shall sprout from the stump of Jesse,
>   and from his roots a bud shall blossom.
> The spirit of the LORD shall rest upon him:
>   a spirit of wisdom and of understanding,
> A spirit of counsel and of strength,
>   a spirit of knowledge and of fear of the LORD. (Is 11:1–2; the Septu-
>   agint and Vulgate translations add "piety," making seven
>   "gifts" of the Spirit.)

§58. The Wisdom and the Word of God Paralleled

It should also be noted that in the Christian tradition the texts concerning the feminine Wisdom in the Hebraic-Judaic tradition are at times associated with the feminine Spirit, as discussed, and also at times with the Word or Logos (masculine in Greek) of God, which in the Gospel of John is identified with both God and Jesus as the Word incarnate. Already in the pre-Christian period a near-identification of Word and Wisdom is made (in Hebraic-Judaic poetry a statement is balanced with the same thought in synonymous terms):

> God of our ancestors, Lord of mercy,
> who by your Word (Logos) have made all things,
> and in your Wisdom (Sophia) fitted humanity to rule . . . (Wisdom
>   9:1–2)

§59. Wisdom, the Goddess Isis, the Word of God, and Jesus Paralleled

Paul speaks of Jesus as the Messiah, the Christ, and then identifies Christ with feminine Wisdom: "We are preaching a crucified Christ . . . who is . . . the Wisdom (Sophia) of God" (1 Cor 1:24–25). In the deutero-Pauline epistle to the Colossians there is a primitive Christian hymn (Col 1:15–20) which speaks of Jesus in terms very like those of the feminine Wisdom of God, e.g., he was with God when all things were created, and through him they were created. In

John's Gospel, Jesus also speaks of himself (Jn 6:35) in language that is likewise very much akin to that of feminine Divine Wisdom, i.e., Jesus, like Wisdom, invites all to come and eat and drink from him (cf. Prov 9:1–6 and Ben Sira 24:19–22). The like is also true of the Prologue of John's Gospel where the Word, Logos, similarly to Hok-mah-Sophia, was said to be from the beginning with God, indeed, was God, through whom all things were created, enlightening all human-ity. The parallel of John's Logos hymn to Hokmah-Sophia is so striking that scholars such as Rudolf Bultmann have suggested the hymn was originally a Sophia hymn and "Logos" was substituted by the author of the Prologue (see Gerhard Kittel, *Theologisches Wörterbuch zum Neuen Testament,* Vol. 4, p. 136; Stuttgart, 1942).

The Catholic scholar Elizabeth Schüssler Fiorenza carried the analysis a step further when she concluded that not only was Jesus identified with the Logos, Word of God, and substituted in place of feminine Sophia in the several New Testament Christological hymns, but because the source of Sophia was the goddess Isis (see p. 36) Jesus Christ also paralleled or assimilated many of the traits of Isis.

Isis virtually took the place of all the other gods and goddesses and she claimed that their names and functions were only names and various titles and functions of her own. Like Isis, Jesus Christ is in the hymn Phil. 2:6–11 given a name which is "above all names." . . . Furthermore: as Isis's true name is "Isis the Queen" *(kyria,* sometimes *kyrios),* so the true name of Jesus Christ is lord *(kyrios).* . . . Just as the Jewish-Hellenistic wisdom speculation appropriated elements from the Isis myth and cult, so too does the Christian proclamation of the cosmic lordship of Jesus Christ borrow its language and categories from the Hellenistic religions, perhaps from the Isis myth and cult. In this milieu where the hymns and aretologies of Isis are found, the Chris-tian community conceives hymns in praise of Jesus Christ as the preexistent one who appeared on earth and is now exalted and enthroned as lord of the whole cosmos. (Elizabeth Schüssler Fiorenza, "Wisdom Mythology and the Christological Hymns of the New Testament," in Robert L. Wilken, ed., *Aspects of Wisdom in Judaism and Early Christianity,* pp. 35f.; University of Notre Dame Press, 1975)

§60. Sophia Christology

In analyzing the Gospel of Matthew, James M. Robinson found that already in the Q materials (putative pre-Matthew and Luke sayings of Jesus—see below, pp. 251ff.) and in the way Matthew used them one finds a Sophia Christology, an identification of the femi-nine Sophia and Jesus. This Sophia Christology continued on into the post-Apostolic Writings (post-New Testament) Christian tradition.

The thanksgiving that in Q culminated in the identification of Jesus with Sophia follows immediately in Matthew, who appends further wisdom material which, like the culmination of that Q section, is applicable to Jesus only because he is Sophia incarnate (11:28–30):

> Come to me all who labor and are heavy laden, and I will give you rest. Take my yoke upon you, and learn from me; for I am gentle and lowly in heart, and you will find rest for your souls. For my yoke is easy, and my burden is light.

These concepts, familiar in wisdom literature, are also applied to the Torah [see §45], and hence point to another trait of Matthew's Sophia christology. Judaism had already identified Sophia with the Torah, by affirming that Sophia, so often rejected by men and having no permanent abode on earth, had come to reside in the Torah (Ecclus. 24). It would fit well with Matthean theology in general to see in the Jewish concept of the "incarnation" of Sophia in the Torah an analogy for carrying through the identification of Sophia with Jesus.

Matthew's Sophia christology is also apparent in his editing of a second wisdom section of Q. The Q saying that began (Luke 11:49): "Therefore also the Wisdom of God said, 'I will send them prophets and apostles,' " is edited by Matthew (23:34): "Therefore I send you prophets and wise men and scribes." It is not enough to say Matthew simply eliminated the reference to Sophia. Rather one must recognize that he identifies Sophia with Jesus, by attributing to Jesus not only a saying previously attributed to Sophia, but by attributing to Jesus the content of the saying, namely, Sophia's role as the heavenly personage who throughout history has sent the prophets and other spokesmen. It is to himself as preexistent Sophia that he refers in saying a few verses later (Matt. 23:37): "How often would I have gathered your children together as a hen gathers her brood under her wings. . . ."

By this time, i.e., the first half of the second century C.E., the identification of Jesus as Sophia had become widespread. In Justin (*Dialogue* 100.4) one reads that Jesus "is also called Sophia . . . in the words of the prophets." (James M. Robinson, "Jesus as Sophos and Sophia: Wisdom Tradition and the Gospels," in Wilken, *Aspects of Wisdom in Judaism and Early Christianity*, pp. 10–12)

Origen (A.D. 185–254) continued the Sophia Christology tradition when, after discussing a number of titles given to Jesus by the Gospels, he concluded that Wisdom was the most ancient and appropriate one.

Thus if we collect the titles of Jesus, the question arises which of them were conferred on him late, and would never have assumed such importance if the saints had begun and had also persevered in blessedness. Perhaps Wisdom would be the only remaining one. . . . (Origen, *Commentary on John* 1.109–113)

§61. Feminine Wisdom, Feminine Holy Spirit,
Sometimes Feminine Word of God

Thus, the feminine divine Wisdom of the Hebraic-Judaic tradition bifurcated in the Christian tradition, partly retaining the usual Hebraic association with the feminine divine Spirit (Ruach) by identification with the Holy Spirit (at times also feminine in Christian tradition), and partly shifting to the rare Judaic association with the masculine Word, Logos, of God. The results were, then, that in Christian tradition one person of the Holy Trinity, the Holy Spirit, is identified with the feminine divine Wisdom and is at times described in feminine imagery, and a second person of the Trinity, the Word, is also identified with the feminine divine Wisdom, but is only rarely described in feminine imagery, as in the following examples.

a. Anselm of Canterbury

The great eleventh-century Western Christian theologian Anselm of Canterbury composed the following prayer:

> But thou also Jesus, good Lord, art thou not also Mother? Art thou not Mother who art like a hen [see §118] which gathers her chicks under her wings? Truly, Lord, thou art also Mother. For what others have labored with and brought forth, they have received from thee. Thou first, for their sake and for those they bring forth, in labor went dead, and by dying hast brought forth. . . . Thou, therefore, soul, dead of thyself, run under the wings of Jesus thy Mother and bewail under her feathers thy afflictions. Beg that she heal thy wounds, and that healed, she may restore thee to life. Mother Christ, who gatherest thy chicks under thy wings, this dead chick of thine puts himself under thy wing. (Anselm, "Oratio ad sanctum Paulum," J. P. Migne, *Patrologia Latina,* Vol. 158, cols. 981f.)

b. Dame Julian of Norwich

The fourteenth-century English mystic Dame Julian of Norwich wrote the following about "Our tender Mother Jesus":

> And thus is Jesus our true Mother in kind [nature] of our first making; and he is our true Mother in grace by his taking of our made kind. All the fair working and all the sweet kindly offices of most dear Motherhood are appropriated to the second Person. (Dame Julian of Norwich, *The Revelations of Divine Love of Julian of Norwich,* tr. by James Walsh, Ch. 59; London: Burns & Oates, 1961)

c. Gregory Palamas

The fourteenth-century Greek Orthodox mystic-theologian Gregory Palamas wrote in the same vein:

> Christ . . . nurses us from his own breast, as a mother, filled with tenderness, does with her babies. (Gregory Palamas, quoted in George H. Tavard, *Woman in Christian Tradition,* p. 158; University of Notre Dame Press, 1973)

§62. An Androgynous God in Catholic Christianity

Very early the term "catholic" came to be used by many Christians to refer to those who had established themselves as orthodox. Among such "orthodox" Christians there was at least one Christian father, Clement of Alexandria (150–215 A.D.—he was listed as a saint in the Roman Catholic Church until the seventeenth century), who wrote of God in androgynous terms. He links essentially God's Fatherhood with Motherhood, love and creation, and speaks of the Father's womb *(kolpon)* which "brought forth" *(exēgēsato)* the only-begotten *(monogenēs)* Son, not of Mother or of Father but of God *(Huios Theou),* underlining both androgyny and unity.

> For what is more essential to God than the mystery of love?
> Look then into the womb *(kolpon)* of the Father,
> Which alone has brought forth the only-begotten Son of God.
>
> God is love,
> And for love of us has become woman *(ethēlynthē).**
> The ineffable being of the Father has out of compassion with us become mother.
> By loving the Father has become woman *(Agapēsas ho Patēr ethēlynthē).* (Clement of Alexandria, "Quis Dives Salvetur," J. P. Migne, *Patrologia Graeca,* Vol. 9, col. 641)
> *[As corrected in Migne; from *thēlynō,* "to become woman."]

C. THE FEMININE GOD IN CHRISTIAN APOCRYPHAL AND GNOSTIC WRITINGS

Because it was only late in the fourth century that the canon of the New Testament was finally fixed as we now have it, many of the writings that are now called apocryphal were for centuries widely accepted and used by Christian churches. Hence, it would be anachronistic to exclude all of them from consideration in matters concerning early Christianity. Still, caution must be exercised in their use, for usually, to a much greater extent than most of the canonical New

Testament writings, most of the apocryphal New Testament writings have very little historical basis—the childhood stories about Jesus, for example, are largely legendary fiction. However, these apocryphal writings are first-class sources for informing us about what many early Christians thought and believed and how they lived: e.g., the extremely anti-sex attitudes of the apocryphal Acts of various apostles—which far exceed any sexual asceticism of the New Testament.

Much, though by no means all, of the Christian writing of these early centuries came under the influence of the broad cultural movement called Gnosticism. Gnosticism, as its name indicated (*gnōsis* —knowledge), taught that salvation was to be attained by means of a secret knowledge lying below the surface of texts, symbols, and events. Thus, in the third-century Gnostic Gospel of Philip it is written: "People do not perceive what is correct but they perceive what is incorrect, unless they have come to know what is correct." (*Nag Hammadi Library*, p. 133.)

Further, Gnosticism tended to be strongly dualistic in its conception of reality (all reality is ultimately made up of two elements: matter, which is evil, and spirit, which is good). In line with that conception it also tended to be very ascetical and anti-sex. But that did not ipso facto mean it was totally anti-woman, as will be seen below when the various apocryphal Acts of apostles are discussed (see §314). Also, partly because of its dualism the masculine and feminine elements were sometimes projected into its conceptualizations of the divinity. Of course there were also other causes of such male-female conceptualizations (e.g., the God and Goddess traditions), and similarly, not every feminine-masculine description of the divinity was necessarily a reflection of Gnosticism. With such cautions in mind we can proceed.

§63. The Triune Thought of God

The Trimorphic Protennoia (the "Three-Form First Thought") is a late second-century Christian (or Christianized) Gnostic tractate about God that in some respects resembles the Hebraic-Judaic traditions about Wisdom (Hokmah-Sophia). Paradoxically the First Thought, *Protennoia*, is at once (1) "The first born of all who exist" and also (2) the one who "exists before the All"; in fact, (3) she "is" the All. The first is reminiscent of Ben Sira 24:9: "From eternity, in the beginning, he created me [Hokmah], and for eternity I shall remain." The second is similar to Prov 8:23: "From everlasting I [Hokmah] was firmly set, from the beginning, before earth came into being." The third is like, but goes beyond, Wisdom 7:25–26: "She [Sophia] is a breath of the power of God, pure emanation of the glory of the Almighty . . . image of his goodness." In this "going beyond," it is analogous to John's utilizing of the Hokmah-Sophia theme and substituting in it the Logos in a way that also continues and "goes beyond" the previous Wisdom tradition (see §59): "In the beginning was the Word [Logos]: The Word was with God and the Word was God. . . . The Word was the true light that enlightens every human being [*anthrōpon*]; and he was coming into the world (Jn 1:1, 9). In the Trimorphic Protennoia, however, the divine "comes the second time in the likeness of a female."

I am Protennoia, the Thought that dwells in the Light. I am the movement that dwells in the All, she in whom the All takes its stand, the first-born among those who came to be, she who exists before the All. She (Protennoia) is called by three names, although she exists alone, since she is perfect. I am invisible within the Thought of the Invisible One. I am revealed in the immeasurable, ineffable things. I am intangible, dwelling in the intangible. I move in every creature. . . . I am the Invisible One within the All. It is I who counsel those who are hidden, since I know the All that exists in it. I am numberless beyond everyone. I am immeasurable, ineffable, yet whenever I wish, I shall reveal myself. I am the movement of the All. I exist before the All, and I am the All, since I exist before everyone. . . .

I am a single one (fem.) since I am undefiled. I am the Mother of the Voice [which is another name for the Father!], speaking in many ways, completing the All. It is in me that knowledge dwells, the knowledge of things everlasting. It is I who speak within every creature and I was known by the All. It is I who lift up the Sound [another name for the Mother] of the Voice to the ears of those who have known me, that is, the Sons of Light.

Now I have come the second time in the likeness of a female and have spoken with them. (Trimorphic Protennoia, *Nag Hammadi Library*, pp. 461, 462, 466)

§64. Mother, Father, Son God — I

In the same Gnostic Christian document, the Trimorphic Protennoia, God is also described as having three dimensions, Mother, Father, and Son. However, there is a certain unclarity because of a language difficulty. The document was originally composed in Greek and was subsequently translated into Coptic (Egyptian). Unfortunately the Greek is lost and the Coptic is obviously not always a precise rendering of the original, leaving us with certain unclarities. Nevertheless, it is sure that the divinity was conceived of as threefold, as Mother, Father, and Son, although it is not clear whether or which, the Father or the Mother, is prior. But perhaps such ambiguity is deliberate. In any case, the feminine, maternal dimension is there at the heart of divinity, as well as the masculine and paternal. The ancient Goddess not only in the form of Wisdom, Knowledge, or Thought (Sophia, Athena) but also as the Mater Magna is present here.

Now the Voice that originated from my Thought exists as three permanences: The Father, the Mother, the Son. . . . He [the Son] gave Aeons for the Father of all Aeons, who is I, the Thought of the Father, for Protennoia, that is, Barbelo [a name often given to the feminine dimension in these Gnostic documents], the perfect Glory and the immeasurable Invisible One who is hidden. I am the Image of the Invisible Spirit and it is through me that the All took shape, and I am the Mother as well as the Light which she appointed as Virgin, she who is called Meirothea [which means "maiden Goddess"], the intangible Womb. . . .
Then the Perfect Son revealed himself to his Aeons. . . . And they gave glory, saying, "He is! He is! The Son of God! The Son of God! It is he who is! (Trimorphic Protennoia, *Nag Hammadi Library*, pp. 463–464)

In the somewhat earlier (before A.D. 185) Gnostic Christian Apocryphon of John the three-form divinity, Father, Mother, Son, is also found. Here, however, the term "spirit" is not feminine but is connected with the Father. The feminine dimension is referred to as Mother, Pronoia (that is, "first thought"), and Barbelo (which may mean "intense radiation"). The Son is also called the Autogenes ("self-generated") and the Christ. Here the Father definitely appears to be prior to the Mother, though she seems to be a perfect image of him and the "womb of everything."

I am the one who is with you forever. I am the Father, I am the Mother, I am the Son. . . . He said to me [John], "The Monad is a monarchy with nothing above it. It is he who exists as God and Father of everything, the invisible one who is above everything, who is imperishability, existing as pure light which no eye can behold.
He is the invisible Spirit. . . . This is the first power which was before all of them and which came forth from his mind, that is the Pronoia of the All. Her light is the likeness of the light, the perfect power which is the image of the invisible, virginal Spirit who is perfect. The first power, the glory, Barbelo, the perfect glory in the aeons, the glory of the revelation, she glorified the virginal Spirit and praised him, because thanks to him she had come forth. This is the first thought, his image; she became the womb of everything for she is prior to them all. (Apocryphon of John, *Nag Hammadi Library*, pp. 99–101)

A third Gnostic Christian document, the Coptic writing called the Gospel of the Egyptians, apparently written somewhat after the above-cited Apocryphon of John, also speaks of a triune God, Father, Mother, and Son. Here the term "Father" does double duty. First it is the great silent unknown Father which is the source of the three powers, the Mother, Son, and Father [the Father being an active force, in this usage]. It should also be noted that in this second sense the Father is also referred to as androgynous (for other examples of androgyny in God, see §§17 and 66). Likewise interesting is the fact that, notwithstanding her "coming forth from the Father," the Mother is also said to have "originated from herself."

> Three powers came forth from him; they are the Father, the Mother, and the Son, from the living silence, what came forth from the incorruptible Father. These came forth from the silence of the unknown Father. . . . The first ogdoad . . . the androgynous Father. The second ogdoad-power, the Mother, the virginal Barbelon. . . . The third ogdoad-power, the Son of the silent silence, and the crown of the silent silence, and the glory of the Father, and the virtue of the Mother. (Gospel of the Egyptians, *Nag Hammadi Library*, p. 196)

§65. Mother, Father, Son God — II

Though Gnosticism was vigorously attacked by catholic Christianity and most of the Gnostic writings were burned, along with as many of the apocryphal writings as could be confiscated, the idea of Motherhood in a triune God either persisted or reappeared in medieval Western Christianity (as also in medieval Judaism, i.e., the Kabbala —see §46). The fourteenth-century English mystic mentioned above, Dame Julian of Norwich, spoke of the properties of Fatherhood, Motherhood, and Lordship (the latter, because it is connected to "Our Lord Jesus," is the equivalent of the Son) in the Trinity. There is here obviously no subordination of Motherhood to the other properties of God.

> I beheld the working of all the blessed Trinity. In which beholding I saw and understood these three properties: the property of Fatherhood, and the property of Motherhood, and the property of the Lordship—in one God. . . . I saw and understood that the high might of the Trinity is our Father, and the deep wisdom of the Trinity is our Mother, and the great love of the Trinity is our Lord. (Dame Julian of Norwich, *Revelations of Divine Love of Julian of Norwich,* tr. by James Walsh, Ch. 58)

§66. The Mother-Father God Once Again

Above in §22 the likelihood of the female and male aspects of the divinity being reflected in the ancient Hebrew names for God *(Eloah, El, Elohim)* was discussed, and in §43 a quotation from the Dead Sea Scrolls was cited as perhaps a further echo of this divine "androgyny." This is of course besides all of the evidence exhibited above showing that the divine in the Judeo-Christian tradition was conceived of in feminine as well as masculine terms; but it was usually rather clearly either feminine or masculine, rather than both at the same time. Even most of the Gnostic Christian material quoted in the pages just above speaks of the Mother and the Father in the divine separately. However, there are other statements from this Gnostic and apocryphal Christian material which refer to the divine as "syzygetic" (paired), "Mother-Father," etc., beginning with the above-cited (§64) Coptic Gospel of the Egyptians reference to "the androgynous Father."

> Then he said to me, "The Mother-Father who is rich in mercy, the holy Spirit in every way, the One who is merciful . . ." (Apocryphon of John, *Nag Hammadi Library*, p. 114)

> I am the Voice [synonym for the Father] that appeared through my Thought, for I am "He who is syzygetic," since I am called "the Thought of the Invisible One." Since I am called "the Unchanging Sound [synonym for the Mother]," I am called "She who is syzygetic." . . . I am androgynous. I am both Mother and Father since I [make love] with myself. I [make love] with myself and with those who love me, and it is through me alone that the All stands firm. I am the Womb that gives shape to the All by giving birth to the Light that shines in splendor. I am the Aeon to come. I am the fulfillment of the All, that is, Meirothea, the glory of the Mother. (Trimorphic Protennoia, *Nag Hammadi Library*, pp. 465–467)

Another second-century Gnostic Christian document, also originally written in Greek but this time available only in a Syriac translation, the Odes of Solomon, also speaks of the divinity in androgynous terms. However, they are different from those previously cited. First, the Odes speak not of Father, Mother, and Son, but of the customary Christian Father, Son, and Holy Spirit. Second, the androgyny appears when the Father is said to have milk-filled breasts!

> A cup of milk was offered to me;
> And I drank it in the sweetness of the delight of the Lord.
> The Son is the cup.
> And He who is milked is the Father;
> And He who milked Him is the Holy Spirit.
> Because His breasts were full;
> And it was not desirable that His milk should be spilt to no purpose.
> And the Holy Spirit opened His [literally, Her] bosom
> And mingled the milk of the two breasts of the Father,
> And gave the mixture to the world without their knowing:
> And they who take it are in the fullness of the right hand.
> (J. R. Harris and A. Mingana, eds., *The Odes and Psalms of Solomon*, Vol. 2, pp. 298f.—19:1–5; London, 1920)

III. Summary: Feminine Imagery of God

§67. Feminine and Masculine Divine
Personifications Co-Identified

Brief summary note should be taken here of the extraordinary contact, and even conflation, in the orthodox Jewish and Christian writings, to say nothing of those outside the mainline traditions, of several of the divine personifications that have been discussed. Mention has already been made of the identification between Hokmah and Ruach (both feminine), Hokmah and Torah (both feminine), and Hokmah-Sophia and Logos (feminine and masculine). In addition, there is also an identification between God's Word (*dabar* in Hebrew and *logos* in Greek, both masculine) and Torah (feminine). This happens in the Hebrew Bible, e.g., in Ps 119, vs. 9, 16, 17, 25, 28, 42, 43, 49, 65, 74, 89. God's Word is praised in parallel with, and identified with, God's Law in vs. 1, 18, 29, 34, 44, 51, 53, 55, 57, 61, 70, 72, 77, 85 (Dabar and Torah and variants are used).

In the Christian tradition there is also a kind of identification that takes place between Logos and Torah. Jesus the Christ is said to be God's Logos; as of old one approached and knew God through the Torah, now such an approach and knowledge is made through the living Logos, Jesus Christ: "Indeed, from his fulness we have, all of us, received—yes, grace in return for grace, since, though the Law [Torah] was given through Moses, grace and truth have come through Jesus Christ [the *logos theou*]. No one has ever seen God; it is the only begotten who is near the Father's heart, who has made him known" (Jn 1:16–18). Indeed, even though in later Christian ecumenical councils a clear distinction between the Christ (the Logos of John) and the Spirit was made, many Scripture scholars and theologians dispute whether such a distinction is biblically sustainable in view of statements like that of Paul in 2 Cor 3:17: "Now this Lord [Christ] is the Spirit, and where the Spirit of the Lord is, there is freedom." In any case, there is no hesitation in the Christian tradition about identifying the masculine Word of God, Logos, and Christ, with the feminine divine personifications of Hokmah, Torah, and Ruach.

Besides these co-identifications in the strictly orthodox Jewish and Christian writings, there are the further manifold conflations of the Mother, Father, Son, Spirit, Light, Voice, Thought (or Logos) cited above from the Gnostic Christian writings. Furthermore, writing of the Jew Philo, Samuel Sandmel said:

> Philo's Logos derives from an earlier encounter of Jewish and Greek ideas, wherein the content of similar terms and ideas resulted in a blending of them. Torah equaled *Hokmah* which equaled *Sophia* ("Wisdom") which equaled Logos ("rationality"). The Divine Logos was a synthesis of these earlier ideas, and were brought together into an amalgam. (Samuel Sandmel, *Judaism and Christian Beginnings,* p. 298; Oxford University Press, 1978)

Something similar was said of Saadia, one of the important kabbalists, by Gershom Scholem:

> According to him [Saadia], God, who remains infinite and unknown also in the role of Creator, has produced the glory as "a created light, the first of all creations." This *Kavod* is "the great radiance called Shekhinah" and it is also identical with the *ruach ha-kodesh,* the "holy spirit," out of whom there speaks the Voice and Word of God. (Scholem, *Major Trends in Jewish Mysticism,* p. 110)

Part Two

WOMAN IN HEBREW-JEWISH TRADITION

IV. Positive Elements in Hebrew-Jewish Tradition

A. THE STATUS OF WOMAN—BIBLICAL PERIOD

1. The First Woman and Man

In Hebrew literature there are at least two traditions about the nature of woman. One, in attempting to describe what the original state of humanity—before the Fall—must have been like, is positive and depicts woman as the equal of man, if indeed not the perfection of humanity. The second tradition, attempting initially to explain the actual subordinate condition of women in society—after the Fall—is negative and describes woman as inferior to man because of disobedience.

§68. God Created Humanity: Genesis 1

There are two accounts of the creation of humanity in the book of Genesis. The later account, composed by the Priestly writer,* is completely egalitarian in its description of human creation. God is described as creating humanity immediately in its dual sexual form; there is no priority or inferiority expressed or implied. It should also

---

*Scholars are basically agreed that the work of at least five writers can be discerned in the first five books of the Bible, the Pentateuch. They are the Yahwist, J (so symbolized because of the personal name of God, Yahweh—sometimes transliterated Jahweh; hence the symbol J), who probably wrote in the tenth century B.C.E.; the Elohist, E (so symbolized because the name Elohim, God, is used almost exclusively when referring to God), who probably wrote during the ninth and tenth centuries; the Deuteronomist, D, who may have written during the seventh century, though the date is much disputed; the Priestly writer, P, who probably wrote during the fifth century; the fifth hand is that of the editors or redactors.

be noted that the word used for "man," as it is often translated in English, is *ha adam,* a generic Hebrew term for humanity, literally "the human"; it is a mistake to translate it in Gen 1 to 2:22 either as man in the male sense or as a proper name, Adam (until Gen 4:25 the definite article *ha* is almost always used with *adam,* precluding the possibility of its being a proper name; in 4:25 it becomes a proper name, *Adam,* without the *ha*). Moreover, it is clearly a *collective* noun in Gen 1 to 2:22, as can be seen in the plural "let *them* be masters" (Gen 1:26).

God said, "Let us make humanity in our own image, in the likeness of ourselves, and let them be masters of the fish of the sea."... God created humanity in the image of himself, in the image of God he created it, male and female he created them. (Gen 1:26–27)

§69. God Created Humanity: Genesis 2

The much older Yahwist writer of Genesis 2 described the same creation of humanity with what became the story of "Adam and Eve." Though interpreted as reflecting man's superiority over woman by apocryphal Jewish writers a century or two before the time of Jesus (see The Books of Adam and Eve, R. H. Charles, ed., *The Apocrypha and Pseudepigrapha of the Old Testament,* Vol. 2, pp. 123–154; Oxford University Press, 1913), Paul (1 Cor 11:7–9—see §332), and the deutero-Pauline writer (1 Tim 2:13—see §334), this late understanding does not reflect the original meaning of the text.

Moreover, such a claim of male superiority made because the male was later, mistakenly, thought to have been created first is based on the assumption that the superior was created first. But not only is that exactly the reverse of what is seen to be reality in modern evolutionary understanding—the higher beings are the last to arise—it is also the reverse of the Genesis 1 story of creation: first God created the heavens and earth, then plants, fish, birds, land animals, and only finally—as a high point, not a low point—humanity. From the perspective of the Priestly writer of Genesis 1, and modern evolutionary thought, the claim that woman was created after man would indicate that she was superior to him. But of course the Priestly writer did not claim woman was created after man, but rather "God created humanity . . . male and female he created them"; the Priestly writer was affirming male and female equality.

Actually the Yahwist writer of Genesis 2 likewise does not speak of the prior creation of male humanity. Rather, he speaks of the creation of humanity, undifferentiated:

Yahweh God fashioned humanity* of dust from the earth.** (Gen 2:7)
*[ha adam—note the definite article *ha*, "the"—here is still not a personal name, but a collective noun.]
**[ha adamah (feminine!); a Hebrew play on words meaning that humanity, *ha adam*, is an earth *(ha adamah)* creature.]

§70. Ishshah and Ish — I

The Yahwist writer, in his story fashion, expresses the idea that it was not good for humanity to be singular, that to be fully human there must be relationships, dialogue between two *equals*, which function the lesser animals cannot fulfill. The Yahwist has God creating the birds and animals after humanity, but they are unable to be an adequate partner to humanity—hence the creation of the sexes, equal though not identical, out of the undifferentiated humanity. The Yahwist uses the word *ha adam*, "the human," or "humanity," all the way to verse 23, where he refers to woman with the word *ishshah* and to the male with the word *ish*, making a definite play on words: "This is to be called wo-man *(ishshah)*, for this was taken from man *(ish)*." Up to that point it is very clear that the creature out of which woman is fashioned is *ha adam*, generic, undifferentiated humanity. But as soon as the Yahwist focuses on the play on words and presents his folk etymology of the Hebrew word for woman, *ishshah*, as "taken from *ish*" (because they sound similar) the possibility of confusion arises; the unwarranted conclusion that woman was "taken from" the male, i.e., that the female was formed from the rib of the male rather than from undifferentiated humanity, is at hand. But the writer's main intent would seem to be that the *word* wo-man *(ishshah)* is taken from the *word* man *(ish;* the word *ishshah* appears—though modern grammarians tell us it is not really so—basically to be the word *ish* with the feminine suffix *ah* added to it. Luther, e.g., translated *ishshah* as *Männin*, a grammatically feminized form of *Mann*, meaning man the male; for *ha adam* he used the generic collective *Mensch*. Paul in 1 Cor 11:7–9 and the deutero-Pauline writer in 1 Tim 2:13 missed this careful, and important, distinction).

Yahweh God said, "It is not good that humanity *(ha adam)* should be singular *(l^ebadda)*. I will make for it a partner."* So from the soil Yahweh God fashioned all the wild beasts and all the birds of heaven. These he brought to humanity *(ha adam)* to see what it would call them; each one was to bear the name humanity *(ha adam)* would give it. Humanity *(ha adam)* gave names to all the cattle, all the birds of heaven and all the wild beasts. But no partner suitable for humanity *(ha adam)* was found for it. So Yahweh

God made humanity *(ha adam)* fall into a deep sleep. . . . Yahweh God built the rib he had taken from humanity *(ha adam)* into a woman *(ishshah)* and presented her to humanity *(ha adam)*. Humanity *(ha adam)* exclaimed:
"This at last is bone from my bones,
and flesh from my flesh!
This is to be called wo-man *(ishshah)*,
for this was taken from man *(ish)*."
That is why a man *(ish)* leaves his father and mother and joins himself to his wife, and they become one body. (Gen 2:18–24)
*[Partner, *ezer neged*, is usually translated "helpmate," but the Hebrew word *ezer* implies no inferiority, as for example in Ps 33:20; 115:9–11; 121:2; 124:8; 146:5–6; Ex 18:4; and Deut 33:7, 26, 29, where God is an *ezer* to humanity; further, the word *neged* adjoining *ezer* indicates equality, meaning literally "alongside of," as is pointed out by E. A. Speiser, *Genesis*, The Anchor Bible p. 17; Doubleday & Co., 1964].

§71. Ishshah and Ish — II

Phyllis Trible has an extremely penetrating analysis of the above key passage (v. 23) which deals with the parallel between *ish/ishshah* and *ha adam/ha adamah:*

As *ishshah* is taken from *ish*, so *ha adam* is taken from *ha adamah* (cf. 2:7). Yet *ha adam* is never portrayed as subordinate to the earth. On the contrary, the creature is given power over the earth so that what is taken from becomes superior to. By strict analogy, then, the line "this shall be called *ishshah* because from *ish* was taken this" would mean not the subordination of the woman to the man but rather her superiority to him.

Yet the practice of determining the nuances of a given word from its usages elsewhere in a text may mislead as well as enlighten. The meanings gleaned from such a procedure must fit the particular context in which the word being studied appears. Since the context for this statement concerning *ishshah* and *ish* is the preceding line, "bone of my bones and flesh of my flesh," the connotation of woman's superiority is inappropriate. The relationship of this couple is one of mutuality and equality, not one of female superiority and certainly not one of female subordination. Nowhere in this entire story is subordination a connotation of the phrase "taken from." Finally, woman is not derived from man, even as the earth creature is not derived from the earth. For both of them life originates with God. Dust of the earth and rib of the earth creature are but raw materials for God's creative activity. Truly, neither woman nor man is an autonomous creature; both owe their origin to divine mystery. (Trible, *God and the Rhetoric of Sexuality*, pp. 100f.)

§72. Humanity and the Fall

After this point, however, the Yahwist becomes ambivalent, for his use of *ha adam* shifts and it now clearly means the male. He states: "and the man *(ha adam)* and his wife *(ishshah)* were not ashamed" (Gen 2:25); "and the man *(ha adam)* and his wife *(ishshah)* hid themselves" (3:8); "and the man *(ha adam)* said, 'the woman *(ishshah)* you gave me' " (3:12); "and he said to the man (*l'adam*, "to the"—with the elision of the preposition the article *ha* disappears), 'Because you listened to the voice of your wife *(ishshah)* . . .' " (3:17); "and Yahweh God made clothes for the man *(l'adam)* and his wife *(ishshah)* . . . (3:21). Then from Gen 4:25 onward the article *(ha)* is not used before *adam* and the word often, though not always (cf. Gen 5:1–2), becomes a proper name, Adam. But in 3:16 the Yahwist did not use any form of *adam*, but rather *ish*, male: "and your desire will be for your man *(ish)*."

However, lest one be tempted to think that, despite the above earlier documentation, this later use of *ha adam* by the Yahwist as meaning "the man" was also intended in the earlier section, Gen 2:7–24, the following should also be recalled: in 3:3 the woman says "God said, 'You (plural) shall not eat the fruit of the tree in the middle of the garden and you shall not touch it lest perhaps you shall die.' " But there is only one previous mention of this command and it is not given to the man and woman after the recorded creation of the woman (and man) in Gen 2:22, but rather to undifferentiated humanity, *ha adam*, in 2:16: "And Yahweh God commanded humanity *(ha adam)*, saying, 'You may eat from every tree in the garden except the tree of the knowledge of good and evil, of which you must not eat, for on the day you eat from it you will surely die.' " Thus for the Yahwist the woman, *ishshah*, was included in undifferentiated humanity, *ha adam*.

§73. Woman and Man After the Fall

Chapter 3 of Genesis is the story of the Fall. It is the Yahwist's (or rather his sources') attempt to account for the misery he sees in the world about him; God is affirmed to be a beneficent creator (ch. 2), and therefore disorder in the world must be caused by someone other than God—that someone is *ha adam*. The Yahwist does not imply that the domination of woman by man is according to the nature of things as God created them. On the contrary, God created woman and man equal (ch. 2); it is because of disobedience that all nature becomes disordered: e.g., the animals and plants are no longer docile before the man, the woman's body in childbirth is no longer completely under her control, woman and man are no longer co-ordinate, but super- and sub-ordinate to one another—all because the anchor of order, humanity's obedience to God, was lost.

It should also be noted that God curses the serpent and the earth, but does not curse either the woman or the man. They both, however, receive a punishment, which is not administered in a command, e.g., "you *must* bear your children in pain," or "you *must* earn your bread by the sweat of your face." Rather, it is the simple future tense of the verbs that is used, telling the man and woman what in fact *will* happen in the future. All this is seen by the biblical writer as evil, resulting from sin, something that according to the order of God's creation ought not be (that includes of course the sub-ordination of the woman to the man), but unfortunately in fact does exist. In other words, the dire words the Yahwist places on the lips of God are not prescriptive, but descriptive—humanity brought its punishment on itself.

The serpent was the most subtle of all the wild beasts that Yahweh God had made. It asked the woman, "Did God really say you were not to eat from any of the trees in the garden?" The woman answered the serpent, "We may eat the fruit of the trees in the garden. But of the fruit of the tree in the middle of the garden God said, 'You must not eat it, nor touch it, under pain of death.' " Then the serpent said to the woman, "No! You will not die! God knows in fact that on the day you eat it your eyes will be opened and you will be like gods, knowing good and evil." The woman saw that the tree was good to eat and pleasing to the eye, and that it was desirable for the knowledge that it could give. So she took some of its fruit and ate it. She gave some also to her husband who was with her, and he ate it. Then the eyes of both of them were opened and they realized that they were naked. So they sewed fig-leaves together to make themselves loin-cloths.

The man and his wife heard the sound of Yahweh God walking in the garden in the cool of the day, and they hid from Yahweh God among the trees of the garden. But Yahweh God called to the man. "Where are you?" he asked. "I heard the sound of you in the garden"; he replied, "I was afraid because I was naked, so I hid." "Who told you that you were naked?" he asked. "Have you been eating of the tree I forbade you to eat?" The man replied, "It was the woman you put with me; she gave me the fruit, and I ate it." Then Yahweh God asked the woman, "What is this you have done?" The woman replied, "The serpent tempted me and I ate."

Then Yahweh God said to the serpent, "Because you have done this, be accursed beyond all cattle, all wild beasts. You shall crawl on your belly and eat dust every day of your life. I will make you enemies of each other: you and the woman, your offspring and her offspring. It will crush your head and you will strike its heel."

To the woman he said: "I will multiply your pains in childbearing, you shall give birth to your children in pain. Your yearning shall be for your husband, yet he will lord it over you."

To the man he said, "Because you listened to the voice of your wife and ate from the tree of which I had forbidden you to eat, accursed be the soil because of you. With suffering shall you get your food from it every day of your life. It shall yield you brambles and thistles, and you shall eat wild plants. With sweat on your brow shall you eat your bread, until you return to the soil, as you were taken from it. For dust you are and to dust you shall return."

The man named his wife "Eve" because she was the mother of all those who live. Yahweh God made clothes out of skins for the man and his wife, and they put them on. Then Yahweh God said, "See, humanity *(ha adam)** has become like one of us, with its knowledge of good and evil. It must not be allowed to stretch its hand out next and pick from the tree of life also, and eat some and live for ever." So Yahweh God expelled it from the garden of Eden, to till the soil from which it had been taken. He banished humanity *(ha adam),* * and in front of the garden of Eden he posted the cherubs, and the flame of a flashing sword, to guard the way to the tree of life. (Genesis 3)

*[Obviously here *ha adam* means not the man but humanity; otherwise not the woman but just the man would have been driven from the garden of Eden. Luther perceived this better than most modern translators, for he rendered *ha adam* here with the plural of the sexless generic term for human beings: *die Menschen.*]

§74. The Shifting Meanings of *ha adam*

As noted above, the term *ha adam* is used in a collective sense in Genesis 1 through 2:22, referring to humanity, as yet undifferentiated sexually. From there to Gen 3:22, *ha adam* refers to the man as distinct from *ishshah*, for the undifferentiated humanity no longer exists. But in Gen 3:22–24, as seen just above, *ha adam* is again meant collectively: humanity is driven out of the Garden of Eden. As Phyllis Trible makes clear,

Ha adam now becomes a generic term that keeps the man visible and renders the woman invisible (3:22–24). . . . The emphasis upon the man in the design of the story shows his rule over the woman in the aftermath of disobedience. What God described to the woman as a consequence of transgression the story not only reports but actually embodies. Generic *ha adam* has subsumed *ishshah*. . . . As a central word in this dissonant ring composition, *ha adam* is used exclusively for humanity at the beginning and end of the story, yet with two very different meanings: at first, the sexually undifferentiated earth creatures (2:7); at last, the generic man who renders the woman invisible (3:24). (Trible, *God and the Rhetoric of Sexuality,* pp. 134–137)

§75. Eve the Seducer

One of the traditional interpretations of the Fall is to see in it proof of woman's inferiority to man; the "proof" is that the serpent, the spirit of evil, realized that the man was too strong to overcome and so he first approached the woman, because she was weaker, less intelligent. In the second century A.D., Tertullian, the Latin Christian church father from North Africa, expressed the argument vigorously:

> The sentence of God on this sex of yours lives on even in our times and so it is necessary that the guilt should live on, also. You are the one who plucked the fruit of the forbidden tree, you are the first who deserted the divine law; you are the one who persuaded him whom the Devil was not strong enough to attack. All too easily you destroyed the image of God, man. (Tertullian [A.D. 160–225], *De cultu feminarum, The Fathers of the Church,* Vol. 40, p. 118; Fathers of the Church, Inc., 1959)

In the fourth century a Greek church father from Palestine, Epiphanius, argued in a similar manner about Eve and women in general: The devil, completely unable to direct the thoughts of the male, who gets his strength from the knowledge of God, from the truth, turned to woman—that is, to the ignorance of humanity—and seduced those who were in ignorance, people without firm ideas—that is, the feminine in humanity. (See Migne, *Patrologia Graeca,* Vol. 41, col. 643.) The eighth-century Greek church father John Damascene presented similar ideas. (See Migne, *Patrologia Graeca,* Vol. 104, col. 706.) Lest one think this line of argument is passé, it should be noted that in 1952 a Christian theologian argued as follows:

> The devil tempted Eve, not Adam, because she—although both possessed the gift of *integritas*—could fall more easily than the man; for she—prescinding from the more abundant grace which Adam doubtless was given—was more easily led astray and weaker in resistance. (I. F. Sagües, *Sacrae Theologiae Summa,* Biblioteca de Autores Cristianos, Vol. 2, p. 887; Madrid, 1952)

§76. Female Superiority

The puzzling, even astounding, thing about this pervasive and persistent line of thought is the total unawareness in its advocates of the self-destructive—to say nothing of the self-contradictory—implications embedded in it. The basic assumption is that one intelligence can lead another astray only when it is superior to it (apparently the serpent/devil was not superior to the man, but was superior to the woman). But that leads to the self-destructive conclusion that, since the woman led the man astray, the woman is superior to the man! An unavoidable, though undesired, conclusion. Clearly there must be a better way to understand the relationship between the woman and the man in the story of the Fall. A contemporary Christian theologian provides a persuasive, feminist one:

The serpent speaks to the woman. Why to the woman and not the man? The simplest answer is that we do not know. . . . But the silence of the text stimulates speculations, many of which only confirm the patriarchal mentality that conceived them. Let a female speculate. If the serpent is "more subtle" than its fellow creatures, the woman is more appealing than her husband. Throughout the myth she is the more intelligent one, the more aggressive one and the one with greater sensibilities. . . . The initiative and the decision are hers alone. She seeks neither her husband's advice nor his permission. She acts independently. By contrast the man is a silent and bland recipient: "She also gave some to her husband and he ate." . . . His one act is belly-oriented, and it is an act of quiescence, not of initiative. The man is not dominant; he is not aggressive; he is not a decision-maker. . . . He follows his wife without question or comment, thereby denying his own individuality. If the woman be intelligent, sensitive, and ingenious, the man is passive, brutish, and inept. These character portrayals are truly extraordinary in a culture dominated by men. I stress this contrast not to promote female chauvinism but to understand patriarchal interpretations alien to the text. (Phyllis Trible, "Depatriarchalizing in Biblical Interpretation," *Journal of the American Academy of Religion,* Vol. 41, No. 1, March 1973, p. 40)

In fact, Professor Trible's analysis probably is more likely correct than she suggests. As was discussed above (see §1), the worship of the deity as Goddess preceded biblical religion by thousands of years and was the target of the most intense hostility by the patriarchal father-God worshipers loyal to Yahweh. What is pertinent to note here is that a very prominent symbol of the Goddess was the Serpent (see, e.g., Gimbutas, *Gods and Goddesses of Old Europe,* pp. 93–101); that the Serpent Goddess was then said to be the source of wisdom (Hokmah—see p. 36) and knowledge; and that priestesses were the mediators of the Goddess, the source of wisdom (Hokmah). Under this also lay the sociological fact that earlier Goddess-worshiping societies were also possibly matriarchal, that is, ruled by women. They were certainly matrilineal (see James, *Cult of the Mother Goddess,* p. 228)—that is, property was inherited through the woman's line; to get at power and property men would have to change the theology of a supreme Goddess as the source of real wisdom [Hokmah], and women as her mediators.

An intention of the Yahwist writer that suggests itself here is that he wishes to show that though the Goddess, in her immediately recognizable symbolic form of the serpent, claims to lead humanity to true knowledge and participation in divine life through the mediation of women—here through "the woman"—such a claim is spurious and leads in fact to death; therefore, man should not follow woman in seeking religious knowledge, i.e., he should forsake the ministrations of the priestesses of the Goddess; moreover, priestesses must forsake the precincts of the Goddess temple where sacred sex was performed as a "holy" act (the priestesses who performed this sacred sex were called *qedeshot* in the Hebrew Bible, meaning literally "holy women") and limit their sexual activity to a single husband: "Your desire shall be for *your* husband."

This latter aspect was patently an attempt to place property in the hands of the man, instead of the woman as it had earlier been. If it had been simply a concern to limit sex to between a single husband and wife, the husband would also have been so constrained; but in the Yahwist's society the man was not limited to one woman. With the woman limited sexually to one man it was possible to know who the man's offspring was and thus have patrilineal inheritance. But if the Hebrew woman could, like the Hebrew man, have more than one spouse, only the mother could be known for certain, and hence matrilineal inheritance would have remained the only choice. Thus did theology serve to reflect, justify, and confirm the "new" patriarchal, patrilineal social structure.

§77. Mutuality Repeated: Genesis 5

Chapter 5 of Genesis is the transition from the story of prehistory to "history," but only the first two verses are pertinent. The chapter was composed by the Priestly writer, who wishes to provide a genealogical link between the first human beings and subsequent historical developments and does so by offering a "roll of humanity's descendants." He basically repeats his statement of ch. 1 about God creating humanity in masculine and feminine form. There is a difficulty about translating P's use of the word *adam.* In ch. 1, P used the word twice, in verses 26 and 27, and in both instances the word had the same meaning, "humanity," even though in one instance the article was used and in one not: "Let us make humanity *(adam)* in our own image. . . . And God created humanity *(ha adam)* in the image of himself, in the image of God he created it, male and female he created them." The presence of the definite article *ha* excludes the possibility that the word *adam* could be meant as a personal name. But its absence does not necessitate understanding the word as a personal name; it merely makes it possible, depending on the context. In ch. 5 the Priestly writer used *adam* without the article, so that only the context can give the correct meaning. In any case, the beginning of ch. 5 reiterates the egalitarian creation of women and men, in almost exactly the same words used in chapter 1.

This is the roll of humanity's *(adam)* descendants:
On the day God created humanity *(adam)* he made it in the likeness of God. Male and female he created them. He blessed them and gave them the name "Humanity" *(adam)* on the day he created them. (Gen 5:1–2)

2. HEBREW WOMEN LEADERS

§78. Women Prophets

There are a variety of characteristics that are attributable to prophets, but basically a prophet is one through whom God speaks. The Hebrew word for prophet is *nabi,* and its feminine form is *nebiah.* It is used to refer to four specific women in the Hebrew Bible. The one other time the word *nebiah* is used is in Is 8:3, where it apparently refers to the prophet's wife, although some scholars suggest it might mean "sacred prostitute."

a. Daughters Prophesy

Perhaps the latest reference in the Hebrew Bible to women prophesying occurs in the writings of the probably postexilic prophet Joel. He does not hesitate to use a form of the verb "to prophesy" *(nb')* in referring to women:

After this I will pour out my spirit on everyone. Your sons and your daughters will prophesy *(nibe'u).* (Joel 2:28)

b. Miriam the Prophet

We are told in Num 26:59 and 1 Chron 5:29 that Miriam, Moses, and Aaron were siblings. Since they were the only ones mentioned, Miriam is presumed to be the sister of Moses referred to in the story of Ex 2:4–9, who offered to find a Hebrew wet nurse for the Pharaoh's daughter's foundling boy—Moses. Miriam was called by the oldest writer of the Bible (J) a woman prophet *(nebiah)* when she sang a victory praise of Yahweh upon the Israelites' escape from Pharaoh's army:

Miriam the prophet *(nebiah),* Aaron's sister, took up a timbrel, and all the women followed her with timbrels, dancing. And Miriam led them in the refrain: "Sing of Yahweh: he has covered himself in glory, horse and rider he has thrown into the sea." (Ex 15:20–21)

That Miriam was a prophet, that is, one through whom God spoke, was also clearly implied in another passage:

Miriam and Aaron too spoke against Moses. . . . They said: "Has Yahweh spoken to Moses only? Has he not spoken to us too?" (Num 12:1–2)

The prophet Micah, who lived in the eighth century B.C.E., was apparently recipient of an ancient tradition that gave Miriam a very significant leadership role in early Israelite history—an independent prominence which some Scripture scholars believe was later downgraded partly in order to raise Moses even higher—could it also have been because women prophets and religious leaders were associated with the priestesses of the Goddess? At any rate, Micah refers to Miriam and Moses and Aaron on a par:

The Lord says, "My people, what have I done to you? How have I been a burden to you? Answer me. I brought you out of Egypt, I rescued you from slavery; I sent Moses, Aaron, and Miriam to lead you." (Mic 6:3–4)

The story of Miriam's rebuke (Num 12:1–16) is somewhat confusing and unbalanced, again raising the question of whether it was designed, or redesigned, to downgrade Miriam vis-à-vis Moses and Aaron. The first element of confusion is that both Miriam and Aaron (with Miriam in the lead) "spoke against" Moses in connection with the Cushite woman he had married (Num 12:1), but what then followed had apparently nothing at all to do with the Cushite woman. Rather, it centered on Miriam's and Aaron's claim also to be leaders, prophets, of the Israelites along with Moses. Conceivably a dispute over the marrying of a foreigner might have precipitated a power confrontation, but that is not clear from the Scriptures. What is clear is that Miriam, a woman, claimed leadership, prophecy, speaking for God, and was put down.

The second problematic element in this story is that although both Miriam and Aaron jointly, equally, challenged Moses' sole leadership, only Miriam was punished—and most severely! She was made a leper, someone who would contaminate others who came into contact with her. The immediate thought is that the resultant isolation of the challengers would keep the contagion of rebellion against the patriarchal Moses from spreading. But why is only the woman "struck with leprosy" and therefore isolated? Was the fear like that of King Ahasuerus in the Book of Esther, who was afraid Queen Vashti's disobedience might "soon become known to all the women and encourage them in a contemptuous attitude towards their husbands"? (Esth 1:17). Was that somehow connected with the relatively high status women had in the Egypt from which the Israelites were escaping, and with the priestesses there who served the powerful Goddess? Some scholars argue that Miriam was one of three independent leaders of the Hebrews escaping from Egypt and that it was only in the later retelling of the story that Miriam is made into Moses' and Aaron's sister and made inferior to Moses.

c. Deborah, Prophet and Judge

As far as one can date the difficult material of the Book of Judges, Deborah is said to have lived perhaps in the twelfth century B.C.E., that is, before the establishment of the Kingdom of Israel under Saul, David, and Solomon. Deborah is called a prophet, *nebiah*. She was a spokesperson for Yahweh:

> At this time Deborah was judge in Israel, a prophet *(nebiah)*. . . . She sent for Barak son of Abinoam from Kedesh in Naphtali. She said to him, "This is the order of Yahweh, the God of Israel: March to Mount Tabor." (Judg 4:4, 6)

As already noted, Deborah was also called a judge, that is, one who dispenses justice and is in a special way an instrument for God's justice. In the former role she exercised the then highest role of potential leadership in Israel:

> At this time Deborah was judge in Israel, a prophet, the wife of Lappidoth. She used to sit under Deborah's Palm between Ramah and Bethel in the highlands of Ephraim, and the Israelites would come to her to have their disputes decided. (Judg 4:4–6)
> [It is interesting to note that as late as the eighth century B.C.E. there are records that women served as judges and magistrates outside of Israel, in Nimrud in northern Mesopotamia—see Stone, *When God Was a Woman*, p. 44.]

In the latter role, as a special instrument of God's justice, Deborah exercised even more decisive leadership, for when Israel was literally oppressed she called forth the men and the will to fight for freedom. The Israelite general said he would fight only if she led the way, which she did. Deborah gave the command to attack, and victory was Israel's. Afterward:

> The land enjoyed rest for forty years. (Judg 5:31)

In what is perhaps the oldest Hebrew literary composition, the Song of Deborah (Judg 5:1–31), Deborah and Barak sang—like Moses and Miriam and so many of the "singing women" and "singing men" of Hebraic culture—of Yahweh's victory:

They sang a song that day, Deborah and Barak. . . . "Dead, dead were Israel's villages until you rose up, O Deborah, you rose up, a mother in Israel. . . . Awake, awake, Deborah! Awake, awake, declaim a song! Take heart, arise Barak, capture your captors, son of Abinoam! Then Israel marched down to the gates; Yahweh's people, like heroes, marched down to fight for him. . . . So perish all your enemies, Yahweh! And let those who love you be like the sun when he arises in all his strength!" (Judg 5:1, 7, 12, 13, 31)

d. Huldah the Prophet

The third woman given the title of prophet, *nebiah*, was Huldah during the reign of Josiah the reforming Yahwist king in the latter part of the seventh century B.C.E. It is the only time she appears in the Bible, but that appearance is quite extraordinary. Josiah was embarked on a religious reform, in the midst of which Hilkiah, the high priest at the Jerusalem Temple, said he had discovered the book of the law of Yahweh—presumably an early form of the present book of Deuteronomy. The book was presented to the pious king, who was deeply impressed by the book and also deeply distressed that its prescriptions were not being lived up to—so much so that he tore his garments, sent for his chief advisers and the high priest and said, "Go and consult Yahweh, on behalf of me and the people. . . ." The extraordinary thing, from one point of view, is that they then went to a woman prophet! It is extraordinary in view of the long-standing, deep hostility between the devotees of Yahweh and the devotees of the Goddess, whether under the name of Asherah, Astarte, or Anath. For example, in 2 Kings 23, where the religious reforms of King Josiah are described, the destruction of shrines to Asherah or Astarte is mentioned specifically six times in verses 4 to 15 (vs. 4, 6, 7, 13, 14, 15). On the other hand, perhaps because Goddess worship was so pervasive and the prominent religious role women naturally played in it so customary, the obvious presumption that Josiah, Hilkiah, and the other Yahwists clearly held about a woman being able to be the deity's, even Yahweh's, spokesperson was not surprising.

Huldah was approached by the king's emmissaries in standard fashion, and she responded in the standard prophetic manner, that is, she began with a phrase like: "Thus says Yahweh." She issued dire warnings for evildoings:

Hilkiah the priest, Ahikam, Achbor, Shaphan and Asiah went to Huldah the prophet *(nebiah)*. . . . She replied, "Yahweh, the God of Israel, says this, 'To the man who sent you to me say this: Yahweh says this: . . . And you are to say to the king of Judah who sent you to consult Yahweh: Yahweh, the God of Israel, says this: . . . It is Yahweh who speaks.' " They took this answer to the king. (2 Kings 22:14–20)

e. Huldah the Founder of Biblical Studies

One scholar has noted that at the beginning of the crucial judgment about which books are to be accepted into the canon of the Bible we find a woman, Huldah.

Josiah as king and head of the Jewish people accepted Huldah's evaluation of the scroll as the authentic word of Yahweh and entered into a covenant with Yahweh to follow all the commandments and decrees in the scroll. This marks the first time any of the Hebrew scriptures were officially recognized as authentic. Josiah's acknowledgement of the Book of the Law, then, represents the first beginnings of our biblical canon. And the authority to pass judgment on this initial entry into the canon was given to a woman. At the beginning of the Bible we find Huldah; in her we discover the first scripture authority, the founder of biblical studies. (Arlene Swidler, "In Search of Huldah," *The Bible Today,* November 1978, p. 1783)

f. Noadiah a False Woman Prophet

The seventh-century, preexilic narrative about Huldah is the last reference in the Hebrew Bible about a woman prophet *(nebiah),* save one (and the more general reference of Joel 2:28, discussed above): an extremely brief reference to Noadiah (whose name, interestingly, means "Yah(weh) assembles"), who is entitled a prophet *(nebiah),* but one who apparently improperly tried to frighten the restorer of Jerusalem, Nehemiah. If women can be prophets, they presumably, like men, can also be false prophets. The Scripture simply says:

Remember Tobiah, my God, for what he has done; and Noadiah the prophet *(nebiah),* and the other prophets who tried to frighten me. (Neh 6:14)

§79. The Wise Women of Tekoa and Abel

As seen above, the Hebrew word for wisdom is *hokmah.* With the same consonants but different vowel pointing (Hebrew is written with only consonants; the vowels—by "pointing"—were added to the biblical text only many centuries later by Hebrew grammarians, the Massoretes) the word becomes *hakamah,* a wise woman.

There are two incidents in the Hebrew Bible which center on a *hakamah,* both in the Second Book of Samuel (2 Sam 14:2–20; 20:16–22). In the first incident King David's general Joab sends for the *hakamah* from Tekoa, some eleven miles from Jerusalem, so that she might act as an intermediary in the bringing back of David's son Absalom from exile. Though she was carefully briefed by Joab, she successfully carried out her task with consummate skill, fully justifying the reputation she had for wisdom, *hokmah.*

The second incident also involves Joab and a *hakamah,* this one from the city of Abel of Beth-maacah. In pursuing the rebel Sheba, Joab laid siege to him in that northern city to which he had fled. Then a *hakamah* from the city negotiated with Joab, who said he did not want to destroy the city, but only Sheba. She persuaded the city leaders to give up the rebel and thus saved the city. Julia F. Beck, doing research at the Religion Department, Temple University, noted that from her "power of counsel in time of war, this woman appears to have wielded, at least locally, the power of a Deborah. . . . Both of these wise women were obviously community leaders and spoke in the name Yahweh." (Unpublished research paper)

§80. Hebrew Queens

Though one does not usually think of Hebrew queens, there were two such reigning queens before the Common Era, Athaliah (842–837) and Salome Alexandra (78–69), both of Judah. Athaliah seized the throne upon the death of her son, putting to death all her grandsons (save one who escaped)—a not infrequent ancient, and not so ancient, pattern of eliminating potential rivals; at the same time Jehu was murdering many scores of rivals in the northern kingdom of Israel. After seven years of rule—relatively long in the list of Hebrew rulers—she was overthrown and put to death by the Yahwist high priest (Athaliah was a devotee of the god Baal and the goddess Asherah).

Salome Alexandra was of a much more irenic nature. At the wish of her dying husband she took over the Jewish realm and ruled until her death some nine years later. Hers was a rare reign of peace and prosperity in Judea, so much so that she is often referred to as "Good Queen Alexandra." After her death her sons fought over the crown, and Rome, in the figure of Pompey, took over the Holy Land. The last really independent Jewish ruler of the Holy Land, until 1948, was a woman.

3. Biblical Love Poetry by Women

In the earliest civilization, the Sumerian, there was a group of professional women, called *naditu,* probably meaning "surrendered to the deity," who worked at the temples of the Goddess, handling its business affairs, etc.; many of them also served as scribes (see Rivkah Harris, "Naditu Women of Sipar I & II," *Journal of Cuneiform Studies*, Vol. 15, 1961, pp. 117–120; Vol. 16, 1962, pp. 1–12). In fact, according to the epic of Gilgamesh a woman is the official recorder of the nether world (James B. Pritchard, ed., *Ancient Near Eastern Texts Relating to the Old Testament*, 2d ed., p. 87; Princeton University Press, 1955). Throughout all the Babylonian periods (running from 1830 to 539 B.C.E.) women served as scribes (see Stone, *When God Was a Woman*, p. 44).

In the Hebrew tradition women played the role of "singing women," that is, singers of ballads, tales, and poetry (e.g., Ex 15:20; Judg 5:1, 12)—not unlike the male troubadors and minnesingers of medieval Europe—as best exemplified in Miriam and Deborah. Dorothy Irvin ("Omnis Analogia Claudet," in Leonard Swidler and Arlene Swidler, eds., *Women Priests: A Catholic Commentary on the Vatican Declaration*, pp. 271–277; Paulist Press, 1977) notes that in the Hebrew Bible references to women as creators and transmitters of the literary culture of that period are numerous (2 Sam 19:35–36; 2 Chron 35:25; Is 23:16; Eccles 2:8; Zeph 3:14; Zech 2:10). Besides songs of the ballad type, about important legendary events mentioned above, religious songs were also part of their repertory (e.g., Ezra 2:65; Neh 7:67). It may well be, as Irvin argues, that the Song of Songs "is more likely than anything else already investigated to be women's written contribution to the Old Testament." She points out that the exclamations addressed in the Song of Songs to other members of the group, "O daughters of Jerusalem," and the references to the mother-daughter relationship—not common in the rest of the Hebrew Bible—both indicate the setting of the women's gathering, an exclusively female group that sang, danced, and in general focused on the prospective bride and her forthcoming wedding.

The biblical book of the Song of Songs as we have it perhaps comes from the third century B.C.E., though much of the material is considerably older. It is simply love poetry of a woman and a man for each other with no particular "religious" content. Perhaps it was attributed to Solomon—who obviously was not the true author—because he had the reputation of being a great lover. Perhaps the reason it was included in the canon of sacred Scriptures was that it was interpreted allegorically, that is, as reflecting the love of Yahweh for Israel, as some rabbis supposedly argued at Jamnia around 100 C.E., although that does not tell us why it was already included in the

Septuagint Greek translation of the Bible (third to second century B.C.E.). In any case, it is love poetry, a candid celebration of full human love, very much including its sensuous, sexual pleasures for both partners. It reflects an image of woman and female-male relations that is extremely positive and egalitarian. To begin with, attention focuses immediately on the woman: the book begins and closes with the woman speaking:

> Your lips cover me with kisses;
>   your love is better than wine.
> There is a fragrance about you;
>   the sound of your name recalls it.
>   No woman could keep from loving you.
> Take me with you, and we'll run away;
>   be my king and take me to your room.
> We will be happy together,
>   drink deep, and lose
>   ourselves in love. (Song of Songs 1:2–4)

> Come to me, my lover, like a gazelle,
>   like a young stag on the mountains where spices grow. (Song of Songs 8:14)

Furthermore, the woman has most of the dialogue by far—eighty-one verses to forty-nine for the man. (See the excellent divisions printed in the Good News Bible translation.) The woman initiates most of the action and is just as active as the man in lovemaking, if not more so. For example:

> On my bed at night, I sought him whom my heart loves . . . I found him. I held him and wouldn't let him go until I took him to my mother's house, to the room where I was born. (Song of Songs 3:1, 4)

In this female initiative in lovemaking the biblical Song of Songs is very like the much more ancient (1920 B.C.E.) Middle Eastern love poetry of Sumer. In writing on this subject anthropologist Jacquetta Hawkes remarked:

> In the subsequent history of human sexual attitudes, there have been the most surprising swings between the view that women are essentially passive in lovemaking, that it is the man who demands and gets full sexual satisfaction, and the opposite opinion that woman's appetite is insatiable, that if allowed she would drain the manhood from her lovers. It is therefore not without interest to find that among the Sumerians, the first people to make some record of sexual passion, it is the second view that seems to prevail. In the sacred marriage texts it is Inanna who utters nearly all the expressions of love, and she who confesses to having sated Dumuzi in lovemaking.

(Jacquetta Hawkes, *The First Great Civilizations,* p. 177; Alfred A. Knopf, 1973)

The poem Hawkes refers to is the Sumerian *Inanna and the King:*

> The sun has gone to sleep, the day has passed,
> As in bed you gaze lovingly upon him. . . .
> She craves it, she craves it, she craves the bed,
> She craves the bed of the rejoicing heart, she craves the bed,
> She craves the bed of the sweet lap, she craves the bed . . .
> (Pritchard, *Ancient Near Eastern Texts,* Vol. 2, pp. 640–641)

A portion of another Sumerian love poem also portraying the woman's initiative in lovemaking is quite like a portion of the Song of Songs with its reference to going to the woman's mother, opening the door of her mother's house for her lover, her lovemaking:

> The priestess directed her feet to the mother who gave birth to her. . . . The lady directed her step, opened the door for Dumuzi. In the house she came forth to him like the light of the moon, gazed at him, rejoiced for him, embraced him. ("Courting, Marriage, Honeymoon," Pritchard, *Ancient Near Eastern Texts,* Vol. 2, p. 639)

> On my bed, at night I sought him whom my heart loves. . . . I found him. I held him and wouldn't let him go until I took him to my mother's house, to the room where I was born. . . . My lover put his hand to the door, and I was thrilled that he was near. I was ready to let him come in. . . . I opened the door for my lover. . . . I would take you to my mother's house, where you could teach me love. (Song of Songs 3:1, 4; 5:4, 6; 8:2)

Another dimension of equality between the woman and the man in the Song is the fact that both are "gainfully employed," and at the same kind of job. They are both shepherds. The woman says to the man: "Tell me, my love, where will you lead your flock to graze?" (1:7). He says to her: "Don't you know the place, loveliest of women? Go and follow the flock; find pasture for your goats near the tents" (1:8).

(It is possible there is here a vestige from the "sacred marriage" rite of Sumer and subsequent Middle Eastern civilizations [see above remarks by Jacquetta Hawkes] wherein the male lover is Dumuzi the shepherd, whose role in the rite was taken by the king—see Song of Songs 3:6–11, where King Solomon is brought into the imagery.)

The woman further explicitly asserts the egalitarianism of mutual love when she twice over says: "My lover is mine, and I am his" (2:16; 6:3).

Though we are quite used to love poetry written by men about the beauty of the women they love, in the Song of Songs the woman is just as eloquent about the beauty of the man she loves—again a fundamental note of egalitarianism:

Like an apple tree among the trees of the forest, so is my dearest compared to other men. I love to sit in its shadow, and its fruit is sweet to my taste. (Song of Songs 2:3)

My lover is handsome and strong; he is one in ten thousand. His face is bronzed and smooth; his hair is wavy, black as a raven. His eyes are as beautiful as doves by a flowing brook, doves washed in milk and standing by the stream. His cheeks are as lovely as a garden that is full of herbs and spices. His lips are like lilies, wet with liquid myrrh. His hands are well-formed, and he wears rings set with gems. His body is like smooth ivory, with sapphires set in it. His thighs are columns of alabaster set in sockets of gold. He is majestic like the Lebanon Mountains with their towering cedars. His mouth is sweet to kiss; everything about him enchants me. This is what my lover is like, women of Jerusalem. (Song of Songs 5:10–16)

The mother plays an extraordinarily important role in the Song of Songs. Is this an echo of a matriarchal, or matrilineal or matrilocal, society? Mother is referred to seven times in the Song, whereas father is not mentioned at all. The mothers of both the woman and the man are mentioned:

She is called the "darling of her *mother*" (6:9).

Of the man reference is made to "where your *mother* conceived you" (8:5).

The woman wishes the man had been her "brother nursed at my *mother's* breast" (8:1).

King Solomon is said to wear the crown "with which his *mother* crowned him: (3:11).

The women's actual brothers are mentioned as "my *mother's* sons" (1:6).

In two places the woman takes the initiative by taking the man "into my *mother's* house" (3:4; 8:2).

At the same time, one scholar notes that in view of the stress on woman's role as wife and mother in Hebrew society, it is remarkable that the Song is not interested in these ways of identifying a woman. The Song does not tell us whether the lovers are married or not; marriage is not an issue here. Moreover, "the woman is *not* a mother, and there are no references to her procreative abilities or interest in childbearing" (Cheryl Exum, "Images of Women in the Bible,"

Women's Caucus—Religious Studies Newsletter, Vol. 2, No. 3, Fall 1974, p. 5).

Some of the most interesting work on the meaning of the Song of Songs has been done by Phyllis Trible, who sees the Song as, if not in intent, then at least in fact, a midrash on the Adam and Eve story, a sort of theme and variations. She concludes by saying:

> In many ways, then, Song of Songs is a midrash on Genesis 2–3. By variations and reversals it creatively actualizes major motifs and themes of the primeval myth. Female and male are born to mutuality and love. They are naked without shame; they are equal without duplication. They live in gardens where nature joins in celebrating their oneness. Neither couple fits the rhetoric of a male-dominated culture. As equals they confront life and death. But the first couple lose their oneness through disobedience. Consequently, the woman's desire becomes the man's dominion. The second couple affirm their oneness through eroticism. Consequently, the man's desire becomes the woman's delight. Whatever else it may be, Canticles is a commentary on Genesis 2–3. Paradise Lost is Paradise Regained. (Trible, "Depatriarchalizing in Biblical Interpretation," pp. 46f.)

The following passages illustrate this point:

> "I am my beloved's, and his desire is for me." (Song of Songs 7:10) "Your desire shall be for your husband, yet he will lord it over you." (Gen 3:16)

B. THE STATUS OF WOMAN—POSTBIBLICAL PERIOD

1. Jewish Women of Elephantine

As noted above (§5), a colony of Jews lived at Elephantine, about four hundred miles south of Cairo on the Nile, perhaps from late seventh century B.C.E. to early fourth century B.C.E. A number of letters from there dated in the fifth century B.C.E. reveal several interesting dimensions of the status of Jewish women in Elephantine that are much more liberal than what apparently obtained in Israel at the same time—the period of Nehemiah and Ezra.

§81. No Polygyny

The worship at Elephantine of the Goddess along with Yahweh is discussed elsewhere (§5). In addition, from extant marriage documents, it appears that polygamy and concubinage, which were allowed to men in Israel in the fifth century, were forbidden in Jewish Elephantine. In a marriage contract from about 441 B.C.E. the groom Ashor promised to his bride Miphtahiah:

And I shall have no right to say I have another wife besides Miphtahiah and other children than the children whom Miphtahiah shall bear me. (Cowley, *Aramaic Papyri*, p. 46)

A similar stipulation made in another Elephantine marriage contract from about 420 B.C.E. repeated this prohibition of polygyny:

Moreover, Anani shall not be able to take another woman beside Ye-hoyishma to him for marriage. If he does he has divorced her. (Kraeling, *Brooklyn Papyri*, p. 207)

It is especially interesting to note that in the same contract it was thought important to also forbid the wife to take another man, again under the threat of divorce. She was equally forbidden to engage in polygamy. Polyandry was so unthinkable in Palestinian Hebrew religion that its prohibition is not even mentioned. But in Egyptian Hebrew religion it is clearly quite thinkable, but along with polygyny is rejected:

But Yehoyishma shall not have power to cohabit with another man beside Anani, and if she does thus, she is divorced. (Kraeling, *Brooklyn Papyri*, p. 207)

§82. Hebrew Women Divorce Their Husbands

In biblical Hebrew religion and Judaism only the man can divorce his spouse, for the wife is the husband's property, but not vice versa. In Elephantine Judaism women could divorce men on equal terms, as is demonstrated by a number of documents, mostly marriage contracts.

The oldest document, 460 B.C.E., is not a marriage contract but a property deed which includes a reference to what would happen if the wife were to divorce the husband:

If tomorrow or another day you lay out this land and then my daughter divorces you and goes away from you. . . . (Cowley, *Aramaic Papyri*, p. 27)

A marriage contract from 449 B.C.E. contains arrangements for the divorce of the husband by the wife, even though she was only another woman's handmaiden:

If tomorrow or another day Tamut rises up and says, "I divorce my husband Anani," a like sum shall be on her head. (Kraeling, *Brooklyn Papyri*, p. 143)

Eight years later in 441 B.C.E. another marriage contract was made out, with typically similar divorce stipulations for both the wife and the husband. It is interesting to note that the wife's divorce right is mentioned first:

> If tomorrow or another day Miphtahiah should stand up in the congregation and say, I divorce Ashor my husband, the price of divorce shall be on her head. . . . Tomorrow or another day if Ashor should stand up in the congregation and say, I divorce my wife Miphtahiah, her price shall be forfeited. (Cowley, *Aramaic Papyri,* p. 46)

We have another partially preserved marriage contract from 425 B.C.E. which as usual includes divorce arrangements for the wife (Cowley, *Aramaic Papyri,* p. 56), and likewise a very elaborate marriage contract from 420 B.C.E. wherein equal divorce rights are stated:

> If tomorrow or another day Anani shall rise up . . . and say: "I divorce my wife Yehoyishma, she shall not be a wife to me," the divorce money is on his head. . . . And if Yehoyishma divorces her husband and says to him, "I divorce thee. I will not be to thee a wife," the divorce money is on her head. (Kraeling, *Brooklyn Papyri,* pp. 205–207)

§83. Jewish Women of Elephantine Receive and Exchange Property

Women in Palestinian Judaism experienced a range of property restrictions, e.g., wives could almost never inherit and daughters usually could not either. (Some reserve in judgment is in order, however, since we do not have contracts and records from fifth- to second-century Palestinian Judaism comparable to Elephantine Judaism of that period.) But in Elephantine Judaism women clearly did regularly receive, hold, and exchange property and goods. In a document dated 495 B.C.E., a property contract, the names of the parties are all feminine, showing that here Jewish women could hold property in their own right and go to court about it:

> On the second day of the month of Epiphi of the twenty-seventh year of King Darius, said Selua daughter of Kenaya and Yethoma her sister to Ya'a' or daughter of Shelomim, We have given to you half the share which was granted to us by the king's judges and Ravaka the commander, in exchange for half the share which accrued to you. (Cowley, *Aramaic Papyri,* p. 2)

In another document, from 447 B.C.E., we find further proof that a woman could hold property and transact business in her own name, independent of her father and husband. This document is a deed for a house which is given by Mahseiah to his daughter Mibtahiah in payment for goods she gave him. They clearly are operating as two independent buyers and sellers in the document, with no father's permission to the daughter sought or given. In fact, we know from another document that the daughter was married at this time and consequently in Palestinian Jewish law she would have come under her husband's control. But he is not even mentioned in this document (Cowley, *Aramaic Papyri*, pp. 37–41).

Still another document, from 420 B.C.E., portrays a woman receiving the deed of part of a house from her father while she was still unmarried, indicating she could operate as a property holder in her own name (Kraeling, *Brooklyn Papyri*, pp. 191–197). The same is also true of "Miphtahiah daughter of Gemariah, a Jew from Yeb the fortress," who paid a sum of money to another woman in return for her earlier support; at the end it said the scribe "wrote this deed at the direction of Miphtahiah" (Cowley, *Aramaic Papyri*, pp. 144–147).

§84. Women: Taxes and Military Service

Equality or near-equality for Jewish women at Elephantine meant sharing both responsibilities as well as privileges with Jewish men. Unlike their Jewish sisters in Palestine, Elephantine Jewish women had equal divorce rights with their husbands, could be parties to litigation and could take oaths, and enjoyed full equality with men in the law of property and obligations. Along with these privileges women also bore the responsibility of serving in the military units, which made up the population of Elephantine—it was a military outpost for the Persian empire while it controlled Egypt in the sixth and fifth centuries B.C.E. (see Reuven Yaron, *Introduction to the Law of the Aramaic Papyri;* Oxford University Press, 1961).

Women also shared in the tax burden, as is indicated by a list of contributors to what was apparently a temple tax. There are about 117 names on the list, 38 of them being clearly women's, since they are referred to as "daughter of . . .," 48 men's, and another 33 indecipherable or missing. In short, of the decipherable names, 44 percent were women's.

It is interesting to note that not all the money here collected was dedicated to Yahu (Elephantine spelling for Yahweh). Rather, it was divided up three ways, with 126 shekels going to Yahu, 120 to Anathbethel, and 70 to Eshembethel. Yahu received slightly more than did the goddess Anath, the consort of Yahu (see §5), just as there were a few more men than women contributing. It is not at all certain who Eshembethel was, though that it was a deity appears definite. Kraeling suggests the name refers to "the consort of Bethel," that is, of the God, presumably synonomous with Yahu; Eshem might have been the spouse-consort of Bethel (Yahu) and Anath the daughter-consort of Bethel (Yahu) (Kraeling, *Brooklyn Papyri,* pp. 87–91). Depending on how the 33 indecipherable names in the list would fall out by sex, it could be that gender served as a basis for the division of the 316 shekels. But this can only be speculative, since the 117 contributors should, at the two shekels apiece mentioned in the document, have raised only 234 shekels—were there additional free-will offerings by the 117 or more names from missing pages?

In any case, it is abundantly clear from the evidence here, and especially from what was discussed above in §5, that the Goddess was worshiped along with the God Yahweh by the Elephantine Jewish community, that Jewish women contributed taxes to her honor—and also fulfilled military service.

2. POSITIVE MODELS OF WOMEN IN RABBINIC JUDAISM

Rabbinic Judaism grows out of the broader Hebrew tradition reaching back into the second millennium B.C.E. It comes closer to focus after the return from exile (587–537 B.C.E.) to Jerusalem mainly of members of the tribe of Judah—hence the name of Judaism. Ideologically it entailed an emphasis on the study and living of the Torah, led by Ezra in the fourth century B.C.E. and by a group that came to be called scribes, on the one hand, and by the Pharisees stemming from the second century B.C.E. who emphasized ritual and Sabbath exactness and purity, on the other. These two elements gradually fused, especially in the crucible of the destruction of the Temple and Jerusalem in 70 and 135 C.E., focusing on the rabbi as student and teacher of the Torah as the linchpin of Jewish religion and society. The teaching and discussions of the rabbis and their students began well before the beginning of the Common Era, but it was only around 200 C.E. that those teachings were first codified in writing. That codification resulted in the Mishnah, that is, the teaching of rabbis up to that time (these rabbis are called *tannaim;* other teachings of *tannaim* were also gathered in a collection called the Tosefta). The succeeding rabbis, called *amoraim,* commented on the Mishnah, and their teachings were gathered into two Talmuds, the Palestinian or Jerusalem Talmud (codified in the fourth century C.E.) and the Babylonian Talmud (codified in the fifth century C.E.). This literature became normative for all subsequent Judaism, and hence it is extremely important to investigate the role of women therein.

The status of women in the formative period of Rabbinic Judaism was very subordinate in general, as will be detailed in brief fashion below (see §106; for a thorough analysis, see Leonard Swidler, *Women in Judaism*). There were a number of rabbinic teachings about women that might be described as positive-negative, or ambivalent. They will also be discussed below (see §96). But there were two women in this period of Judaism who projected quite positive images, one of them very much so. They shall be discussed in detail here. The first is Beruria.

§85. Beruria the Unordained Rabbi

Beruria lived in Palestine during the first part of the second century C.E., a time when the Roman empire was exerting maximum oppression on the numerous Jews (perhaps eight million of a total one hundred million population) within its borders. She was the daughter of one rabbi, Hananya ben Teradyon, and the wife of another, Meir. But Beruria's claim to fame lies not in her relationship to men, but in her own self and accomplishments. As the *Encyclopaedia Judaica* (Vol. 4, col. 701; Jerusalem, 1971) states, "she is famous as the only woman in talmudic literature whose views on halachic matters [religious law] are seriously reckoned with by the scholars of her time." She provides an extraordinary, indeed unique, model of religious and intellectual profundity and strength in Rabbinic Judaism.

Beruria became an avid student of Torah, although we do not know who taught her to read or with what rabbi she studied; she may have studied with her father, but perhaps also with other rabbis. Apparently she went through the intensive three-year course of study customary for disciples of rabbis at the time:

> Rabbi Simlai came before Rabbi Johanan and requested him: Let the master teach me the Book of Genealogies. . . . Let us learn it in three months, he proposed. Thereupon he (Rabbi Johanan) took a clod and threw it at him, saying: If Beruria, wife of Rabbi Meir and daughter of Rabbi Hananya ben Teradyon, who studied three hundred laws from three hundred teachers in one day could nevertheless not do her duty in three years, yet you propose to do it in three months! (Talmud bPesachim 62b)

Beruria not only put in the canonical three-year program of study but also did it in such an exemplary manner that she was held up as an example of how to study Torah. Indeed, her reputation as an avid student was so great that it spawned legends about her studiousness, as in the clearly hyperbolic reference to the three hundred laws studied from three hundred teachers every day for three years. Such a legend was quite a compliment to her reputation, and triply so when it is also recalled that Beruria was being held up to be emulated by Rabbi Simlai who himself was a very renowned rabbi, and that Rabbi Simlai lived over a hundred years after Beruria.

Beruria also took part in the discussions and debates among the rabbis and their more able followers. In one such debate over a very technical matter of ritual purity, she opposed, and bested, her brother: in referring to Beruria, Rabbi Judah ben Baba said, "His daughter has answered more correctly than his son" (Tosephta Kelim B. K. 4, 17).

Another debate was recorded in which two rabbinical schools were ranged on opposite sides, whereupon Beruria gave her solution. "When these words were said before Rabbi Judah, he commented, 'Beruria has spoken rightly' " (Tosephta Kelim B. M. 1, 6). The striking thing about these reports, and others elsewhere in the Talmud, is that a woman's opinion on Torah became law, halacha. At least one woman penetrated to the heart of Judaism, Torah, and not only as an absorbent student but also as a rabbinical disputant and a decisive maker of law.

But beyond these accomplishments Beruria also followed the path of all other really able students of Torah and became a teacher of Torah:

> Beruria once discovered a student who was learning in an undertone. Rebuking him, she exclaimed: Is it not written, "ordered in all things and sure?" If it (the Torah) is "ordered" in your 248 limbs it will be "sure," otherwise it will not be "sure." (Talmud bErubin 53b)

The then common mode of studying Torah was to recite it aloud to memorize it more effectively. Here Beruria not only drilled the student as a schoolmistress, but did so in a peculiarly rabbinic fashion: she quoted from the Torah and argued her position by explaining and applying the scriptural passage. Her rebuke of the student was gentle; she tried to lead him more deeply into his studies. As one modern Jewish woman scholar states, "One gets the impression that Beruria had the personality of a master-rebbe who was seriously concerned with the spiritual and educational welfare of people" (Anne Goldfeld, "Women as Sources of Torah in the Rabbinic Tradition," *Judaism,* Spring 1975, pp. 245–256). That this story of Beruria, together with one of her teaching the famous rabbi

Jose the Galilean on the road to Lydda, is grouped with a number
of other rabbinical stories about teaching, indicates that the editors
of the Babylonian Talmud were aware of her teaching prowess as late
as the fifth century—three centuries after her death.

Still another story recorded in the Talmud portrays Beruria teaching Torah in the customary rabbinical manner—quoting, explaining,
and applying Scripture:

> A certain *min* (Sadducee) said to Beruria: It is written: "Sing, O barren,
> thou that didst not bear." Because she did not bear, she should sing? She
> said to him: Fool! Look at the end of the verse, where it is written, "for more
> are the children of the desolate than the children of the married wife, saith
> the Lord." Rather, what is the meaning of "O barren, thou that didst not
> bear"?—Sing O community of Israel, who resembles a barren woman, for not
> having borne children like you, who are damned to hell. (Talmud bBerakhoth
> 10a)

Beruria clearly did not suffer fools gladly, as this story and the one
about Rabbi Jose the Galilean related below indicate. She could also
be extremely sympathetic and sensitive to those she felt were sincere,
but here she faced a man she thought was helping to destroy true
Judaism (*min* is to be understood here either as a Sadducee opponent
of the Pharisees/rabbis or as a Jewish-Christian) and who apparently
was expounding Scripture in an ignorant way. If there was anything
Beruria could not tolerate, it was a man being pretentious about
Torah.

Beruria likewise had an intense moral fervor and sensitive concern
for persons, as illustrated by the following story about her and her
famous husband, Rabbi Meir:

> Certain highwaymen living in the neighborhood of Rabbi Meir annoyed
> him greatly, and Rabbi Meir prayed for them to die. His wife Beruria said
> to him: What is your view? Is it because it is written: "Let the sinners be
> consumed?" Is "sinners" written? "Sins" is written. Moreover, look at the
> end of the verse: "and let the wicked be no more." Since the sins will cease,
> the wicked will be no more. He prayed for them and they repented. (Talmud
> bBerakhoth 10a)

This is clearly high moral advice, presented with the usual scriptural quotation, analysis, and application of its meaning. Beruria here
showed herself the superior of the best male rabbinical mind and
moral spirit; the hard proof of that is that Rabbi Meir took her advice,
with success. A modern male Jewish scholar has commented on this
passage: "Students sufficiently familiar with Hebrew would profit
greatly by following Beruria's argument in the Talmud's original text,

also looking up the Hebrew of the verse." (B. M. Lerner, in A. Ehrman, ed., *The Babylonian and Jerusalem Talmuds Translated Into English with Commentary,* bBerakhoth 10a, p. 189; Jerusalem, 1965ff.)

If Beruria was a brilliant student and teacher of Torah, a decider of halacha, and one who lived and taught an intensely moral life, did she not have all the qualities of a rabbi? Rabbi, after all, simply meant "master" or "teacher"; it was a term of respect given to the teachers of Torah who were expected to decide the law and live morally. She clearly did, but in the documents as we have them she is never referred to as rabbi. Presumably she never received the "ordination" *(semikhah)* to the rabbinate that promising young men normally received at the completion of their studies. (At least one man, Ben Azzai, of the first century, was also learned in the Law, taught law, decided law, and was of high moral character, and was also not "ordained," and hence not referred to as rabbi.) There was no legal reason why she could not have been "ordained"; rather, the generally very low rabbinic estimate of women is the most likely reason, though from the documents which are available we cannot know that for certain.

Beruria, as she appears in the pages of rabbinic writings, is a person who lived a very full human life with perhaps more than her measure of suffering. Hers was the time of the final destruction of the Jewish homeland in Palestine by the Romans in 135 C.E., until it was reestablished in the twentieth century. She lost her father Rabbi Hananya ben Teradyon in these same Hadrianic persecutions. Her brother, whom she had bested in a Torah dispute, disgraced the family by turning to banditry and subsequently was murdered by his gang for trying to inform on them. Her sister was forced into a brothel by the conquering Roman authorities, although Beruria contrived to have her husband, Rabbi Meir, rescue her. But perhaps the most tragic suffering of her life was the death of two of her sons. Her endurance and response to their sudden deaths is recalled in the following rabbinic story:

When two of their sons died on Sabbath, Beruria did not inform Meir of their children's death upon his return from the academy in order not to grieve him on the Sabbath! Only after the Havdalah prayer did she broach the matter, saying: Some time ago a certain man came and left something in my trust; now he has called for it. Shall I return it to him or not? Naturally Meir replied in the affirmative, whereupon Beruria showed him their dead children. When Meir began to weep, she asked: Did you not tell me that we must give back what is given on trust? "The Lord gave, and the Lord has taken away." (Midrash Proverbs 30, 10)

In the midst of extraordinary suffering we see her rabbinic style coming to the fore once more, as she tells a story and applies it to the present situation with a Scripture quotation. Likewise, the stereotypical sex roles are reversed as the strong Beruria takes the more intellectual approach, and Rabbi Meir weeps.

In all the stories recorded about Beruria, she is always set over against a man; the only story involving another woman is really not a tale about Beruria but about her husband, who was asked by Beruria to rescue her sister from the brothel (Talmud bAboda Zara 176–182). In the rabbinic writings Beruria is seen only as a rabbinic student, disputant, halachic decision maker, and above all a teacher—always with men. Moreover, she is always superior to the men, whether as a model of studiousness, a teacher, or as a superior and even at times triumphant disputant and exegete. This is the case even in regard to her husband, the most learned and renowned rabbi of his age. If such a strong and positive image comes through even the totally male memorized, written, and edited rabbinic materials, what must Beruria have been like?

Beruria had to be an unusual—a rabbinical—woman to make a broad mark on that massive male work, the Talmud. Clearly she did not fit the female stereotype of her day. But she was more than that. She very keenly felt the oppressed, subordinate position women held in the Jewish society around her, and struck out against it. Her consciousness was extremely sensitized:

> Rabbi Jose the Galilean was once on a journey when he met Beruria. "By what road," he asked her, "do we go to Lydda?" "Foolish Galilean," she replied, "did not the Sages say this: Engage not in much talk with women? You should have asked: By which to Lydda?" (Talmud bErubin 53b)

What is irritating Beruria is woman's second-class status, here reflected in the rabbinic law that a man should not speak much with women, who are too "lightheaded" to waste time on, and sexually tempting besides. Here was a chance to throw verbal acid in the face of one of her "oppressors." A student she treated gently; the rabbi she called a fool. But with her keen wit she did not simply vituperate the rabbi (one wonders if he had earlier delivered himself of some pompous sage quotation on the frivolity and inferiority of women to have earned this breathtaking attack); instead, she carefully followed the traditional rabbinic pattern of disputation by rebutting a statement with a quotation from the written or oral Law. Always she remained the intellectual.

What a weight Beruria's reputation must have had in talmudic times for this vitriolic putdown of a rabbi to be noted, remembered for hundreds of years, and ultimately made permanent in the final redaction of the Talmud. That there was obviously also a counter feeling among the early rabbis is reflected only in a shadowy fashion in the last line of the talmudic story about Rabbi Meir's rescue of Beruria's sister from a brothel. There was a backlash to his rescue efforts and "he then arose and ran away and came to Babylon; others say because of the incident about Beruria" (Talmud bAboda Zara 182). No further information about the "incident" is given in the Talmud. There is merely this dark reference, sheer innuendo.

A thousand years later, we find a full-blown legend about the incident in the commentary on this passage by the famous Jewish medieval talmudic scholar Rashi:

> Beruria once again made fun of the saying of the Sages that women are lightheaded. Then Meir said to her: With your life you will have to take back your words. Then he sent one of his students to test her to see if she would allow herself to be seduced. He sat by her the whole day until she surrendered herself to him. When she realized (what she had done) she strangled herself. Thereupon Rabbi Meir ran away (to Babylonia) on account of the scandal. (Rashi, quoted in Hans Kosmala, "Gedanken zur Kontroverse Farbstein-Hoch," *Judaica*, 1948, pp. 225–227)

There is nothing at all in the intelligence, perceptiveness, and moral character of Beruria to make this in any way credible. Would she not have perceived that her husband had set a trap for her? Is it not incomprehensible that the great Rabbi Meir could have commissioned his rabbinic student to commit one of the three deadly sins in its most serious form: sexual immorality with a married Jewish woman? Finally, why would it take a thousand years for this story, so out of character with all of the previously known documentation, to surface? It clearly was invented simply to morally annihilate Beruria, the one woman of superior stature in the Talmud, Beruria the feminist—for it was exactly on that point that she was attacked. Because she took an overtly feminist stance of rejecting the rabbinic stereotyping of women as intellectually inferior she was told she would have to give up her life. Feminism was a capital crime! In male chauvinist fashion the moral destruction planned for her would reduce her to the female stereotype, a weak sexual creature who could not resist a determined Don Juan.

Despite the historical bankruptcy of this late legend, it does under-line Beruria's towering reputation in her lifetime and for centuries afterward. The very attempt to destroy it is evidence of its power. Although the opposition was already there in talmudic times, as is seen in the innuendo about the "incident," the later hatchet job suggests that the enemies of what she stood for grew stronger in time. Fortunately the character assassination attempt was far from com-pletely successful, for the clearly historically based evidence of the earlier talmudic stories remains today. Less fortunately, the fact that the talmudic evidence was not erased bears witness not only to the vigorous reputation of Beruria but also to the faithful honesty of the generations of rabbis who memorized, handed on—and finally wrote down, collected, and edited the stories about Beruria. This latter means that there were no other women who entered and advanced in the heartland of Judaism, the study of the Torah, otherwise we would have talmudic stories of them as well. Beruria was the "excep-tion that proves the rule" that in talmudic days women did not study Torah.

A medieval dictum has it: "If it happened, it's possible"—*ab esse ad posse*. If in the midst of a very male-dominated society and religion, as Rabbinic Judaism certainly was, Beruria could lead a full human life, could reach the highest level of "religious" life by becom-ing a renowned and redoubtable student and teacher of Torah, then really anything within Judaism is "possible" for Jewish women. Beruria continues to be a preeminent teacher through the example of her life. A key lesson was her essentially linking feminism to a commitment to live a full Jewish life.

§86. The Anonymous Maidservant of Rabbi Judah the Prince

Of much less importance as a model for Jewish women, but never-theless of significance as an example of a woman who despite the obstacles attained visibility in the formative period of male-centered Rabbinic Judaism (end of the second century C.E., when the first rabbinic writings, the Mishnah, were being codified) is the image of the maid of Rabbi Judah the Prince.

Perhaps the first thing to notice about this maidservant of Rabbi Judah (the codifier of the Mishnah) is that she is nameless; in the five, or possibly six, places in the Babylonian Talmud where she is men-tioned she is always referred to only as Rabbi Judah's maidservant or domestic. Our evidence concerning her is very meager. We do know that she had learned at least some Hebrew, something of the symbolic style of speaking current among rabbis and their students, and was an imposing and responsible enough member of Rabbi Judah's household to be able to levy an excommunication and exercise a powerful prayer at the death of the rabbi—no mean accomplishments for a woman servant. However, given the slimness of the documentation, one must be careful neither unduly to expand nor contract its significance. It is necessary to look at each portion separately before attempting an overall evaluation.

If the reference in Talmud bShabbath 152a, about a ninety-two-year-old domestic of Rabbi Judah's household serving as a food taster, refers to the female domestic in question, as seems reasonably likely, and if it is coupled with the stories of her exercising significant household responsibilities, one gets the picture of an intelligent, perceptive woman servant who for many decades must have heard the great Rabbi Judah, and perhaps even his father, Rabbi Simon III, teaching his students and discussing halachic matters with his colleagues:

> She even had charge of the tables reserved by the patriarch for the numerous pupils who received free board at his house; and as circumstances or her whims dictated, she would either immediately dismiss the students after the meals were over or invite them to remain a while longer. In such company she adopted the technical language known only to the initiated, and employed exclusively by the Rabbis, who scarcely ever expressed the principal idea literally, but nearly always resorted to symbols and figures of speech. (Henry Zirndorf, *Some Jewish Women*, p. 200; Philadelphia, 1892)

> When Rabbi's maid indulged in enigmatic speech she used to say this: The ladle strikes against the jar [all the wine in the jar has been used up]; let the eagles fly to their nests [the students may now leave the dining room for their lodgings]; and when she wished them to remain at table she used to tell them, The crown of her friend [the bung of the adjoining jar] shall be removed and the ladle will float in the jar like a ship that sails in the sea. (Talmud bErubin 53b)

That such a woman in that setting would have learned some Hebrew is not at all surprising, especially those terms dealing with kitchen and domestic matters. However, when we look at the passage in Talmud bMegilla 18a, it is a little difficult to conclude with some scholars (e.g., Shalom Ben Chorin, *Mutter Mirjam*, p. 99; Munich: Paul List Verlag, 1971) that she "commented on Bible verses which were difficult to understand." The passage reads as follows:

> The Rabbis did not know what was meant by *serugin*, until one day they heard the maidservant of Rabbi's household, on seeing the Rabbis enter at intervals, say to them, How long are you going to come by *serugin?*

The Rabbis did not know what was meant by *halugelugoth,* til one day they heard the handmaid of the household of Rabbi, on seeing a man peeling portulaks, say to him, How long will you be peeling your portulaks? *(halugelugoth).*

The Rabbis did not know what was meant by *salseleah* (and it shall exalt). One day they heard the handmaid of the house of Rabbi say to a man who was curling his hair, How long will you be measalsel with your hair? . . . [Then comes a similar example which does not involve Rabbi Judah's maidservant.]

The Rabbis did not know what was meant by *we-tetethia bematate* (of destruction), til one day they heard the handmaid of the household of Rabbi say to her companion, Take the *tatitha* (broom) and *tati* (sweep) the house. (Talmud bMegilla 18a; cf. bNazir 3a, bRosh Hashanah 26b, pShebiit 9, 1, and pMegilla 2, 2)

To be sure, Ben Chorin is not alone in making the sort of claim he does: "She used to help the great scholar and his students to interpret difficult biblical passages by muttering clues to their interpretations as she cleaned the room" (Susan Wall, "Forgotten Jewish Women in Jewish History," *The Jewish Digest,* November 1974, p. 9). Likewise: "In almost one breath this sensible woman once explained the meaning of four separate rabbinical expressions in the presence of the learned. The ingenious, roundabout way in which this was done, and her half playful manner of concealing the act, are matters not without interest" (see Zirndorf, *Some Jewish Women,* p. 198).

There are difficulties with these explanations of this passage. First, those who were aided by the maidservant's Hebrew utterances did not include Rabbi Judah himself. Secondly, that these word difficulties all occurred and were solved "in almost one breath" is quite unlikely. What is likely is that several different occasions were involved and that these four at any rate were remembered and (almost) brought together in this one passage—after all, they were also recorded singly elsewhere in the Talmud. The Talmud simply records that a group of rabbis who gathered around the household of Rabbi Judah the Prince were inadvertently assisted in understanding some unusual Hebrew words when they *overheard* the maidservant on different occasions using a form of these words—which concerned household matters that a maidservant would deal with. It is *just possible* that the maid was circumspectly passing on some of her household Hebrew to perhaps relatively newly arrived rabbis, but there is nothing in the text that positively indicates that this was the case; rather, the contrary is true. If she was "commenting on Bible verses which were difficult to understand," then neither the rabbis who overheard her utterances nor those who recorded them in the Talmud were aware that she was doing so. Still, it is possible.

This same maidservant also wielded an extraordinary degree of responsibility, as the following story of her banishing a malefactor from the company of the rabbi's household indicates:

> Then R. Samuel b. Nahmani got up on his feet and said: Why, even a "separation" imposed by one of the domestics in Rabbi's house was not treated lightly by the Rabbis for three years; how much more so one imposed by our colleague, Rab Judah! . . . What (was the incident) of the domestic in Rabbi's house? It was one of the maidservants in Rabbi's house that had noticed a man beating his grown-up son and said, Let that fellow be under a *shammetha!* because he sinned against the words (of Holy Writ): *Put not a stumbling-block before the blind.* For it is taught: *and not put a stumbling-block before the blind;* that text applies to the one who beats his grown-up son (and this caused him to rebel). (Talmud bMoed Katan 17a)

Obviously not only rabbis could "exclude" wrongdoers at that time, but obviously, too, the maidservant's reputation must have carried some weight. It should also be noted that she also knew the rabbinic style of backing things up with a Scripture quotation—she doubtless had heard many such bannings issued over the decades.

The final story about Rabbi Judah's maidservant reveals again her strength of character in a most dramatic manner:

> On the day when Rabbi died the Rabbis decreed a public fast and offered prayers for heavenly mercy. They, furthermore, announced that whoever said that Rabbi was dead would be stabbed with a sword.
> Rabbi's handmaid ascended the roof and prayed: The immortals desire Rabbi (to join them) and the mortals desire Rabbi (to remain with them); may it be the will (of God) that the mortals may overpower the immortals. When, however, she saw how often he resorted to the privy, painfully taking off his tefillin and putting them on again, she prayed: May it be the will (of the Almighty) that the immortals may overpower the mortals. As the Rabbis incessantly continued their prayers for (heavenly) mercy she took up a jar and threw it down from the roof to the ground. (For a moment) they ceased praying and the soul of the Rabbi departed to its eternal rest. (Talmud bKethuboth 104a)

Rabbi Henry Zirndorf explained this passage thus:

> According to a prevailing belief of the time, so long as the sick man heard these impassioned prayers—and as he lay in the upper chamber he could scarcely help hearing them—it was impossible for him to draw his last breath. This belief is no conclusive proof of faith in miracles; the prolongation of life through intense momentary excitement is readily explained on psychological, and perhaps also on physiological grounds. But, however this may be, on the roof stood the maid-servant . . . trying in vain to make her voice heard below.

Then, seizing a jug all of a sudden, she threw it in the midst of the earnest crowd of suppliants. A dreadful pause ensued and, in the inimitable language of the Talmud, "the soul of Rabbi Judah the Patriarch reposed." (Zirndorf, *Some Jewish Women,* pp. 203f.)

In sum, it is likely that the same maidservant is spoken of in all the passages quoted, although one cannot be absolutely certain, since no name is ever given—a fact which in itself reveals a good deal about the inferior status of women, even those of strong character. This maidservant was a strong character who learned at least some Hebrew, could banter with rabbinic students in the "in" language, and at least once wielded effectively the "separation" in the approved manner. For all of her strength of character, however, she is not evidence that women studied Torah. In fact, she is evidence that, except for Beruria, they did not, for if such a servant had been male, he would doubtless have eventually been pulled into the ranks of the rabbinic students and then the rabbis, and would not have been nameless, or known simply as a man's servant. Still, against the odds of her being a woman on the edges of an exclusively male club, the rabbinate, she significantly and positively influenced the lives of those around her, and, through her memory recorded in the Talmud, those who came after.

V. Ambivalent Elements
in Hebrew-Jewish Tradition

A. AMBIVALENT MODELS OF WOMEN—HEBREW
BIBLE AND APOCRYPHA

There are at least four other women of note in the Hebrew Bible that are held up by the Bible itself for praise, who provide ambivalent models of women. Three of them (Ruth, Judith, and Esther) accomplish their ends largely through the stereotypical characteristics, sexual attractiveness. Three of them (Jael, Judith, and Esther) have the stereotypical impact on men (since the interpretation of the Fall as having meant Eve's bringing death to Adam—see §104)—namely, death.

§87. Jael the Deadly Hostess

The Book of Judges contains a story about Jael, who is celebrated as the killer of Sisera, Israel's enemy. After the battle of Taanach, presumably in 1125 B.C.E., wherein Deborah and Barak led the Israelites in a crushing victory over Sisera and the Canaanites, Sisera fled for his life to the tent of the non-Israelite woman Jael. Her people were at peace with the Canaanites, which meant that the code of hospitality, with its extraordinary rigor in favor of the guest, should have applied. Sisera thought it did.

As repugnant as Jael's conduct seems to us today, just how much it was a violation of the mores of that time and place can be appreciated only when the centrality of the virtue of hospitality in that culture is perceived:

In the desert hospitality is a necessity for survival; and since this necessity falls on all alike, any guest is entitled to hospitality from any host. Should

111

host and guest be at enmity, the acceptance of hospitality involves a recon-
ciliation. The guest, once the host has accepted him, is sacred and must be
protected from any danger, even at the cost of the life of members of the
family. (John L. McKenzie, *Dictionary of the Bible,* p. 374; Bruce Publishing
Co., 1965)

But the breach of the code of hospitality, the deception, and the
cowardly murder are all waived aside in the Book of Judges and Jael
is held up in great praise both in a song of great antiquity and in a
prose account. McKenzie laconically remarks: "actually she seems to
have violated the customs of hospitality" (ibid., p. 410). In her
deceitful, cowardly assassination Jael was very much like the later
Judith. Unethical deeds done by women, if carried out for the sake
of the Jewish people, are condoned. This ethical stance, however, is
at variance with ethical principles of truthfulness, etc., elsewhere in
the Hebrew Bible. The Jael story clearly reflects an earlier stage of
ethical development and as such offers little for emulation.

Sisera meanwhile fled on foot towards the tent of Jael, the wife of Heber
the Kenite. For there was peace between Jabin the king of Hazor and the
family of Heber the Kenite. Jael came out to meet Sisera and said to him,
"My lord, stay here with me; do not be afraid!" He stayed there in her tent,
and she covered him with a rug. He said to her, "Please give me a little water
to drink, for I am thirsty." She opened the skin that had milk in it, gave him
some to drink and covered him up again. Then he said to her, "Stand at the
door, and if anyone comes and questions you—if he asks, 'Is there a man
here?' say, 'No.' " But Jael the wife of Heber took a tent-peg, and picked up
a mallet; she crept up softly to him and drove the peg into his temple right
through to the ground. He was lying fast asleep, worn out; and so he died.
And now Barak came up in pursuit of Sisera. Jael went out to meet him and
said, "Come in, and I will show you the man you are looking for." He went
into her tent; Sisera lay dead, with the tent-peg through his temple.

. . . .
"Blessed be Jael among women
(the wife of Heber the Kenite);
among all the women that dwell in tents may she be blessed.
He asked for water; she gave him milk;
in a precious bowl she brought him cream.
She stretched out her hand to seize the peg,
her right hand to seize the workman's mallet.
She struck Sisera, crushed his head,
pierced his temple and shattered it.
At her feet he tumbled, he fell, he lay;
at her feet he tumbled, he fell.
Where he tumbled, there he fell dead." (Judg 4:17–22; 5:24–27)

§88. Judith, a Femme Fatale

Judith seems a more attractive person than Jael. After all, it took quite a bit of courage to sally forth almost alone into an enemy army camp. (She left the besieged Jewish city, went to the enemy camp, seduced the leader and cut off his head while he slept.) Her story reads much like a modern spy adventure. But still in the end she murders a man by deception.

The Book of Judith is deuterocanonical, that is, although it is found in the ancient Jewish version of the Old Testament in Greek, it is no longer accepted by either Judaism or Protestantism as canonical. Catholicism and Orthodox Christianity do accept it as canonical. It was originally written in Hebrew or Aramaic, but only a Greek translation is extant. It probably was written in the second century B.C.E.

When it is asked what the image of woman is in the Book of Judith, the answer is stereotypical: woman accomplishes her end by adorning her physical beauty and seducing men, and in this instance in killing men. The highly respected Jewish scholar Solomon Zeitlin corroborated this point when he paraphrased the Talmud (Aboda Zara 25b):

> Judith had no army. She had charm and beauty and with this she was sure she could conquer the enemy by beguiling Holofernes. The Talmud said well that woman had an army with her, that is sex. This is her main armor. (Solomon Zeitlin, Introduction to Morton S. Enslin, *The Book of Judith*, p. 14; Leiden: E. J. Brill, 1972)

As in much of the Wisdom and apocalyptic Jewish literature (see §§93 and 104), the implicit message here in Judith too is: beware of beautiful women—they will unman you and lead you to death. The redeeming factor in this case again of course is that Judith puts her evil womanly wiles at the service of her nation.

Judith is also quite unusual in the following way. Although she was a widow from her youth and was extremely beautiful, she did not take another husband either before killing Holofernes or afterward. Perhaps the placing of her seductive sexual powers at the service of her nation, and God, demanded, in this obviously fictional story, both that she not be "defiled" by Holofernes, or by any other man subsequently.

Jerome, who in the late fourth century C.E. translated the Bible

into Latin (the Vulgate), used an ancient Aramaic manuscript of the
Book of Judith, which since has been lost, leaving us with the Septuagint Greek as our oldest text. On the question of Judith's "chastity" Jerome's translation differs from the Septuagint; in a rather
mixed metaphor it says that in acting so continently Judith "behaved
like a man":

> Since you behaved like a man (quia fecisti *viriliter*), your heart was
> strengthened, because you loved chastity and have known no other man since
> your husband. Hence the hand of the Lord gave you strength. So you will
> be blessed forever. (Judith 15:11—Vulgate)

The moral of the Book of Judith is not that women are good
creatures of God, but rather that God is so great that he can bring
good out of evil; not that women are to be valued greatly, but rather
that God is so great that he can humble Israel's enemies even through
the lowliest of instruments, women—and the weapon women use
against men, beguiling beauty and sex:

> Assyria came down from the mountains of the north. . . . But the Lord
> Almighty has thwarted them by a woman's hand. For their hero did not fall
> at the young men's hands, it was not the sons of Titans who struck him down,
> no proud giants made that attack, but Judith the daughter of Merari, who
> disarmed him with the beauty of her face. She laid aside her widow's dress
> to rally those who were oppressed in Israel; she anointed her face with
> perfume, bound her hair under a turban, put on a linen gown to seduce him.
> Her sandal ravished his eye, her beauty took his soul prisoner . . . and the
> scimitar cut through his neck! (Judith 16:3, 5–9)

On the positive side it must be noted that in the story Judith was
thereafter highly thought of. But even the description of this praise
betrays the inferior position in which women lived in that society.
Had a male hero married after his glorious feat he would have continued in high honor in the society. But a female hero would immediately have been placed under the dominance of her husband—just
as in the famous description of the perfect wife in Proverbs who
worked from dawn to dusk all year, with the result that she should
be given "a share in what her hands have worked for, and let her
works tell her praise at the city gates," but *"her husband* is respected
at the city gates, taking his seat among the elders of the land" (Prov
31:31, 23). To avoid this eclipse of the heroine the writer of the Book
of Judith had to keep her celibate—but still alluring:

> As long as she lived, she enjoyed a great reputation throughout the coun-
> try. She had many suitors, but all her days, from the time her husband
> Manasseh died and was gathered to his people, she never gave herself to

another man. Her fame spread more and more the older she grew in her husband's house; she lived to the age of a hundred and five years. (Judith 16:21–23)

§89. Esther the Beauty Queen

The Book of Esther, a largely fictional story written perhaps in the second century B.C.E., begins, unintentionally it would seem, with an admirable model of a woman, on the one hand, and the most explicit kind of male supremacist attitude on the other. The admirable model is not Esther, the second, the Jewish, queen of the Persian king Ahasuerus, but his first queen, Vashti. Vashti is a woman of dignity, courage, and independence of spirit which included a willingess to take the consequences of her decisions.

After a seven-day-long celebration King Ahasuerus was drunk and ordered his eunuchs to fetch Queen Vashti, "in order to display her beauty to the people and the officers" (Esth 1:11). She declined to come, an understandable decision given the probably riotous conditions of what by then must have been a somewhat sodden drinking bout. This infuriated the king and disturbed his advisers, for they thought that when word got abroad among the other wives in the kingdom, "there will be endless disrespect and insolence!" Hence, Queen Vashti had to be deposed, so that "all the women will henceforth bow to the authority of their husbands . . . ensuring that each man might be master in his own house" (Esth 1:20, 22).

On the seventh day, when the king was merry with wine, he commanded . . . the seven eunuchs in attendance . . . to bring Queen Vashti before the king crowned with her royal diadem, in order to display her beauty to the people and the administrators, for she was very beautiful. But Queen Vashti refused to come at the king's command delivered by the eunuchs. The king was very angry at this and his rage grew hot. He then consulted the wise men who were versed in the law, since it was the practice to refer matters affecting the king to expert lawyers and jurists. He summoned . . . the seven administrators of Persia and Media. . . . "According to the law," he said, "what is to be done to Queen Vashti for not obeying the command of King Ahasuerus delivered by the eunuchs?" In the presence of the king and of the administrators Memucan answered, "Vashti has wronged not only the king, but also all the administrators and nations inhabiting the provinces of King Ahasuerus. The queen's conduct will soon become known to all the women and encourage them in a contemptuous attitude towards their husbands, since they will say, 'King Ahasuerus ordered Queen Vashti to appear before him and she did not come.' The wives of all the Persian and Median administrators will hear of the queen's answer before the day is out, and will start talking to the king's administrators in the same way; that will mean contempt and anger all round. If it is the king's pleasure, let him issue a royal edict, to be irrevocably incorporated into the laws of the Persians and Medes, to the effect that Vashti is never to appear again before King Ahasuerus, and let the king confer her royal dignity on a worthier woman. Let this edict issued by the king be proclaimed throughout the length and breadth of his realm, and all the women will henceforth bow to the authority of their husbands, both high and low alike." (Esth 1:10–20)

One contemporary Jewish woman writes that,

Further, in order to insure that we really have no shred of sympathy left for Vashti, several sources credit her with responsibility for preventing the king from giving his consent to the rebuilding of the Temple. These legends are very significant, for they reflect popular and rabbinic feeling. And it is very clear that in no way was Vashti's refusal to debase herself seen by succeeding Jews as noble or courageous. Quite the contrary. The Rabbis must have found themselves in somewhat of a bind initially. On the one hand they couldn't possibly approve the demand Ahasuerus makes on Vashti. On the other hand, to support her would be to invite female disobedience in other situations, an idea they apparently could not tolerate. They solve this by condemning Ahasuerus as foolish and by creating legends whereby Vashti is shown as getting exactly what she deserves. (Mary Gendler, "The Vindication of Vashti," *The Jewish Woman. Response,* 18, Summer 1973, pp. 156f.)

After the deposition of Vashti, the Persian king held a beauty contest, which Hadassah, or Esther, a Jewish girl (though that fact was not known), won.

The king's courtiers-in-waiting said, "Let beautiful girls be selected for the king. Let the king appoint commissioners throughout the provinces of his realm to bring all these beautiful young virgins to the citadel of Susa, to the harem under the authority of Hegai the king's eunuch, custodian of the women. Let him provide them with what they need for their adornment, and let the girl who pleases the king take Vashti's place as queen." This advice pleased the king and he acted on it. . . . [Esther] had a good figure and a beautiful face. . . . She was brought to King Ahasuerus . . . and the king liked Esther better than any of the other women; none of the other girls found so much favour and approval with him. So he set the royal diadem on her head and proclaimed her queen instead of Vashti. (Esth 2:2–4, 7, 16, 17)

In the rest of the story the Jew Mordecai, who secretly gives instructions to his niece Esther, refuses to bow before Haman, a high official, who then plots the death of Mordecai and a pogrom against the Jews. At Mordecai's insistence Esther risks a breach of court custom to see the king. She succeeds in turning the tables on Haman, who instead is executed and seventy-five thousand of his countrymen are killed by the Jews—with her aid.

The image of woman projected here is that "good" women are beautiful and submissive; but the beauty of women is dangerous and leads to the death of many. Here again, as with Judith, the redeeming factor was that Esther put this death-dealing female power at the service of her people.

Aviva Cantor Zuckoff made a similar point when she wrote of Esther:

> In doing so she must act aggressively toward her husband. She must engage in the same type of behavior that was condemned in Vashti—assertiveness, willingness to risk her life for her values, aggressiveness. But since she's doing this not for herself but for her people, and with Mordecai's approval and on his orders, it is condoned. Esther's aggressiveness is praised and she becomes a role model for Jewish women.

> Esther's aggressiveness is approved because it is altruistic, as were the actions of Deborah, who judged the people, and Judith, who cut off the head of the Syrian-Greek general besieging her city. What it all adds up to is that it's good for Jewish women to be strong and aggressive when the Jews are in danger and she's acting in the people's interest, in other words, when it's "good for the Jews." If we go through the Bible and legends carefully, we see that whenever Jewish survival is at stake, the Jewish woman is called upon to be strong and aggressive. When the crisis is over, it's back to patriarchy. (Aviva Cantor Zuckoff, "The Oppression of the Jewish Woman," *The Jewish Woman. Response,* 18, Summer 1973, p. 49)

The point of this whole story concerns the providence of God which preserves his people from annihilation—and by the most unlikely means, a woman, just as happened with Judith. The fact that in both these stories the "heroines" were women indicates not that women were often heroines or highly thought of in Jewish society at that time, but just the opposite, that women were not heroines or highly thought of in that society; otherwise the stories would not have been interesting or worth telling. They were of interest exactly because they displayed God's providence for his people by having them saved by the most unlikely and lowly means available—women.

In comparing Vashti and Esther, Mary Gendler wrote:

> Ahasuerus can be seen not only as an Ultimate Authority who holds vast power over everyone, but more generally as male, patriarchal authority in relation to females. As such, Vashti and Esther serve as models of how to deal with such authority. And the message comes through loud and clear: women who are bold, direct, aggressive and disobedient are not acceptable; the praiseworthy are those who are unassuming, quietly persistent, and who gain their power through the love they inspire in men. These women live almost vicariously, subordinating their needs and desires to those of others. We have only to look at the stereotyped Jewish Mother to attest the still-pervasive influence of the Esther-behavior-model. . . . What I am interested in here, however, is pointing up typical male and female models of behavior and, at that level, it is clear that society rewards men for being direct

and aggressive while it condemns women, like Vashti, for equivalent behavior. For, in a sense, Mordecai and Vashti have behaved identically: both refuse to debase themselves by submitting to illegitimate demands. For this Mordecai is praised and Vashti is condemned. (Gendler, "Vindication of Vashti," p. 158)

Gendler added an interesting proposal at the end of her article:

I propose, then, that Vashti be reinstated on the throne along with her sister Esther, together to rule and guide the psyches and actions of women. Women, combining the attributes of these two remarkable females—beauty softened by grace; pride tempered by humility; independence checked by heartful loyalties; courage; dignity—such women will be much more whole and complete than are those who simply seek to emulate Esther. The Lillith, the Vashti in us is valuable. It is time that we recognize, cultivate and embrace her! (Ibid., p. 160)

§90. Ruth: Subservient to Men, but Loyal to a Woman

The Book of Ruth presents a pleasant contrast to the bloody adventures of the books of Judges, Judith, and Esther. The story is quite idyllic. Nothing bad is said about anyone! There are no villains in the story. It is largely the tale of the loyalty and selfless love of one woman for another. It is its positive, fetching quality, however, that makes the Book of Ruth somewhat "dangerous," for because of it the reader is likely to accept its image of women and their role uncritically.

A Hebrew woman, Naomi, has moved to a foreign country with her husband and two sons, who marry wives from there. After her husband's and sons' childless deaths Naomi returns home and one daughter-in-law, Ruth, selflessly follows. They live a hard life, but Ruth provides for them both. She meets, attracts, and wins to marriage a Hebrew kinsman of Naomi's, thereby ensuring the bloodline of her dead husband from which line springs King David.

Clearly one of the purposes of this book is to show how the selfless loyalty of a foreigner, Ruth, served to continue the line of the Hebrew Elimelech (Naomi's husband) and Mahlon (Ruth's dead husband). It was of great consequence in Hebrew society that a man's bloodline not die out; as a result the law of levirate (Deut 25:5ff.) was developed. By this law, if a married man dies childless, his next of kin has an obligation to marry his widow; children from that couple would be viewed as in the bloodline (and inheritance!) of the dead husband. All this is obviously in the structure of a patriarchal society rather than the earlier matrilineal society of the Goddess worshipers. On one level, the narrator's, there is Ruth sacrificing her self-interest to continue a male line—no similar concern is exhibited, for example, about her own mother's line. It obviously was not thought important enough to be even mentioned.

This dimension is reinforced by the clear parallels in the story of Ruth with that of Tamar (Genesis 38), who is specifically mentioned in Ruth (Ruth 4:2). Both Tamar and Ruth are foreigners (the former a Canaanite, the latter a Moabite), both are widows of Hebrews in the same family, both have children by a levir, but not the "proper" levir, both get their man by sexual seduction—Tamar clearly played the prostitute on the roadside (Gen 38:15–19), and Ruth followed Naomi's instructions:

> Naomi said to Ruth, "I must find a husband for you. . . . Remember that this man Boaz . . . is our relative. Now listen. This evening he will be threshing the barley. So wash yourself, put on some perfume, and get dressed in your best clothes. . . . After he falls asleep, go and lift the covers and lie down at his feet [a number of scholars note that in ancient Hebrew "feet" was often a euphemism for genitals]. He will tell you what to do." . . . Ruth slipped over quietly, lifted the covers and lay down at his feet. . . . "Who are you?" he asked. "It's Ruth, . . . please marry me." . . . "May Yahweh bless you," he said. . . . "You might have gone looking for a young man, either rich or poor, but you haven't. . . . Now lie down and stay here till morning." So she lay there at his feet, but she got up before it was light enough for her to be seen, because Boaz did not want anyone to know that she had been there. (Ruth 3:1–4, 7, 9–10, 13, 14)

To be sure, in that patriarchal society both Tamar and Ruth needed to find a man to support them, either husband or son. But as the two stories are told, there is an overriding concern that the two widows conceive a son by a levir, a relative of the dead husband, so his line might continue—that is, the value of women, besides their labor (like the "perfect wife" of Proverbs 31), was in the bearing of *sons.* In these two cases what was of paramount importance was that they led to King David. The elders of the village said to Boaz:

> "And through the children Yahweh will give you by this young woman, may your House become like the House of Perez [Boaz' ancestor] whom Tamar bore to Judah." So Boaz took Ruth and she became his wife. And when they came together, Yahweh made her conceive and she bore a son. And the women said to Naomi, "Blessed be Yahweh who has not left the dead man without next of kin this day to perpetuate his name in Israel." . . . And they named him Obed. This was the father of Jesse, the father of David. (Ruth 4:12–14, 17)

There are of course some extremely positive elements in the Book of Ruth. Note has already been taken of its nonviolent nature and the fact that it has only good to say about everyone. Also highlighted in the story is the virtue of loyalty beyond all demand of duty. What is of special interest here is that this supererogatory loyalty was exhibited by a woman, indeed by two women, and beyond that, the loyalty was toward another woman. This latter was not at all something that could be taken for granted in a patriarchal society.

The two Moabite women, Orpah and Ruth, obviously had developed a deep affection for their mother-in-law, Naomi, for after the death of their husbands they started out with Naomi on the road back to Judea (Ruth 1:7), and when Naomi told them that for their own good they should return "each . . . to her mother's house" (interesting that she did not say father's house—is there a remnant of earlier matrilocality here?) they *both* cried aloud and refused. Orpah was clearly no slacker in altruistic loyalty to another woman. Naomi had to press much harder before she could force at least one of them, Orpah, to go back. But even this further effort was to no avail with Ruth, who uttered her immortal words of undying love of one woman for another.

And they took the road back to the land of Judah. Naomi said to her two daughters-in-law, "Go back each of you to her mother's house. . . ." And she kissed them. But they wept aloud and said to her, "No, we will go back with you to your people." And Naomi said, "You must return, my daughters; why come with me? . . . No, my daughters, I should then be deeply grieved for you, for the hand of Yahweh has been raised against me." And once more they started to weep aloud. Then Orpah kissed her mother-in-law and went back to her people, but Ruth clung to her. Naomi said to her, "Look, your sister-in-law has gone back to her people and to her god. You must return too; follow your sister-in-law." But Ruth said, "Do not press me to leave you and to turn back from your company, for
   wherever you go, I will go,
   wherever you live, I will live.
   Your people shall be my people,
   and your God, my God.
   Wherever you die, I will die
   and there I will be buried.
   May Yahweh's worst punishment
   come upon me,
   if ever death should come between us." (Ruth 1:7–11, 13–17)

The other women in Naomi's home village also recognized Ruth's incredible love for and loyalty to Naomi and were clearly appreciative of it, for they remarked:

Your daughter-in-law . . . loves you and is to you more than seven sons. (Ruth 4:15)

There is at least one other very important positive dimension to the Book of Ruth, and, although it does not have immediate bearing on women as such, it does have a very significant indirect import. The universality of Yahweh's power and grace is strongly stamped on the very structure of the Book of Ruth. There was a stringent strand of nationalism, even at times of xenophobia, that ran through swaths of ancient Hebrew literature and life. For example, in almost direct opposition to the willing acceptance of Ruth the Moabite stood Deuteronomy's dictum:

No Ammonite or Moabite is to be admitted to the assembly of Yahweh; . . . and this for all time. (Deut 23:3)

The response in Nehemiah's fifth-century B.C.E. period to the reading of this portion of the Torah was as follows:

As soon as the people had heard the Torah they excluded all of foreign descent from Israel. (Neh 13:3)

In the fifth century B.C.E. the Jewish "scribe" Ezra launched a vigorous, even vicious, drive to rid the Jewish population, recently returned from Persian exile, of all foreign wives and children (including Moabites), whatever the hardship and agony involved. The fear of course was that foreign customs and foreign deities would infiltrate the Jewish population through the foreign women—presumably especially Goddess worship, as all preexilic evidence suggests.

"The people of Israel, the priests and the Levites, have not broken with the natives of the countries who are steeped in abominations—Canaanites, Ammonites, . . . Moabites . . . but have found wives among these foreign women for themselves and for their sons; the holy race has been mingling with the natives of the countries; in this act of treachery the chief men and officials have led the way. . . . So you must not give your daughters to their sons nor take their daughters for your sons; you must not be concerned for their peace or their prosperity. . . . We will make a solemn promise before our God to put away our foreign wives and the children born to them." . . . Among the members of the priesthood, these are the names of those who were found to have married foreign women [there follow 112 names of Jewish men]. . . . All these had married foreign wives; they put them away, both women and children. (Ezra 9:1, 2, 12; 10:3, 18, 44)

Another Jewish leader, Nehemiah, about the same time as Ezra, also acted strenuously against Jews marrying foreign women, including Moabites like Ruth:

At that time I again saw Jews who had married women from Ashdod, Ammon and Moab. . . . I reprimanded them and called down curses on them;

I struck several of them and tore out their hair. . . . Are we then to follow your example and commit this grave sin, playing traitor to our God by marrying foreign women? One of the sons of Jehoiada, son of the high priest Eliashib, had married a daughter of Sanballat the Horonite; therefore I drove him out of my presence. . . . And so I purged them of everything foreign. (Neh 13:23, 25, 27–28, 30)

The Book of Ruth stands in stark contradiction to this vitriolic attitude toward foreign women. Ruth, a Moabite, is shown as an extremely selfless and loving person, and an essential link (along with that other foreign wife, Tamar) in the genealogy leading to David, the greatest king of Israel. But the author of the Book of Ruth is even more explicit in the praise of a foreign wife who so far outshines most persons that Israel's God, Yahweh, is called upon to bless her abundantly:

"You take notice of me, even though I am a foreigner?" And Boaz answered her, "I have been told all you have done for your mother-in-law since your husband's death, and how you left your own father and mother and the land where you were born to come among a people whom you knew nothing about before you came here. May Yahweh reward you for what you have done!" (Ruth 2:10–12)

For linguistic reasons and because the Book of Ruth so opposes the xenophobic attitude of Ezra and Nehemiah, a number of scholars, though by no means all, are convinced that though the book is set in the time of Judges (eleventh century B.C.E.), it really was written, at least in its final form, in the fifth century, the time of Ezra and Nehemiah, as a counter voice to them; it would have been then a voice both in favor of Yahweh's universalism, of irenicism, the quiet, deep virtue of women, and the need for women to be loyal to women.

If this late dating is correct, it can be said that fortunately the Book of Ruth is not the only one written then that has an emphasis on Yahweh's universalism. The Book of Jonah, perhaps also written in the immediate postexilic period, is about the conversion of Nineveh, the capital city of the hated Assyrians, to Yahweh. McKenzie says of the book:

Jonah, like Ruth, is a protest against the narrowness and exclusivism which often appeared in postexilic Judaism. This narrowness frequently expressed itself in a hate of foreign nations, a desire for their destruction rather than their recognition of the divinity of Yahweh. Hence Jonah marks one of the greatest steps forward in the spiritual advancement of biblical religion. (McKenzie, *Dictionary of the Bible*, p. 451)

A similar openness to foreigners is also found in Third Isaiah, likewise written in this period after the return from exile in opposition to the exclusivist position. It is interesting to note that Third Isaiah also opens Yahwism to eunuchs, who along with foreigners were excluded from the community of Israel by Deuteronomy; the eunuchs did not produce offspring. The same theme is repeated in the first century B.C.E. deuterocanonical Book of Wisdom, which pronounces blessed not only the eunuch but also the barren woman —virtue is better than children. In the Book of Wisdom the doctrine of the immortality of the soul is expounded; perhaps it is also hinted at in Third Isaiah. The person's immortality is no longer located in offspring; therefore, not having children is not an unmitigated disaster, and the barren woman's and the eunuch's value can be affirmed.

> Let no foreigner who has attached himself to Yahweh say, "Yahweh will surely exclude me from his people." Let no eunuch say, "And I, I am a dried-up tree."
> For Yahweh says this: To the eunuchs who observe my sabbaths, and resolve to do what pleases me and cling to my covenant, I will give, in my house and within my walls, a monument and a name better than sons and daughters; I will give them an everlasting name that shall never be effaced.
> Foreigners who have attached themselves to Yahweh to serve him and to love his name and be his servants—all who observe the sabbath, not profaning it, and cling to my covenant—these I will bring to my holy mountain. I will make them joyful in my house of prayer. Their holocausts and their sacrifices will be accepted on my altar, for my house will be called a house of prayer for all the peoples.
> It is the Lord Yahweh who speaks, who gathers the outcasts of Israel: there are others I will gather besides those already gathered. (Is 56:3-8)

> Blessed the barren woman. . . . Her fruitfulness will be seen at the scrutiny of souls. Blessed too the eunuch. . . . For his loyalty special favour will be granted him, a most desirable portion in the temple of the Lord. (Wisdom 3:13-14)

§91. Good Wives and Mothers

As will be briefly discussed below, much of what the Wisdom literature in the Bible has to say about women is extremely negative, even misogynist. But that same literature does also contain a number of positive statements about wives and mothers. This material is found basically in two books, Proverbs and Ben Sira (also called Ecclesiasticus). The latter is not accepted in the Jewish and Protestant canon but is in the Catholic and Orthodox canon. Ben Sira is in the Greek Septuagint, but was originally written in Hebrew in 190 B.C.E. Proverbs is a collection of Wisdom writings, some of which were written before the sixth century B.C.E. exile and some after.

Proverbs has two brief sayings about the honor due a mother, as well as a father:

Listen to your father who begot you, do not despise your mother in her old age. . . . May you be the joy of your father, the gladness of her who bore you! (Prov 23:22, 25)

There are also four short aphorisms about the value of a good wife in the book of Proverbs:

A gracious woman brings honour to her husband.
A good wife, her husband's crown.
Who finds a wife finds happiness, receiving a mark of favour from
    Yahweh.
From Yahweh [comes] a wife who is discreet. (Prov 11:16; 12:4; 18:
    22; 19:14)

Ben Sira has a number of sayings about honoring father and mother (he also has several about fathers alone, but never about mothers alone):

The Lord honours the father in his children,
    and upholds the rights of a mother over her sons.
Whoever respects his father is atoning for his sins,
    he who honours his mother is like someone amassing a fortune. . . .
Long life comes to him who honours his father,
    he who sets his mother at ease is showing obedience to the
        Lord. . . .
A man's honor derives from the respect shown to his father,
    and a mother held in dishonour is a reproach to her children. . . .
The man who deserts his father is no better than a blasphemer,
    and whoever angers his mother is accursed of the Lord. . . .
With all your heart honour your father,
    never forget the birthpangs of your mother. . . .
Remember your father and mother
    when you are sitting among princes. (Ben Sira 3:2–4, 6, 7, 11, 16;
    7:27; 23:14)

Even more than Proverbs, Ben Sira has several sayings on what a boon it is to have a good wife—she is placed very high on the list of values:

Happy the husband of a really good wife;
    the number of his days will be doubled.
A perfect wife is the joy of her husband,
    he will live out the years of his life in peace.
A good wife is the best of portions,

reserved for those who fear the Lord. . . .
Like the sun rising over the mountains of the Lord
  is the beauty of a good wife in a well-kept house.
The man who takes a wife has the makings of a fortune,
  a helper that suits him, and a pillar to lean on. . . .
When a man has no wife, he is aimless and querulous. (Ben Sira
26:1–3, 16; 36:24, 25)

Ben Sira also has something to say about the desirable virtues of a wife. They presumably are meant as compliments, but really require genteel subservience from the woman:

The grace of a wife will charm her husband,
  her accomplishments will make him the stronger.
A silent wife is a gift from the Lord,
  no price can be put on a well-trained character.
A modest wife is a boon twice-over,
  a chaste character cannot be weighed on scales.
. . . .
If her tongue is kind and gentle,
  her husband has no equal among the sons of men. (Ben Sira 26:
13–15; 36:23)

Despite his fears of and warnings against beauty in women, Ben Sira also had an appreciative eye, and pen, for feminine beauty:

Like the lamp standing on the sacred lamp-stand
  is a beautiful face on a well-proportioned body.
Like golden pillars on a silver base
  are shapely legs on firm-set heels.
. . . .
A woman's beauty delights the beholder,
  a man likes nothing better. (Ben Sira 26:17–18; 36:22)

As laudatory of women as some of these biblical sayings are, it should be noted that women are praised only in their roles as related beneficially to men, that is, as mothers and wives. (It is also interesting that, although fathers are praised here, good husbands are never lauded or even mentioned—only good wives: a clear sign of total male orientation.) Further, nothing good is ever said in these books about women in any other roles, or about women as such, although bad things are said about women as such. To the extent that women can help men they are appreciated, not otherwise.

This is made dramatically clear in the widely known poem in Proverbs 31 honoring the "Perfect Wife," understandably often used at weddings and similar occasions. The husband's enthusiasm can be appreciated, for he "will derive no little profit from her. Advantage and not hurt she will bring him all the days of her life" (Prov 31:11–12). The wife works uncommonly hard, exercising a great deal of business judgment and responsibility (not in her own name, however, as can be seen in 31:31); the result is not that she is given some religious responsibility or honorific title or position—rather, her husband is: "Her husband is respected at the city gates, taking his seat among the elders of the land" (31:23). It is no wonder she is appreciated; she is the model for the "Perfect Servant." Indeed, the impression given by this poem is that thanks to the diligence of the wife the husband is a man of leisure. In return for her complete self-sacrifice she is given praise by the men: "Her sons stand up and proclaim her blessed, her husband too sings her praises" (31:28), and those men gathered at the city gates "let her works tell her praises at the city gates" (31:31). She is allowed to share in the fruits of her labor: "Give her a share in what her hands have worked for" (31:31).

The paean of praise of the "Perfect Wife" is in the form of an alphabetic poem, each verse beginning with the next letter of the Hebrew alphabet.

Aleph	A perfect wife—who can find her? She is far beyond the price of pearls.
Beth	Her husband's heart has confidence in her, from her he will derive no little profit.
Ghimel	Advantage and not hurt she brings him all the days of her life.
Daleth	She is always busy with wool and with flax, she does her work with eager hands.
He	She is like a merchant vessel bringing her food from far away.
Wau	She gets up while it is still dark giving her household their food, giving orders to her serving girls.
Zain	She sets her mind on a field, then she buys it; with what her hands have earned she plants a vineyard.
Heth	She puts her back into her work and shows how strong her arms can be.
Teth	She finds her labour well worth while; her lamp does not go out at night.
Yod	She sets her hands to the distaff, her fingers grasp the spindle.
Kaph	She holds out her hand to the poor, she opens her arms to the needy.
Lamed	Snow may come, she has no fears for her household, with all her servants warmly clothed.

Mem   She makes her own quilts,
      she is dressed in fine linen and purple.

Nun   Her husband is respected at the city gates,
      taking his seat among the elders of the land.

Samek   She weaves linen sheets and sells them,
      she supplies the merchant with sashes.

Ain   She is clothed in strength and dignity,
      she can laugh at the days to come.

Pe   When she opens her mouth, she does so wisely;
      on her tongue is kindly instruction.

Sade   She keeps good watch on the conduct of her household,
      no bread of idleness for her.

Qoph   Her sons stand up and proclaim her blessed,
      her husband, too, sings her praises:

Resh   "Many women have done admirable things,
      but you surpass them all!"

Shin   Charm is deceitful, and beauty empty;
      the woman who is wise is the one to praise.

Tau   Give her a share in what her hands have worked for,
      and let her works tell her praises at the city gates. (Prov 31:10–31)

§92. Bad Wives

Not all the remarks about wives, however, are positive. Some are vaguely ominous, as: "Do not turn against a wise and good wife. . . . Have you a wife to your liking? Do not turn her out; but if you dislike her, never trust her" (Ben Sira 7:19, 26). Some are rather threatening comparisons:

A godless wife is assigned to a transgressor as his fortune, but a devout wife given to the man who fears the Lord. A shameless wife takes pleasure in disgracing herself, a modest wife is diffident even with her husband. A headstrong wife is a shameless bitch, but one with a sense of shame fears the Lord. A wife who respects her husband will be acknowledged wise by all, but the one who proudly despises him will be known by all as wicked. (Ben Sira 26:23–26)

In many instances pure vitriol is poured on the wife, as in the book of Proverbs:

A woman's scolding is like a dripping gutter. . . . The steady dripping of a gutter on a rainy day and a scolding woman are alike. Whoever can restrain her, can restrain the wind, and with right hand grasp oil. . . . Better the corner of a loft to live in than a house shared with a scolding woman. . . . Better to live in a desert land than with a scolding and irritable woman. (Prov 19:13; 27:15–16; 21:9; 25:24; 21:19)

Ben Sira easily matches Proverbs in anti-wife acid:

I would sooner keep house with a lion or a dragon than keep house with a spiteful wife. A wife's spite changes the appearance of her husband and makes him look like a bear. When her husband goes out to dinner with his neighbours, he cannot help heaving bitter sighs. . . . Low spirits, gloomy face, stricken heart: such the achievements of a spiteful wife. Slack hands and sagging knees indicate a wife who makes her husband wretched. . . . A bad wife is a badly fitting ox yoke, trying to master her is like grasping a scorpion. A drunken wife will goad anyone to fury, she makes no effort to hide her degradation. (Ben Sira 25:16–18, 23; 26:7–8)

§93. Misogynism

One other biblical book in the Wisdom literature collection is pertinent here. Ecclesiastes, written in 250 B.C.E., is an unusually short book, twelve brief chapters, and also has unusually little to say about women. Except for a few metaphorical references to women and an exhortation to marital fidelity (Eccles 9:9), the only reference to women is an especially vitriolic and bitter one: "I find woman more bitter than death; she is a snare, her heart a net, her arms are chains" (Eccles 7:26). Here the remarks are not like the statements praising women; that is, they are not directed toward women in relationships, as mothers or wives of men. Rather, the statements are directed toward women as such: "I find woman," not *"my* woman." This would seem to fulfill the definition of misogynism, of woman-hating. The author then raises misogynism to the level of a religious virtue: "He who is pleasing to God eludes her, but the sinner is her captive" (Eccles 7:26). Here there is no pretense of a virtuous rejection of woman as a prostitute or adulteress; *all* women have been reduced to essential evil. Of course, in general Ecclesiastes is very pessimistic, as is reflected, among other places, in his remark that only one man in a thousand is "better than the rest." This is surely a relatively low estimate of men; but his condemnation of women is absolute: "but *never* a woman" (Eccles 7:28).

In similar fashion Ben Sira pours invective on prostitutes, adulteresses, daughters in general, and all but submissive wives. He also bitterly abuses women in general with an intensity that surpasses previous biblical misogynism. It would also seem that for Ben Sira all women are nymphomaniacs, at least in the passive sense: "A woman will accept any husband, but some daughters are better than others" (Ben Sira 36:21). For Ben Sira it also seems that all women are spiteful by nature: "Do not let water find a leak, do not allow a spiteful woman free rein for her tongue. If she will not do as you tell her, get rid of her. . . . For moth comes out of clothes, and woman's spite out of woman" (25:25–26; 42:13). He pushes the matter further: "Any spite rather than the spite of a woman!" (25:13). And still further: "A man's spite is preferable to a woman's kindness; women give rise to shame and reproach" (42:14). Indeed, to Ben Sira women are the greatest evil in the world by far! "No wickedness comes anywhere near the wickedness of a woman, may a sinner's lot be hers!" (25:19). Woman is not only the greatest of evils, but in fact the cause of all evil: "Sin began with a woman, and thanks to her we all must die" (25:24).

§94. Great Women Behind Great Men

The next passage is much more positive toward women, though it is still ambivalent. The setting of the story is at the court of Darius, king of Persia, where the Jews were in exile (sixth century B.C.E.). Three pages dispute before the king as to what is the strongest thing. The first argues for wine, the great leveler; the second argues for the king; the third—Zerubbabel, future leader of the Jews—argues for women:

Then the third, that is Zerubbabel, who had spoken of women and truth, began to speak: "Gentlemen, is not the king great, and are not men many, and is not wine strong? Who then is their master, or who is their lord? Is it not women? Women gave birth to the king and to every people that rules over sea and land. From women they came; and women brought up the very men who plant the vineyards from which comes wine. Women make men's clothes; they bring men glory; men cannot exist without women. If men gather gold and silver or any other beautiful thing, and then see a woman lovely in appearance and beauty, they let all those things go, and gape at her, and with open mouths stare at her, and all prefer her to gold or silver or any other beautiful thing. A man leaves his own father, who brought him up, and his own country, and cleaves to his wife. With his wife he ends his days, with no thought of his father or his mother or his country. Hence you must realize that women rule over you!

"Do you not labor and toil, and bring everything and give it to women? A man takes his sword, and goes out to travel and rob and steal and to sail the sea and rivers; he faces lions, and he walks in darkness, and when he steals and robs and plunders, he brings it back to the woman he loves. A man loves his wife more than his father or his mother. Many men have lost their minds because of women, and have become slaves because of them. Many have perished, or stumbled, or sinned, because of women. And now do you not believe me?

"Is not the king great in his power? Do not all lands fear to touch him? Yet I have seen him with Apame, the king's concubine, the daughter of the illustrious Bartacus; she would sit at the king's right hand and take the crown from the king's head and put it on her own, and slap the king with her left hand. At this the king would gaze at her with mouth agape. If she smiles at him, he laughs; if she loses her temper with him, he flatters her, that she may be reconciled to him. Gentlemen, why are not women strong, since they do such things?" (1 Esdras 4:13–32)

Zerubbabel then proceeded to argue that the truth is nevertheless the victor over all. This would seem to be an early version of the notion that *behind* every great man is a great woman. It does not indicate that women had a high status. On the contrary. Women seem to have been relegated to bearing men—who then did all the important things of the world—and to being the object of men's sexual desires. Women's humanity and their sexuality were coextensive. Not so with men.

The book of 1 Esdras is part of the Apocrypha, not the Pseudepigrapha. It is found in the Septuagint Greek Bible, but not in the Masoretic Hebrew text. Jerome included it in his Latin Vulgate translation, but since the Council of Trent in the sixteenth century the Catholic Church has not included it in the regular part of the Bible.

The First Book of Esdras is largely the story of the return of the Jews from exile and the subsequent events, mostly all found in the canonical book Ezra-Nehemiah. Hence, either it is largely derived from Ezra-Nehemiah; or vice versa; or both are from a common source, or parallel sources. It is judged to have been composed in the second century B.C.E. (see Herbert G. May and Bruce M. Metzger, eds., *The Oxford Annotated Bible with the Apocrypha*, The Apocrypha, p. 1; Oxford University Press, 1965), and quite likely in Egypt (see McKenzie, *Dictionary of the Bible*, p. 42). Since this story is missing from the Ezra-Nehemiah account, it probably was added from non-Jewish sources, e.g., Egyptian: "The story probably originated outside the Jewish community as a popular tale praising the relative strength of wine, kings, and women (the original order was perhaps kings, wine, and women). The praise of the strength of truth (4:33–41; compare 3:12) was added later in the transmission of the story, perhaps by a Greek-speaking editor (this part of the story has close parallels to Greek thought and literature)" (*Oxford Annotated Bible*, Apocrypha, pp. 5f.).

The alternate theory is that earlier this story had been included in the Ezra-Nehemiah account, but then was excised: "Although our O.T. has lost the story of Zerubbabel and the Praise of Truth, there is no doubt that there is something 'unbiblical' in the orations. In the course of the growth of the O.T., compilers and revisers have not unfrequently obscured or omitted that to which they took exception, and some light is thus often thrown upon other phases of contemporary Palestinian or Jewish thought." (R. H. Charles, *The Apocrypha and Pseudepigrapha of the Old Testament,* Vol. 1, p. 19; Oxford University Press, 1913. It should also be noted that the Jewish historian Josephus in the late first century C.E. also records the same story. See Flavius Josephus, *Antiquities of the Jews* XI.iii.5.)

In either case, if the story could be said to reflect a high status for women, the reflected reality was not evident in Palestinian Judaism, and in the second theory, even that reflection was removed by the redactor of the canonical Ezra-Nehemiah.

B. AMBIVALENT MODELS OF WOMEN—
POSTBIBLICAL WRITINGS

§95. Therapeutae: Jewish Women and Men Contemplatives

The Therapeutae ("healers") were a sect of Jewish ascetic contemplatives who lived near Alexandria, Egypt, in the first century C.E. What we know about them comes from Philo alone. In their monastic, celibate, ascetic, contemplative life-style they were very like the Essenes in Palestine. However, they were dramatically different from the Essenes in that among the celibate contemplatives of the Therapeutae there were women. When speaking of the celebration of a religious feast Philo describes the women Therapeutae as quite on a par with the men, though it is clear from elsewhere that the leading teachers of the sect were men:

> The feast is shared by women also, most of them aged virgins, who have kept their chastity not under compulsion, like some of the Greek priestesses, but of their own free will in their ardent yearning for wisdom. Eager to have her for their life mate they have spurned the pleasures of the body and desire no mortal offspring but those immortal children which only the soul that is dear to God can bring to the birth unaided because the Father has sown in her spiritual rays enabling her to hold the verities of wisdom.
> IX. The order of reclining is so apportioned that the men sit by themselves on the right and the women by themselves on the left. (Philo, *On the Contemplative Life* 68f.; Loeb Classical Library, *Philo,* Vol. 9, p. 155)

Though each ascetic had her or his own small house and there spent most of the time studying and praying over allegorical interpretations of Scripture, all the members did come together every Sabbath, the men and women, to hear lectures by their (male) teachers. However, the meeting place partitioned the men and women from each other, or rather, the women from the men:

This common sanctuary in which they meet every seventh day is a double enclosure, one portion set apart for the men, the other for the women. For women too regularly make part of the audience with the same ardour and the same sense of their calling. The wall between the two chambers rises up from the ground to three or four cubits [four and a half to over six feet] built in the form of a breast work, while the space above up to the roof is left open. This arrangement serves two purposes; the modesty becoming to the female sex is preserved, while the women sitting within ear-shot can easily follow what is said since there is nothing to obstruct the voice of the speaker. (Philo, *On the Contemplative Life* 32ff.; Loeb Classical Library, *Philo*, Vol. 9, pp. 131, 133)

Here is exhibited a mingling of Jewish and Hellenistic influences —which one would expect in the then perhaps most flourishing of Hellenistic cities (founded by Alexander the Great), which was at the same time perhaps the then most flourishing Jewish city in the world. The men and the women were separated in the synagogue, according to the Jewish custom (see §106); even today one can see in the synagogue in the very Orthodox section of Jerusalem, Mea Shearim, the same kind of wall (though higher) between the room for men and the room for women, with a separate entrance for each room; a somewhat similar division exists at the Western or "Wailing" Wall. The separation in the synagogue meant, of course, that the women could only listen, not speak, in the services. However, it was untraditional that the women should have committed themselves to the life of this sect with a devotion equal to that of the men, for that meant devoting the greatest part of their lives to being in their cells studying allegorical interpretations of the Scriptures; women traditionally did not devote themselves, like men, to a study of the Scriptures (see §106), whereas in Hellenist Mystery religions and the Egyptian Isis cult women did take prominent and even priestly roles (see p. 17).

There was, however, one regular occasion when the female Therapeutae did take an active part in a religious service. Every seventh week there was a sacred feast day with a meal. (Some scholars, e.g., Colson, suggest that the feast did not take place every fifty days, but rather once a year at Pentecost.) The men would recline on one side of the table and the women on the other; with the meal there were readings, prayers, and hymn-singing—and the women participated in the latter. Afterward the men and the women grouped themselves in two separate choirs and sang in alternating fashion, accompanied with various hand and body movements, like a sacred dance. At the end the men and women mixed to form a single choir.

Thus they prayed, sang, and danced, filled with pious enthusiasm, until morning, when they returned to their cells.

XI. After the supper they hold the sacred vigil which is conducted in the following way. They rise up all together and standing in the middle of the refectory form themselves first into two choirs, one of men and one of women, the leader and precentor chosen for each being the most honored amongst them and also the most musical. Then they sing hymns to God composed of many measures and set to many melodies, sometimes chanting together, sometimes taking up the harmony antiphonally, hands and feet keeping time in accompaniment, and rapt with enthusiasm reproduce sometimes the lyrics of the procession, sometimes of the halt and of the wheeling and counter-wheeling of a choric dance.

Then when each choir has separately done its own part in the feast, having drunk as in the Bacchic rites of the strong wine of God's love they mix and both together become a single choir, a copy of the choir set up of old beside the Red Sea in honor of the wonders there wrought. . . . This wonderful sight and experience, an act transcending word and thought and hope, so filled with ecstasy both men and women that forming a single choir they sang hymns of thanksgiving to God their Saviour, the men led by the prophet Moses and the women by the Prophetess Miriam.

It is on this model above all that the choir of the Therapeutae of either sex, note in response to note and voice to voice, the treble of the women blending with the bass of the men, create an harmonious concert, music in the truest sense. Lovely are the thoughts, lovely the words and worthy of reverence the choristers, and the end and aim of thoughts, words and choristers alike is piety. Thus they continue till dawn, drunk with this drunkenness in which there is no shame, then not with heavy heads or drowsy eyes but more alert and wakeful than when they came to the banquet, they stand with their faces and whole body turned to the east and when they see the sun rising they stretch their hands up to heaven and pray for bright days and knowledge of the truth and the power of keen sighted thinking. And after the prayers they depart each to his private sanctuary once more to ply the trade and till the field of their wonted philosophy. (Philo, *On the Contemplative Life* 83–89; Loeb Classical Library, *Philo,* Vol. 9, pp. 165–169)

Johannes Leipoldt noted that this seven-week feast of the Therapeutae had all the characteristics of a Greek Mystery religion feast, clearly reflecting the influence of Hellenism. He continued:

Then the Greeks reflected a past fateful event by imitation, men and women participated equally—in Mystery religions something accepted as obvious. When the Therapeutae take this over they may not exclude the women Therapeutae, so much more so may they not since in the Old Testament model the prophetess Miriam steps forward so decisively. Hence, one may not view the participation of the women Therapeutae in the worship service as indicative of the Jewish manner [but rather of the Greek manner]. (Johannes Leipoldt, *Die Frau in der antiken Welt und im Urchristentum,* p. 86; Leipzig, 1954)

It should be noted that if, despite all the massive Hellenistic influences present in Alexandria and among the Therapeutae, the women were still so strictly separated in the weekly synagogue service and relegated to listening, then the force of the Jewish custom must have been very strong.

Thus we find a blending of Jewish and Greek traditions among the Therapeutae. As far as women are concerned, the stronger influence of Greek customs—in contrast to the apparently relatively weaker Greek influence among the Essenes—worked to their advantage: they were full-fledged members, "having adopted the same sect with equal (to the men) deliberation and decision"; they spent their time studying the Scriptures; they took an active part in the sacred banquet, vigil, and dance every seven weeks. None of these things was true of the position of women in the Essenes. Nevertheless, all women Therapeutae were segregated in the Sabbath synagogue, did not have the right to speak there, and in other ways appeared subordinate to men, which was not the case with women in many contemporary Greek Mystery religions. The misogynism of much of contemporary Palestinian Judaism seems to have been greatly modified by Greek influence in the Therapeutae, though we know from other evidence that this modifying influence on the restrictions in the lives of married Jewish women in Egypt was not so effective (see §106).

§96. Ambivalent Rabbinic Attitudes Toward Women

In the rabbinic writings there are a number of positive evaluations of women. For example, "It was taught: He who has no wife dwells without good, without help, without joy, without blessing, and without atonement" (Genesis Rabbah 18, 2). There is a series of sayings gathered together in one place in the Talmud, mostly concerning the sadness caused by the death, or divorce, of one's wife: "Rabbi Alexandri said: The world is darkened for him whose wife has died in his days [i.e., predeceased him]. . . . Rabbi Jose ben Hanina said: His steps grow short. . . . Rabbi Johanan also said: He whose first wife has died (is grieved as much) as if the destruction of the Temple had taken place in his days. . . . Rabbi Samuel ben Nahman said: For him who divorces the first wife, the very altar sheds tears" (Talmud bSanhedrin 22a).

Two things should be kept in mind in evaluating these positive statements. First, as with the Wisdom literature noted above, almost all the positive things said about women by the rabbis are not about women as such, but rather about women as they are related to men, namely, as wives. In fact, at the same place in the Talmud as the above appreciative statements about the loss of one's wife, it is also stated: "Rabbi Samuel ben Unya said in the name of Rab: A woman (before marriage) is a shapeless lump, and concludes a covenant only with him who transforms her (into) a (useful) vessel" (Talmud bSanhedrin 22b). Secondly, although a good wife is highly valued and receives deep affection, this appreciation very frequently is expressed, as in the Wisdom literature, in terms of what the wife does for the husband, and family. This attitude was expressed well by a modern rabbi writing on the subject of the Jewish woman:

> Only the life of the woman contains even more renunciation. Her whole life is a self-denying devotion to the welfare of others, especially of her husband and children. The true woman is the performance of duty personified. . . . Renunciation, sacrifice for the joy of her husband and children becomes her joy. . . . This will-subordination of the wife to the husband is a necessary condition of the unity which man and wife should form together. The subordination cannot be the other way about, since the man . . . has to carry forward the divine and human messages. (Samson Raphael Hirsch, *Judaism Eternal*, Vol. 2, pp. 57f.; London: Soncino Press, 1959)

In addition to the laudatory statements already mentioned, the ancient rabbinic literature also contains the following rabbinic teachings which are likewise in praise of women, or rather, of wives and marriage. "Rabbi Eleazar said: Any man who has no wife is no proper man," that is, as Rabbi Eliezer is recorded in the same place as having taught: "Anyone who does not engage in the propagation of the race is as though he shed blood." Also in the same place Rabbi Hiyya taught about wives: "It is sufficient for us that they rear up our children and deliver us from sin," i.e., satisfy the male's sexual drive within the "ethically acceptable" context of marriage. "Our Rabbis taught: Concerning a man who loves his wife as himself, who honors her more than himself . . ." "Rabbi Hama ben Hanina stated: "As soon as a man takes a wife his sins are stopped up," that is, concupiscence is "legitimately" channeled. A man was advised: "Be quick in buying land, but deliberate in taking a wife. Come down a step in choosing your wife"; since the wife was to be in the subordinate position it was thought important that she come from a lower social position. In the same place in the Talmud there is also the appreciative saying: "Happy is the husband of a beautiful wife; the number of his days shall be double," which is immediately followed by a warning against all other beautiful women: "Turn away thy eyes from (thy neighbor's) charming wife lest thou be caught in her net. Do not turn in to her husband to mingle with him wine and strong drink; for, through the form of a beautiful woman, many were destroyed and a mighty host are all her slain." (All these quotations are from Talmud bYebamoth 63a–b.)

If a good wife was appreciated by the rabbis, a bad wife was equally unappreciated:

> Raba said: (If one has a) bad wife it is a meritorious act to divorce her. . . . Raba further stated: A bad wife . . . (should be given) a rival at her side [that is, a second wife should be taken]. . . . Raba further stated: A bad wife is as troublesome as a very rainy day; for it is said, A continual dropping on a very rainy day and a contentious woman are alike. . . . How baneful is a bad wife with whom Gehenna is compared. . . . Behold I will bring evil upon them, which they shall not be able to escape. Rabbi Nahuan said in the name of Rabbah ben Abbuha: This refers to a bad wife, the amount of whose kethubah is large. (Talmud bYebamoth 63a–b)

In arguing for the high estimation of women held by the ancient rabbis, some scholars refer to the rabbinic teaching about the beneficent or maleficent influence a wife has on a husband:

> It once happened that a pious man was married to a pious woman, and they did not produce children. Said they, "We are of no use to the Holy One, blessed be He," whereupon they arose and divorced each other. The former went and married a wicked woman, and she made him wicked, while the latter went and married a wicked man, and made him righteous. This proves that all depends on the woman. (Genesis Rabbah 17, 7)

However, the fact that this truly appreciative story about a pious wife is immediately followed by a whole series of rather deprecatory statements about women in general somewhat modifies the force of that story as evidence of high appreciation of women by the rabbis as a group (although clearly *individual* rabbis at least at times expressed themselves more positively about women):

> And why must a woman use perfume, while a man does not need perfume? . . . And why has a woman a shrill voice but not a man? . . . And why does a man go out bareheaded while a woman goes out with her head covered? She is like one who has done wrong and is ashamed of people; therefore she goes out with her head covered. Why do they (the women) walk in front of the corpse (at a funeral)? Because they brought death into the world, they therefore walk in front of the corpse. . . . And why was the precept of menstruation given to her? Because she shed the blood of Adam (by causing death), therefore was the precept of menstruation given to her. And why was the precept of the "dough" given to her? Because she corrupted Adam, who was the dough of the world, therefore was the precept of dough given to her. And why was the precept of the Sabbath lights given to her? Because she

extinguished the soul of Adam, therefore was the precept of the Sabbath lights given to her. (Genesis Rabbah 17, 8)

Similarly weakened, or at least put in an ambivalent light as evidence concerning the rabbis as a group, are several sets of rabbinic teachings favorable toward wives:

Rabbi Helbo said: One must always observe the honor due to his wife, because blessings rest on a man's home only on account of his wife. . . . Thus did Raba say to the townspeople of Mahuza, Honor your wives, that ye may be enriched. . . . Rab said: One should always be heedful of wronging his wife, for since her tears are frequent she is quickly hurt. (Talmud bBaba Mezia 59a)

These are all truly sensitive sentiments. But in the same place the same "Rab also said: He who follows his wife's counsel will descend into Gehenna." At this the Talmud adds the part which Rabbi Hirsch in the above-quoted book only partially cited as proof of the rabbis' high estimation of women: "Rabbi Papa objected to Abaye: But people say, If your wife is short, bend down and hear her whisper!" He did not write the following resolution of what the rabbis saw as a contradiction between the teachings of Rab and Papa just quoted:

There is no difficulty: the one refers to general matters; the other to household affairs. Another version: the one refers to religious matters, the other to secular questions. (Talmud bBaba Mezia 59a)

Apparently the translator of the English Soncino edition was somewhat embarrassed by this teaching, for he noted: "A man should certainly consult his wife on the latter, but not on the former,—not a disparagement of woman; her activities lying mainly in the home," which meant that rabbinic "high estimation of women" was here limited to a valuing of women as housekeepers.

The noble statement: "Who is wealthy? . . . He who has a wife comely in deeds" (Talmud bShabbath 25b), takes on a somewhat intimidating quality when it is realized that it was made by Rabbi Akiba, who allegedly allowed his wife to spend twenty-four years in living widowhood while he studied Torah, and who was "the founder of the peculiar institution of married 'monasticism.' . . . After marriage they would devote themselves completely to their studies while their wives supported them" (Louis Finkelstein, *Akiba: Scholar, Saint and Martyr,* p. 80; Meridian Books, 1962—not unlike what happens in the Mea Shearim section of Jerusalem today). It was Akiba who also taught that a man may divorce his wife merely on the grounds that "he finds another woman more beautiful than she is" (Mishnah Gittin 9, 10).

It also says in the Talmud: "The Holy One . . . endowed the woman with more understanding then the man" (Talmud bNiddah 45b). However, since this statement comes in the midst of a discussion about the age at which vows can be made and is used as an argument that girls can make vows a year earlier than boys because they mature sooner, its intended meaning seems to be limited to this particular case. This is clearly confirmed in an early midrash where the very same discussion is taken up and carried further as follows: "Some reverse it, because a woman generally stays home, whereas a man goes out into the streets and learns understanding from people" (Genesis Rabbah 18, 1).

Rabbi Hirsch in the above-quoted book also notes that the Talmud says that women are promised greater bliss—after death—but he does not note what it then says about *how* women are to merit this bliss. The following first sentence Rabbi Hirsch refers to; the rest he does not:

[Our Rabbis taught]: Greater is the promise made by the Holy One, blessed be He, to the women than to the men; for it says, "Rise up, ye women that are at ease; ye confident daughters, give ear unto my speech." Rab said to Rabbi Hiyya: Whereby do women earn merit? By making their children go to the synagogue to learn Scripture and their husbands to the Beth Hamidrash to learn Mishnah, and waiting for their husbands till they return from the Beth Hamidrash. (Talmud bBerakhoth 17a)

The latter half of this passage would seem to dilute at least somewhat the strength of the former half as evidence of the rabbis' high estimation of women.

VI. Negative Images of and Attitudes Toward Women in Hebrew-Jewish Tradition

As noted at the outset, the main purpose of this book is to draw together and analyze the positive statements about women in the Bible and immediately related materials. However, in order not to give a grossly distorted picture of the status of women in the Bible, it was felt imperative that not only should the positive and ambivalent materials on women be presented in detail; also at least a sample survey of the negative materials should be set forth. No attempt at thoroughness will be made, as that lies outside the scope of this book, and because this negative side, which in fact in some areas is so much more predominant than the positive, has already been amply presented elsewhere (see, e.g., Phyllis Bird, "Images of Women in the Old Testament," in Rosemary Radford Ruether, ed., *Religion and Sexism*, pp. 41–88; Simon & Schuster, 1974; and Leonard Swidler, *Women in Judaism*). What follows will be a brief survey first of the negative material on women in the Hebrew Bible, Apocrypha, and Pseudepigrapha, and then of the early rabbinic literature.

A. NEGATIVE IMAGES AND ATTITUDES— HEBREW BIBLE

§97. Women at the Disposal of Men

To begin with, women were almost inevitably subordinate creatures in Hebrew society, coming first under the control of the father, and passing from the father's dominance to the husband's. For example, the wife is listed along with the *rest* of the husband's property in the Decalogue, but not vice versa:

You shall not covet your neighbour's wife, nor his male or female slave, nor his ox or ass, nor anything else that *belongs* to him. (Ex 20:17)

Children were almost totally at the disposal of the father, but daughters were so in a special way. The daughter and the son could be sold into slavery, but after six years of service all male Hebrew slaves had to be freed by Hebrew masters. However, "if a man sells his daughter as a slave, she shall not regain her liberty like male slaves" (Ex 21:7). A more startling sexual disposal of daughters is found in the story of Lot and his daughters. Lot met two men on the road and invited them to spend the night at his house.

The house was surrounded by the men of the town, the men of Sodom both young and old, all the people without exception. Calling to Lot they said, "Where are the men who came to you tonight? Send them out to us!" The men of Sodom wanted to have sex with them. Lot came out to them at the door, and having closed the door behind him said, "I beg you, my brothers, do no such wicked thing. Listen, I have two daughters who are virgins. I am ready to send them out to you, to treat as it pleases you. But as for the men, do nothing to them." (Gen 19:4–8)

A similar story occurs in the Book of Judges where the visiting man himself, a Levite no less, shoves his concubine out the door to the mob to save himself; she is raped and beaten to death! A particularly poignant part of the story is that the Levite's concubine had run away from her "husband" back to her home. After four months he went to fetch her and bring her back. It was on the first night's journey back that she met her grim fate:

As they were at their meal, some men from the town, scoundrels, came crowding together round the house; they battered on the door and said to the old man, the master of the house, "Send out the man who has come into your house! We want to have sex with him!" Then the master of the house went out to them and said, "No, my brothers, I implore you, do not commit this crime. This man has become my guest; do not commit such an infamy against this man. Behold, here are my virgin daughter and his concubine. I bring them out now. Ravish them and do with them what you will, but do not commit such an infamy against this man. But the men would not listen to him, so the Levite seized his concubine and put her outside with them. And they raped and abused her all night long and did not stop until morning. At dawn the woman came and fell down at the door of the old man's house, where her husband *('adon)* was. She was still there when daylight came. Her husband got up that morning, and when he opened the door to go on his way, he found his concubine lying in front of his house with her hands reaching for the door. He said, "Get up. Let's go." But there was no answer. So he put

her body across his donkey and began his journey. Having reached his
house, he picked up his knife, took hold of his concubine, and limb by
limb cut her into twelve pieces; then he sent her all through the land of
Israel. (Judg 19:22–29)

In the following passages the perpetrators of the crime, that is, the
whole Hebrew tribe of Benjamin, were severely punished. But nothing happens, or is even said, to the Levite who shoved his concubine
out to her death or the father who offered up his daughter to the same
fate. Women were almost totally at the disposal of men in that
society.

This is borne out further by the fact that the Hebrew verb *b'l*,
meaning at root, "to master," is at times used to mean "the man
marries" (e.g., Deut 21:13 and Jer 31:32). The noun form, *ba'al*, at
root means "master": fifteen times it is used as "husband." That is,
the wife addresses her husband as *ba'al*, "master" (e.g., Ex 21:4, 22;
Deut 22:22; 24:4; 2 Sam 11:26; Esth 1:17, 20; Prov 12:4; 31:11, 23,
28; Joel 1:8), or as Lord, *'adon*, as in Judg 19:26 just quoted, and
elsewhere.

§98. Women Inheriting
Normally a woman could not inherit property in Israel. A daughter
could inherit from her father only if there were no son (Num 27:
1–11), but she had to marry within the clan so the property would
not move out of it (Num 36:1–9); the women simply served as blood
links to pass property from male to male within the family line. The
wife normally received nothing, but was always dependent on a man
for her support: first on her father, then on her husband, then when
a widow on her son, or on her father again if she had no son—or into
dire straits, as with Naomi of the Book of Ruth. It was because of
this complete financial dependence of women that the prophets so
often railed against the oppression of widows, for widows were normally of themselves helpless—this is why Judith as a widow would
normally be thought of as the most helpless of the helpless (women),
and through this weakest of all possible instruments Yahweh saves his
people (see §88).

§99. Sexual Transgressions
Since in ancient society women were thought of as men's posses-
sions (e.g., as noted just above, in the Decalogue it was forbidden to
covet a neighbor's wife but not a neighbor's husband, because in this

regard a wife was not a person but a possession—cf. Jeffrey Howard Togay, "Adultery," *Encyclopaedia Judaica,* Vol. 2, col. 313), in patriarchal days it was the husband's right, or at least the head of the family's right, to punish the adulterous woman (see Gen 38:24, where Judah ordered Tamar burned). "It was only when adultery was elevated to the rank of a grave offense against God as well that the husband was required to resort to the priests or to the courts" (Chaim Hermann Cohn, "Adultery," *Encyclopaedia Judaica,* Vol. 2, col. 315).

There was no punishment for the man having sex unless a married or betrothed woman was involved. In adultery both the adulterer and the adulteress were to be executed (because the husband's property rights had been violated). Of course since only the woman could become pregnant, she alone would be caught many more times than the man—and punished. However, the Book of Proverbs indicated that at least for the adulterer it was possible to "compound" his offense, that is, pay the wronged husband a sum of money in lieu of undergoing the death penalty (Prov 6:35). Since this portion of the Book of Proverbs was probably composed only in the third or fourth century B.C.E., this may be an indication of the lessening of the rigor of the earlier biblical injunctions. According to the available evidence, this lessening of the death penalty was apparently applied only to the man; the woman, who was often not likely to have any money available anyhow, was presumably still put to death.

The usual means of execution was by stoning, but in preexilic days it may at times have been different for adulteresses. In a metaphorical description of wayward Jerusalem as an adulterous woman by the prophet Ezekiel, which may or may not have any historical referent, stripping and exposure is seen as one form of punishment:

> I will gather all those lovers to whom you made advances. . . . I will put you on trial for adultery. . . . Then I will hand you over to them. . . . They will strip your clothes off, take away your splendid ornaments, and leave you naked and exposed. They will bring up the mob against you and stone you, they will hack you to pieces with their swords . . . and many women shall see it. (Ezek 16:37–41)

That women were also burned for adultery, as was required in the case of a priest's daughter (Lev 21:9), as late as the first century C.E. (probably 62 C.E.) is testified to in Mishnah and Talmud:

Rabbi Eliezer ben Zadok said: It happened once that a priest's daughter committed adultery and they encompassed her with bundles of branches and burnt her. (Mishnah Sanhedrin 7, 3)

Rabbi Eleazar ben Zadok said, "I remember when I was a child riding on my father's shoulder that a priest's adulterous daughter was brought (to the place of execution) surrounded by faggots, and burnt." (Talmud bSanhedrin 52b)

Still later, in late third-century Babylon, a similar execution was reported:

Imarta the daughter of Tali, a priest, committed adultery. Therefore Rabbi Hama ben Tobiah had her surrounded by faggots and burnt. (Talmud bSanhedrin 52b)

Another instance in the ancient biblical law concerning sexual immorality where the woman was again the victim of a double moral standard is found in Deut 22:13–21. There, if a man claimed that his wife was not a virgin, the father of the bride was expected to bring out a garment with bloodstains resulting from the breaking of the hymen during the first marital intercourse and "spread the garment before the elders of the town." If the elders were satisfied, they fined the husband one hundred pieces of silver—payable to the father!—and he would not be allowed to divorce the girl ever. However, if the elders were not satisfied with the evidence—the obtaining of which must have presented no little difficulty at times—"They shall bring her out of the door of her father's house and the *men* of her town shall stone her to death." The young bride, often less than a teen-ager, was in a no-win situation: if she lost her case, she was put to death; if she won, she had to live for-ever with—under—a husband who was furious enough with her to try to have her killed, but was frustrated and had to pay a huge fine on her account. On the other hand, no man suffered a penalty for his lack of virginity.

All of these punishments took place only if there was hard evidence that adultery had occurred, usually including the testimony of two witnesses. However, even simply on the basis of a suspicion, or only as the result of a fit of jealousy, a husband could force his wife to submit to an extremely humiliating and terrorizing trial by ordeal. The priestly portion of the Book of Numbers (fifth century B.C.E.), i.e., Num 5:11–31, is the only specific account in the Bible of trial by ordeal. The essential prescriptions there are as follows:

When in such a case a fit of jealousy comes over the husband which causes him to suspect his wife, she being in fact defiled; or when, on the other hand, a fit of jealousy comes over a husband which causes him to suspect his wife, when she is not in fact defiled; then in either case, the husband shall bring his wife to the priest. . . . The priest shall bring her forward and set her before the Lord. He shall take clean water in an earthenware vessel, and shall take dust from the floor of the Tabernacle and add it to the water. He shall set the woman before the Lord, uncover her head . . . [He then tells her in a formal manner that if she is innocent, she will be unharmed.] "But if you have gone astray, . . . may the Lord make an example of you among your people in adjurations and in swearing of oaths by bringing upon you miscarriage and untimely birth; and this water that brings out the truth shall enter your body . . ." The priest shall write these curses on a scroll and wash them off into the water of contention; he shall make the woman drink the water that brings out the truth, and the water shall enter her body . . .   If she has let herself become defiled and has been unfaithful to her husband, then when the priest makes her drink the water that brings out the truth and the water has entered her body, she will suffer a miscarriage and untimely birth, and her name will become an example in adjuration among her kin. But if the woman has not let herself become defiled and is pure, then her innocence is established and she will bear her child. (Num 5:14–28)

Either way, the experience is horrible for the woman, but "no guilt will attach to the husband, but the woman shall bear the penalty of her guilt" (Num 5:31).

§100. Polygyny

Polyandry was not explicitly forbidden in the Hebrew Bible—it was never considered as a possible choice. A renowned Orthodox Jewish scholar, Louis Epstein, noted that the Bible generally assumed a patrilineal family organization among the early Hebrews and that consequently marriage represented acquisition, ownership on the part of the husband. Such a marriage was called *ba'al* marriage, where the husband was the owner of his wife in the same sense as he owned his slaves. "Polygamy is the logical corollary of ba'al marriage, for as one may own many slaves, so he may espouse many wives" (Louis M. Epstein, *Marriage Laws in the Bible and the Talmud*, p. 7; Harvard University Press, 1942). Epstein further stated that though upon their return to the Land of Canaan from Egypt the Hebrews did not at first take up polygamy:

With better times, however, even the masses indulged in polygamy, and it is so reported especially of the tribe of Issachar. In that formative period, it seems bigamy became common among the Hebrews. Noble and wealthy families had full polygamy and larger or smaller harems, but the common folk were satisfied with two wives. . . . We find the teachings of the Pharisees a continuation of the biblical attitude to polygamy, and the teaching of the rabbis thereafter an extension of the pharisaic tradition. This tradition accepted polygamy as legally permissible and did not even imply a policy of monogamy as did the Church; for while the Church shifted its center to the West, where monogamy was the rule, the Synagogue continued in its oriental setting, where polygamy was native. Any resistance to polygamy in talmudic times as in biblical days was created by life itself and was not formulated into law. . . . The Jewish family during that period was very like its counterpart in the biblical period. Rulers permitted themselves plural wives; bigamy was not infrequent, but the people as a rule practiced monogamy. (Epstein, *Marriage Laws in the Bible and the Talmud,* pp. 12–17)

§101. Divorce

Since in Israel the man possessed the woman and not vice versa, the man could dis-possess, that is, divorce, the woman, but she could not divorce him. The Orthodox Israeli scholar Ze'ev Falk notes that in ancient Israelite days divorce was "an arbitrary, unilateral, private act on the part of the husband and consisted of the wife's expulsion from the husband's house" (Ze'ev Falk, *Hebrew Law in Biblical Times,* p. 154; Jerusalem: Wahrmann Books, 1964), the very term usually used to refer to a divorced wife being *gerushah,* "expelled." "At a later stage (but before Deut 24:1; Is 50:1; and Jer 3:8) the husband was required to deliver a bill of divorce to his wife at her expulsion" (ibid.). The whole ceremony of the man handing the wife a writ of divorce was done privately, before two witnesses, down through the early rabbinic period.

Already a number of decades before the beginning of the rabbinic period, and down through the time of the rabbinic writings, it was even considered obligatory to divorce a "bad wife," though of course the opposite, the divorce of a bad husband, was not possible. In the midst of vitriolic misogynism Ben Sira stated the obligation clearly and forcefully:

A bad wife brings humiliation, downcast looks, and a wounded heart. Slack of hand and weak of knee is the man whose wife fails to make him happy. Woman is the origin of sin, and it is through her that we all die. Do not leave a leaky cistern to drip or allow a bad wife to say what she likes. If she does not accept your control, divorce her and send her away. (Ben Sira 25:23–26)

The basic expression in law of the divorce procedure is stated only indirectly in Deuteronomy:

Supposing a man has taken a wife and consummated the marriage; but she has not pleased him and he has found some impropriety [*dabar erwat,* literally, "a word of nakedness" or "shame"] of which to accuse her; so he has made out a writ of divorce for her and handed it to her and then dismissed her from his house. (Deut 24:1)

A dispute developed by the end of the Hebrew biblical period about how the term *erwat* was to be understood. Two rabbinic schools developed, one following Hillel and the other Shammai, both of whom lived in the first century B.C.E. (Akiba, who followed Hillel, lived in the late first and early second century C.E.). The Hillel-Akiba school won out:

> The school of Shammai says: A man may not divorce his wife unless he has found something unseemly in her, for it is written, Because he hath found in her *indecency* in anything. And the school of Hillel says (he may divorce her) even if she spoiled a dish for him, for it is written, Because he hath found in her indecency in *anything*. Rabbi Akiba says: Even if he found another more beautiful than she, for it is written, And it shall be if she find no favor in his eyes. (Mishnah Gittin 9, 10)

§102. Religious Disabilities

Basically, laws in the Hebrew Bible were directed at men, which can be seen not only in the general use of the second-person masculine form for the verbs but also in a number of specific laws that inadvertently make the assumption clear:

> You shall not afflict any widow or orphan. If you do, . . . then your wives shall become widows and your children fatherless. (Ex 22:22–24)

Women could not receive the sign of membership in the religious community, circumcision (Gen 17:10ff.). Only men could become priests. Women were not obliged by the law of Deut 16:16 to attend the three annual pilgrim feasts. This non-obligation of women grew with time, with the predictable result that many things women originally were not required to do, they eventually were required not to do. One modern Jewish scholar makes the same point bluntly:

> A logical consequence of female exemption from the time-geared features of the liturgical round is the ineligibility of women to take an active role in them, for example, as leaders of prayer for congregations including men. (Raphael Lowe, *The Position of Women in Judaism*, p. 44; London, 1966)

No information is available about the courts of the Temple built by Solomon in the tenth century B.C.E., or of the one built by Zerubbabel in the sixth century B.C.E. For its replacement, however, built by Herod starting in 19 B.C.E. and completely finished only in 64 C.E., six years before its destruction, we do have information from several sources. The outermost ring was the Court of the Gentiles, within which was the Court of the Women and within it the Court of Israel, into which only the men of Israel were admitted. The Court of the Women was nineteen steps above the Court of the Gentiles, but fifteen below the Court of Israel. Women were allowed in both the Gentiles' court and the women's court, but even this latter was further restricted:

Beforetime (the Court of the Women) was free of buildings, and (afterwards) they surrounded it with a gallery so that the women should observe from above and the men from below and that they should not mingle together. (Mishnah Middoth 2, 5)

If for those who no longer have the evil inclination the men must be separated from the women, how much more is that separation necessary for those who have not overcome the evil inclination at all. (Palestinian Talmud Sukka 55b, *Le Talmud de Jerusalem,* tr. by Moise Schwab, Vol. 6, pp. 43f.; Paris, 1883).

Moreover, the women were allowed to enter their own court only by certain gates, and indeed this privilege, as well as entrance to the Court of the Gentiles, was denied to them if they were within seven days following the end of their menstruation, or within forty days following the birth of a boy, or eighty days following the birth of a girl.

Each Jewish community in Palestine and throughout the Diaspora usually had at least one synagogue, an institution whose origins go back to the time of Ezra, and possibly to the exile. As a building, the synagogue was a meeting place for prayer and for study of the Law; at least by the time of the Roman emperor Augustus the synagogues tended to have two separate areas: the *sabbateion* for worship services and the *andron* for lectures on and discussion of the Law by the scribes and their students. The latter room, as the name makes clear, was exclusively for males. But even in the prayer hall the sexes were separated, either by some sort of barrier or grillwork or moderately high wall, as with the Therapeutae discussed above; or in a separate adjoining room, as in the synagogue of Delos (from the first century B.C.E.); or, later, in a gallery around the two sides and the rear, complete with a separate entrance, as can be seen from the oldest extant ruins in Palestine, those at Capernaum. The latter stem from the third century C.E.; presumably all earlier synagogues were destroyed by the Romans after the rebellions of 70 C.E. and 135 C.E. For details and bibliography, see Leonard Swidler, *Women in Judaism,* pp. 88–91. At present there is some questioning about how early this segregation took place in the synagogue.

§103. Impure Menstruous Women

As the *Encyclopaedia Judaica* points out, the state of ritual impurity "is considered hateful to God, and man is to take care in order not to find himself thus excluded from his divine presence" (Vol. 13, col. 1405). In Lev 11:43–44, purity and holiness are clearly linked together:

> You shall not contaminate yourselves through any crawling creature. You shall not defile yourselves with them and make yourselves unclean by them. For I am Yahweh your God; you shall make yourselves holy and keep yourselves holy, because I am holy. (Lev 11:43–44)

The consequence of ritual impurity could be dire in the extreme:

> A polluted person is always in the wrong. He has developed some wrong condition or simply crossed some line which should not have been crossed and this displacement unleashes danger for some. (Mary Douglas, *Purity and Danger,* quoted in Rachel Adler, "Tum'ah and Toharah," *The Jewish Woman. Response,* 18, Summer 1973, p. 118)

While the Temple in Jerusalem yet existed, the concern of the priestly class about ritual purity became so overriding that it was said: "To render a knife impure was more serious to them than bloodshed" (Tosephta Yoma 1, 12). In fact, the Mishnah notes that "if a priest served (at the Altar) in a state of uncleanness his brethren priests did not bring him to the court, but the young men among the priests took him outside the Temple Court and split open his brain with clubs" (Mishnah Sanhedrin 9, 6). At the same time it must be remembered that by the beginning of the Common Era, "the prohibition against contracting impurity and the obligation of purity extend also to all Jews and to all localities" (*Encyclopaedia Judaica,* Vol. 13, col. 1411).

There were three main causes of impurity: leprosy, dead bodies of certain animals, and particularly human corpses, and issue from sexual organs (these laws were based mainly on Leviticus 11–17 composed by priestly writers in the fifth century B.C.E.). Of the three, the last is the most important and frequent, and clearly it is the woman that is mostly involved. If a man has an emission of semen outside of intercourse, he is unclean; but if a man has intercourse with a woman, both are unclean—in both instances, however, only until the evening of the day of the emission.

The Levitical laws concerning the impurity of women are much more restrictive. When a woman has a menstruous discharge of blood, she is unclean for seven days, or as long as it lasts, whichever is longer. In addition, whoever she touches becomes unclean for a day, as does anything she touches. Further,

Whoever touches anything on which she sits shall wash his clothes, bathe in water and remain unclean till evening. If he is on the bed or seat where she is sitting, by touching it he shall become unclean till evening. If a man goes so far as to have intercourse with her and any of her discharge gets on him, then he shall be unclean for seven days, and every bed on which he lies down shall be unclean. (Lev 15:23–24)

In the latter case a further, more severe punishment is specified: "If a man lies with a woman during her monthly period and brings shame upon her, he has exposed her discharge and she has uncovered the source of her discharge; they shall both be cut off from their people" (Lev 20:18). In the end, the biblical threat against disregarding these laws concerning ritual purity was dire: "In this way you shall warn the Israelites against uncleanness, in order that they may not bring uncleanness upon the Tabernacle where I dwell among them, and so die" (Lev 15:31). The young priests referred to above apparently took it upon themselves to be God's executioners.

After giving birth, a woman was also considered unclean for a period of time and in need of still further "purification" for an even longer period. What is especially interesting is that both periods of "impurity" were twice as long if a girl was born than if a boy was—which would seem to indicate that a girl was considered twice as defiling as a boy:

When a woman conceives and bears a male child, she shall be unclean for seven days; as in the period of her impurity through menstruation. . . . The woman shall wait for thirty-three days because her blood requires purification; she shall touch nothing that is holy, and shall not enter the sanctuary till her days of purification are completed. If she bears a female child, she shall be unclean for fourteen days as for her menstruation and shall wait for sixty-six days. (Lev 12:2–5)

Originally, in biblical times, intercourse was forbidden only during the seven- or fourteen-day period after childbirth, but by rabbinic times there were many attempts to expand that restriction to the entire forty- and eighty-day periods—with substantial success.

B. NEGATIVE IMAGES AND ATTITUDES— "INTERTESTAMENTAL" LITERATURE

§104. Pseudepigrapha

In the last century or two before the Common Era and in the first century C.E., Jewish writers poured out a large number of religious writings, often giving fictitious names as authors. Hence, such writings are referred to as pseudepigrapha. This literature continued the very negative attitude toward women that was found in the biblical Ecclesiastes and Ben Sira (see §§92 and 93).

In the Book of the Secrets of Enoch, probably written in the first century C.E., the author expresses the notion that Eve alone was the cause of death in humanity—a notion that would have to be read into and not out of the Genesis 3 account of the Fall. This notion was part of the general atmosphere in the Judaism of that period which was apocalyptic, full of fears, anti-body, anti-sex, and anti-woman:

> And I put sleep into him and he fell asleep. And I took from him a rib, and created him a wife, that death should come to him by his wife. (The Book of the Secrets of Enoch 30:17–18, Charles, Vol. 2, p. 450)

Another Jewish book written about the same time, The Life of Adam and Eve, also lays the cause of death at the feet of Eve alone:

> And Adam saith to Eve: "Eve, what hast thou wrought in us? Thou hast brought upon us great wrath which is death (lording it over all our race)."
> . . . And Adam said to him [his son Seth]: "When God made us, me and your mother, through whom I also die . . ." (The Books of Adam and Eve, Charles, Vol. 2, pp. 145, 141)

In the Book of Jubilees, probably written at the end of the second century B.C.E., there is an extraordinary concern with fornication as the greatest of all sins (presumably surpassing thereby in gravity such sins as idolatry, murder, robbing the poor and helpless, etc.):

> There is no greater sin than the fornication which they commit on earth. (Book of Jubilees 33:20, Charles, Vol. 2)

The one to suffer most of all from such sins was the woman:

> And if any woman or maid commit fornication amongst you, burn her with fire. (Book of Jubilees 20:4, Charles, Vol. 2)

There is no mention here of any punishment whatsoever to be meted out to the man involved. Such a fundamental grounding of evil in sex and meting out punishment to the woman alone tended to imply and further a misogynist attitude in males—and in females by way of self-hatred. That development becomes very clear in another Jewish book written at the same time.

The Testaments of the Twelve Patriarchs is likewise greatly concerned about fornication as the "mother of all evils" (Testament of Simeon 5:3). It warns that a man should not "gaze on the beauty of women" (Testament of Judah 17:1), "lest he should pollute his mind with corruption" (Testament of Issachar 4:4). From this attitude of the need to avoid women out of fear, it is but a brief step to outright misogynism, of seeing women as such as evil; *every* wc in leads the essentially "good" man down to evil. The author ta. s that step:

> For evil are women, my children; and since they have no power or strength over man, they use wiles by outward attractions, that they may draw him to themselves. And whom they cannot bewitch by outward attractions, him they overcome by craft. (Testament of Reuben 5:1–2, Charles, Vol. 2)

Somewhat as in Ben Sira, the author proceeds to describe how women in general go about spreading their evil:

> By means of their adornment . . . they instil the poison, and then through the accomplished act they take them captive. For a woman cannot force a man openly, but by a harlot's bearing she beguiles him. (Testament of Reuben 5:3–4, Charles, Vol. 2)

The "logical" conclusion is then drawn by the author, namely, that all women should reject attractive clothing, jewelry, and cosmetics:

> Command your wives and your daughters, that they adorn not their heads and faces [and woe to the woman who nevertheless does], because every woman who useth these wiles hath been reserved for eternal punishment. (Testament of Reuben 5:5, Charles, Vol. 2)

In the end the principle, which was already seen in Ben Sira, was put forth, namely, that every woman is a nymphomaniac. It is expressed in the Testament of Reuben in the strongest possible form:

> Moreover, concerning them (women), the angel of the Lord told me, and taught me, that women are overcome by the spirit of fornication more than men, and in their heart they plot against men. (Testament of Reuben 5:3, Charles, Vol. 2)

Conclusion? "Guard your senses from every woman. And command the women likewise not to associate with men" (Testament of Reuben 6:1–2, Charles, Vol. 2). Contact between men and women, "even though the ungodly deed be not wrought," was seen as "an irremediable disease" for the women and as a "destruction of Beliar and an eternal reproach" for the men (Testament of Reuben 6:3–4, Charles, Vol. 2).

§105. Essene and Qumran Misogynism

The Essenes were a Jewish sect that probably originated in the second century B.C.E. and died out in the second century C.E. Some of them were married, but some lived a celibate, monastic kind of life. Philo, a Jewish contemporary (first century C.E.), described the attitude of the celibate Essenes toward women:

> They eschew marriage because they clearly discern it to be the sole or the principal danger to the maintenance of the communal life, as well as because they particularly practice continence. For no Essene takes a wife, because a woman *(gynē)* is a selfish creature, excessively jealous and an adept at beguiling the morals of her husband and seducing him by her continued impostures. For by the fawning talk which she practices and the other ways in which she plays her part like an actress on the stage she first ensnares the sight and hearing, and when these subjects as it were have been duped she cajoles the sovereign mind. And if the children come, filled with the spirit of arrogance and bold speaking she gives utterance with more audacious hardihood to things which before she hinted covertly and under disguise, and casting off all shame she compels him to commit actions which are all hostile to the life of fellowship. For he who is either fast bound in the love lures of his wife or under the stress of nature makes his children his first care ceases to be the same to the others and unconsciously has become a different man and passed from freedom into slavery. (Philo, *Hypothetica* 11, 14–17)

The Jewish sect of Qumran, which has left us the Dead Sea Scrolls, flourished about the same time as the Essenes and has been identified with them by many scholars. In any case, the misogynist pattern is continued:

> The association of women with trouble-making belongs quite naturally to the Wisdom literature of the Old Testament. At Qumran, not only the Old Testament Wisdom literature, but also Ben Sira and even properly Essene Wisdom texts were copied; and one of the unpublished texts from Cave IV attests, among other things, that the sapiential depreciation of women was not forgotten but developed startlingly. (John Strugnell, "Flavius Josephus and the Essenes: *Antiquities* XVIII.18–22," *Journal of Biblical Literature,* Vol. 77, 1958, p. 110)

The earlier descriptions of the ways of prostitutes from Proverbs and elsewhere, or indeed any description of the seductive ways of women in ancient Jewish literature, is far outstripped by this Essene diatribe. There is obviously a fascination here with that forbidden thing, sex, and its personification, woman; but since it is forbidden, there is also expressed a deep hatred of the unattainable, woman, here in the form of a harlot. Here is the fountainhead of misogynism:

The harlot utters vanities,
   and [. . .] errors;
She seeks continually [to] sharpen [her] words,
   [. . .] she mockingly flatters
and with *emp[tiness]* to bring altogether into derision.
   Her heart's perversion prepares wantonness,
and her emotions [. . .].
   In perversion they seized the fouled (organs) of passion,
they descended the pit of her legs to act wickedly,
   and behave with the guilt of [*transgression*
. . .] the foundations of darkness,
   the sins in her skirts are many.
Her [. . .] is the depths of the night,
   and her clothes [. . .].
Her garments are the shades of twilight,
   and her adornments are touched with corruption.
Her beds are couches of *corruption,*
   [. . .] depths of the Pit.
Her lodgings are beds of darkness,
   and in the depths of the nigh[t] are her [do]minions.
From the foundations of *darkness* she takes her dwelling,
   and she resides in the tents of the underworld,
in the midst of everlasting fire,
   and she has no inheritance (in the midst of) among all who gird
      themselves with light.
She is the foremost of all the ways of iniquity;
   Alas! ruin shall be to all who possess her,
And desolation to a[ll] who take hold of her.
   For her ways are the ways of death,
and her path[s] are the roads to sin;
   her tracks lead astray to iniquity,
and her paths are the guilt of transgression.
   Her gates are the gates of death,
in the opening of her house it stalks.
   To Sheol a[l]l [. . .] will return,
and all who possess her will go down to the Pit.
   She lies in wait in secret places,
[. . .] all [. . .].
   In the city's broad places she displays herself,
and in the town gates she sets herself,

and there is none to distur[b her] from [. . .].
Her eyes glance keenly hither and thither,
    and she wantonly raises her eyelids
to seek out a righteous man and lead him astray,
    and a perfect man to make him stumble;
upright men to divert (their) path,
    and those chosen for righteousness from keeping the
        commandment;
those sustained with [. . .] to make fools of them with wantonness,
    and those who walk uprightly to change the st[atute];
to make the humble rebel from God,
    and to turn their steps from the ways of righteousness;
to bring presumptuousness [. . .]
    those not arraign[ed] in the tracks of uprightness;
to lead mankind astray in the ways of the Pit,
    and to seduce by flatteries the sons of men. (John M. Allegro, with
the collaboration of Arnold A. Anderson, *Discoveries in the Judaean Desert of Jordan*, Vol. 5, *Qumrân Cave 4*, pp. 82–84; Oxford University Press,
1968)

C. NEGATIVE IMAGES AND ATTITUDES— POSTBIBLICAL WRITINGS

§106. Negative Rabbinic Attitudes Toward Women

The growth of Rabbinic Judaism out of the traditions of the scribes
and the Pharisees in the last centuries before and the first century of
the Common Era was discussed briefly above (see pp. 99ff.). Both the
positive and the ambivalent aspects of Rabbinic Judaism's attitudes
toward women were detailed (see pp. 99ff. and §106). However, it
must be noted that the status of women in Rabbinic Judaism is
predominantly negative (for a thorough analysis, see Leonard Swidler, *Women in Judaism*). As indicated before, only a brief outline of
the negative aspect of Rabbinic Judaism's attitude toward women
will be provided here.

The heart of Judaism is the study and living of Torah—the Law
—and the differing status of men and women is expressed here quite
explicitly, for women were all but forbidden to study the Scriptures
(Torah). The first-century rabbi Eliezer put the point sharply:

Rather should the words of the Torah be burned than entrusted to a
woman. . . . Whoever teaches his daughter the Torah is like one who teaches
her obscenity. (Mishnah Sotah 3, 4)

In the vitally religious area of prayer, women were so little thought
of as not to be given obligations of the same seriousness as men. For

example, women, along with children and slaves, were not obliged to recite the Shema, the morning prayer, nor prayers at meals (Mishnah Berakhoth 3, 3). In fact, the Talmud states: "Let a curse come upon the man who [must needs have] his wife or children say grace for him" (Talmud bBerakhoth 20b).

In the daily prayers prescribed for Jewish males there is a threefold thanksgiving which graphically illustrated where women stood in Rabbinic Judaism:

> Praised be God that he has not created me a gentile; praised be God that he has not created me a woman; praised be God that he has not created me an ignorant man. (Tosephta Berakhoth 7, 8)

Because of the blunt male superiority expressed in this prayer one might be tempted to discount it as a single hyperbolic statement of an obscure rabbi. But this is not the case. No less than three separate direct quotations of this prayer occur in three of the most ancient rabbinic collections (Tosephta Berakhoth 7, 8; Talmud pBerakhoth 13b; Talmud bMenakhoth 43b). The fact that this statement in not simply a teaching but rather a prayer increases its significance considerably. Moreover, it is not recommended as a once-a-year or occasional prayer, but rather as a daily prayer. In the Tosephta, Rabbi Judah recommends that this prayer be said daily. The Babylonian Talmud attributes the prayer to Rabbi Judah's contemporary, Rabbi Meir (of the first part of the second century), who claims that he faithfully passed on what he learned from Rabbi Akiba, a first-century rabbi.

It should also be noted that there are three commandments directed specifically to women, which result in the following dire consequences if they are disregarded, according to the earliest rabbinical document, the Mishnah:

> For three transgressions do women die in childbirth: for heedlessness of the laws concerning their menstruation, the dough-offering *(hallah)*, and the lighting of the (Sabbath) lamp. (Mishnah Shabbath 2, 6)

The reasons given for these three commands—in no less than four ancient sources: Tosephta Shabbath 2, 19(112); Talmud pShabbath 2, 5b, 34; Talmud bShabbath 31b; Genesis Rabbah 17, 8—all lead back to the charge that Eve caused the death of Adam (as did also the Life of Adam and Eve and the Book of the Secrets of Enoch— see §104):

Concerning menstruation: the first man was the blood and the life of the world . . . and Eve was the cause of his death; therefore has she been given the menstruation precept. The same is true concerning *hallah* (leaven): Adam was the pure *hallah* for the world . . . and Eve was the cause of his death; therefore she has been given the *hallah* precept. And concerning the lighting of the (Sabbath) lamp: Adam was the light of the world . . . and Eve was the cause of his death; therefore has she been given the precept about lighting the (Sabbath) lamp. Rabbi Jose [early second century] said: there are three causes of death and they were transmitted to women, namely, the menstruation precept, the *hallah* precept, and the precept about lighting the (Sabbath) lamp. (Talmud pShabbath 2, 5b, 34)

Though the precept concerning menstruation could be seen by some as degrading for women and the precept concerning *hallah* might be seen as bothersome, the lighting of the Sabbath lamp in the home on Friday evening would normally be viewed as an honor. It is therefore somewhat surprising to learn that the ancient rabbinic reason offered for the commandment is that it is a punishment for Eve's having caused Adam's death.

Women were also grossly restricted in public prayer. It was not possible for them to be counted toward the number necessary for a quorum *(minyan)* to form a congregation to worship communally (Mishnah Aboth 3, 6). They were here again, as often in other cases in rabbinic literature, classified with children and slaves, who similarly did not qualify. As noted above, in the great Temple at Jerusalem women were limited to the Gentiles' court and the women's court, the latter being fifteen steps below the court for the men (see §102); in the synagogues the women were also separated from the men, and of course they were not allowed to read aloud or perform any leading function.

Besides the disabilities that women suffered in the areas of prayer and worship there were many others in the private and public forums of society. A man regarded it as beneath his dignity, as indeed positively disreputable, to speak to a woman in public. The "Proverbs of the Fathers" contain the injunction:

"Speak not much with a woman." Since a man's own wife is meant here, how much more does not this apply to the wife of another? The wise men say: "Who speaks much with a woman draws down misfortune on himself, neglects the words of the law, and finally earns hell." (Mishnah Aboth 1, 5)

If it were merely the too free intercourse of the sexes which was being warned against, this would perhaps signify nothing derogatory to woman. But since the man was not to speak even to his own wife, daughter, or sister in the street (Talmud bBerakhoth 43b), then only male arrogance can be the motive; association with uneducated company was warned against in exactly the same terms. "One is not so much as to greet a woman" (ibid.). In addition, save in the rarest instances, women were not allowed to bear witness in a legal sense (Mishnah Shabbath 4, 1). Some Jewish thinkers, as for example, Philo, of the first century c.e., thought women ought not leave their households except to go to the synagogue—and that only at a time when most of the other people would be at home (*Against Flaccus* 89; *De specialibus legibus* III.171)—and girls ought not even cross the threshold that separated the male and female apartments of the household (*De specialibus legibus* III.169).

Rabbinic sayings about women also provide an insight into the attitude toward women. "It is well for those whose children are male, but ill for those whose children are female" (Talmud bKiddushin 82b); "At the birth of a boy all are joyful, but at the birth of a girl all are sad" (Talmud bNiddah 31b); "When a boy comes into the world, peace comes into the world; when a girl comes, nothing comes" (ibid.); "Even the most virtuous of women is a witch" (Mishnah Terum 15); "Our teachers have said: Four qualities are evident in women: They are greedy at their food, eager to gossip, lazy and jealous" (Genesis Rabbah 45, 5); "A woman is a pitcher full of filth with its mouth full of blood, yet all run after her" (Talmud bShabbath 152a).

VII. Summary:
Woman in Hebrew-Jewish Tradition

Earlier it was noted that there was a dual tradition on women in the Hebraic nation, one positive and one negative, somehow connected with Goddess worship and higher status for women on the one hand and Yahweh worship and dominant status for men on the other, and that with the passage of time the negative came to dominate more and more. It is clear that whatever the restrictions on Hebrew women were in the times reflected in the writings about the patriarchs and their wives (Abraham-Sarah, Isaac-Rebecca, Jacob-Rachel) and the Judges (Deborah), they had considerably more status and freedom than at the beginning of the Common Era when men were warned not to speak much to women, even their own wives. An intensification of the restriction on Jewish women took place after the return of a Jewish remnant from the Babylonian exile in the sixth century B.C.E., as seen in the demands of Ezra and Nehemiah that the Jewish men drive away their non-Jewish wives and children (Ezra 10:3; Neh 13:23–28), and in the growing anti-woman literature in the later books of the Hebrew Bible and the postbiblical Jewish writings, the Apocrypha and Pseudepigrapha.

It is not difficult to understand why a pattern of restrictiveness against women developed in Judaism. Their felt need to develop in-group/out-group defenses in the early centuries after the exile, in view of the return of such a relatively small group of Jews to a land surrounded by peoples of different cultures and religions, particularly Goddess worship, is psychologically and sociologically understandable. The traditional stress within a patriarchal society, such as that of the Hebrews, on continuing the male line in general leads to the sexual restriction of women far beyond that of men (e.g., polygyny but not polyandry being allowed). But the condition of the embattled remnant obviously forced the Jews to take even more drastic measures to retain group identity and unity, as is evidenced by the radical negative actions of Ezra and Nehemiah. After the conquest of the area by Alexander the Great toward the end of the fourth century B.C.E. and the subsequent spread of Hellenistic culture, the restrictive Jewish attitude intensified even more, as can be seen in Ecclesiastes, Ben Sira, and the Testaments of the Twelve Patriarchs. The Hellenistic culture proved increasingly attractive and pervasive, and those Jews who saw it as a threat to Jewish identity felt that they had to insulate the Jewish community from its enervating influences. By increasing restrictions, half the population—the female half—was thereby more surely removed from Hellenism's baleful blandishments; such moves would also tend to lessen the Hellenizing influence non-Jewish women would have on the male half of the Jewish community. Such an approach was also doubtless reinforced by the knowledge that a significant element in the to-be-rejected Hellenistic culture was the relatively much higher status women held in religion and society and the Goddess worship connected with it.

Despite the extraordinary exceptions like the Therapeutae and Beruria, the necessarily defensive stance of Judaism, including the restriction of its women, only rigidified after the destruction of the Jewish homeland in 70 C.E. and 135 C.E. and the increasing persecution of Jews throughout the Roman empire, first by the pagans and after the fourth century by Christians. Jewish women have since then basically remained severely subordinated to men within Judaism until the most recent times.

Rabbinic Judaism, whose roots go back to the origin of the synagogue and the Pharisees in the centuries before the Common Era, reinforced this practice of separation—the very name of the Pharisees means "Separatists." The destruction of Temple Judaism in 70 C.E. greatly magnified the sociological pressure for a policy of Jewish separateness. Without a homeland, the Jews found such a policy absolutely necessary for survival. Hence the separation and restriction of women tended to be proportionately increased.

Still, the positive elements of the Hebraic tradition on women were there, are recorded, and are to be cherished.

Part Three

WOMAN IN CHRISTIAN TRADITION

VIII. Positive Elements in Christian Tradition

A. THE APOSTOLIC WRITINGS (NEW TESTAMENT)— THE GOSPELS

The Apostolic Writings (New Testament) are a series of writings mostly written by Jews, initially even mainly for Jews, about Jews, in largely Jewish conceptual language and imagery, and full of quotations from the Jewish Scriptures, which these writings claim to fulfill. Obviously then, it will be impossible to understand the Apostolic Writings (New Testament) properly except within the context of its Jewish milieu. This is also true as far as the role and status of women is concerned. Hence it is essential that the earlier Hebrew and Jewish traditions concerning women be borne in mind, especially the late biblical, intertestamental, and early rabbinic traditions, which tended to be so very negative on women (see §106). At the same time, however, it must also be kept in mind that Judaism did not exist in isolation from surrounding cultures.

By the time of Jesus, Judaism existed almost entirely within first a Hellenistic world (i.e., the cultural world succeeding the Greek empire of Alexander the Great after 323 B.C.), and then a Greco-Roman world. In Jesus' lifetime perhaps 8 percent of the Roman empire was Jewish, and most of these eight million Jews lived scattered (in dispersion, "diaspora") throughout the cities of the empire. But the center of Judaism was still the Palestinian homeland. Naturally Greco-Roman influences on Judaism were very strong in the Diaspora, but they were also strong in Palestine. Hence, it is likewise essential for the understanding of the Apostolic Writings that the Hellenistic, Greco-Roman world also be recalled (see pp. 15ff.). This is important in matters concerning women, even if the

161

Greco-Roman influence is at times reflected only by way of nega-
tion and rejection.

The Apostolic Writings can be divided up in a number of ways.
One obvious way, and one that is helpful to the study of women, is
to divide them into two major groupings: the four Gospels, which
focus on the life and teaching of Jesus, and the rest of the twenty-
seven books of the Apostolic Writings, which focus on the activities
and teachings of the followers of Jesus. Since Jesus is the "founder"
of Christianity, there is a certain primacy about the Gospels, that is,
it is logical that the life and teaching of Jesus should determine how
the teaching of the followers of Jesus should be interpreted, not the
other way around. Thus, for example, if Jesus strongly stressed justice
for women, but Paul or Peter did not, it would be "logical" for
subsequent Christians—who by definition are followers of Jesus, the
Christ—to place great stress on justice for women, and to interpret
Paul's and Peter's lack of stress as something to be expected in
followers, a falling short of the example of the leader.

However, history is not always logical, and it is almost never simple.
In this case too it was neither so simple nor so logical. In fact, in
Christian history, the restrictive statements concerning women in
the Pauline and Petrine writings (discussed below, pp. 332ff.) often
were much more influential than the very liberating statements and
actions of Jesus concerning women. Furthermore, what we know of
the life and teachings of Jesus has come down to us already filtered
through his followers, so that the distinction between Jesus' teaching
and that of his followers is not always as simple as was earlier thought.
Still, with careful, painstaking work, we can learn much about Jesus'
life and teaching.

Hence, the plan to be followed here is to treat first the four
Gospels, then the rest of the Apostolic Writings. In dealing with the
Gospels, the material will be treated in twofold fashion: first, a presentation of Jesus' teaching about and interaction with women *as
imaged* in the materials of all four Gospels; second, a systematic
presentation of the materials concerning women found in each of the
four Gospels successively, which will open up to us something of the
impact that Jesus' life and teaching, as pertaining to women, had on
his first hearers and followers—who have bequeathed to us the Apostolic Writings.

1. THE GOSPELS' IMAGE OF JESUS' ATTITUDE TOWARD WOMEN

The first thing to be noticed about Jesus and women is that in all of the four Gospels, nowhere does Jesus treat women as inferior. In fact, as shall be seen, Jesus clearly felt especially sent to the typical classes of "inferior beings," such as the poor, the lame, sinners—and women—to call them all to the freedom and equality of the "reign of God." The twentieth-century reader will perhaps think, "of course." But when it is recalled that religious men in that Jewish culture thought just the opposite (e.g., Paul: "Man is the head of woman . . . man is the image of God . . . but woman is a reflection of man's glory"—1 Cor 11:3, 7; Josephus: "The woman, says the law, is in all things inferior to the man"—*Against Apion* II.201), and that in fact women were treated as inferiors by Jesus' fellow rabbis (e.g., "Rabbi Eliezer [first century C.E.] said: Rather should the words of the Torah be burned than entrusted to a woman!"—Mishnah Sotah 3, 4), this negative fact is quite startling. It becomes still more extraordinary when in addition the nature of the Gospels is considered.

§107. The Nature of the Gospels

The Gospels, of course, are not the straight factual reports of eyewitnesses of the events in the life of Jesus of Nazareth that one might expect to find in the columns of *The New York Times* or the pages of a critical biography. Rather, they are four different faith statements reflecting at least four primitive Christian communities which believed that Jesus was the Messiah, the Lord and Savior of the world. They were composed from a variety of sources, written and oral, over a period of time and in response to certain needs felt by the communities and individuals at the time; consequently they are many-layered. Since the Gospel writer-editors were not twentieth-century critical historians they were not particularly intent on recording the words of Jesus verbatim, nor were they concerned to winnow out all of their own cultural biases and assumptions. Indeed, it is doubtful whether they were particularly conscious of them.

This modern critical understanding of the Gospels, of course, does not impugn the historical character of the Gospels; it merely describes the type of historical documents they are so that their historical significance can more accurately be evaluated. Its religious value lies in the fact that modern Christians are thereby helped to know much more precisely what Jesus meant by certain statements and actions as they are reported by the first Christian communities in the Gospels. With this new knowledge of the nature of the Gospels it is easier to make the vital distinction between the religious truth that is to be handed on and the time-conditioned categories and customs involved in expressing it.

We find that no negative attitudes by Jesus toward women are portrayed in the Gospels. When this fact is set side by side with the recently discerned "communal faith-statement" understanding of the nature of the Gospels, the importance of the former is vastly enhanced. For whatever Jesus said or did comes to us only through the lens of the first Christians. If there were no very special religious significance in a particular concept or custom, we would expect that current concept or custom to be reflected by Jesus. But we know from the above analysis of the late biblical, pseudepigraphical, early rabbinic and contemporaneous Jewish materials like those of Philo, Josephus, and the Dead Sea Scrolls, that women were generally held to be very inferior to men; there is no reason to assume that Jesus' followers and the Jewish-Christian sources of the Gospels would not also have held these common views—except for Jesus' influence. The fact that this overwhelmingly negative attitude toward women in Palestine did not come through the primitive Christian communal lens by itself underscores the clearly great religious importance Jesus attached to his positive attitude—his feminist attitude—toward women: feminism, that is, personalism extended to women, is a constitutive part of the gospel, the good news, of Jesus.

a. Women in Jesus' Language

Jesus' attitude toward women is expressed by the Gospel language attributed to him in an extraordinarily vigorous and manifold fashion. First, in the Gospels Jesus often uses women in his stories and sayings, something most unusual for his culture—and others. Secondly, the images of women Jesus uses are never negative, but rather always positive—in dramatic contrast to his predecessors and contemporaries. Thirdly, these positive images of women are often very exalted, at times being associated with the "reign of heaven," likened to the chosen people, and even to God herself! Fourthly, Jesus often teaches a point by telling two similar stories or using two images, one of which features a man and one a woman. This balance, among other things, indicates that Jesus wanted it to be abundantly clear that his teaching, unlike that of other rabbis, was intended for both women and men—and he obviously wanted this to be clear to the men as well as the women, since he told these stories to all his disciples and at times even to crowds. These sexually parallel stories and images also confirm the presence of women among his hearers; they were used to bring home the point of a teaching in an image that was familiar to the women.

The sexually parallel stories and images used by Jesus range from very brief pairings to lengthy parables. Their frequency of occurrence is impressive, and it is therefore worth gathering them together here where the focus will be mainly on what they can tell us about Jesus' attitude toward women. The significance of the variations in the recording of the stories and what they tell us of the attitude of the several evangelists and their sources toward women will be analyzed later.

§108. Lamp on a Lampstand

In ch. 8 of his Gospel, Luke recorded that Jesus taught in parables, i.e., stories with a message (Luke 8:10). Luke then related two parables. It is very likely they are sexually parallel stories: the first is about a sower in a field; the second, about a person placing a lamp on a lampstand instead of covering it with a bowl or putting it under a bed. The first story is in the context of the outdoor worker; the second is set indoors. In the first, the masculine gender is used all the way through: the sower *(ho speirōn)*, his seed *(sporon autou)*, he sowed *(en tō speirein auton)*. In the second story the Greek uses no genders at all: "no one" *(oudeis)* is the sole subject of the sentence, with no personal pronouns, which would reflect gender, being used. Since in the first the occupation was culturally male and the gender of the language was masculine, and since the context of the second was culturally female and no gender was reflected in the language, we may conclude that the stories were almost certainly meant by Luke to be sexually parallel stories, and, in the light of other sexually parallel stories and images used by Jesus, were also most probably so meant by Jesus. The first story would immediately be understood existentially by the men of the time, and the second likewise by the women. Both were clearly among Jesus' listeners. He spoke to each of them.

Though both Mark and Matthew record the saying about putting a lamp on a lampstand (and indeed Luke himself repeats it in another context—Lk 11:33–36), their report of it does not have the clearly sexually parallel quality that it so manifestly does in Luke 8.

With a large crowd gathering and people from every town finding their way to him, he used this parable: "A sower went out to sow his seed. As he sowed, some fell on the edge of the path and was trampled on; and the birds of the air ate it up. Some seed fell on rock, and when it came up it withered away, having no moisture. Some seed fell amongst thorns and the thorns grew with it and choked it. . . ."

"No one lights a lamp to cover it with a bowl or to put it under a bed. No, it is put on a lamp-stand so that people may see the light when they come in. For nothing is hidden but it will be made clear, nothing secret but it will be known and brought to light." (Lk 8:4–8, 16–17; cf. Mk 4:1–9, 21–22; Mt 13:4–9; 5:15; Lk 11:33–36)

§109. The Widow and the Unjust Judge

In one pair of stories illustrating the need for perseverance in prayer Jesus used two tales remarkably similar in structure. The one about the man is given here so it can be compared with the one about the woman; the man is given no qualities superior to the woman:

> He also said to them, "Suppose one of you has a friend and goes to him in the middle of the night to say, 'My friend, lend me three loaves, because a friend of mine on his travels has just arrived at my house and I have nothing to offer him,' and the man answers from inside the house, 'Do not bother me. The door is bolted now, and my children and I are in bed; I cannot get up to give it to you.' . . . I tell you, if the man does not get up and give it to him for friendship's sake, persistence will be enough to make him get up and give his friend all he wants. So I say to you: Ask, and it will be given to you; search, and you will find." (Lk 11:5–9)

In the parallel story about the woman Jesus uses the image of a widow. She is up against the powerful male establishment, self-confessedly corrupt, at that; her opponent most probably was also a male property holder—her property! She is commended by Jesus for her popularly tagged "masculine" traits of aggressiveness and stick-to-itiveness. This is a comparison story and the widow is the image of, is like, the chosen people *(tōn eklektōn)*. [Cf. 2 John, which is addressed to the chosen mistress, *eklekta kyria*. See below, p. 316.]

> Then he told them a parable about the need to pray continually and never lose heart. "There was a judge in a certain town," he said, "who had neither fear of God nor respect for humans. In the same town there was a widow who kept on coming to him and saying, 'I want justice from you against my enemy!' For a long time he refused, but at last he said to himself, 'Maybe I have neither fear of God nor respect for humans, but since she keeps pestering me I must give this widow her just rights, or she will persist in coming and worry me to death.'"
>
> And the Lord said, "You notice what the unjust judge has to say? Now will not God see justice done to his chosen who cry to him day and night

even when he delays to help them? I promise you, he will see justice done to them, and done speedily." (Lk 18:1–8)

§110. A Prophet in His Own Country

In illustrating his statement, "No prophet is ever accepted in his own country," Jesus again used two brief stories, one centering on women and the other on men. Again the widow is the most down-and-out example of women, matched in the male realm only by outcast lepers. Not only is Luke the only recorder of this sexually paired set of stories, but he also relates the women's story first, both subtle signs of Luke's sympathy for the women's cause.

And he went on, "I tell you solemnly, no prophet is ever accepted in his own country. There were many widows in Israel, I can assure you, in Elijah's day, when heaven remained shut for three years and six months and a great famine raged throughout the land, but Elijah was not sent to any one of these: he was sent to a widow at Zarephath, a Sidonian town. And in the prophet Elisha's time there were many lepers in Israel, but none of these was cured, except the Syrian, Naaman." (Lk 4:24–27)

§111. Women at the "End of Days" — I

Three of the pairs of sexually parallel stories concern aspects of the end of the world. One clear point of the first pair is that there is no ultimate importance in the distinction between men and women; important human distinctions are founded on bases other than sex.

"It will be like this when the Son of Man comes. Then of two men in the fields one is taken, one left. Of two women at the millstone grinding, one is taken, one left." (Mt 24:39–41)

§112. Women at the "End of Days" — II

Luke, with slightly different pairings, makes the same point. (Though the great majority of the best ancient Greek manuscripts do *not* contain v. 36 about the two men in the field, some do; but this is most likely due to scribes transferring that verse from the parallel in Matt 24:40, quoted just above.) From the Greek it is clear that the two persons referred to in v. 34 are male and the two in v. 35 are female.

"I tell you, on that night two [men] will be in one bed: one will be taken, the other left. Two women will be grinding corn together: one will be taken, the other left. [There will be two men in the fields: one will be taken, the other left.]" (Lk 17:34–36)

§113. The Queen of the South

The second pair of images concerning the final day is an interesting but strange coupling. The image of the men of Nineveh condemning Jesus' generation fits well with the preceding reference to Jonah. But the reference to the Queen of the South (Sheba) can be connected only because of a similar condemnation of Jesus' generation for not accepting him. Jesus would not have made these two statements at the same time. But the statement about the Queen of the South probably was on a list of sayings of Jesus which both Luke and Matthew had access to (or one did and the other copied from him). It is likely that Jesus actually made something like both statements —otherwise why would the Queen of Sheba be brought up by Luke or his predecessor at all?—and it is likely that the two statements were linked together here partly because of the similar condemnation. But again, it is still another example of sexually parallel stories that probably go back to Jesus, even if the evangelists, or their sources, are responsible for putting them together here. It is also interesting to note that pro-feminist Luke places the image of the women first, while Matthew gives first place to the man.

Then some of the scribes and Pharisees spoke up. "Master," they said, "we should like to see a sign from you." He replied, "It is an evil and unfaithful generation that asks for a sign! The only sign it will be given is the sign of the prophet Jonah. For as Jonah was in the belly of the sea-monster for three days and three nights, so will the Son of Man be in the heart of the earth for three days and three nights. On Judgement day the men of Nineveh will stand up with this generation and condemn it, because when Jonah preached they repented; and there is something greater than Jonah here. On Judgement day the Queen of the South will rise up with this generation and condemn it, because she came from the ends of the earth to hear the wisdom of Solomon; and there is something greater than Solomon here." (Mt 12:38–42; cf. Lk 11:29–32)

§114. Wise and Foolish Bridesmaids

The unknown or uncertain quality of the final day is likewise illustrated by the third pair of images concerning the end of time, but it focuses on the uncertainness of when that day will be. The first story is of an honest and dishonest male servant:

"What sort of servant, then, is faithful and wise enough for the master to place him over his household to give them their food at the proper time? Happy that servant if his master's arrival finds him at his employment. I tell you solemnly, he will place him over everything he owns. But as for the dishonest servant who says to himself, "My master is taking his time," and sets about beating his fellow servants and eating and drinking with drunkards, his master will come on a day he does not expect him and at an hour he does not know. The master will cut him off and send him to the same fate as the hypocrites, where there will be weeping and grinding of teeth." (Mt 24: 45–51; cf. Lk 12:42–46)

Immediately following is the second story, about the wise and foolish bridesmaids. The structure of the story is almost exactly the same as the one about the men, again illustrating the parity women and men held in Jesus' eyes. It is difficult to believe that these two stories, or something very like them, were not told by Jesus, for who else would have been at such pains to compose two such similar stories illustrating the same point with one focusing on women, if not Jesus? Of course Matthew, or the source Matthew used, might well be credited with setting down this parallel pair together:

> "The reign of heaven will be like this: Ten bridesmaids took their lamps and went to meet the bridegroom. Five of them were foolish and five were sensible: the foolish ones did take their lamps, but they brought no oil, whereas the sensible ones took flasks of oil as well as their lamps. The bridegroom was late, and they all grew drowsy and fell asleep. But at midnight there was a cry, 'The bridegroom is here! Go out and meet him.' At this, all those bridesmaids woke up and trimmed their lamps, and the foolish ones said to the sensible ones, 'Give us some of your oil: our lamps are going out.' But they replied, 'There may not be enough for us and for you; you had better go to those who sell it and buy some for yourselves.' They had gone off to buy it when the bridegroom arrived. Those who were ready went in with him to the wedding hall and the door was closed. The other bridesmaids arrived later. 'Lord, Lord,' they said, 'open the door for us.' But he replied, 'I tell you solemnly, I do not know you.' So stay awake, because you do not know either the day or the hour." (Mt 25:1–13)

It is interesting to note that here Luke does not have the story of the ten bridesmaids, but rather one of servants waiting for the master to return from a wedding feast. Luke uses the generic *anthrōpois* for "men" and the "generic" masculine gender for servants *(douloi)*, so that there is no clear indication that men or both men and women were involved; it could not have been just women. In Mark almost certainly just men are involved in the single brief story of the servants (masculine *doulois*) and the doorkeeper (masculine *thyrōroi*). Cf. Lk 12:35–40 and Mk 13:34–37.

§115. Heaven the Leaven in Dough

Even the reign of heaven is depicted in a pair of sexually parallel images: one is a man sowing mustard seed, and the other a woman mixing leaven in flour. The main point of the second comparison is that the realm of heaven, like leaven in flour, is initially very small, but in the end it transforms the whole. Jesus was clearly telling women that though they might seem insignificant in this world, they could by association with the "reign of heaven" share in the transformation of the whole world. Another dimension of meaning is also possible. In that religious culture leaven was seen as an agent of corruption, and *un*leaven was a sign of God's purity and rule—this can be best seen in the Feast of the Passover. Jesus' use of leaven not as a sign of corruption and the lack of God's rule, but the opposite, as a sign of the "reign of heaven," was probably a deliberate choice on his part to show that what often was thought to be a source of sin was really a source of salvation—and this was done with the intimate association of a woman as the provider of the key image, leaven. Meaning: woman is not the provider of the source (or occasion) of sin, as was usually thought, but the provider of the source of salvation.

Luke apparently thought this second dimension was intended in Jesus' saying, for he immediately followed it with another set of sayings of Jesus which make that point—or a similar one—primary: that is, those who thought they certainly would find salvation do not, and those who were not expected to, do.

He put another parable before them, "The reign of heaven is like a mustard seed which a man took and sowed in his field. It is the smallest of all the seeds, but when it has grown it is the biggest shrub of all and becomes a tree so that the birds of the air come and shelter in its branches."
He told them another parable, "The reign of heaven is like the leaven a woman took and mixed in with three measures of flour till it was leavened all through." (Mt 13:31–33; cf. Lk 13:18–21)

§116. God Is Likened to a Woman

The ultimate in sexually parallel stories told by Jesus includes one in which God is cast in the likeness of a woman. This was extraordinary in the Jewish culture of Jesus' time. Luke recorded that the despised tax collectors and sinners were gathering around Jesus, and consequently the Pharisees and scribes complained. According to Luke, Jesus therefore related three parables in a row, all of which depicted God's being deeply concerned for that which was lost. The first story was of the shepherd who left the ninety-nine sheep to seek the one that was lost—God is like that shepherd. The third story is of the prodigal son—God is like the father. The second story is of the woman who sought the lost coin—God is like that woman. Jesus did not shrink from the notion of God as feminine. In fact, it would appear that Jesus included this womanly image of God quite deliberately at this point, for the scribes and Pharisees were among those who most of all denigrated women—just as they did the "tax collectors and sinners." (It should be noted that although Matthew has the story about the lost sheep, Mt 18:12–14, only Luke has the stories of the prodigal son and the woman whom God is like.)

There have been some instances in Christian history when the Holy Spirit has been associated with a feminine character (see pp. 57ff.). For example, the Syrian Didascalia (third century), in speaking of various offices in the church, states: "The deaconess, however, should be honored by you as the image of the Holy Spirit." But in the history of later Christian biblical interpretation nowhere are these images of God presented here by Luke ever used in a Trinitarian manner—i.e., thereby giving the Holy Spirit a feminine image. Yet after the establishment of the doctrine of the Trinity, in the fourth century, this passage would seem to have been particularly apt for Trinitarian interpretation: the prodigal son's father is God the Father (this interpretation has in fact been quite common in Christian history); since Jesus elsewhere identified himself as the Good Shepherd, the shepherd seeking the lost sheep is Jesus, the Son (this standard interpretation is reflected in, among other things, the often seen picture of Jesus carrying the lost sheep on his shoulders); the woman who sought the lost coin should "logically" be the Holy Spirit, but she has not been so interpreted. Should such lack of "logic" be attributed, as is often suggested, to the Christian abhorrence of pagan goddesses? But then why did Christian abhorrence of pagan gods not also result in a Christian rejection of a male image of God? The only answer can be an underlying widespread Christian deprecatory attitude toward women that blinded most Christian theologians and commentators to the strong feminism of Jesus in the Gospels.

The tax collectors and the sinners, meanwhile, were all seeking his company to hear what he had to say, and the Pharisees and the scribes complained. "This man," they said, "welcomes sinners and eats with them." So he spoke this parable to them:

(1) "What person among you with a hundred sheep, losing one, would not leave the ninety-nine in the wilderness and go after the missing one till he found it? . . .

(2) "Or again, what woman with ten drachmas would not, if she lost one, light a lamp and sweep out the house and search thoroughly till she found it? And then, when she had found it, call together her friends and neigh-

bours? 'Rejoice with me,' she would say, 'I have found the drachma I lost.'
In the same way, I tell you, there is rejoicing among the angels of God over
one repentant sinner."
(3) He also said, "A man had two sons. The younger said to his father,
'Father, let me have the share of the estate that would come to me.' . . ."
(Lk 15:1-5, 8-12)

§117. Extracanonical Sexually Parallel Stories of Jesus

Whether any of the "new" sayings attributed to Jesus found in the
third-century Gnostic Christian Gospel of Thomas can in any de-
monstrable way be plausibly traced back to Jesus is debated by scholars. Much of this "Gospel" is a variation of what is found in the four
canonical Gospels, but it is nevertheless interesting to find two quite
different stories attributed to Jesus that describe what the reign of the
Father (rather than God or heaven, as in the canonical Gospels) is
like in sexually parallel fashion. It is difficult to be certain exactly what
the meaning of the stories is, but that one is directed primarily at
women and the other at men is clear, indicating a continuation of
the pattern of sexually parallel stories, if not by Jesus himself, then
at least by some of his followers who must have thought it was "in
keeping" with his style. After Logion ("Saying") number 96, which
relates how the reign of the Father is like a woman who mixed leaven
in some dough, Logia 97 and 98 are as follows:

(Logion 97) Jesus said: "The Kingdom of the [Father] is like a woman who
was carrying a jar full of meal. While she was walking (on a) distant road,
the handle of the jar broke. The meal streamed out behind her on the road.
She did not know (it), she had noticed no accident. When she came into
her house, she put down her jar, she found it empty."
(Logion 98) Jesus said: "The Kingdom of the Father is like a man who
wished to kill a powerful man. He drew the sword in his house, he stuck it
into the wall, in order to know whether his hand would carry through; then
he slew the powerful man." (Gospel of Thomas, *New Testament Apocrypha*, Vol. 1, pp. 289-290)

§118. Jesus in a Female Image — I

Jesus did not shrink from applying a female image to himself
either; he likened himself to a hen gathering her chicks under her
wings. Such an image is interesting because throughout the Hebrew
Bible the image of protecting wings is often used in connection with
God (e.g., Ps 17:8; 36:7; 57:1; 61:4; 63:7; 91:4; Ruth 2:12; Is 31:5;
Deut 32:11). But in all these images there is never any intimation of
the feminine. It is usually a prayer asking for shelter under God's
wings. There is one reference to birds hovering in protection (Is

31:5) and one to an eagle "hovering over its young" (Deut 32:11), but nowhere to a female bird. The use of that image in the Jewish tradition was left to Jesus. (See §61 for a discussion of later Christian reference to Jesus with female imagery.)

"Jerusalem, Jerusalem, you that kill the prophets and stone those who are sent to you! How often have I longed to gather your children, as a hen gathers her brood under her wings, and you refused!" (Lk 13:34; cf. Mt 23:37)

§119. Jesus in a Female Image — II

When Jesus was in the Temple on the last day of the Feast of Succoth, at which there was a procession bringing "living" water from the fountain of Shiloh to the Temple as a sign of the future messianic salvation, he uttered a saying that cast him in a female image. He said, "If anyone is thirsty, let him come to me and drink!" The image of drinking from a human being can only be that of a mother (the fourteenth-century English mystic, Dame Julian of Norwich, did have a scriptural basis for her vision of Christ the mother —see §61*b*).

Jesus went on to apply a Scripture paraphrase to himself: "From his *koilia* shall flow fountains of living water." *Koilia* basically means a hollow place and is used to refer to the whole or part of the abdomen. In the context of feeding from within, the reference would be to the upper part of the body cavity, and the word *koilia* could properly be translated "breast." But modern translations generally are fearful of doing the obvious and projecting Jesus in a maternal image —although Jesus was not.

On the last and greatest day of the festival, Jesus stood there and cried out: "If anyone is thirsty, let him come to me! Let him come and drink who believes in me! As scripture says: 'From his breast *(koilia)* shall flow fountains of living water.' " He was speaking of the Spirit which those who believed in him were to receive; for there was no Spirit as yet because Jesus had not yet been glorified. (Jn 7:37–39)

b. Women in Jesus' Teaching

§120. Marriage and the Dignity of Women — I

One of the most important stands Jesus took in relation to the dignity of women was his position on marriage. His attitude toward marriage was unpopular (see Mt 19:10: "The disciples said to him, 'If such is the case of a man with his wife, it is not expedient to marry' "). It presupposed a feminist view of women; they had rights and responsibilities equal to men's; indeed Mk 10:12 even has Jesus saying: "and if a woman divorces her husband . . ." It was quite possible in Jewish law for men to have more than one wife (this practice was probably not common in Jesus' time, but there are recorded instances, e.g., Herod, Josephus), though the reverse was not possible. Divorce, of course, also was a simple matter, to be initiated *only* by the man. In both situations women were basically chattel. A man was free to collect or dismiss them if he was able and wished to do so; the double moral standard was flagrantly apparent. Jesus rejected both customs by insisting on monogamy and the elimination of divorce; both the man and the woman were to have the same rights and responsibilities in their relationship toward each other (cf. Mk 10:2–12; Mt 19:3–6). This stance of Jesus was one of the few that were rather thoroughly assimilated by the Christian church. (In fact, it was often applied in an overly rigid way concerning divorce in Western Catholic Christianity, where divorce *eventually* was almost never allowed, even in the case permitted by Jesus according to Mt 19:9: "Whoever divorces his wife, except for unchastity"—*mē epi porneiai;* cf. also Mt 5:28. Such was not the case in Eastern Orthodox Christianity, where divorce continues to be allowed, for Jesus' ethical prescriptions were, correctly, understood to be goals to be striven toward, not minimums to be rigidly administered.)

And Pharisees came up to him and tested him by asking, "Is it lawful to divorce one's wife for any cause?"* He answered, "Have you not read that the creator from the beginning made them male and female, and said, 'For this reason a man shall leave his father and mother and be joined to his wife, and the two shall become one'? So they are no longer two but one. What therefore God has joined together, let no human put asunder." They said to him, "Why then did Moses command one to give a certificate of divorce, and to put her away?" He said to them, "For your hardness of heart Moses allowed you to divorce your wives, but from the beginning it was not so. And I say to you: whoever divorces his wife, except for unchastity, and marries another, commits adultery."

The disciples said to him, "If such is the case of a man with his wife, it is not expedient to marry." (Mt 19:3–10) [Cf. also Mt 5:32; Mk 10:2–9; and Lk 16:18; the latter two do not provide any reason for divorce.)

*[A rabbinic dispute then raged between the school of Shammai, who said a wife can be divorced only for adultery (Jesus here agrees), and the school of Hillel, who said a wife can be divorced for any reason; this latter became the accepted position in subsequent Judaism—see §101.]

§121. Marriage and the Dignity of Women — II

Special note should be taken of the version of Jesus' words recorded by Mark, judged by many scholars most likely the closest to Jesus' original words and certainly faithful to the early tradition that here Jesus set forth a new teaching, clearly in favor of putting women on the same level as men in the crucial matter of marriage fidelity. As we have noted, in Jewish law adultery could be committed *only* against a husband, i.e., sex between a husband and an unmarried woman was *not* adultery against his wife, but sex between a wife and any man other than her husband was adultery against her husband (deserving the death penalty). But here Jesus speaks of a husband "being guilty of adultery against *her* [his wife]"—in that culture a revolutionary egalitarianism. It is clear that the parallel accounts in Matthew and Luke also describe the husband as capable of adultery. But to underscore the newness of this teaching Mark's version includes "against her" *(ep' autēn)*.

> He said to them, "The man who divorces his wife and marries another is guilty of adultery against her. And if a woman divorces her husband and marries another she is guilty of adultery too." (Mk 10:11–12; cf. Mt 19:9; Lk 16:18)

§122. Marriage and the Dignity of Women — III

Jesus clearly saw women as having equal rights and responsibilities within marriage. This was because he did not see a woman's existence as totally defined by her relationship to a man, i.e., as someone's daughter, wife, mother, widow, or harlot; her total being was not caught up in marriage. Rather, Jesus saw women as being first of all individual persons, which view was expressed in his response to the Sadducees that at the fulfillment of human history each human being will be simply an individual person, that "men and women do not marry; no, they are like the angels in heaven." The Sadducees' question about who the woman would belong to was rejected as containing a false assumption.

> That day some Sadducees—who deny that there is a resurrection—approached him and they put this question to him, "Master, Moses said that if a man dies childless, his brother is to marry the widow, his sister-in-law, to raise children for his brother. Now we had a case involving seven brothers; the first married and then died without children, leaving his wife to his brother; the same thing happened with the second and the third and so on to the seventh, and then last of all the woman herself died. Now at the

resurrection to which of those seven will she be wife, since she had been married to them all?" Jesus answered them, "You are wrong, because you understand neither the scriptures nor the power of God. For at the resurrection men and women do not marry; no, they are like the angels in heaven. And as for the resurrection of the dead, have you never read what God said to you: I am the God of Abraham, the God of Isaac and the God of Jacob? God is God, not of the dead, but of the living." (Mt 22:23–30; cf. Mk 12:18–27; Lk 20:27–38)

§123. Marriage and the Dignity of Women — IV

It is interesting to note here the remarks of a modern Jewish scholar commenting on the theme of divorce in Mt 5:31–32.

In these verses the originality of Jesus is made manifest. So far, in the Sermon on the Mount, we have found nothing which goes beyond Rabbinic religion and Rabbinic morality, or which greatly differs from them. Here we do. The attitude of Jesus towards women is very striking. He breaks through oriental limitations in more directions than one. For (1) he associates with, and is much looked after by, women in a manner which was unusual; (2) he is more strict about divorce; (3) he is also more merciful and compassionate. He is a great champion of womanhood, and in this combination of freedom and pity, as well as in his strict attitude to divorce, he makes a new departure of enormous significance and importance. If he had done no more than this, he might justly be regarded as one of the great teachers of the world. (Claude G. Montefiore, *Rabbinic Literature and Gospel Teaching*, pp. 217f.; London, 1930)

§124. Jesus at Cana

According to the Gospel of John the first of the public signs of Jesus was worked by him at the, at least indirect, bidding of a woman, his mother. Also to be noted in John's account is Jesus' coupling his respect for his mother with a distancing of himself from her, part of his attempt to loosen the too-often oppressive bonds of family in that culture. Jesus addresses his mother as "woman," a polite and proper enough public usage with other women, but, according to contemporary literature, surely not usual with one's mother. This "distancing" move is reinforced by his remark, "How does this concern of yours involve me?"

Jesus' presence at and support of the wedding at Cana also confirms his affirmation of marriage and rejection of hyper-asceticism. Perhaps John had this particularly in mind when he decided to include this account, as a counterweight to the encratic and gnostic elements that were springing up at the time of the composition of his Gospel, for those movements tended to be anti-marriage and/or anti-sex.

On the third day there was a wedding at Cana in Galilee, and the mother of Jesus was there. Jesus and his disciples had likewise been invited to the celebration. At a certain point the wine ran out and Jesus' mother told him, "They have no more wine." Jesus replied, "Woman, how does this concern of yours involve me? My hour has not yet come." His mother instructed those waiting on table, "Do whatever he tells you." As prescribed for Jewish ceremonial washings, there were at hand six stone water jars, each one holding fifteen to twenty-five gallons. "Fill those jars with water," Jesus ordered, at which they filled them to the brim. "Now," he said, "draw some out and take it to the waiter in charge." They did as he instructed them. The waiter in charge tasted the water made wine, without knowing where it had come from; only the waiters knew, since they had drawn the water. Then the waiter in charge called the groom over and remarked to him: "People usually serve the choice wine first; then when the guests have been drinking awhile, a lesser vintage. What you have done is keep the choice wine until now." Jesus performed this first of his signs at Cana in Galilee. Thus did he reveal his glory, and his disciples believed in him. (Jn 2:1–11)

§125. Jesus Affirms Parents

Jesus affirmed parenthood. Luke notes that Jesus "lived under the authority" of his mother and father (Lk 2:51). And Jesus reiterated the traditional affirmation of parenthood in his own words on one occasion when he accused his opponents of avoiding their obligations to their mothers and fathers. However, in this support of parents Jesus in no way set the father's prerogatives above those of the mother.

Pharisees and scribes from Jerusalem then came to Jesus and said, "Why do your disciples break away from the tradition of the elders? They do not wash their hands when they eat food." "And why do you," he answered, "break away from the commandment of God for the sake of your tradition? For God said: Do your duty to your father and mother, and: Anyone who curses father or mother must be put to death. But you say, 'If anyone says to his father or mother: Anything I have that I might have used to help you is dedicated to God,' he is rid of his duty to father or mother. In this way you have made God's word null and void by means of your tradition. Hypocrites!" (Mt 15:1–7; cf. Mk 7:1–13)

§126. Jesus' Problems with His Family

Despite Jesus' affirmation of marriage and parenthood, he had severe problems with his family. Early in his public life they tried to pack him off because they thought he was insane. More than that, he was rejected by his home community simply because they knew his family. His family not only tried to lock him in, but their very existence also tended to lock the community out.

He went home again, and once more such a crowd collected that they could not even have a meal. When his family heard of this, they set out to take charge of him, convinced he was out of his mind. (Mk 3:20–21)

Going from that district, he went to his home town and his disciples accompanied him. With the coming of the sabbath he began teaching in the synagogue and most of them were astonished when they heard him. They said, "Where did the man get all this? What is this wisdom that has been granted him, and these miracles that are worked through him? This is the carpenter, surely, the son of Mary, the brother of James and Joset and Jude and Simon? His sisters, too, are they not here with us?" And they would not accept him. And Jesus said to them, "A prophet is only despised in his own country, among his own relations and in his own house"; and he could work no miracle there, though he cured a few sick people by laying his hands on them. He was amazed at their lack of faith. (Mk 6:1–6; cf. Mt 13:53–58; Lk 4:16–30)

§127. Spiritual Bonds Above Blood Bonds

In Near Eastern society, despite positive qualities, the demands of the patriarchal family relationships were at times overwhelming, often crushing individual personal growth, and most especially was this so for women. Almost any rule could be bent or broken, but not the obligations to family. Jesus, having experienced family repression himself, clearly and often fought this social form of oppression, which weighed most often and most heavily on women. He insisted on personal, spiritual bonds as being more important than blood bonds.

He was still speaking to the crowds when his mother and his brothers appeared; they were standing outside and were anxious to have a word with him. But to the man who told him this Jesus replied, "Who is my mother? Who are my brothers?" And stretching out his hand towards his disciples he said, "Here are my mother and my brothers. Anyone who does the will of my Father in heaven, he is my brother and sister and mother." (Mt 12:46–50; cf. Mk 3:31–35; Lk 8:19–21; 11:27–28)

§128. Jesus Dismantles Restrictive Family Bonds

A number of sayings of Jesus stress following him as rising above the bonds of family obligations so vigorously as to be clearly hyperbolic in tone at times, as, for example, "hating" one's parents (in Aramaic "hating" really has the meaning of "loving less"). What is apparent is Jesus' setting himself the task of dismantling the awesomely powerful restrictive forces of the patriarchal family, whose most obvious victims were women.

(1) Peter took this up. "What about us?" he asked him. "We have left everything and followed you." Jesus said, "I tell you solemnly, there is no one

who has left house, brothers, sisters, father, children or land for my sake and for the sake of the gospel who will not be repaid a hundred times over, houses, brothers, sisters, mothers, children and land—not without persecutions— now in this present time, and in the world to come eternal life." (Mk 10:28–30)

(2) "Do not suppose that I have come to bring peace to the earth: it is not peace I have come to bring, but a sword. For I have come to set a man against his father, a daughter against her mother, a daughter-in-law against her mother-in-law. A man's enemies will be those of his household." (Mt 10:34–36)

(3) "Anyone who prefers father or mother to me is not worthy of me. Anyone who prefers son or daughter to me is not worthy of me." (Mt 10:37–38)

(4) "And everyone who has left houses, brothers, sisters, father, mother, children or land for the sake of my name will be repaid a hundred times over, and also inherit eternal life." (Mt 19:29)

(5) "Do you suppose that I am here to bring peace on earth? No, I tell you, but rather division. For from now on a household of five will be divided: three against two and two against three; the father divided against the son, son against father, mother against daughter, daughter against mother, mother-in-law against daughter-in-law, daughter-in-law against mother-in-law." (Lk 12:51–53)

(6) "If anyone comes to me without hating his father, mother, wife, children, brothers, sisters, yes and his own life too, he cannot be my disciple." (Lk 14:26)

(7) Then Peter said, "What about us? We left all we had to follow you." He said to them, "I tell you solemnly, there is no one who has left house, wife, brothers, parents or children for the sake of the reign of God who will not be given repayment many times over in this present time and, in the world to come, eternal life." (Lk 18:28–30)

§129. The Widow's Mite

One of the essential lessons that Jesus taught, in words and actions, was that what is important about a human being is the intention, integrity, and inner spirit of the person rather than the outward forms of strength, beauty, wealth, power, piety, etc. But because the reverse was most often adhered to, Jesus clearly took up the cause of the oppressed, insisting: "Blessed are the poor"; "The last shall be first"; "The humble shall be exalted." Jesus combined both these lessons in one when he contrasted the giving of money by the rich (*plousioi*— masculine!) on the one hand and by a poor widow on the other. Jesus depicted the extremes by rich men on one side, and the lowest of the oppressed on the other, a poor widow, a woman whose almost sole value in society, being a man's wife, was gone. Jesus was clearly aware of women's oppressed state in society—and took their side: "I tell you solemnly, this poor widow has put more in than all who have contributed to the treasury."

He sat down opposite the treasury and watched the people putting money into the treasury, and many of the rich put in a great deal. A poor widow came and put in two small coins, the equivalent of a penny. Then he called his disciples and said to them, "I tell you solemnly, this poor widow has put more in than all who have contributed to the treasury; for they have all put in money they had over, but she from the little she had has put in everything she possessed, all she had to live on." (Mk 12:41–44; cf. Lk 21:1–4)

§130. Healing of Women by Jesus

Unlike other Jewish rabbis about whom stories of miraculous healing, and raising from the dead, are recorded, Jesus does heal women. They are seen by him first as persons with both physical needs and spiritual strengths (faith), the two of which call forth his healing action. Perhaps the reason there is recorded no instance of a Jewish woman ever asking Jesus for a cure is that Jewish women were conditioned by their culture to assume they would not be recognized by a public religious figure.

It is significant that the first healing by Jesus recorded by the oldest Gospel, Mark (and followed in this by Lk 4:38–39, but not Mt 8:14–15), at the very beginning of Jesus' public life, was the healing of a woman, Simon Peter's mother-in-law.

On leaving the synagogue, he went with James and John straight to the house of Simon and Andrew. Now Simon's mother-in-law had gone to bed with fever, and they told him about her straightaway. He went to her, took her by the hand and helped her up. And the fever left her and she began to wait on them. (Mk 1:29–31; cf. Mt 8:14–15; Lk 4:38–39)

§131. Healing of the Woman with an Issue of Blood

All three of the Synoptic Gospels record the healing of the woman who had an issue of blood for twelve years. Especially touching is the fact that the woman was so reluctant to project herself into public attention that she "said to herself, 'If I only touch his garment, I shall be made well.'" As a woman with a flow of blood, whether menstrual or other, she had been constantly, for twelve years, ritually unclean (Lev 15:19–30). This not only made her incapable of participation in any cultic action and made her in some sense "displeasing to God," it also rendered anyone and anything she touched (or anyone who touched what she had touched!) similarly unclean. But Jesus not only healed the woman, he also made a great to-do about the event, calling extraordinary attention to the publicity-shy woman. It seems clear that Jesus wanted to call attention to the fact that he did not shrink from the ritual uncleanness incurred by being touched by the "unclean" woman, and by immediate implication that he rejected the concept of the "uncleanness" of a woman who had a flow of blood. Jesus apparently placed a greater importance on the dramatic making of this point, both to the afflicted woman herself and to the crowd, than he did on avoiding the temporary psychological discomfort of the embarrassed woman, which in the light of Jesus' extraordinary concern to alleviate the pain of the afflicted meant he placed a great weight on the teaching of this lesson about the dignity of women.

Jesus went with him and a large crowd followed him; they were pressing all round him. Now there was a woman who had suffered from a haemorrhage for twelve years; after long and painful treatment under various doctors, she had spent all she had without being any the better for it; in fact, she was getting worse. She had heard about Jesus, and she came up behind him through the crowd and touched his cloak. "If I can touch even his clothes," she had told herself, "I shall be well again." And the source of the bleeding dried up instantly, and she felt in herself that she was cured of her affliction. Immediately aware that power had gone out from him, Jesus turned round in the crowd and said, "Who touched my clothes?" His disciples said to him, "You see how the crowd is pressing round you and yet you say, 'Who touched me?'" But he continued to look all round to see who had done it. Then the woman came forward, frightened and trembling because she knew what had happened to her, and she fell at his feet and told him the whole truth. "My daughter," he said, "your faith has restored you to health; go in peace and be free from your affliction." (Mk 5:24–34; cf. Mt 9:18–26; Lk 8:40–56)

§132. Healing on the Sabbath

Luke, whose Gospel exhibits the greatest sympathy for women by the relatively large number of events and stories involving women he includes, reports three healings on the Sabbath—which caused Jesus difficulties. Two were healings of men, the other, the healing of a woman. John also records the healing of two men on the Sabbath (Jn 5:10; 9:14–17), whereas both Mark (Mk 3:1–6) and Matthew (Mt 12:9–14) report only the healing of one man; none of the three report the healing of any women on the Sabbath. Perhaps Luke's Hellenistic background and intended audience explain his emphasizing Jesus' feminism, since the Hellenistic world experienced an extended "women's liberation" movement (see above, pp. 15ff., for further analysis). It should also be noted that in Luke's story Jesus not only healed the woman on the Sabbath, he also spoke to her in public, an unseemly thing for any man in that culture, especially a rabbi. He also referred to her as a *"daughter* of Abraham,"* an almost unheard of honorific, although *son* of Abraham (cf. "sons of the covenant," *bnei brith*) is a standard phrase used throughout Hebrew and Jewish literature as well as by Jesus (e.g., Lk 19:9) as a way of referring to a member (male) of the chosen people. For Jesus, women were also clearly full-fledged participants of the people and covenant of God.

One sabbath day he was teaching in one of the synagogues, and a woman was there who for eighteen years had been possessed by a spirit that left her enfeebled; she was bent double and quite unable to stand upright. When Jesus saw her he called her over and said, "Woman, you are rid of your infirmity," and he laid his hands on her. And at once she straightened up, and she glorified God.

But the synagogue official was indignant because Jesus had healed on the sabbath, and he addressed the people present. "There are six days," he said, "when work is to be done. Come and be healed on one of those days and not on the sabbath." But the Lord answered him. "Hypocrites!" he said. "Is there one of you who does not untie his ox or his donkey from the manger on the sabbath and take it out for watering? And this woman, a *daughter* of Abraham whom Satan has held bound these eighteen years—was it not right to untie her bonds on the sabbath day?" When he said this, all his adversaries were covered with confusion, and all the people were overjoyed at all the wonders he worked. (Lk 13:10–17; cf. Lk 6:6–11; 14:1–6)

§133. The Syrophoenician Woman and Jesus

According to Matthew, Jesus conceived of his mission as being directed first of all to God's chosen people, the Jews. The first recorded instance of his going beyond the limits of his commission was to heal a female, at the persistent insistence of a woman. It was her human quality, her "faith," that Jesus perceived and that moved him to extend himself; she was not treated as an inferior category, a woman, but as a "person," who had "great faith." It is also interesting to note that this is the only recorded instance wherein Jesus was bested in a verbal exchange—and it is by a woman.

Jesus left that place and withdrew to the region of Tyre and Sidon. Then out came a Canaanite woman from that district and started shouting, "Sir, Son of David, take pity on me. My daughter is tormented by a devil." But he answered her not a word. And his disciples went and pleaded with him. "Give her what she wants," they said, "because she is shouting after us." He said in reply, "I was sent only to the lost sheep of the House of Israel." But the woman had come up and was kneeling at his feet. "Lord," she said, "help me." He replied, "It is not fair to take the children's food and throw it to the house-dogs." She retorted, "Ah yes, sir; but even house-dogs can eat the scraps that fall from their master's table." Then Jesus answered her, "Woman, you have great faith. Let your wish be granted." And from that moment her daughter was well again. (Mt 15:21–28; cf. Mk 7:24–30)

§134. Jesus' Concern for Widows — I

Jesus felt himself especially sent to the poor and oppressed, and that clearly included in a preeminent way the largest class of that group, women. However, if women were a more oppressed class among the oppressed, the most oppressed of women were widows, for they had almost no means of livelihood or standing before the law, nor anyone to provide them. Jesus was clearly most concerned about these most oppressed of the most oppressed class of the oppressed, and his concern was translated into action. It should be noted that all the following accounts concerning Jesus and widows, save the final one, are recorded in Luke, again reflecting Luke's sensitivity to this dimension of Jesus' mission.

§135. Jesus' Concern for Widows — II

It is recorded by Luke that almost at the beginning of his life Jesus was prophesied over by a widow.

There was a *woman prophet* also, Anna the daughter of Phanuel, of the tribe of Asher. She was well on in years. Her days of girlhood over, she had been married for seven years before becoming a *widow*. She was now eighty-four years old and never left the Temple, serving God night and day with fasting and prayer. She came by just at that moment and began to praise God; and she spoke of the child to all who looked forward to the deliverance of Jerusalem. (Lk 2:36–38)

§136. Jesus' Concern for Widows — III

Jesus set before his disciples the example of a widow's minute contribution as being greater than the largesse of the rich (see §129):

As he looked up he saw rich people putting their offerings into the treasury; then he happened to notice a poverty-stricken widow putting in two small coins, and he said, "I tell you truly, this poor widow has put in more than any of them; for these have all contributed money they had over, but she from the little she had has put in all she had to live on." (Lk 21:1–4; cf. Mk 12:41–44)

§137. Jesus' Concern for Widows — IV

Jesus publicly vigorously condemned the scribes (part of the male establishment) for their oppression of widows—thereby earning himself many enemies.

In his teaching he said, "Beware of the scribes who like to walk about in long robes, to be greeted obsequiously in the market squares, to take the front seats in the synagogues and the places of honour at banquets; these are the men who swallow the property of widows, while making a show of lengthy prayers. The more severe will be the sentence they receive." (Mk 12:38–40; cf. Lk 20:45–47)

§138. Jesus' Concern for Widows — V

In his teaching Jesus used the image of widows when illustrating how a prophet is not accepted in his own country.

"There were many widows in Israel, I can assure you, in Elijah's day, when heaven remained shut for three years and six months and a great famine raged throughout the land, but Elijah was not sent to any one of these: he was sent to a widow at Zarephath, a Sidonian town. And in the prophet Elisha's time there were many lepers in Israel, but none of these was cured, except the Syrian, Naaman." (Lk 4:25–27)

§139. Jesus' Concern for Widows — VI

Also in his teaching Jesus used the image of a widow as one in the weakest and most hopeless of positions to illustrate the need for perseverance in prayer. (Lk 18:1–8; see §109 for text)

§140. Jesus' Concern for Widows — VII

Also recorded is Jesus' curing of a widow, Simon Peter's mother-in-law. The fact that she was living at Peter's house is a clear indication that she was widowed (also see §130).

Leaving the synagogue he went to Simon's house. Now Simon's mother-in-law was suffering from a high fever and they asked him to do something for her. Leaning over her he rebuked the fever and it left her. And she immediately got up and began to wait on them. (Lk 4:38–39; cf. Mt 8:14–15; Mk 1:29–31)

§141. Jesus' Concern for Widows — VIII

Perhaps the most moving action of Jesus for the sake of a widow was his raising to life the only son of the widow of Nain; she, unlike Peter's mother-in-law, had no one to provide for and protect her. Jesus was "moved with pity" for her "and said to her, 'Do not cry.'"

Soon afterward he went to a town called Nain, and his disciples and a large crowd accompanied him. As he approached the gate of the town a dead man was being carried out, the only son of a widowed mother. A considerable crowd of townsfolk were with her. The Lord was moved with pity upon seeing her and said to her, "Do not cry." Then he stepped forward and touched the litter; at this, the bearers halted. He said, "Young man, I bid you get up." The dead man sat up and began to speak. Then Jesus gave him back to his mother. Fear seized them all and they began to praise God. "A great prophet has risen among us," they said; and, "God has visited his people." This was the report that spread about him throughout Judea and the surrounding country. (Lk 7:11–17)

§142. Jesus' Concern for Widows — IX

Just as there was a widow (Anna) and his mother at the beginning of his life (Lk 2:36–38), so also at the end of Jesus' life there was a widow and his mother—and the two were one. According to John, even in his death agony Jesus looked to the welfare of his beloved most oppressed, widows; he provided for his mother's future home with his "beloved disciple."

Near the cross of Jesus stood his mother and his mother's sister, Mary the wife of Clopas, and Mary of Magdala. Seeing his mother and the disciple he loved standing near her, Jesus said to his mother, "Woman, this is your son." Then to the disciple he said, "This is your mother." And from that moment the disciple made a place for her in his home. (Jn 19:25–27)

§143. The Woman Taken in Adultery

The story of Jesus and the woman taken in adultery is found in the Gospel of John, although scholars agree that he did not write the story. It is not found in the earliest Greek manuscripts and comes into the canonical scriptures through the manuscripts of the Western Latin church, although there is a reference to the story in the third-century Didascalia, of Syrian origin. Why the long resistance to this story? Probably partly because Jesus was totally forgiving of adultery and much of early Christianity took an extremely severe stance against sexual offenses. Also, Jesus' treating of the woman in the story as a person rather than simply as a creature of sex probably drew forth resistance from certain elements in the church; other elements (women?) persisted in retaining the story, and ultimately succeeded.

We have in this story the crass use by a group of scribes and Pharisees of a woman, reduced entirely to a sex object, to set a legal trap for Jesus. In fact, it is difficult to imagine a more callous use of a human person than the way the enemies of Jesus treated the adulterous woman. First, the woman was surprised in the intimate act of sexual intercourse. According to Deut 19:15 there had to have been two or more witnesses other than the husband. The witnesses, of course, had to be male. Unless the scribes and the Pharisees were themselves the witnesses, it would seem that the poor woman was dragged before them, and they perhaps in turn, along with the witnesses, were dragging her to the Sanhedrin. Since Jesus was teaching in the area of the Temple at the time, the scribes and the Pharisees apparently took the opportunity to use the woman to trap Jesus.

Most scholars suggest that the trap set up for Jesus was to present him with the dilemma of a woman caught in the very act of adultery, which according to Mosaic law should have resulted in her being put to death, on the one hand, and the restriction of capital punishment to Roman authorities at that time, on the other. It is also clear that the enemies of Jesus would not have thought of this case as presenting Jesus with some kind of trap if Jesus did not already have a reputation among them as a champion of women. There apparently was no question but that the woman was guilty of the "crime" of adultery, since she was caught *in delicto,* and therefore was subject to the Mosaic punishment of death. The question was, would Jesus retain his reputation as the great rabbi, the teacher of the Torah, or would he retain his reputation as the champion of women?

Jesus of course avoided the horns of the dilemma by refusing to become involved in legalisms and abstractions. Rather, he dealt with the persons involved, both the woman herself and her accusers. He spoke to the latter not as a lawyer, nor as to lawyers, but rather as one who was concerned with their humanness, their mind, spirit, and heart: "Let him who is without sin cast the first stone." He spoke similarly to the woman when he said that he also would not condemn her, but that she should from now on avoid that sin.

At daybreak he appeared in the Temple again; and as all the people came to him, he sat down and began to teach them. The scribes and Pharisees brought a woman along who had been caught committing adultery; and making her stand there in full view of everybody, they said to Jesus, "Master, this woman was caught in the very act of committing adultery, and Moses has ordered us in the Law to condemn women like this to death by stoning. What have you to say?" They asked him this as a test, looking for something to use against him. But Jesus bent down and started writing on the ground with his finger. As they persisted with their question, he looked up and said, "If there is one of you who has not sinned, let him be the first to throw a stone at her." Then he bent down and wrote on the ground again. When they heard this they went away one by one, beginning with the eldest, until

Jesus was left alone with the woman, who remained standing there. He looked up and said, "Woman, where are they? Has no one condemned you?" "No one, sir," she replied. "Neither do I condemn you," said Jesus, "go away, and don't sin any more." (Jn 8:2–11)

§144. Jesus and the Penitent Woman

Scholars have always found the story of Jesus and the penitent woman difficult to understand and translate (especially the key portion, v. 47); Joachim Jeremias provides perhaps the most helpful suggestion when he supposes that Jesus had just delivered a powerful sermon that moved the Pharisee Simon to see Jesus as a prophet and the sinful woman to confess and repent of her sins and be filled with gratitude for the forgiveness she received in the sermon. Several things should be recalled here in the relationship between the woman and Jesus. First, in that culture one did not publicly speak to one's own wife, let alone to a strange woman, indeed a known "sinner," probably a prostitute! Jesus not only spoke with her but let her touch him and kiss him. Further, a woman was never to let her hair be uncovered, and to loose it in public was grounds for mandatory divorce; this woman uncovered her hair, loosed it, and wiped Jesus' feet with it, without thereby scandalizing Jesus—although Simon was clearly scandalized. Jesus rebuked the Pharisee and treated the woman not as a sexual creature but as a person; he spoke of her human and spiritual actions, her love, her unlove (her sins), her being forgiven, and her faith.

One of the Pharisees invited him to a meal. When he arrived at the Pharisee's house and took his place at table, a woman came in, who had a bad name (*ēn hamartōlos*, was a sinner) in the town. She had heard he was dining with the Pharisee and had brought with her an alabaster jar of ointment. She waited behind him at his feet, weeping, and her tears fell on his feet, and she wiped them away with her hair; then she covered his feet with kisses and anointed them with the ointment.

When the Pharisee who had invited him saw this, he said to himself, "If this man were a prophet, he would know who this woman is that is touching him and what a bad name she has." Then Jesus took him up and said, "Simon, I have something to say to you." "Speak, Master," was the reply. "There was once a creditor who had two men in his debt; one owed him five hundred denarii, the other fifty. They were unable to pay, so he pardoned them both. Which of them will love him more?" "The one who was pardoned more, I suppose," answered Simon. Jesus said, "You are right."

Then he turned to the woman. "Simon," he said, "you see this woman? I came into your house, and you poured no water over my feet, but she has poured out her tears over my feet and wiped them away with her hair. You gave me no kiss, but she has been covering my feet with kisses ever since I came in. You did not anoint my head with oil, but she has anointed my feet with ointment. For this reason I tell you that her sins, her many sins, must have been forgiven her, or she would not have shown such great love. It is the person who is forgiven little who shows little love." Then he said to her, "Your sins are forgiven." Those who were with him at table began to say to themselves, "Who is this man, that he even forgives sins?" But he said to the woman, "Your faith has saved you; go in peace." (Lk 7:36–50)

§145. Prostitutes and the Reign of God

On at least one other occasion Jesus reached out in his teaching specifically to the most despised of human creatures, prostitutes. Jesus made it clear in both his words and actions that he understood his mission to be to preach in word and deed the "good news," the coming of the reign of God, to the poor and oppressed. In a debate with the chief priests and the elders of the people Jesus named two of the presumably most unlikely classes of these "oppressed" as entering into the reign of God ahead of the chief priests and elders, namely, tax collectors and prostitutes, the two most despised groups of that society. A sexual parallelism should be noted here: the male tax collector and the female prostitute. It is difficult to believe that such a sexual balance was not struck deliberately by Jesus, for the Synoptic Gospels usually connect tax collectors and *sinners,* a much broader term than prostitutes, with Jesus ten different times and only on this occasion are tax collectors and prostitutes mentioned. In fact (except in the parable of the prodigal son), this is the only time the term "prostitutes" is used in any of the Gospels. The source for the term "prostitutes" in this connection could then, almost certainly, only be Jesus.

Upon reflection, it is really quite extraordinary that Jesus would picture prostitutes as in the reign of God, as being "saved." Clearly for him a woman reduced completely to a sex object is seen as the object, not of disdain, but rather of exploitation, who nevertheless is a *person,* one among those who can "make their way into the reign of God."

He had gone into the Temple and was teaching, when the chief priests and the elders of the people came to him. . . . Jesus said to them, "I tell you solemnly, tax collectors and prostitutes are making their way into the reign of God before you. For John came to you, a pattern of true righteousness, but you did not believe him, and yet the tax collectors and prostitutes did." (Mt 21:23, 31–32)

§146. The Samaritan Woman

On another occasion Jesus again deliberately and flagrantly violated the then common code concerning men's relationship to women. It is recorded in the story of the Samaritan woman at the well of Jacob. Jesus was waiting at the well outside the village while his disciples were getting food. A Samaritan woman approached the well to draw water. Normally a Jew would not address a Samaritan, as the woman pointed out: "Jews, in fact, do not associate with Samaritans." But, of course, also normally a man would not speak to a woman in public (doubly so in the case of a rabbi). However, Jesus startled the woman by initiating a conversation. The woman was aware that on both counts, her being a Samaritan and being a woman, Jesus' action was out of the ordinary, for she replied: "How is it that you, a Jew, ask a drink of me, a *woman* of Samaria?" As hated as the Samaritans were by the Jews, it is nevertheless clear that Jesus' speaking with a woman was considered a much more flagrant breach of conduct than his speaking with a Samaritan, for John related: "His disciples returned, and were shocked to find him speaking to a *woman,* though none of them asked, 'What do you want from her?' or, 'Why are you talking to her?' " Of course the woman's being a Samaritan more than doubled the shocking quality of Jesus' conversing with her, and especially his taking a drink from her, for she was considered certainly ritually unclean since customarily Jews considered Samaritan women as menstruants (and hence unclean: Lev 15:19) from their cradle! However, Jesus' rejection of the woman's uncleanness and his bridging of the gap of inequality between men and women continued further, for in the conversation with the woman he revealed himself in a straightforward fashion as the Messiah for the first time (according to John): "The woman said to him, 'I know that the Messiah is coming.' . . . Jesus said to her, 'I who speak to you am he.' "

Just as when Jesus revealed himself to Martha as "the resurrection," and to Mary Magdalene as the "risen one" and bade her to bear witness to the disciples, Jesus here also revealed himself in one of his key roles, as Messiah, to a woman (all these instances recorded in the Gospel of John)—who immediately *bore witness* of the fact to her fellow villagers. It is interesting to note that apparently the testimony of women carried greater weight among the Samaritans than among the Jews, for the villagers came out to see Jesus: "Many

Samaritans of that town believed in him on the strength of the woman's testimony. . . ." It would seem that John the Gospel writer deliberately highlighted this contrast in the way he wrote about this event, and also that he clearly wished thereby to reinforce Jesus' stress on the equal dignity of women.

This stress on the witness role of the Samaritan woman is further underscored by John's language. He says the villagers "believed . . . because of the woman's word" *(episteusan dia ton logon),* almost the identical words he records in Jesus' "priestly" prayer at the Last Supper when Jesus prays not only for his disciples "but also for those who believe in me through their word" (. . . *pisteuontōn dia tou logou,* Jn 17:20). As Raymond E. Brown notes, "the Evangelist can describe both a woman and the (presumably male) disciples at the Last Supper as bearing witness to Jesus through preaching and thus bringing people to believe in him on the strength of their word." (Raymond E. Brown, "Roles of Women in the Fourth Gospel, *"Theological Studies,* December 1975, p. 691.)

One other point should be noted in connection with this story. As the crowd of Samaritans was walking out to see Jesus, Jesus was speaking to his disciples about the fields being ready for the harvest and how he was sending them to reap what others had sown. He was clearly speaking of the souls of humans, and most probably was referring directly to the approaching Samaritans. Such exegesis is standard. It is also rather standard to refer to "others" in general and only to Jesus in particular as having been the sowers whose harvest the apostles were about to reap (e.g., in the Jerusalem Bible). But it would seem that the evangelist also meant specifically to include the Samaritan woman among those sowers, for immediately after he recorded Jesus' statement to the disciples about their reaping what others had sown he added the above-mentioned verse: "Many Samaritans of that town had believed on the strength of the woman's testimony. . . ." The Samaritan woman preached the "Good News," the *euangelion,* of Jesus, that is, she was an "evangelist."

When Jesus heard that the Pharisees had found out that he was making and baptising more disciples than John—though in fact it was his disciples who baptised, not Jesus himself—he left Judaea and went back to Galilee. This meant that he had to cross Samaria.

On the way he came to the Samaritan town called Sychar, near the land that Jacob gave to his son Joseph. Joseph's well is there and Jesus, tired by the journey, sat straight down by the well. It was about the sixth hour. When a Samaritan woman came to draw water, Jesus said to her, "Give me a drink." His disciples had gone into the town to buy food. The Samaritan woman said to him, "What? You are a Jew and you ask me, a woman of Samaria, for a drink?—Jews, in fact, do not associate with Samaritans." Jesus replied: "If you only knew what God is offering and who it is that is saying to you: 'Give me a drink,' you would have been the one to ask, and he would have given you living water." "You have no bucket, sir," she answered, "and the well is deep: how could you get this living water? Are you a greater man than our father Jacob who gave us this well and drank from it himself with his sons and his cattle?" Jesus replied: "Whoever drinks this water will get thirsty again; but anyone who drinks the water that I shall give will never be thirsty again: the water that I shall give will turn into a spring inside him, welling up to eternal life."

"Sir," said the woman, "give me some of that water, so that I may never get thirsty and never have to come here again to draw water." "Go and call your husband," said Jesus to her, "and come back here." The woman answered, "I have no husband." He said to her, "You are right to say, 'I have no husband'; for although you have had five, the one you have now is not your husband. You spoke the truth there." "I see you are a prophet, sir," said the woman. "Our fathers worshipped on this mountain, while you say that Jerusalem is the place where one ought to worship." Jesus said: "Believe me, woman, the hour is coming when you will worship the Father neither on this mountain nor in Jerusalem. You worship what you do not know; we worship what we do know; for salvation comes from the Jews. But the hour will come —in fact it is here already—when true worshippers will worship the Father in spirit and truth: that is the kind of worshipper the Father wants. God is spirit, and those who worship must worship in spirit and truth."

The woman said to him, "I know that Messiah—that is, Christ—is coming, and when he comes he will tell us everything." "I who am speaking to you," said Jesus, "I am he."

At this point his disciples returned, and were surprised to find him speaking to a woman, though none of them asked, "What do you want from her?" or, "Why are you talking to her?" The woman put down her water jar and hurried back to the town to tell the people, "Come and see a man who has told me everything I ever did; I wonder if he is the Christ?" This brought people out of the town and they started walking towards him.

Meanwhile, the disciples were urging him, "Rabbi, do have something to eat"; but he said, "I have food to eat that you do not know about." So the disciples asked one another, "Has someone been bringing him food?" But Jesus said: "My food is to do the will of the one who sent me, and to complete his work. Have you not got a saying: Four months and then the harvest? Well, I tell you: Look around you, look at the fields; already they are white, ready for harvest! Already the reaper is being paid his wages, already he is bringing in the grain for eternal life, and thus sower and reaper rejoice together. For here the proverb holds good: one sows, another reaps; I sent you to reap a harvest you had not worked for. Others worked for it; and you have come into the rewards of their trouble."

Many Samaritans of that town had believed in him on the strength of the woman's testimony when she said, "He told me all I have ever done," so, when the Samaritans came up to him, they begged him to stay with them.

He stayed for two days, and when he spoke to them many more came to believe; and they said to the woman, "Now we no longer believe because of what you told us; we have heard him ourselves and we know that he really is the saviour of the world." (Jn 4:1–42)

§147. Martha and Mary

Perhaps the strongest and clearest affirmation on the part of Jesus that the intellectual and "spiritual" life was just as proper to women as to men is recorded in Luke's Gospel in the description of a visit of Jesus to the house of his friends Martha and Mary. The first thing to be noted is that Jesus allowed himself to be served by a woman, which was contrary to strict custom, although it might have been somewhat mitigated because it took place in the less rigid village area. Jesus here clearly rejected the prevalent notion that the only proper place for women was "in the home." Martha took the woman's typical role and "was distracted with much serving." Mary, however, took the supposedly male role: she "sat at the Lord's feet and listened to his teaching." To sit at someone's feet is a rabbinic phrase indicating studying with that person. That phrase, coupled with the second half, "listened to his teaching," makes it abundantly clear that Mary was acting like a disciple of a teacher, a rabbi. Martha apparently thought Mary was out of place in choosing the role of the "intellectual," for she complained to Jesus. But Jesus' response was a refusal to force all women into the stereotype; he treated Mary first of all as a person (whose highest faculty is the intellect, the spirit) who was allowed to set her own priorities, and who in this instance had "chosen the better part." And Jesus applauded her: "It is not to be taken from her." Again, when one recalls the Palestinian restriction on women studying the Scriptures or studying with rabbis, that is, engaging in the intellectual life or acquiring any "religious authority," it is difficult to imagine how Jesus could possibly have been clearer in his insistence that women were called to the intellectual, the spiritual, life just as were men.

In the course of their journey he came to a village, and a woman named Martha welcomed him into her house. She had a sister called Mary, who sat down at the Lord's feet and listened to him speaking. Now Martha who was distracted with all the serving said, "Lord, do you not care that my sister is leaving me to do the serving all by myself? Please tell her to help me." But the Lord answered: "Martha, Martha," he said, "you worry and fret about so many things, and yet few are needed, indeed only one. It is Mary who has chosen the better part; it is not to be taken from her." (Lk 10:38–42)

§148. Intellectual Life for Women

There is at least one other instance recorded in the Gospels when Jesus clearly taught that the intellectual and spiritual life was definitely for women. One day as Jesus was preaching, a woman from the crowd apparently was very deeply impressed and, perhaps imagining how happy she would be to have such a son, raised her voice to pay Jesus a compliment. She did so by referring to his mother, and did so in a way that was probably not untypical at that time and place. But her image of a woman was sexually reductionist in the extreme (one that largely persists to the present): female genitals and breasts. "Blessed is the womb that bore you, and the breasts that you sucked!" Although this was obviously meant as a compliment, and although it was even uttered by a woman, Jesus clearly felt it necessary to reject this "baby machine" image of women and insist again on the personhood, the intellectual and moral faculties, being primary for all: "But he said, 'Blessed rather are those who hear the word of God and keep it!' " It is difficult to see how the primary point of this text could be anything substantially other than this. Luke and the sources he depended on must also have been quite clear about the sexual significance of this event. Otherwise, why would he (and they) have kept and included such a small event from all the months of Jesus' public life? It was not retained *merely* because Jesus said those who hear and keep God's word are blessed, for Luke had already recorded that statement of Jesus in 8:21 (cf. Mt 12:46–50 and Mk 3:31–35). Rather, it was probably retained because keeping God's word was stressed by Jesus as being primary in comparison to a woman's sexuality. Luke seems to have had a discernment here, as well as elsewhere, concerning what Jesus was about in his approach to the question of women's status that has not been shared by subsequent Christians (and perhaps was not shared by many of Luke's fellow Christians), for, in the explanation of this passage, Christians for two thousand years apparently have not seen its plain meaning—doubtless because of unconscious presuppositions about the status of women inculcated by their cultural and religious milieu.

Now as he was speaking, a woman in the crowd raised her voice and said, "Happy the womb that bore you and the breasts you sucked!" But he replied, "Blessed rather are those who hear the word of God and keep it!" (Lk 11:27–28) *c. Women in the Life of Jesus*

§149. The Prophet Anna

Luke records at least seven sexually parallel images or stories, one about a man and one about a woman, used by Jesus. The same sexual parallelism is found in his account of the presentation of the child Jesus in the Temple. The parents are met there by Simeon, "an upright and devout man," who, though he is not called a prophet, nevertheless prophesies concerning Jesus. They are also met by a woman who is specifically called a prophet *(prophētis)* and who also spoke of Jesus as the Messiah.

There was a woman prophet also, Anna the daughter of Phanuel, of the tribe of Asher. She was well on in years. Her days of girlhood over, she had been married for seven years before becoming a widow. She was now eighty-four years old and never left the Temple, serving God night and day with fasting and prayer. She came by just at that moment and began to praise God; and she spoke of the child to all who looked forward to the deliverance of Jerusalem. (Lk 2:36–38)

§150. Women Disciples of Jesus — I

The disciples of Jesus were those who followed Jesus about, listening to and living with him. This group of disciples included in a prominent way a number of women (some are specifically named), mainly from the more rural area of Galilee where the restrictive rules against women would have been less stringent than in Jerusalem. Still, they had to leave home and family and travel openly with a "rabbi," an unheard of breach of custom. Jesus not only condoned but obviously encouraged this flouting of sexist custom. These women disciples were such a prominent part of Jesus' life that all three of the Synoptic Gospels mention them.

Now after this he made his way through towns and villages preaching, and proclaiming the Good News of the reign of God. With him went the Twelve, as well as certain women who had been cured of evil spirits and ailments: Mary surnamed the Magdalene, from whom seven demons had gone out, Joanna the wife of Herod's steward Chuza, Susanna, and several others who ministered *(diēkonoun)* to them out of their own resources. (Lk 8:1–3; cf. Mk 15:40–41; Mt 27:55–56)

§151. Women "Minister to" *(Diakoneō)* Jesus

All three of the Synoptic Gospels use a form of the verb *diakoneō* (to minister or serve) to describe what these women did in addition to saying that they "followed" Jesus. It is the same basic word as "deacon"; indeed, apparently the tasks of the deacons in early Christianity were much the same as what these women undertook.

> There were some women watching from a distance. Among them were Mary of Magdala, Mary who was the mother of James the younger and Joset, and Salome. These used to follow him and minister *(diēkonoun)* to him when he was in Galilee. And there were many other women there who had come up to Jerusalem with him. (Mk 15:40–41)

> And many women were there, watching from a distance, the same women who had followed Jesus from Galilee and ministered *(diakonousai)* to him. Among them were Mary of Magdala, Mary the mother of James and Joseph, and the mother of Zebedee's sons. (Mt 27:55–56)

§152. Women Disciples of Jesus — II

That early Christians thought of and referred to the women who are mentioned by name in the above three citations as "disciples" of Jesus is attested to by at least three early apocryphal Christian documents (see pp. 66f. for a brief discussion of the significance of apocryphal writings). The first, the Sophia Jesu Christi, was probably written during the second century; it puts these seven holy women followers of Jesus terminologically on a par with the twelve men followers. It calls the men not only apostles but also disciples *(mathētēs)*, and it says of the women that they had followed him "as disciples" *(mathēteuein)*.

> After he had risen from the dead, when they came, the twelve disciples *(mathētēs)* and seven women who had followed him as disciples *(mathēteuein)*, into Galilee, . . . there appeared to them the Redeemer. (Sophia Jesu Christi, *New Testament Apocrypha*, Vol. 1, p. 246)

The second document, the second-century Gospel of Thomas, contains a rather obscure exchange between Jesus and Salome, in the midst of which Salome announces that she is Jesus' disciple, and he does not contradict her.

> Jesus said: "Two will rest on a bed: the one will die, the one will live." Salome said: "Who art thou, man, and whose son? Thou didst take thy place upon my bench and eat from my table." Jesus said to her: "I am He who is from the Same, to me was given from the things of my Father." Salome said: *"I am thy disciple."* Jesus said [to her]: "Therefore I say, if he is the Same, he will be filled with light, but if he is divided, he will be filled with darkness." (Gospel of Thomas, *New Testament Apocrypha*, Vol. 1, p. 298)

The third document is the early third-century Pistis Sophia, wherein Mary Magdalene is not specifically called a disciple, but Jesus predicts that she "will surpass all my disciples."

> But Mary Magdalene and John, the maiden *(parthenos)*, will surpass all my disciples *(mathētai)* and all men who shall receive mysteries in the Ineffable, they will be on my right hand and on my left, and I am they and they are I. (Pistis Sophia, *New Testament Apocrypha*, Vol. 1, pp. 256–257)

§153. Anointment of Jesus by Mary of Bethany — I

It was customary that women did not eat with men when guests were present, nor, indeed, did they even enter the dining area. Nevertheless, when a woman (Mary of Bethany according to Jn 12:3) entered the room where Jesus was dining and anointed him, he neither resisted nor rebuked her. To be sure, others showed unhappiness at her intrusion, expressed especially at her "wasting" the expensive ointment. But, as in the "Martha and Mary" story of Lk 10:38–42, Jesus defended Mary's act of special discipleship to him.

> Jesus was at Bethany in the house of Simon the leper; he was at dinner when a woman came in with an alabaster jar of very costly ointment, pure nard. She broke the jar and poured the ointment on his head. Some who were there said to one another indignantly, "Why this waste of ointment? Ointment like this could have been sold for over three hundred denarii and the money given to the poor"; and they were angry with her. But Jesus said, "Leave her alone. Why are you upsetting her? What she has done for me is one of the good works. You have the poor with you always, and you can be kind to them whenever you wish, but you will not always have me. She has done what was in her power to do: she has anointed my body beforehand for its burial. I tell you solemnly, wherever throughout all the world the Good News is proclaimed, what she has done will be told also, in remembrance of her." (Mk 14:3–9; cf. Mt 26:6–13; Jn 12:1–8)

§154. Anointment of Jesus by Mary of Bethany — II

John's account of the anointment of Jesus by Mary confirms the all-male character of the banquet, in accordance with the custom of the day, for it states that Lazarus (brother of Martha and Mary) was at table, and that Martha, as usual, served. (See §151 for an analysis of the significance of the word "served," *diēkonei*, used here.) Also as usual, Mary did not serve but related to Jesus in a very special way, both poignantly personal and "transcendent," apparently oblivious of, or disregarding, her intrusion into a male sanctum, probably because she knew from experience that Jesus would support her—which he did.

> Six days before the Passover, Jesus went to Bethany, where Lazarus was, whom he had raised from the dead. They gave a dinner for him there; Martha waited on them and Lazarus was among those at table. Mary brought in a pound of very costly ointment, pure nard, and with it anointed the feet of Jesus, wiping them with her hair; the house was full of the scent of the ointment. Then Judas Iscariot—one of the disciples, the man who was to betray him—said, "Why wasn't this ointment sold for three hundred denarii, and the money given to the poor?" He said this, not because he cared about the poor, but because he was a thief; he was in charge of the common fund and used to help himself to the contributions. So Jesus said, "Leave her alone; she had to keep this scent for the day of my burial. You have the poor with you always, you will not always have me." (Jn 12:1–8; cf. Mk 14:3–9; Mt 26:6–13)

§155. Pilate's Wife

We know nothing of Pilate's wife except that she sent a message to her husband in support of Jesus during his trial. As the wife of a Roman procurator of Judea she doubtless was not Jewish but rather a pagan. We have no reason to doubt the historicity of her intervention; in fact elsewhere in the contemporary world there are recorded instances of similar interventions by women. She apparently was so upset by the attempt to destroy Jesus that she had dreamed a bad dream about him. Bad dreams were taken very seriously by most if not all people then, the vast majority being inclined toward superstition. Such a disturbing dream, bringing her to the point of intervening in a public proceeding of the most serious and formal kind ("as he was seated in the chair of judgement"), and of interrupting a husband who was known for his vicious and brutal temper, tells us something about Pilate's wife and Jesus. Jesus obviously was known to her, and most probably not simply by general, or even detailed, reputation. For her to have become so disturbed as to attempt to interfere in Jesus' behalf where such a tumult was being raised would make it most likely that she had personally been deeply impressed by Jesus. She would not have been the only woman whom Jesus deeply affected, nor the only pagan—nor indeed the only "Roman" (cf. the centurion from Capernaum, Mt 8:5; and the centurion under the cross, Mt 27:54)—nor the only pagan woman (cf. the Phoenician woman, Mt 15:21–28).

Now as he was seated in the chair of judgement, his wife sent him a message, "Have nothing to do with that man; I have been upset all day by a dream I had about him." (Mt 27:19)

§156. Jerusalem Women on the Via Dolorosa

Luke, again, is the only one of the Gospel writers who mentions the women of Jerusalem meeting Jesus as he was carrying his cross to the place of execution. He records that they mourned and cried for him. The Talmud notes that the noble women used to prepare a soothing drink for the condemned, but that is far different from what is described by Luke. These women clearly must have been devoted followers of Jesus who were overwhelmed with grief. They are a group distinct from the "large numbers of people" who followed Jesus; the Greek makes it clear that only the women were said to mourn and lament for Jesus. They obviously responded with a profound attachment to this Jesus who had taught them. Nowhere in any of the Gospels is there a similar report of a group of male followers of Jesus lamenting for him publicly or risking their limbs and lives by meeting and mourning for him in the open. Jesus' response was typical in that he showed greater concern for them than for himself. Luke would have him speak with foreknowledge of the coming destruction of Jerusalem (A.D. 70); hence most scholars hold that these specific words were provided by the evangelist, though with a historical basis.

As they were leading him away they seized on a man, Simon from Cyrene, who was coming in from the country, and made him shoulder the cross and carry it behind Jesus. Large numbers of people followed him, and of women too, who mourned and lamented for him. But Jesus turned to them and said, "Daughters of Jerusalem, do not weep for me; weep rather for yourselves and for your children. For the days will surely come when people will say, 'Happy are those who are barren, the wombs that have never borne, the breasts that have never suckled!' Then they will begin to say to the mountains, 'Fall on us!'; to the hills, 'Cover us!' For if men use the green wood like this, what will happen when it is dry?" Now with him they were also leading out two other criminals to be executed. (Lk 23:26–32)

§157. Only Women Remain by Jesus Through His Death

It should first be noted that there is no record of any women seeking the death of Jesus; all those in any way involved in promoting Jesus' death are men. Such noninvolvement of women in the violent death of others was by no means a foregone conclusion in Jewish tradition: cf. Deborah, Jael, Esther, Judith, Salome.

On the positive side, the response of the women disciples to Jesus was extraordinary. He taught and fought for them and they responded by following him to his bitter end, even at risk to their own limb and life. All Jesus' male disciples deserted him: "Then all the disciples deserted him and ran away" (Mt 26:56); "And they all deserted him and ran away" (Mk 14:49). Luke, almost certainly a later Gospel than Mark and perhaps also Matthew, says that "those who knew" Jesus stood afar and watched the crucifixion. John, which is the latest of all the Gospels, places "the disciple Jesus loved," traditionally thought to be John the Apostle, below the cross with women. Many scholars believe that both Luke and John here contain unhistorical additions to the Mark and Matthew report. Following this historical judgment, and Mark and Matthew, we have to conclude that only the women stayed with Jesus in his moment of despair and humiliation.

(1) There were some women watching from a distance. Among them were Mary of Magdala, Mary who was the mother of James the younger and Joset, and Salome. These used to follow him and minister to him when he was in Galilee. And there were many other women there who had come up to Jerusalem with him. (Mk 15:40–41)

(2) And many women were there, watching from a distance, the same women who had followed Jesus from Galilee and ministered to him. Among them were Mary of Magdala, Mary the mother of James and Joseph, and the mother of Zebedee's sons. (Mt 27:55–56)

(3) All those who knew him stood at a distance; so also did the women who had accompanied him from Galilee, and they saw all this happen. (Lk 23:49)

(4) Near the cross of Jesus stood his mother and his mother's sister, Mary the wife of Clopas, and Mary of Magdala. Seeing his mother and the disciple he loved standing near her, Jesus said to his mother, "Woman, this is your son." Then to the disciple he said, "This is your mother." And from that moment the disciple made a place for her in his home. (Jn 19:25–27)

§158. Women Witness the Burial of Jesus

The women disciples of Jesus remained by him through his death and also his burial—when all was despair. All three of the Synoptic Gospels report the presence of the women at the burial of Jesus. Joseph of Arimathaea and, probably, Nicodemus were members of the Council which participated in the trial of Jesus. Hence they had the political weight to obtain Jesus' body. Except for them, apparently only the women disciples were present for the burial—faithful to the end.

(1) It was now evening, and since it was Preparation Day (that is, the vigil of the sabbath), there came Joseph of Arimathaea, a prominent member of the Council, who himself lived in the hope of seeing the reign of God, and he boldly went to Pilate and asked for the body of Jesus. Pilate, astonished that he should have died so soon, summoned the centurion and enquired if he was already dead. Having been assured of this by the centurion, he granted the corpse to Joseph who bought a shroud, took Jesus down from the cross, wrapped him in the shroud and laid him in a tomb which had been hewn out of the rock. He then rolled a stone against the entrance to the tomb. Mary of Magdala and Mary the mother of Joset were watching and took note of where he was laid. (Mk 15:42–47)

(2) When it was evening, there came a rich man of Arimathaea, called Joseph, who had himself become a disciple of Jesus. This man went to Pilate and asked for the body of Jesus. Pilate thereupon ordered it to be handed over. So Joseph took the body, wrapped it in a clean shroud and put it in his own new tomb which he had hewn out of the rock. He then rolled a large stone across the entrance of the tomb and went away. Now Mary of Magdala and the other Mary were there, sitting opposite the sepulchre. (Mt 27:57–61)

(3) Then a member of the council arrived, an upright and virtuous man named Joseph. He had not consented to what the others had planned and carried out. He came from Arimathaea, a Jewish town, and he lived in the hope of seeing the reign of God. This man went to Pilate and asked for the body of Jesus. He then took it down, wrapped it in a shroud and put him in a tomb which was hewn in stone in which no one had yet been laid. It was Preparation Day and the sabbath was imminent. Meanwhile the women who had come from Galilee with Jesus were following behind. . . . They returned and prepared spices and ointments. And on the sabbath day they rested, as the Law required. (Lk 23:50–56)

§159. Empty Tomb — I

Perhaps because the women disciples followed Jesus to his bitter end on the cross and his burial and came back to his grave after the Sabbath, they were privileged to be the first witnesses to the empty tomb and first appearances of the "resurrected one." This last element doubtless helps explain the prominent place women held in the early Christian community. Though their testimony was then rejected by the male disciples (according to the Jewish custom of the time, which did not allow women to bear witness), all four evangelists record the women's witness to the risen Jesus and/or the empty tomb as primary, obviously reflecting the consensuses of the different primitive Christian communities in the midst of which they wrote their

Gospels. But because these traditions differed in the details of how the witnessing of the women took place, it will be helpful to look at each one.

§160. Empty Tomb — II

The account by Mark is probably the earliest, but somehow the original ending of the Gospel after Mk 16:8 probably has been lost and the story is incomplete, e.g., the women are silent after witnessing the empty tomb (see §182 for a discussion of this problem).

When the sabbath was over, Mary of Magdala, Mary the mother of James, and Salome, bought spices with which to go and anoint him. And very early in the morning on the first day of the week they went to the tomb, just as the sun was rising.

They had been saying to one another, "Who will roll away the stone for us from the entrance to the tomb?" But when they looked they could see that the stone—which was very big—had already been rolled back. On entering the tomb they saw a young man in a white robe seated on the right-hand side, and they were struck with amazement. But he said to them, "There is no need for alarm. You are looking for Jesus of Nazareth, who was crucified: he has risen, he is not here. See, here is the place where they laid him. But you must go and tell his disciples and Peter, 'He is going before you to Galilee; it is there you will see him, just as he told you.' " And the women came out and ran away from the tomb because they were frightened out of their wits; and they said nothing to a soul, for they were afraid. (Mk 16:1–8)

§161. Empty Tomb — III

In Matthew's account, perhaps the second oldest Gospel, the women are commissioned by an angel to give witness to the male disciples that Jesus had risen. Thus in a basic sense they were "apostles," ones sent *(apostoloi)* to bear witness to the resurrection.

After the sabbath, and towards dawn on the first day of the week, Mary of Magdala and the other Mary went to visit the sepulchre. And all at once there was a violent earthquake, for the angel of the Lord, descending from heaven, came and rolled away the stone and sat on it. His face was like lightning, his robe white as snow. The guards were so shaken, so frightened of him, that they were like dead men. But the angel spoke; and he said to the women, "There is no need for you to be afraid. I know you are looking for Jesus, who was crucified. He is not here, for he has risen, as he said he would. Come and see the place where he lay, then *go quickly and tell his disciples, 'He has risen from the dead* and now he is going before you to Galilee; it is there you will see him.' Now I have told you." Filled with awe and great joy the women came quickly away from the tomb and ran to tell the disciples. (Mt 28:1–8)

§162. Empty Tomb — IV

The third account, by Luke, not only describes the women reporting what they had seen and heard to the male disciples, but, in customary fashion, being disbelieved by them.

On the first day of the week, at the first sign of dawn, they went to the tomb with the spices they had prepared. They found that the stone had been rolled away from the tomb, but on entering discovered that the body of the Lord Jesus was not there. As they stood there not knowing what to think, two men in brilliant clothes suddenly appeared at their side. Terrified, the women lowered their eyes. But the two men said to them, "Why look among the dead for someone who is alive? He is not here; he has risen. Remember what he told you when he was still in Galilee: that the Son of Man had to be handed over into the power of sinful men and be crucified, and rise again on the third day?" And they remembered his words.

When the women returned from the tomb they told all this to the Eleven and to all the others. The women were Mary of Magdala, Joanna, and Mary the mother of James. The other women with them also told the apostles, but this story of theirs seemed pure nonsense, and they did not believe them.

Peter, however, went running to the tomb. He bent down and saw the binding cloths but nothing else; he then went back home, amazed at what had happened. (Lk 24:1–12)

§163. Empty Tomb — V

John the Evangelist, writing considerably later than the other three Gospel writers, describes only Mary Magdalene's visit to the tomb and her report to the male disciples. Though he does not say explicitly, as does Luke, that they disbelieved her, their actions would fit within that assumption.

It was very early on the first day of the week and still dark, when Mary of Magdala came to the tomb. She saw that the stone had been moved away from the tomb and came running to Simon Peter and the other disciple, the one Jesus loved. "They have taken the Lord out of the tomb," she said, "and we don't know where they have put him."

So Peter set out with the other disciple to go to the tomb. They ran together, but the other disciple, running faster than Peter, reached the tomb first; he bent down and saw the linen cloths lying on the ground, but did not go in. Simon Peter who was following now came up, went right into the tomb, saw the linen cloths on the ground, and also the cloth that had been over his head; this was not with the linen cloths but rolled up in a place by itself. Then the other disciple who had reached the tomb first also went in; he saw and he believed. Till this moment they had failed to understand the teaching of scripture, that he must rise from the dead. The disciples then went home again. (Jn 20:1–10)

§164. The Risen Jesus and Women — I
Three of the four Gospels report that the first appearance of the risen Jesus was to Mary Magdalene, or to a group of women disciples, in addition to the women's being the first witnesses of the empty tomb and the speech and commission by an angel or angels to witness to the resurrection. Writing before any of the evangelists, Paul in 1 Cor 15:5–8 described five of the appearances of the risen Jesus, "that he appeared *first* to Cephas (Peter) and secondly to the Twelve." Nowhere does Paul refer to Jesus' appearance to Mary Magdalene or the other women disciples. Could this be a reflection of the Jewish custom of disallowing the testimony of women, manifested by the Pharisee Paul and not yet counteracted by the women disciples through the oral traditions that fed three of the Gospel writers?

§165. The Risen Jesus and Women — II
In any case it is "the gospel truth" that the risen Jesus appeared first to a woman. The earliest Gospel, Mark, records the appearance of Jesus to Mary Magdalene, but that whole final section (Mk 16:9–20) is universally held by scholars not to have been written by the author of the Gospel of Mark, but rather added later, perhaps in the second century. As it stands, the Gospel of Mark reports simply that Jesus appeared to Mary Magdalene and also that the male disciples refused to believe her—which a woman might have expected.

Having risen in the morning on the first day of the week, he appeared first to Mary of Magdala from whom he had cast out seven devils. She then went to those who had been his companions, and who were mourning and in tears, and told them. But they did not believe her when they heard her say that he was alive and that she had seen him. (Mk 16:9–11)

§166. The Risen Jesus and Women — III
According to Matthew, Jesus appeared first to Mary Madgalene and "the other Mary." He gives more concrete details and a commission by Jesus to "go and tell my brothers" about the resurrection; they, women, were being "sent" *(apostellein)* by Jesus to men, to the male disciples, to bear witness (despite women's inability in Jewish law) to the resurrection—in a word, women were made "apostles" by Jesus.

Filled with awe and great joy the women came quickly away from the tomb and ran to tell the disciples.

And there, coming to meet them, was Jesus. "Greetings," he said. And the women came up to him and, falling down before him, clasped his feet. Then Jesus said to them, "Do not be afraid; *go and tell my brothers* that they must leave for Galilee; they will see me there." (Mt 28:8–10)

§167. The Risen Jesus and Women — IV

John, the last Gospel writer, is the most detailed, and touching, in his description of Jesus' appearance to Mary Magdalene. She obviously had a deep affection for Jesus: he had cured her and she followed him throughout Galilee and down to Jerusalem, "ministering" *(diēkonoun)* to him; she stayed by him through his bitter death (which, according to some Gospel accounts, the male disciples did not do), attended his burial, returned to his tomb to mourn, "weeping"; when she recognized him she threw her arms around his feet and called him "rabbi," teacher. Jesus reciprocated by appearing to her first of all; after addressing her as "woman," a frequent form of address, he called her by her proper name, Mary; he commissioned her "to go to the brothers and tell them" of his resurrection, commissioning her as an "apostle to the apostles"—in that sense, the "first of the apostles!"

Meanwhile Mary stayed outside near the tomb, weeping. Then, still weeping, she stooped to look inside, and saw two angels in white sitting where the body of Jesus had been, one at the head, the other at the feet. They said, "Woman, why are you weeping?" "They have taken my Lord away," she replied, "and I don't know where they have put him." As she said this she turned round and saw Jesus standing there, though she did not recognize him. Jesus said, "Woman, why are you weeping? Who are you looking for?" Supposing him to be the gardener, she said, "Sir, if you have taken him away, tell me where you have put him, and I will go and remove him." Jesus said, "Mary!" She knew him then and said to him in Hebrew, "Rabbuni!"— which means Teacher. Jesus said to her, "Do not cling to me, because I have not yet ascended to the Father. But *go to the brothers, and tell them:* I am ascending to my Father and your Father, to my God and your God." So Mary of Magdala went and told the disciples that she had seen the Lord and that he had said these things to her. (Jn 20:11–18)

§168. The Risen Jesus and Women — V

In the several evangelists' accounts Jesus is depicted as one learned in the Law, and therefore obviously aware of the stricture against women serving as witnesses. Hence their describing his first appearing to and commissioning of women to bear witness to the most important event of his career cannot be understood as anything but deliberate; it was a dramatic linking of a very clear rejection of the second-class status of women with the center of Jesus' gospel, his resurrection. The portrayal of Jesus' effort to connect centrally these two points is so obvious that it is an overwhelming tribute to *man's* intellectual myopia not to have discerned it effectively in two thousand years.

§169. The Risen Jesus and Women — VI: Apocryphal Writings

As mentioned above (pp. 66f.), apocryphal New Testament writings, especially the earlier ones, may well be the vehicles of certain historical traditions, though it may be difficult at times to discern the historically based element amid the legendary accretions. Further, they tell us something historical about what and how some Christians believed and lived at the time they were written. Hence, it is very interesting to find several apocryphal writings (running from perhaps the time of the writing of the canonical Gospels in the latter part of the first century to the third or fourth centuries) which continue both the traditions concerning the women followers of Jesus, still always including Mary Magdalene: that it was they who first found the empty tomb and they to whom Jesus first appeared, commissioning them to witness to the male disciples—to no avail, of course.

(1) The earliest of these apocryphal writings is the Gospel of Peter, composed anywhere from the latter part of the first century to the middle of the second century. It is strikingly like the three Synoptic Gospels, especially Mark's first "ending," where the women "fearfully fled the tomb" (Mk 16:8), suggesting that the apocryphal Gospel of Peter was written before the "long ending" of Mark (Mk 16:9–20) was composed—probably early in the second century. It should be noted that Mary Magdalene is especially named here a woman disciple of the Lord.

Early in the morning of the Lord's day Mary Magdalene, a woman disciple of the Lord—for fear of the Jews, since (they) were inflamed with wrath, she had not done at the sepulchre of the Lord what women are wont to do for those beloved of them who die—took with her her women friends and came to the sepulchre where he was laid. And they feared lest the Jews should see them, and said, "Although we could not weep and lament on that day when he was crucified, yet let us now do so at his sepulchre. But who will roll away for us the stone also that is set on the entrance to the sepulchre, that we may go in and sit beside him and do what is due? For the stone was great,—and we fear lest any one see us. And if we cannot do so, let us at least put down at the entrance what we bring for a memorial of him and let us weep and lament until we have again gone home." So they went and found the sepulchre opened. And they came near, stooped down and saw there a young man sitting in the midst of the sepulchre, comely and clothed with a brightly shining robe, who said to them, "Wherefore are ye come? Whom seek ye? Not him that was crucified? He is risen and gone. But if ye believe not, stoop this way and see the place where he lay, for he is not here. For he is risen and is gone thither whence he was sent." Then the women fled affrighted. (Gospel of Peter, *New Testament Apocrypha*, Vol. 1, pp. 186–187)

(2) In the second apocryphal writing, the Letter of the Apostles, or Epistula Apostolorum, also written early in the second century, the women, including Mary Magdalene, were not only the first to go and find the empty tomb but also the first to see Jesus. Moreover, here at this very early period stress is placed not only on the women being the first to see the risen Jesus but also very heavily on the fact that they were sent to witness to the male disciples, who were so recalcitrant that Jesus sent a second woman, and finally went along with all of them to convince the male disciples of the resurrection. Was the expansion on this theme here both a reflection of the growing restrictions that women were experiencing in the church at that time and also a rebuke of those male leaders responsible for those restrictions?

He of whom we are witnesses we know as the one crucified in the days of Pontius Pilate and of the prince Archelaus, who was crucified between two thieves and was taken down from the wood of the cross together with them, and was buried in the place of the skull, to which three women came, Sarah, Martha, and Mary Magdalene. They carried ointment to pour out upon his body, weeping and mourning over what had happened. And they approached the tomb and found the stone where it had been rolled away from the tomb, and they opened the door and did not find his body. And as they were mourning and weeping, the Lord appeared to them and said to them, "Do not weep; I am he whom you seek. But let one of you go to your brothers and say 'Come, our Master has risen from the dead.'"

And Mary came to us and told us. And we said to her, "What have we to do with you, O woman? He that is dead and buried, can he then live?" And we did not believe her, that our Saviour had risen from the dead.

Then she went back to our Lord and said to him, "None of them believed me concerning your resurrection." And he said to her, "Let another one of you go to them." And Sarah came and gave us the same news, and we accused her of lying. And she returned to our Lord and spoke to him as Mary had.

Then the Lord said to Mary and to her sisters, "Let us go to them." And he came and found us inside. . . . And . . . he said to us, "Come, and do not be afraid. I am your teacher whom you, Peter, denied three times; and now do you deny again?" (Epistula Apostolorum, *New Testament Apocrypha*, Vol. 1, pp. 195–196)

(3) The third document was written significantly later and was the product of a definitely Gnostic Christian group, the followers of Mani (Manicheans); it was probably written in the third or fourth

century. Only fragments are still extant, and the only portion of them dealing with the resurrection concerns Jesus' appearance to Mary Magdalene, apparently a development of the story at the end of the canonical Gospel of John. There are several points of special interest in it. For one thing, Mary Magdalene is specifically made "a messenger *(angelos)* for me to these wandering orphans *(orphanos)*," meaning the eleven male disciples. Further, she is asked to do this as a service, a *leitourgia* to Jesus. Could there be a deliberate support here for women's involvement in leadership roles in liturgy and an implicit rebuke for those church leaders who did not allow it?

Something similar may perhaps also be the case with the reference to Mary Magdalene's being made a "messenger," as far as women having a leadership role over men is concerned. The male disciples, spoken of as "wandering orphans," are really put down as badly in need of the guidance of this woman. For the women, however, it is noted that they no doubt will meet stiff resistance from the men and that consequently they must develop all their "skill *(technē)* and advice until thou hast brought the sheep to the shepherd," again placing the woman in a much superior, indeed, "pastoral," position vis-à-vis the male disciples, who are suspected by Jesus of "having their wits gone." Even Peter is placed under Mary Magdalene's evangelistic *(eu-angelios)* tutelage.

"Mariam, Mariam, know me: do not touch me. Stem the tears of thy eyes and know me that I am thy master. Only touch me not, for I have not yet seen the face of my Father. Thy God was not stolen away, according to the thoughts of thy littleness; thy God did not die, rather he mastered death. I am not the gardener. . . . Cast this sadness away from thee and do this service *(leitourgia):* be a messenger *(angelos)* for me to these wandering orphans *(orphanos)*. Make haste rejoicing, and go unto the Eleven. Thou shalt find them gathered together on the bank of the Jordan. The traitor persuaded them to be fishermen as they were at first and to lay down their nets with which they caught men unto life. Say to them: 'Arise, let us go, it is your brother that calls you.' If they scorn my brotherhood, say to them: 'It is your Master.' If they disregard my mastership, say to them: 'It is your Lord.' Use all skill *(technē)* and advice until thou hast brought the sheep to the shepherd. If thou seest that their wits are gone, draw Simon Peter unto thee; say to him, 'Remember what I uttered between thee and me . . . in the Mount of Olives: I have something to say, I have none to whom to say it.' " (Gospel of Mani, *New Testament Apocrypha*, Vol. 1, pp. 353–354)

§170. Mary Magdalene

It should be noted that Mary Magdalene, that is, Mary from the town of Magdala, is named in all four of the canonical Gospels.

(There is no solid reason to identify her with the sinful woman of Lk 7:37–50 or Mary of Bethany.) In every instance (there are a total of twelve in the four Gospels) except Lk 8:2, the reference is in connection either with her being at the crucifixion and observing Jesus' burial, or with her seeing the empty tomb and the risen Jesus—the former being mentioned as a preparation to recording the latter. Each time, Mary Magdalene is either named alone or is at the head of the list (with the exception of the special situation of Jn 19:25, where the focus is specifically on Jesus' mother Mary). Moreover, all of the lists vary from evangelist to evangelist, no two lists ever being the same; however, Mary Magdalene is always listed. Scholars conclude that there was a strong and widespread tradition that Jesus appeared first of all to Mary Magdalene and that she therefore held a place of honor in the early Christian community—thereby explaining her appearance on all the lists of women in the Gospels, and her being first on all save one.

(1) And many women were there, watching from a distance, the same women who had followed Jesus from Galilee and ministered to him. Among them were Mary of Magdala, Mary the mother of James and Joseph, and the mother of Zebedee's sons. (Mt 27:55–56)

(2) So Joseph took the body, wrapped it in a clean shroud and put it in his own new tomb which he had hewn out of the rock. He then rolled a large stone across the entrance of the tomb and went away. Now Mary of Magdala and the other Mary were there, sitting opposite the sepulchre. (Mt 27:59–61)

(3) After the sabbath, and towards dawn on the first day of the week, Mary of Magdala and the other Mary went to visit the sepulchre. (Mt 28:1)

(4) There were some women watching from a distance. Among them were Mary of Magdala, Mary who was the mother of James the younger and Joset, and Salome. These used to follow him and minister to him when he was in Galilee. (Mk 15:40–41)

(5) He granted the corpse to Joseph who bought a shroud, took Jesus down from the cross, wrapped him in the shroud and laid him in a tomb which had been hewn out of the rock. He then rolled a stone against the entrance to the tomb. Mary of Magdala and Mary the mother of Joset were watching and took note of where he was laid. (Mk 15:45–47)

(6) When the sabbath was over, Mary of Magdala, Mary the mother of James, and Salome, bought spices with which to go and anoint him. And very early in the morning on the first day of the week they went to the tomb, just as the sun was rising. (Mk 16:1–2)

(7) Having risen in the morning on the first day of the week, he appeared first to Mary of Magdala from whom he had cast out seven devils. (Mk 16:9)

(8) With him went the Twelve, as well as certain women who had been cured of evil spirits and ailments: Mary surnamed the Magdalene, from whom seven demons had gone out, Joanna the wife of Herod's steward Chuza, Susanna, and several others who ministered to them out of their own resources. (Lk 8:1-3)

(9) When the women returned from the tomb they told all this to the Eleven and to all the others. The women were Mary of Magdala, Joanna, and Mary the mother of James. The other women with them also told the apostles, but this story of theirs seemed pure nonsense, and they did not believe them. (Lk 24:9-11)

(10) Near the cross of Jesus stood his mother and his mother's sister, Mary the wife of Clopas, and Mary of Magdala. Seeing his mother and the disciple he loved standing near her, Jesus said to his mother, "Woman, this is your son." Then to the disciple he said, "This is your mother." And from that moment the disciple made a place for her in his home. (Jn 19:25-27)

(11) It was very early on the first day of the week and still dark, when Mary of Magdala came to the tomb. She . . . saw Jesus standing there. . . . Jesus said to her, . . . "Go to the brothers, and tell them . . ." So Mary of Magdala went and told the disciples that she had seen the Lord and that he had said these things to her. (Jn 20:1,15,17,18)

§171. The Apostle to the Apostles

As a result of Mary Magdalene's role as one sent *(apostellein)* by Jesus to witness to the male apostles, as recorded in the canonical Gospel of John 20:17, she was the only woman besides Jesus' mother on whose feast the Creed was recited in the Western Church (Josef Andreas Jungmann, *The Mass of the Roman Rite,* p. 470, n. 55; Benziger Brothers, 1951). The term "apostle" in reference to Magdalene occurs often in the well-known ninth-century life of her by Rabanus Maurus: Jesus commissioned her an apostle to the apostles *(apostola apostolorum)*—cf. Migne, *Patrologia Latina,* Vol. 112, col. 1474B; she did not delay in carrying out the office of the apostolate to which she was commissioned (col. 1475A); her fellow apostles were evangelized with the news of the resurrection of the Messiah (col. 1475B); she was raised to the honor of the apostolate and was commissioned an evangelist *(evangelisto)* of the resurrection (col. 1479C). Even the acerbic Bernard of Clairvaux (twelfth century) refers to her as the "apostle to the apostles" (Migne, *Patrologia Latina,* Vol. 183, col. 1148).

Rabanus Maurus really simply carried on a tradition attested to many centuries earlier. Around the end of the second century or the beginning of the third, Hippolytus of Rome also commented on Jesus' appearing first to Mary Magdalene, and the other women, and spoke of Mary Magdalene, and the other women—and symbolically, Eve—as *apostles* and *evangelists* (proclaimers of the gospel, *evangelium*). The extant text is in a Slavonic translation, with variations in an Armenian translation:

Christ himself sent [Mary Magdalene], so that even women become the apostles of Christ and the deficiency of the first Eve's disobedience was made evident by this justifying obedience. O wondrous adviser, Eve becomes an apostle! Already recognizing the cunning of the serpent, henceforth the tree of knowledge did not seduce her, but having accepted the tree of promise, she partook of being judged worthy to be a part of Christ. . . . Now Eve is a helpmate through the Gospel! Therefore too the women proclaimed the Gospel [from here on the Armenian translation has a few differences; see below]. But the basic fact was this, that Eve's custom was to proclaim lies and not truth. What's this? For us the women proclaim the resurrection as the Gospel. Then Christ appeared to them and said: Peace be with you. I have appeared to the women and have sent them to you as apostles.

[The differences in the Armenian translation are as follows:]
Therefore women too proclaimed the Gospel to the disciples. Therefore, however, they believed them mistaken. . . . What kind of a new thing is it for you, O women, to tell of the resurrection? But that they might not be judged mistaken again, but as speaking in truth, Christ appeared to them and said: Peace be with you. Wherewith he showed it as true: As I appeared to the women, sending them to you, I have desired to send them as apostles. (Hippolytus, in *Die griechischen christlichen Schriftsteller der ersten drei Jahrhunderte*, 1, 1, pp. 354f.; Berlin, 1897)

§172. Mary Magdalene in Gnostic Christian Literature

Besides the strong, positive tradition about Mary Magdalene in the canonical Gospels and the orthodox Christian writers quoted above, and others, there is a similarly strong tradition about her among Gnostic Christians, already amply displayed above (§169) in the third- or fourth-century Manichean document wherein Mary Magdalene is sent by Jesus as a messenger *(angelos)* to "evangelize" *(euangelizein)* the male disciples with all possible skill.

a. Mary Magdalene, Teacher of the Apostles

This tradition of Mary Magdalene's superiority to the male disciples begins even earlier in the apocryphal Gospel named after her, the Gospel of Mary, probably a second-century Gnostic Christian document. In it, after Jesus commanded the disciples to go and preach the gospel and then left them, the men played the stereotypical female role—not knowing what to do and crying; whereas Mary played the stereotypical male role—confidently knowing what to do and encouraging the men. At first she succeeded admirably, but then, as she expounded her specialized knowledge from Jesus, jealousy was engendered among the male disciples, particularly Andrew and Peter, who attacked her for thinking that she, a woman, might have better access to the truths of Christ than they, the men, did. Mary responded bluntly and was supported by another apostle, Levi, who rebuked Peter for being so hot-tempered and attacking Mary Magdalene. In the end they all went off to preach the gospel, so that Mary Magdalene prevailed.

But they were grieved and wept sore, saying: "How shall we go to the heathen and preach the Gospel of the Kingdom of the Son of man? If he was not spared at all, how shall we be spared?"

Then arose Mary, saluted them all, and spake to her brethren: "Weep not, be not sorrowful, neither be ye undecided, for his grace will be with you all and will protect you. Let us rather praise his greatness, for he hath made us ready, and made us to be men."

When Mary said this, she turned their mind to good, and they began to discuss the words of the [Saviour].

[Peter now says to Mary, "We know that the Saviour loved you above all other women." He asks her to recount the revelations that she has received from the Savior, which he and the others have not heard. Mary tells how she saw the Lord in a vision and spoke with him. There follows a lengthy, complicated Gnostic conversation between Jesus and Mary.]

When Mary had said this, she was silent, so that (thus) the Saviour had spoken with her up to this point. But Andrew answered and said to the brethren: "Tell me, what think ye with regard to what she says? I at least do not believe that the Saviour said this. For certainly these doctrines have other meanings." Peter in answer spoke with reference to things of this kind, and asked them about the Saviour: "Did he then speak privily with a woman rather than with us, and not openly? Shall we turn about and all hearken unto her? Has he preferred her over against us?"

Then Mary wept and said to Peter: "My brother Peter, what dost thou then believe? Dost thou believe that I imagined this myself in my heart, or that I would lie about the Saviour?" Levi answered (and) said to Peter: "Peter, thou hast ever been of a hasty temper. Now I see how thou dost exercise thyself against the woman like the adversaries. But if the Saviour hath made her worthy, who then art thou, that thou reject her? Certainly the Saviour knows her surely enough. Therefore did he love her more than us. Let us rather be ashamed, put on the perfect Man, [form ourselves (?)] as he charged us, and proclaim the Gospel, without requiring any further command or any further law beyond that which the Saviour said (Gr.: neither limiting nor legislating, as the Saviour said)."

But [when Levi had said this,] they set about going to preach and to proclaim (Gr.: When he had thus spoken, Levi went away and began to preach). (Gospel of Mary, *New Testament Apocrypha*, Vol. 1, pp. 342–344)

b. Mary Magdalene, Most Beloved Disciple

In the above citation Peter admits that "the Saviour loved [Mary Magdalene] above all other women." He could not bring himself to say that Jesus loved Mary Magdalene more than him, but a little later Levi does make such an admission: "But if the Saviour hath made her worthy, who then art thou, that thou reject her? Certainly the Saviour knows her surely enough. Therefore did he love her more than us." Earlier it was noted (see §152) that in the early third-century Gnostic Christian document Pistis Sophia, Jesus said, "But Mary Magdalene and John, the maiden *(parthenos)*, will surpass all my disciples and all men who shall receive mysteries." Beyond these there is a further Gnostic Christian apocryphal Gospel, the third-century Gospel of Philip, in which Mary Magdalene is said to be called the companion of Jesus and loved by Christ "more than all the disciples." There is also a startling passage in which Christ is said to "kiss her often on the mouth." In this Gnostic Christian document this action obviously has a spiritualized significance, but still, Mary Magdalene is the recipient of the most intimate favors (graces) of Christ.

There were three who always walked with the Lord: Mary his mother and her sister and Magdalene, the one who was called his companion. His sister and his mother and his companion were each a Mary. . . . And the companion of the [Savior is] Mary Magdalene. [But Christ loved her] more than [all] the disciples [and used to] kiss her [often] on her [mouth]. The rest of the [disciples were offended] by it and [expressed disapproval]. They said to him, *"Why do you love her more than all of us?"* The Savior answered and said to them, *"Why do I not love you like her?"* When a blind man and one who sees are both together in darkness, they are no different from one another. When the light comes, then he who sees will see the light, and he who is blind will remain in darkness. (Gospel of Philip, *Nag Hammadi Library*, pp. 135–136, 138; italics added)

c. Peter's Jealousy of Mary Magdalene

In the canonical Gospel of John, Mary Magdalene, rather than Peter, is the one to whom the risen Christ first appears, just as it is Martha rather than Peter who declares Jesus to be the Son of God, giving in the Johannine Christian community a certain priority of Mary Magdalene and other women over Peter (see §180). This does not reflect anything negative toward Peter in the Johannine Christian community, but it does probably indicate a conscious stress on the importance of women, especially Mary Magdalene, rather than

Peter, whose importance in the other Gospels was probably known to the final redactor of John. As will be discussed further below, it should also be recalled that there are several lengthy and important passages in John's Gospel which focus on women, including Mary Magdalene's first discovery of the empty tomb, her reporting of it to Peter and the others, and Jesus' appearing to her alone and commissioning her to "go to the brothers, and tell them." It was probably the next sentence (or the tradition behind the sentence) in John, which said, "So Mary of Magdala went and told the disciples that she had seen the Lord and that he had said these things to her" (Jn 20:18), that gave rise to the expanded report in the apocryphal Gospel of Mary about Mary Magdalene reporting her conversation with Jesus to Peter and the other disciples. Further, the Gospel of John would have been found very attractive by Gnostic Christians, for, like them, it stressed light and life and a very "spiritual" kind of theology—with many long and complicated discourses placed in the mouth of Jesus. Hence it is not surprising to find Gnostic Christians, like John's Gospel, giving a prominence to Mary Magdalene and also speaking of Peter's fits of jealousy toward her.

Besides the male disciples' in general taking offense at Mary Magdalene's favored position with Jesus recorded in the Gospel of Philip, cited just above, and the specific resentment voiced by Andrew and Peter in the above-cited Gospel of Mary, there is also the extremely vicious attack on women prophets attributed to Peter in the apocryphal Kerygmata Petrou (see §291). Further, Peter's hostility toward women in general and Mary Magdalene in particular is referred to twice (chs. 36 and 72) in the early third-century Gnostic Christian Pistis Sophia, and reaches a kind of climax in the statement attributed to him in the third-century Gnostic Christian Gospel of Thomas, wherein Peter wants to excommunicate Mary Magdalene, *because she is a woman,* but Jesus defends her (in a way peculiar to the later ascetic time). Again the question naturally arises: was this a protest on the part of some Christian women, and their male sympathizers, against what they saw to be the rising restriction of women and even misogynism exercised by church leaders, who prided themselves on their rootage in the apostles, the chief of whom was Peter, as over against the feminism of Jesus? The solution for many non-Gnostic as well as Gnostic Christian women (as will be discussed below, §314 and pp. 341ff.) was in becoming a man, a male *(vir)*—that is, celibate. However, the celibate Gnostic Christian women were less willing

to accept subordination to the male hierarch than were the orthodox catholic women.

> Simon Peter said to them: Let Mary go forth from among us, for women
> are not worthy of the life. Jesus said: Behold, I shall lead her, that I may make
> her male, in order that she also may become a living spirit like you males.
> For every woman who makes herself male shall enter into the kingdom of
> heaven. (Gospel of Thomas, *New Testament Apocrypha*, Vol. 1, p. 522)

§173. Resurrection and Jairus' Daughter

The intimate connection of women with resurrection from the
dead is not limited in the Gospels to the resurrection of Jesus. There
are accounts of three other resurrections in the Gospels—each closely
involving a woman (as does also the resurrection of Tabitha by Peter,
Acts 9:36–42). In one Jesus raised a young girl from the dead; in the
other two he raised persons from the dead largely because of women.

The most obvious connection of a woman with a resurrection
account is that of the raising of the daughter of Jairus. In this story,
which is contained in all three Synoptic Gospels, the daughter is
initially said only to be extremely ill; but Jesus is delayed, and she is
reported dead. Jesus had already agreed to come to her; he is not
deterred by the death report. He raises her to life. Thus Jesus makes
clear that the resurrection is for women as well as for men.

A small detail is of particular interest here. Only in the case of
Jairus' daughter did Jesus touch the corpse—which made him ritually
unclean. In the cases of the two men Jesus did not touch them, but
merely said, "Young man, I say to you, arise," or, "Lazarus, come
out." One must at least wonder why Jesus chose to violate the laws
for ritual purity in order to help a woman, but not a man. That this
point is intended by Jesus, or at least so understood by all the early
Christian communities, is corroborated by the fact that in the middle
of the account of the raising of Jairus' daughter in all three of the
Synoptic Gospels is placed the story of the curing of the woman with
the twelve-year flow of blood, which carries a similar message: that,
as far as Jesus is concerned, touching, or being touched by, a woman
with a flow of blood does not make one unclean before God.

> When Jesus had crossed again in the boat to the other side, a large crowd
> gathered round him and he stayed by the lakeside. Then one of the syna-
> gogue officials came up, Jairus by name, and seeing him, fell at his feet and
> pleaded with him earnestly, saying, "My little daughter is desperately sick.
> Do come and lay your hands on her to make her better and save her life."
> Jesus went with him and a large crowd followed him. . . . [here is inserted

the account of the curing of the woman with the twelve-year flow of blood].

While he was still speaking some people arrived from the house of the synagogue official to say, "Your daughter is dead: why put the Master to any further trouble?" But Jesus had overheard this remark of theirs and he said to the official, "Do not be afraid; only have faith." And he allowed no one to go with him except Peter and James and John the brother of James. So they came to the official's house and Jesus noticed all the commotion, with people weeping and wailing unrestrainedly. He went in and said to them, "Why all this commotion and crying? The child is not dead, but asleep." But they laughed at him. So he turned them all out and, taking with him the child's father and mother and his own companions, he went into the place where the child lay. And taking the child by the hand he said to her, "Talitha, kum!" which means "Little girl, I tell you to get up." The little girl got up at once and began to walk about, for she was twelve years old. At this they were overcome with astonishment, and he ordered them strictly not to let anyone know about it, and told them to give her something to eat. (Mk 5:21–24, 35–43; cf. Mt 9:18–26; Lk 8:40–56)

§174. The Widow of Nain

Again Luke alone records an event dealing with Jesus and a woman, the raising from the dead of the son of the widow of Nain. The plight of this woman should be recalled: she was now alone in the world; she had no male to provide for her or to protect her with legal guardianship, which were almost absolute necessities in that society. For this reason, widows were considered the poorest of the poor. Further, despite the large crowd in the funeral procession who would be there to perform a good deed, a *mitzvah,* she was by custom thought to have caused the early death of her child (he is called "young man," *neaniskē,* by Jesus) by her sins—and this on top of the loss of her husband. Jesus sees all this and is touchingly described by Luke as being moved with pity for her and asking her not to cry. When Jesus raises the young man, he *gives him back to his mother;* she is clearly the center of concern. Scholars note that this story is very similar to the raising of the only son of a widow by the prophet Elijah (1 Kings 17:17–24), even to the use of the phrase "gave him to his mother." Those who reject the miraculous suggest here is the source of the story, especially since resurrections are also attributed to Tannaitic rabbis (rabbis of Jesus' time) in remembrance of Elijah and Elisha. Those who don't reject the miraculous out of hand would see the Elijah story as a source of some of the *form* of Luke's description. Even the former would often grant a historical kernel of Jesus' great concern for the welfare of sonless widows, and doubtless some particular instance. Luke of course affirms the resurrection.

Soon afterward he went to a town called Nain, and his disciples and a large crowd accompanied him. As he approached the gate of the town a dead man was being carried out, the only son of a widowed mother. A considerable crowd of townsfolk were with her. The Lord was moved with pity upon seeing her and said to her, "Do not cry." Then he stepped forward and touched the litter; at this, the bearers halted. He said, "Young man, I bid you get up." The dead man sat up and began to speak. Then Jesus gave him back to his mother. Fear seized them all and they began to praise God. "A great prophet has risen among us," they said; and, "God has visited his people." This was the report that spread about him throughout Judea and the surrounding country. (Lk 7:11–17)

§175. The Resurrection of Lazarus

The third, and in some ways most important, account of a resurrection by Jesus is that of Lazarus, at the request of his sisters, Martha and Mary. From the first it was Martha and Mary who sent for Jesus because of Lazarus' illness. But when Jesus finally came, Lazarus was four days dead. Martha met Jesus and pleaded for his resurrection: "Lord, if you had been here, my brother would not have died. And even now I know that whatever you ask from God, God will give you." Mary, who had been *sitting,* in mourning, hastened to Jesus and fell *at his feet* in supplication (both italicized elements reminiscent of Mary's posture in the Lk 10:38–42 story of Martha and Mary) and said much the same—it is interesting that Jesus sent a special call to Mary. John then records how Jesus was deeply moved by a woman's, Mary's, suffering and weeping—as with the widow of Nain. Jesus was so moved that he also cried, and then proceeded to raise Lazarus to life.

A further important point to be observed in this account is in Jesus' conversation with Martha after she pleaded for the resurrection of Lazarus. Jesus declared himself to be the resurrection ("I am the resurrection and the life"), the only time he did so that is recorded in the Gospels. According to John, Jesus here revealed the central event, the central message, in the Gospel—the resurrection, his resurrection, his being the resurrection—to a woman! and thereafter performed a resurrection at least partially at her request.

It should be further noted that Martha here also makes the same public profession of Jesus being the Messiah and the Son of God (*su ei ho christos ho huios tou theou*—Jn 11:27) as Peter is recorded to have made (*su ei ho christos ho huios tou theou*—Mt 16:16). It is especially impressive that exactly the same words are used in Greek, since there normally is very little relationship or similarity between the Gospel of John and any of the three Synoptic Gospels. This striking identity is further underlined by the fact that in the passages parallel to Mt 16:16, found in Mark (Mk 8:27–30) and Luke (Lk 9:18–21), the confession by Peter is considerably less in magnitude, i.e., Peter confesses Jesus to be the Messiah, but not the Son of God. (Luke, however, does record that evil spirits driven out of sick persons by Jesus proclaimed, " 'You are the Son of God' . . . because they knew that he was the Messiah"—Lk 4:41.) According to Matthew, several of the disciples together had earlier proclaimed Jesus "a son of God" (*theou huios ei*—Mt 14:33), but since no definite article was used *(ho huios theou),* as in both Mt 16:16 by Peter and in Jn 11:27 by Martha, this declaration has a lesser significance. Raymond E. Brown ("Roles of Women in the Fourth Gospel," pp. 692f.), after noting that according to John, Jesus first appeared to Mary Magdalene, rather than to Peter, as Luke (Lk 24:34) and his missionary colleague Paul (1 Cor 15:5) report, stated: "Giving to a woman a role traditionally associated with Peter may well be a deliberate emphasis on John's part, for substitution is also exemplified in the story of Lazarus, Mary, and Martha. . . . Thus, if other Christian communities thought of Peter as the one who made a supreme confession of Jesus as the Son of God and the one to whom the risen Jesus first appeared, the Johannine community associated such memories with heroines like Martha and Mary Magdalene."

There was a man named Lazarus who lived in the village of Bethany with the two sisters, Mary and Martha, and he was ill. It was the same Mary, the sister of the sick man Lazarus, who anointed the Lord with ointment and wiped his feet with her hair. The sisters sent this message to Jesus, "Lord, the man you love is ill." On receiving the message, Jesus said, "This sickness will end, not in death but in God's glory, and through it the Son of God will be glorified."

Jesus loved Martha and her sister and Lazarus, yet when he heard that Lazarus was ill he stayed where he was for two more days before saying to the disciples, "Let us go to Judaea." The disciples said, "Rabbi, it is not long since the Jews wanted to stone you; are you going back again?" Jesus replied: "Are there not twelve hours in the day? A man can walk in the daytime without stumbling because he has the light of this world to see by; but if he walks at night he stumbles, because there is no light to guide him."

He said that and then added, "Our friend Lazarus is resting, I am going to wake him." The disciples said to him, "Lord, if he is able to rest he is sure to get better." The phrase Jesus used referred to the death of Lazarus, but they thought that by "rest" he meant "sleep," so Jesus put it plainly, "Lazarus is dead; and for your sake I am glad I was not there because now you will believe. But let us go to him." Then Thomas—known as the Twin—said to the other disciples, "Let us go too, and die with him."

On arriving, Jesus found that Lazarus had been in the tomb for four days already. Bethany is only about two miles from Jerusalem, and many Jews had come to Martha and Mary to sympathise with them over their brother. When Martha heard that Jesus had come she went to meet him. Mary remained sitting in the house. Martha said to Jesus, "If you had been here, my brother would not have died, but I know that, even now, whatever you ask of God, he will grant you." "Your brother," said Jesus to her, "will rise again." Martha said, "I know he will rise again at the resurrection on the last day." Jesus said: "I am the resurrection. If anyone believes in me, even though he dies he will live, and whoever lives and believes in me will never die. Do you believe this?" "Yes, Lord," she said, "I believe that you are the Christ, the Son of God, the one who was to come into this world."

When she had said this, she went and called her sister Mary, saying in a low voice, "The Master is here and wants to see you." Hearing this, Mary got up quickly and went to him. Jesus had not yet come into the village; he was still at the place where Martha had met him. When the Jews who were in the house sympathising with Mary saw her get up so quickly and go out, they followed her, thinking that she was going to the tomb to weep there.

Mary went to Jesus, and as soon as she saw him she threw herself at this feet, saying, "Lord, if you had been here, my brother would not have died." At the sight of her tears, and those of the Jews who followed her, Jesus said in great distress, with a sigh that came straight from the heart, "Where have you put him?" They said, "Lord, come and see." Jesus wept; and the Jews said, "See how much he loved him!" But there were some who remarked, "He opened the eyes of the blind man, could he not have prevented this man's death?" Still sighing, Jesus reached the tomb: it was a cave with a stone to close the opening. Jesus said, "Take the stone away." Martha said to him, "Lord, by now he will smell; this is the fourth day." Jesus replied, "Have I not told you that if you believe you will see the glory of God?" So they took away the stone. Then Jesus lifted up his eyes and said: "Father, I thank you for hearing my prayer. I knew indeed that you always hear me, but I speak for the sake of all these who stand round me, so that they may believe it was you who sent me."

When he had said this, he cried in a loud voice, "Lazarus, here! Come out!" The dead man came out, his feet and hands bound with bands of stuff and a cloth round his face. Jesus said to them, "Unbind him, let him go free." (Jn 11:1–44)

2. THE ATTITUDE TOWARD WOMEN REFLECTED BY THE GOSPEL WRITERS AND THEIR SOURCES

As outlined earlier, one of the contributions of modern scriptural scholarship is the notion that the Gospels are not simple accounts of the words and actions of Jesus as related by several different eyewitnesses. The fact that they are many-layered faith statements brought together from several sources, written and oral, and put into their present four forms by at least four different Gospel writers means that they will tell us something not only of the attitude of Jesus toward women but also of the attitudes of the evangelists and their sources. At times, in certain accounts, it is difficult to determine whether it is Jesus' or the evangelists' or their sources' attitudes that are reflected, but for the most part those passages which rather clearly reveal Jesus' own attitude have been treated above. However, many passages that in some way deal with women still remain to be dealt with. They will be listed below by Gospel, and will be analyzed where pertinent for any additional light they cast on the attitude toward women expressed by the Gospel writer and his sources. Often this will have to be traced in some form ultimately back to Jesus.

By presenting the material systematically according to each Gospel, we anticipate that a picture of the attitude toward women of each evangelist and his sources will emerge. The attitude of each can be compared to that of the others, and to that of Jesus—insofar as his attitude can be distilled out and seen separately from those of the evangelists and their sources.

The first Gospel to be presented will be John's, because it has by far the smallest number of accounts that deal with women, and they are almost totally unrelated to the material in the three Synoptic Gospels, outside of the final section of all the Gospels which treat the passion and resurrection of Jesus. Next treated will be Mark, since it is thought by most scholars to be the oldest of the Gospels, and it is third in number of passages dealing with women. Then will come Matthew, because it is second in number of women passages, followed by Luke with the highest number.

a. The Gospel According to John

John's Gospel was the last of the four Gospels to be written (probably between A.D. 90 and 100). Much of its material is different from the other three Gospels, the Synoptics, and it tends to report the teaching of Jesus in long discourses. It is third in overall length, being about 75 percent of the length of Luke, the longest Gospel. However, John contains far fewer accounts that deal with women or the "feminine"—only nine. On the other hand, several of these accounts are quite long, are important, and are very sympathetic toward women. In fact, these nine passages are 122 verses in length, compared to Mark's 114 (Matthew has 180 verses and Luke 220).

§176. Wedding at Cana

See pp. 176f. for an analysis of Jesus' attitude toward his mother, his support of marriage, and John's probable balancing of that against ascetic elements of his time which denigrated marriage. John alone records this event. (Jn 2:1–12)

§177. Samaritan Woman

See §146 for a discussion of this long and important account, which only John records. Here we find Jesus going out of his way to enter into a conversation with a strange woman, to reveal himself to her as the Messiah, and to make her an instrument for the preaching of his "good news." (Jn 4:5–42)

§178. Jesus in a Female Image

See §119 for an analysis of the passage in which Jesus referred to himself with the maternal image of giving drink at the breast. (Jn 7:37–39)

§179. Woman Taken in Adultery

Although the report of Jesus' encounter with the woman seized in the act of adultery is usually located in John (Jn 7:53 to 8:11), it is the scholarly consensus that John certainly did not write it, that it has many characteristics akin to the Synoptics' style, and that there is some manuscript evidence that it originally might have been located in Luke, after Lk 21:38. See §143 for a discussion of this passage.

§180. The Resurrection of Lazarus

See §175, where we have analyzed the profound involvement of women in the raising of Lazarus by Jesus, Jesus' revealing of himself as "the resurrection," to a woman, and his being proclaimed by her to be the Messiah and the Son of God. Only John has this account. (Jn 11:1–44)

§181. The Anointment of Jesus by Mary of Bethany

See §§153 and 154 for a discussion of Mary's "wasteful" anointing of Jesus and the defense of her by Jesus. (Jn 12:1–8; cf. Mk 14:3–9; Mt 26:6–13)

§182. Women in Jesus' Passion and Resurrection

a. Women at the Foot of the Cross

See §157 for an analysis of John's account of the women present at Jesus' crucifixion and death. Even though many scholars believe that John's adding the presence of the one male disciple to the group of women at the crucifixion is unhistorical, it should be noted that with all the other evangelists John does locate the women there. John, like Mark and Matthew, lists three women's names; they are not exactly the same as those on the other lists, but Mary Magdalene is there, as in all the lists. This is the only list on which Mary Magdalene is not placed first (see §170). In John's account, Jesus' concern to find his widowed mother a home was almost the last thing he spoke of. (Jn 19:25–27; cf. Mk 15:40–41; Mt 27:55–56; Lk 23:49)

b. Women First Witnesses to the Empty Tomb

See §170 for analyses of Mary Magdalene's witness to the empty tomb. All the other evangelists also record this event, and, as in the other accounts, Mary Magdalene is named first in the list of women at the empty tomb—only in John the list begins and ends with Mary Magdalene. (Jn 20:1–10; cf. Mk 16:1–2; Mt 28:1–8; Lk 24:1–8)

c. Women Testify to Male Disciples About Jesus' Resurrection

See §166 for a discussion of the women's testifying about the resurrection of Jesus to the male disciples. The traditions are extremely various on this matter. (1) The earliest of the accounts in the Apostolic Writings, i.e., Paul's First Letter to the Corinthians, ch. 15:5–8, does not even mention the women in connection with the resurrection. (2) The earliest Gospel, Mark, says the women were frightened, ran away and "said nothing to a soul," though obviously they did eventually say something to someone—how else could the existence of the Gospel account be explained? (3) In Matthew it simply says they "ran to tell the disciples," and on the way were met by Jesus and commissioned by him to "go and tell my brothers"— no indication of the brothers' reaction. (4) Luke, written, like Matthew, between the time of the writing of Mark and John, records that a whole group of women told the apostles of the empty tomb, "but this story of theirs seemed pure nonsense, and they did not believe them; Peter, however, went running to the tomb." (5) In John, the latest Gospel, Mary Magdalene ran and told Peter and "the other disciple"; their response was simply to run and see for themselves, not necessarily implying that they did not believe her, but it seems likely so. (6) The ending added to Mark's Gospel (Mk 16:1–9), written probably early in the second century, sounds in some ways much like Luke's account and in some ways like John's. "But they did not believe her [Mary Magdalene] when they heard her say that he was alive and that she had seen him."

Furthermore, of the four Gospels' accounts, Mark records that an angel in the empty tomb commissioned the women to testify to the male disciples; Matthew does so as well, but also adds that Jesus himself likewise commissioned the women; Luke mentions two angels in the empty tomb but records no commissioning at all, though in fact the women do testify to the male disciples; John reports the presence of the angels, but records only Jesus' commissioning of Mary Magdalene. Thus, three of the four Gospels speak of a commissioning of the women: one (Mark) by an angel, one (John) by Jesus, and one (Matthew) by both; one (Luke) does not record such a commissioning. In fact, however, according to Luke the women did nevertheless testify, and according to Mark they did not, despite the commission —though the matter is confused here because of the strong possibility of a lost original ending and because the second-century ending does record a testifying by Mary Magdalene.

It is perhaps not possible to speak of an original version of the account of the women's commissioning and testifying. Rather, perhaps it is best to speak of several traditions that fed into the different Gospel accounts and that may or may not have been significantly adapted by the Gospel writers. What is clear is that all three elements —(1) the commissioning of the women to testify concerning the empty tomb and/or resurrection to the male disciples; (2) their actual testifying; (3) a disbelieving response to the women by the men—are strongly represented in the Gospel accounts (though not at all in Paul). Mark, without the "lost" or added ending, is the least supportive of the women's role in these matters; the other three are equally, though differently, supportive. One would have to conclude that the tradition concerning this *very* significant involvement of women in this most essential matter of Christian belief and their put-down by the men grew so much stronger—either in times after, or places other, or both—than when Paul and Mark wrote that they found a prominent place in the later three Gospels, and in the later ending of Mark. (Jn 20:18; Mk 16:7, 11; Mt 28:16–20; Lk 24:9–11)

d. The Risen Jesus Appears to Women

See pp. 203ff. for a discussion of the risen Jesus' appearance first to women (one or more). (Jn 20:11–18; cf. Mk 16:9; Mt 28:9–10)

Raymond E. Brown notes ("Roles of Women in the Fourth Gospel," p. 692) that "essential to the apostolate in the mind of Paul were the two components of having seen the risen Jesus and having been sent to proclaim him; this is the implicit logic of 1 Cor 9:1–2; 15:8–11; Gal 1:11–16. A key to Peter's importance in the apostolate was the tradition that he was the first to see the risen Jesus (1 Cor 15:5; Lk 24:34). More than any other Gospel, John revises this tradition about Peter. . . . In John (and in Matthew) Mary Magdalene is sent by the risen Lord. . . . True, this is not a mission to the whole world; but Mary Magdalene comes close to meeting the basic Pauline requirements of an apostle; and it is she, not Peter, who is the first to see the risen Jesus. . . . The tradition that Jesus appeared first to Mary Magdalene has a good chance of being historical—he remembered first this representative of the women who had not deserted him during the Passion. The priority given to Peter in Paul and Luke is a priority among those who became official witnesses to the Resurrection. The secondary place given to the tradition of an appearance to a woman or women probably reflects the fact that women did not serve at first as official preachers of the Church—a fact that would make the creation of an appearance to a woman unlikely."

§183. Conclusion

Although John's Gospel has the least number of passages about women (the number of verses is slightly more than Mark's, however), it takes a strongly pro-woman stance. It contains a large number of events peculiar to it in which women played extremely important roles: According to John, Jesus performed his first miracle at the bidding of a woman (wedding feast at Cana, Jn 2:1–12); the first recorded effective woman evangelist is sent out by Jesus (the Samaritan woman, Jn 4:5–42); Jesus revealed himself uniquely to a woman as the resurrection (Martha, Jn 11:25), and for the first time, in John's Gospel, as the Messiah (the Samaritan woman, Jn 4:26); Jesus was proclaimed publicly by a woman (Martha, Jn 11:27)—rather than Peter—to be the Messiah, and also the Son of God. Likewise, rather than appearing first to Peter, the risen Jesus is reported by John as having appeared first to a woman (Mary Magdalene, Jn 20:11–18), who then was sent by Jesus to bear witness to Peter! This latter point, the first appearance of the risen Jesus to a woman, however, John's Gospel has in common with Matthew's, although there the account is not nearly so detailed and moving as John's. Moreover, Jesus described himself with a very female, maternal, image (Jn 7:37–38).

It is perhaps also worth noting that although the account about Jesus and the adulterous woman (Jn 7:53 to 8:11) was clearly not written by John, in the greatest number of manuscripts it ended up being located there, indicating perhaps that many early Christians felt that John's Gospel was so sensitive toward women as to be thought the most appropriate place to locate that "orphaned" story. John's Gospel contains long accounts about Mary Magdalene and Mary of Bethany—including the accounts of the latter at her own home (Jn 11:1–44) and as the anointer of Jesus' feet (Jn 12:1–8). Perhaps this fact—coupled with the tradition which (incorrectly) considered Mary Magdalene, Mary of Bethany, and the penitent harlot of Lk 7:36–50 who anointed Jesus' feet to be one and the same person—encouraged the early Christians to locate this story of Jesus' befriending another female sexual sinner in John's Gospel.

In any case, it is clear that John's Gospel (the last of the four to be written) was, not quantitatively, but certainly qualitatively, very strongly pro-woman.

b. The Gospel According to Mark

Mark is thought by most scholars to be the earliest of the four Gospels we have. It is also the shortest, being about 62 percent of the length of Luke. (Matthew is about 92 percent of Luke's length, and John 75 percent.) Of the three Synoptic Gospels, Mark has by far the least to say about women. In Mark there are twenty passages of a total of 114 verses that deal with one or more women, or with the feminine.

§184. Jesus' First Cures: Men and Women

See §130 for an analysis of the account of the cure of Peter's mother-in-law, and §201 for a discussion of how Matthew makes use of this account. In Mark's Gospel the cure of Peter's mother-in-law is paired with the cure of a man with an "unclean spirit." These two cures were the first signs of Jesus' power, as recorded by Mark. It does not seem possible that it could be an accident that here at the opening of Jesus' public life stand the cures of a man and a woman. Clearly Mark, or his source here, took this opportunity to show Jesus' equal commitment to both women and men in his mission.

Luke follows exactly Mark's structure in this matter by recording these two cures at the beginning of Jesus' public life.

a. Jesus Teaches in Capernaum and Cures a Demoniac

They went as far as Capernaum, and as soon as the sabbath came he went to the synagogue and began to teach. And his teaching made a deep impression on them because, unlike the scribes, he taught them with authority.

In their synagogue just then there was a man possessed by an unclean spirit, and it shouted, "What do you want with us, Jesus of Nazareth? Have you come to destroy us? I know who you are: the Holy One of God." But Jesus said sharply, "Be quiet! Come out of him!" And the unclean spirit threw the man into convulsions and with a loud cry went out of him. The people were so astonished that they started asking each other what it all meant. "Here is a teaching that is new," they said, "and with authority behind it: he gives orders even to unclean spirits and they obey him." And his reputation rapidly spread everywhere through all the surrounding Galilean countryside.

b. Cure of Simon's Mother-in-law

On leaving the synagogue, he went with James and John straight to the house of Simon and Andrew. Now Simon's mother-in-law had gone to bed with fever, and they told him about her straightaway. He went to her, took her by the hand and helped her up. And the fever left her and she began to wait on them. (Mk 1:21-28, 29-31; cf. Lk 4:31-37, 38-39; Mt 8:14-15)

§185. Jesus' Mother, Brothers, and Sisters

See §§126, 204, 209, and 215 for a discussion of Jesus' attitude toward his family. Here it should be simply noted that Mark, and Matthew following him, refers to sisters as well as mother and brothers. Luke, for some reason, does not.

His mother and brothers now arrived and, standing outside, sent in a message asking for him. A crowd was sitting round him at the time the message was passed to him, "Your mother and brothers and sisters are outside asking for you." He replied, "Who are my mother and my brothers?" And looking round at those sitting in a circle about him, he said, "Here are my mother and my brothers. Anyone who does the will of God, that person is my brother and sister and mother." (Mk 3:31-35; Mt 12:46-50; Lk 8:19-21)

§186. Lamp on a Lampstand

See §108 for a discussion. The story of a person placing a lamp on a lampstand rather than under a tub or bed is in a household context and more likely to be familiar to women than men, and in Luke it makes a clearly sexually parallel story to match the preceding outdoors story of the sower in the field, which is in a context more likely to be familiar to men. In Mark, however, these two stories are not an isolated pair as in Luke. Rather, they are the first two of five consecutive stories in Mark. Hence the quality of the pair being parallel is considerably diluted in Mark as compared with Luke.

He taught them many things in parables, and in the course of his teaching he said to them, "Listen! Imagine a sower going out to sow . . ." [after relating the parable Jesus explained it, and the text continues].

He also said to them, "Would you bring in a lamp to put it under a tub or under the bed? Surely you will put it on the lamp-stand? For there is nothing hidden but it must be disclosed, nothing kept secret except to be brought to light." (Mk 4:2–4, 21–22; cf. Lk 8:4–8, 16–17; Mt 13:1–9; 5: 14–15)

§187. Jairus' Daughter and the Woman with a Flow of Blood

See §131 for an analysis of these two spliced accounts of cures of women—one from death! Here we should simply focus on the fact that Mark has juxtaposed this spliced account of the cures of women next to the account of a cure of a man—the cleansing of a man of an "unclean spirit." These are the only cures recorded by Mark in this portion of his Gospel; both preceding and following them are other kinds of matters: a series of parables by Jesus, accounts of Jesus' traveling and the beheading of John the Baptist. Though we cannot be certain, it seems likely that Mark—perhaps the arrangement of the materials is as he found them in his written or oral sources—placed these accounts of cures side by side because they showed Jesus curing both women and men. Because this set so very closely parallels the earlier cures of, first, a man possessed of an "unclean spirit" in Capernaum (Mk 1:21–28), and second, Peter's mother-in-law (Mk 1:29–31), it again seems most likely that Mark placed these accounts of cures side by side because they likewise showed Jesus curing both women and men. It is possible that here, and in the earlier set, Mark found these accounts already so arranged in his written or oral sources. We cannot know that, but if it was so, it would simply be evidence that an awareness of Jesus' sexual egalitarianism preceded the composition of the Gospel of Mark, and that Mark affirmed it and handed it on.

Also as in the earlier sexually parallel set of cures, Luke here likewise follows Mark's structure, thereby also handing on this evidence of Jesus' sexual egalitarian attitude and confirming it with his own. Matthew again rearranged Mark's structure here for other purposes:

a. The Gerasene Demoniac

They reached the country of the Gerasenes on the other side of the lake, and no sooner had he left the boat than a man with an unclean spirit came out from the tombs towards him. . . .

b. Cure of the Woman with a Hemorrhage. The Daughter of Jairus Raised to Life

When Jesus had crossed again in the boat to the other side, a large crowd gathered round him and he stayed by the lakeside. Then one of the synagogue officials came up, Jairus by name, and seeing him, fell at his feet and pleaded with him earnestly, saying, "My little daughter is desperately sick. Do come and lay your hands on her to make her better and save her life." Jesus went with him and a large crowd followed him; they were pressing all round him.

Now there was a woman who had suffered from a haemorrhage for twelve years; after long and painful treatment under various doctors, she had spent all she had without being any the better for it, in fact, she was getting worse. She had heard about Jesus, and she came up behind him through the crowd and touched his cloak. "If I can touch even his clothes," she had told herself, "I shall be well again." And the source of the bleeding dried up instantly, and she felt in herself that she was cured of her complaint. Immediately aware that power had gone out from him, Jesus turned round in the crowd and said, "Who touched my clothes?" His disciples said to him, "You see how the crowd is pressing round you and yet you say, 'Who touched me?'" But he continued to look all round to see who had done it. Then the woman came forward, frightened and trembling because she knew what had happened to her, and she fell at his feet and told him the whole truth. "My daughter," he said, "your faith has restored you to health; go in peace and be free from your complaint."

While he was still speaking some people arrived from the house of the synagogue official to say, "Your daughter is dead: why put the Master to any further trouble?" But Jesus had overheard this remark of theirs and he said to the official, "Do not be afraid; only have faith." And he allowed no one to go with him except Peter and James and John the brother of James. So they came to the official's house and Jesus noticed all the commotion, with people weeping and wailing unrestrainedly. He went in and said to them, "Why all this commotion and crying? The child is not dead, but asleep." But they laughed at him. So he turned them all out and, taking with him the child's father and mother and his own companions, he went into the place where the child lay. And taking the child by the hand he said to her. "Talitha, kum!" which means, "Little girl, I tell you to get up." The little girl got up at once and began to walk about, for she was twelve years old. At this they were overcome with astonishment, and he ordered them strictly not to let anyone know about it, and told them to give her something to eat. (Mk 5:1–2, 21–43; cf. Mt 8:28–34; 9:18–26; Lk 8:26–39, 40–56)

§188. Jesus' Problems with His Family

See §§126, 204, 209, and 215 for an analysis of the difficulties Jesus had with his family, including—as Mark and Matthew record it—his mother and his sisters. (Mk 6:1–6; cf. Mt 13:53–58. In the parallel passage in Luke, Jesus' family is not mentioned.)

§189. Herodias, Salome, John the Baptist

This is the only story in Mark which is not in some way about Jesus; Mark tells it because he saw John the Baptist as the prophet Elijah returning (Mk 9:11–13) as a precursor to the Messiah, Jesus. It projects a very evil picture of women: Herodias who indirectly asked for the head of John the Baptist, and Salome her daughter who asked for it directly. It is from Josephus, the first-century Jewish historian, that we learn Salome's name (*Antiquities* XVIII.136). Josephus also records a different description of the execution of John the Baptist —ordered by Herod for political reasons (*Antiquities* XVIII.5.1–2). Mark parallels Queen Jezebel, who wished to kill Elijah (1 Kings 21) with Herodias, who "was furious with him [John the Baptist—'Elijah returned'] and wanted to kill him" (Mk 6:19). Mark also was influenced by the story of Esther (see §89), with the woman called to "perform" before a crowd of tipsy courtiers, the king's promise of half his kingdom (Esth 5:6), and the woman's beauty leading to the death of her enemy.

Thus we have projected one of the few negative images of women in all the Gospels, but it is in a story that is not even about Jesus. The fact, however, that it is recorded in Mark is simply a reflection of the culturally pervasive negative attitude toward women, perhaps indicating that Jesus' positive attitude was not completely shared by Mark, or perhaps reflecting also the tradition Mark represented.

Matthew summarizes Mark's twenty-seven-verse account in twelve verses—he in fact often abbreviates Mark's accounts (some scholars speculate that these short Matthean accounts are really the residues of the earlier Aramaic-language Matthew which Mark later expanded). In doing so, he places the desire to kill John the Baptist not in Herodias but in Herod, thereby very slightly mollifying the image of women that is projected; perhaps he too knew of the tradition of Herod's political motivation for killing John that Josephus mentions. Luke, however, simply refers to John's criticism of Herod "for his relations with his brother's wife Herodias" (Lk 3:19), and later mentions that Herod had had John beheaded (Lk 9:7–9)—no negative image of women whatsoever. It would seem that, in this instance at least, Jesus' positive attitude toward women was not sufficiently persuasive to convince either Mark or Matthew not to write the story of Herodias and Salome, but it did convince Luke not to include it. Matthew, however, did partly shift the guilt from the women alone and did shorten the account by about 40 percent. Apparently Luke's sensitivity about women led him to find the vicious popular story about Herodias and Salome offensive, or at least irrelevant to the gospel of Jesus as he understood it.

Now it was this same Herod who had sent to have John arrested, and had him chained up in prison because of Herodias, his brother Philip's wife whom he had married. For John had told Herod, "It is against the law for you to have your brother's wife." As for Herodias, she was furious with him and wanted to kill him; but she was not able to, because Herod was afraid of John, knowing him to be a good and holy man, and gave him his protection. When he had heard him speak he was greatly perplexed, and yet he liked to listen to him.

An opportunity came on Herod's birthday when he gave a banquet for the nobles of his court, for his army officers and for the leading figures in Galilee. When the daughter of this same Herodias came in and danced, she delighted Herod and his guests; so the king said to the girl, "Ask me anything you like and I will give it you." And he swore her an oath, "I will give you anything you ask, even half my kingdom." She went out and said to her mother, "What shall I ask for?" She replied, "The head of John the Baptist." The girl hurried straight back to the king and made her request, "I want you to give me John the Baptist's head, here and now, on a dish." The king was deeply distressed but, thinking of the oaths he had sworn and of his guests, he was reluctant to break his word to her. So the king at once sent one of the bodyguards with orders to bring John's head. The man went off and beheaded him in prison; then he brought the head on a dish and gave it to the girl, and the girl gave it to her mother. When John's disciples heard about this, they came and took his body and laid it in a tomb. (Mk 6:17–29; cf. Mt 14:3–12; Lk 3:19–20; 9:7–9)

§190. Jesus Affirms Parents

See §125 for a discussion of Jesus' affirmation of parenthood. There Matthew's version of Jesus' angry retort to some of his opponents was given. The commentary there applies equally to the Markan version here.

[Jesus said to some Pharisees and scribes:] "You put aside the commandment of God to cling to human traditions." And he said to them, "How ingeniously you get round the commandment of God in order to preserve your own tradition! For Moses said: Do your duty to your father and your mother and, Anyone who curses father or mother must be put to death. But you say, 'If a man says to his father or mother: Anything I have that I might have used to help you is Corban (that is, dedicated to God), then he is forbidden from that moment to do anything for his father or mother.' In this way you make God's word null and void for the sake of your tradition which you have handed down. And you do many other things like this." (Mk 7:8–13; cf. Mt 15:1–7)

§191. Jesus' Mission to Non-Jews Through a Woman

Mark was writing for a Gentile readership, and, according to a number of scholars, wished to develop a section on Jesus' mission to Gentiles. Mark wrote in ch. 7:24, "He set out for the [Gentile] territory of Tyre," and then told the story of the cure of the daughter of the Gentile woman (Mk 7:24–30). But then immediately Mark recorded Jesus' trip farther north to Sidon (also a largely Gentile area) and back to the shores of the Sea of Galilee, a Jewish area: "Returning from the district of Tyre, he went by way of Sidon towards the Sea of Galilee, right through the Decapolis region" (Mk 7:31). Thus, the only evidence Mark could find in the tradition for Jesus' missionary tour of Gentile territory was this trip to Tyre and Sidon and back. The really interesting fact is that this trip produced nothing memorable other than the encounter with the Syrophoenician woman, whose daughter Jesus cured at her insistence (see §133). Is it because the status of women in the Roman world, for whom Mark wrote, was much higher than in Jewish society that Mark chose this story to show Jesus reaching out to the Gentiles? Or was it that Mark simply found no other story in the tradition he knew which exemplified Jesus' mission tour of pagan areas? Given Mark's readership, it seems most likely he would have included other such stories from the trip of Jesus if there were any, and so the second explanation is the more likely. But the first should not be ruled out as at least a contributing motive as well. In the end, however, all we know from the evidence available is that Jesus' mission to the Gentile world consisted of the healing of a woman at the persistent request of another woman.

He left that place and set out for the territory of Tyre. There he went into a house and did not want anyone to know he was there, but he could not pass unrecognised. A woman whose little daughter had an unclean spirit heard about him straightaway and came and fell at his feet. Now the woman was a pagan, by birth a Syrophoenician, and she begged him to cast the devil out of her daughter. And he said to her, "The children should be fed first, because it is not fair to take the children's food and throw it to the house-dogs." But she spoke up: "Ah yes, sir," she replied, "but the house-dogs under the table can eat the children's scraps." And he said to her, "For saying this, you may go home happy; the devil has gone out of your daughter." So she went off to her home and found the child lying on the bed and the devil gone. (Mk 7:24–30; cf. Mt 15:21–28)

§192. Marriage and the Dignity of Women — I
See pp. 173ff. for an analysis of Jesus' revolutionary egalitarian attitude toward marriage, adultery, and divorce, particularly as expressed in Mark's account. In Mark, Jesus flatly contradicts the Jewish law and custom of his time by saying that a husband can be "guilty of adultery against her [his wife]." Jesus also speaks about a woman divorcing her husband, an impossibility in Jewish law, although possible in Hellenistic and Roman law of the time. Of course such divorcing women were known in Palestine around the time of Jesus, and he may well have included them in his remarks. Hence it is not necessary to suggest that Mark's writing in Rome was responsible for that phrase—if the Roman Mark, then why not the Hellenistic Luke? In any case, Jesus' sexual egalitarianism in marriage comes through here very strongly, and correspondingly Mark's corroboration of it.

Some Pharisees approached him and asked, "Is it against the law for a man to divorce his wife?" They were testing him. He answered them, "What did Moses command you?" "Moses allowed us," they said, "to draw up a writ of dismissal and so to divorce." Then Jesus said to them, "It was because you were so unteachable that he wrote this commandment for you. But from the beginning of creation God made them male and female. This is why a man must leave father and mother, and the two become one body. They are no longer two, therefore, but one body. So then, what God has united, man must not divide." Back in the house the disciples questioned him again about this, and he said to them, "The man who divorces his wife and marries another is guilty of adultery against her. And if a woman divorces her husband and marries another she is guilty of adultery too." (Mk 10:2–12; cf. Mt 19:1–9; 5:32; Lk 16:18)

§193. Jesus Dismantles Restrictive Family Bonds
See §127 for a discussion of the extraordinarily powerful restrictions and obligations which extended-family bonds placed on persons in the Near East (which is still largely to be seen today). By far the most restricted group of persons in the patriarchal family are women. Hence they have the most to gain in human freedom by a loosening of such restrictions, as Jesus advocated. (Note that Mark records only one such reference, relatively mild; Matthew has two, and Luke three. The significance of this will be discussed below, §234.)

Peter took this up. "What about us?" he asked him. "We have left everything and followed you." Jesus said, "I tell you solemnly, there is no one who has left house, brothers, sisters, father, children or land for my sake and for the sake of the gospel who will not be repaid a hundred times over, houses, brothers, sisters, mothers, children and land—not without persecutions—now in this present time and, in the world to come, eternal life." (Mk 10:28–30; cf. Mt 19:27–30; Lk 18:28–30)

§194. Marriage and the Dignity of Women — II

See §122 for an analysis of Jesus' response to the question of some Sadducees about a woman married seven times—to whom would she belong in heaven? Jesus' answer presumed that she was a person and belonged to no one.

Then some Sadducees—who deny that there is a resurrection—came to him and they put this question to him, "Master, we have it from Moses in writing, if a man's brother dies leaving a wife but no child, the man must marry the widow to raise up children for his brother. Now there were seven brothers. The first married a wife and died leaving no children. The second married the widow, and he too died leaving no children; with the third it was the same, and none of the seven left any children. Last of all the woman herself died. Now at the resurrection, when they rise again, whose wife will she be, since she had been married to all seven?"

Jesus said to them, "Is not the reason why you go wrong, that you understand neither the scriptures nor the power of God? For when they rise from the dead, men and women do not marry; no, they are like the angels in heaven. Now about the dead rising again, have you never read in the Book of Moses, in the passage about the Bush, how God spoke to him and said: I am the God of Abraham, the God of Isaac and the God of Jacob? He is God, not of the dead, but of the living. You are very much mistaken." (Mk 12:18–27; cf. Mt 22:23–33; Lk 20:27–40)

§195. The Oppression of Widows

See pp. 183ff. for a discussion of Jesus' slashing condemnation of the oppression of the most downtrodden element of the male-dominated society in which he lived, widows. (Mk 12:40; cf. Lk 20:47)

§196. The Widow's Mite

See §129 for an analysis of Jesus' holding up a widow as a model to be emulated. (Mk 12:41–44; cf. Lk 21:1–4)

§197. Jesus' Concern for Women's Welfare

There have been many scholarly suggestions for the real sources of the apocalyptic-sounding predictions of the end of the world that are found in all three of the Synoptic Gospels; these suggestions include solidly represented arguments that a prophetic statement of Jesus is the source—just as the Gospels represent. There is rather general agreement that there has been some editorial adaptation by the evangelists, but usually disagreement on exactly what. No one, however, denies that the statement, "Alas for those with child, or with babies at the breast, when those days come!" was in the original version. Since there is no reason why Jesus could not have made the original prophetic statement, however it may have been differently adapted by the evangelists, and since the documents claim that he did, it is logical to conclude that it is at least probable that he did. In that case Jesus would be the utterer of the cry of concern for women.

There is a certain sexual parallelism where the references to a man on the housetop and a man in the fields are "balanced" by references to expectant mothers and nursing mothers. The desolation described is so sudden and devastating that only immediate flight offers some chance of safety; hence, relatively immobilized mothers are at a severe disadvantage, and Jesus expresses great concern for them— about no one else does he so express his concern.

Both Matthew and Luke use basically the same words concerning the women as does Mark.

"When you see the disastrous abomination set up where it ought not to be (let the reader understand), then those in Judaea must escape to the mountains; if a man is on the housetop, he must not come down to go into the house to collect any of his belongings; if a man is in the fields, he must not turn back to fetch his cloak. Alas for those with child, or with babies at the breast, when those days come! Pray that this may not be in winter. For in those days there will be such distress as, until now, has not been equalled since the beginning when God created the world, nor ever will be again. And if the Lord had not shortened that time, no one would have survived; but he did shorten the time, for the sake of the elect whom he chose." (Mk 13:14–20; cf. Mt 24:15–25; Lk 21:20–24)

§198. Anointment of Jesus at Bethany
See §153 for an analysis of the account of Jesus' anointment by a woman while he was at table and his defense of her against grumbling men. (Mk 14:3–9; cf. Mt 26:6–13; Jn 12:1–8)

§199. Women in Jesus' Passion and Resurrection
See pp. 198ff. for analyses of the extraordinary supportive involvement of women in Jesus' passion, death, and burial; their presence

at the empty tomb; their seeing the risen Jesus; and their reporting to the rest of the disciples. Almost all of these elements are reported by each of the four Gospels—an extraordinary near-unanimity.

Only Women Remain by Jesus Through His Death
Mk 15:40–41; cf. Mt 27:55–56; Lk 23:49; Jn 19:25

Women Witness the Burial of Jesus
Mk 15:47; cf. Mt 27:61; Lk 23:55

Women First Witnesses to the Empty Tomb
Mk 16:1–8; cf. Mt 28:1–8; Lk 24:1–8; Jn 20:1–10

Women Testify About Resurrection to Male Disciples
Mk 16:7,11; cf. Mt 28:8; Lk 24:9–11; Jn 20:18

The Risen Jesus Appears to Women First
Mk 16:9; cf. Mt 28:9–10; Jn 20:11–17

§200. Conclusion

Mark's Gospel has the least number of passages dealing with women of the three Synoptic Gospels (20 to Matthew's 36 and Luke's 42) and the smallest number of verses concerning women of all four Gospels (114 to John's 119, Matthew's 180, and Luke's 220). Of course it is the shortest Gospel in overall size, but proportionately it nevertheless has the least emphasis on women of the three Synoptics, but still more than John's in terms of proportionate quantity. Because it is the earliest Gospel it apparently was available to both Matthew and Luke, and consequently almost all of it reappears in one form or another in either Matthew or Luke or both, and that includes all the passages dealing with women. Hence in comparison to the other two Synoptics, Mark seems much less pro-woman in the number of accounts dealing with women he records. Still, the extremely important fact that nothing negative about women is recorded (with the exception of the non-Jesus story of the beheading of John the Baptist discussed above, §189) and the significant number of positive accounts about women which Mark does record lead to the conclusion that Mark's Gospel is pro-woman in its stance, though not nearly as much so as Matthew and Luke, or even John.

c. The Gospel According to Matthew

It is true that there are no negative statements, attitudes, or actions concerning women by Jesus in the Gospel of Mark. That in itself has a great significance. And while there is a relatively smaller amount of positive evidence of Jesus' attitude toward women provided by Mark, this evidence nevertheless would indeed support a claim that Jesus was a champion of women—but only modestly so.

However, the situation is quite different when we come to the next two Synoptic Gospels, Matthew and Luke. Not only in neither of them are there no negative attitudes toward women expressed by Jesus, but also every one of the above accounts in Mark dealing with women is found in either Matthew or Luke, or in both, and sometimes even in John as well. Furthermore, Matthew records eighteen additional accounts significantly concerned with women that Mark does not mention—making a total of thirty-six accounts in Matthew dealing with women. Of these non-Marcan accounts, ten are peculiar to Matthew; eight of them Luke also records along with Matthew (John records none of these eighteen accounts). The ten passages peculiar to Matthew, plus the four he has in common with Mark which Luke does not have, make fourteen accounts concerning women that Matthew records and that Luke does not.

(1) Passages Common to Matthew and Mark

§201. Women Included in the Reign of God

The first matter that reveals something of Matthew's attitude toward women that should be noted here concerns a passage Matthew has in common with both Mark and Luke. Because Matthew was writing for a Hebrew community he consciously drew attention to Hebrew Scripture parallels. For Matthew the Sermon on the *Mount* is the starting point for the new "assembly" *(qahal, ekklesia)*, paralleling the calling out and forming of the first "assembly" by the teaching and laws on *Mount* Sinai. For Matthew, Jesus formed this new "assembly" by the healings he performed following his preaching; the cures specifically benefited a leper, a pagan, a woman—the three categories excluded from the Hebrew cultic assembly. According to Matthew, then, these three categories were obviously intended by Jesus to be included in his new "assembly." To communicate this in his Gospel, Matthew relocated the account of the cure of Peter's mother-in-law from where it apparently was originally situated (in both Mark's and Luke's Gospels) to group it with the cure of the leper and the centurion's servant immediately after the close of the Sermon on the Mount.

And going into Peter's house Jesus found Peter's mother-in-law in bed with fever. He touched her hand and the fever left her, and she got up and began to wait on him. (Mt 8:14–15; cf. Mk 1:29–31; Lk 4:38–39)

§202. Jairus' Daughter and the Woman with a Flow of Blood

See §131 for analyses of Jesus' cures of two women, one with a long-term hemorrhage and one dead. The account is shorter in Matthew than in Mark, as happens in a number of other instances. This fact gave rise to the earlier theory that Matthew was prior in time and that Mark expanded the account; most (but not all) scholars now, however, hold Mark to be prior and that Matthew abbreviated the account. In any case, in Matthew these cures of women are grouped with two others, all of which are immediately followed by the statement, "Jesus made a tour through all the towns and villages, teaching in their synagogues, proclaiming the Good News of the reign of God" and its healing effects (Mt 9:35). This structural message is the same, and is similarly communicated, as in Matthew's placing of the cure of Peter's mother-in-law where he did, discussed above. The highlighting of this sexual egalitarianism in Jesus' gospel and in the reign of God by structural placement of stories and statements could come from Matthew's sources, written and oral, where he found things so arranged, or from Matthew himself, or a combination. Hence, Matthew either further affirmed Jesus' pro-woman stance by his own editorial arranging, or at least corroborated that affirmation in his sources by transmitting it in his editorial arrangement.

While he was speaking to them, up came one of the officials, who bowed low in front of him and said, "My daughter has just died, but come and lay your hand on her and her life will be saved." Jesus rose and, with his disciples, followed him.

Then from behind him came a woman, who had suffered from a haemorrhage for twelve years, and she touched the fringe of his cloak, for she said to herself, "If I can only touch his cloak I shall be well again." Jesus turned round and saw her; and he said to her, "Courage, my daughter, your faith has restored you to health." And from that moment the woman was well again.

When Jesus reached the officials' house and saw the flute-players, with the crowd making a commotion he said, "Get out of here; the little girl is not dead, she is asleep." And they laughed at him. But when the people had been turned out he went inside and took the little girl by the hand; and she stood up. And the news spread all round the countryside. (Mt 9:18–26; cf. Mk 5:21–43; Lk 8:40–56)

§203. Jesus' Mother, Brothers, and Sisters

See §§127 and 128 for a discussion of Jesus' spiritualizing of the bonds of kinship, his dismantling of the oppressive restrictions of family ties which were so especially burdensome to women in that society. Note again that Matthew along with Mark mentions sisters, in addition to mother and brothers (though Luke does not), perhaps thereby reflecting quantitatively the special oppression women experienced in family restrictions. (Mt 12:46–50; cf. Mk 3:31–35; Lk 8:19–21)

§204. Jesus' Problems with His Family — I

See §127 for a discussion of the problems Jesus had with his family, and his response that had a freeing effect on women.

When Jesus had finished these parables he left the district; and, coming to his home town, he taught the people in their synagogue in such a way that they were astonished and said, "Where did the man get this wisdom and these miraculous powers? This is the carpenter's son, surely? Is not his mother the woman called Mary, and his brothers James and Joseph and Simon and Jude? His sisters, too, are they not all here with us? So where did the man get it all?" And they would not accept him. But Jesus said to them, "A prophet is only despised in his own country and in his own house," and he did not work many miracles there because of their lack of faith. (Mt 13:53–58; cf. Mk 6:1–6) [In the parallel passage in Luke, Jesus' family is not mentioned.]

§205. Herodias, Salome, John the Baptist

See §189 for an analysis of the implications of Matthew's inclusion of this story which projects such an evil image of women.

Now it was Herod who had arrested John, chained him up and put him in prison because of Herodias, his brother Philip's wife. For John had told him, "It is against the Law for you to have her." He had wanted to kill him but was afraid of the people, who regarded John as a prophet. Then, during the celebrations for Herod's birthday, the daughter of Herodias danced before the company, and so delighted Herod that he promised on oath to give her anything she asked. Prompted by her mother she said, "Give me John the Baptist's head, here, on a dish." The king was distressed but, thinking of the oaths he had sworn and of his guests, he ordered it to be given her, and sent and had John beheaded in the prison. The head was brought in on a dish and given to the girl who took it to her mother. John's disciples came and took the body and buried it; then they went off to tell Jesus. (Mt 14:3–12; cf. Mk 6:17–29; Lk 3:19–20; 9:7–9)

§206. Jesus Affirms Parents

See §125 for a discussion of Jesus' affirmation of parents, mother as well as father. This position, of course, stands in the Hebraic tradition. (Mt 15:1–7; cf. Mk 7:1–13)

§207. Jesus' Mission to Non-Jews Through a Woman

See §133 for an analysis of Jesus' "mission to the Gentiles" through a woman, and also the special role this account plays in Mark's Gospel. (Mt 15:21–38; cf. Mk 7:24–30)

§208. Marriage and the Dignity of Women — I

See §120 for the analysis of Jesus' revolutionary egalitarian attitude toward women in marriage by eliminating the husband's right to divorce his wife. Matthew alone of the three Gospels that discuss divorce includes the exception, "except for immorality." Most scholarship tends to see this exception clause either as (1) an additional interpretative phrase stemming from the Christian communities that served as Matthew's sources; or (2) possibly—under later and more complex circumstances than those which prevailed when Mark and Luke were written—Matthew's sources' recollection and preservation of this helpful exception clause of Jesus'; or (3) as a phrase of Jesus' which really did not constitute an exception and therefore also did not contradict his absolute prohibition of divorce recorded in the Gospels. This latter interpretation is supported by Paul's report on Jesus' teaching on divorce—Paul's epistle was written before any of the Gospels: "For the married I have something to say, and this is not from me but from the Lord: a wife must not leave her husband —or if she does leave him, she must either remain unmarried or else make it up with her husband—nor must a husband send his wife away"—1 Cor 7:10–11. (Paul himself, however, went beyond this restriction in the case of a Christian and non-Christian couple when the non-Christian wished a divorce: "If the unbelieving partner does not consent [to live together], they may separate; in these circumstances, the brother or sister is not tied"—1 Cor 7:15.) It should be noted that Paul reports an equal balance between the woman's and the man's rights here stemming from Jesus—and maintains the balance himself in his extension, the so-called "Pauline Privilege."

The fact that the Matthew exception clause refers only to the man divorcing his wife, and not vice versa, also seems out of character with Jesus' egalitarian attitude as recorded in the Mark and Luke divorce passages and many other places in the Gospels. This factor would also make it likely that the editor of the Greek version of Matthew (see §216d for a discussion of a possible earlier Aramaic version of Matthew) received the recollection or interpretation from his sources and felt a special need in the circumstances of the time and place to insert the clause in the account already at hand which did not contain it —perhaps to address a dispute pressing in Greek Matthew's source communities—but in inserting it did not do so in a sexually balanced manner, as one would have expected from Jesus and as Matthew (perhaps the earlier Aramaic Matthew?) does elsewhere in his Gospel.

"And I say to you: whoever divorces his wife, except for unchastity, and marries another, commits adultery." (Mt 19:9)

"But I say to you that every one who divorces his wife, except on the ground of unchastity, makes her an adulteress; and whoever marries a divorced woman commits adultery." (Mt 5:32; cf. Mk 10:1–12; Lk 16:18)

§209. Jesus' Problems with His Family — II
See §127 for an analysis of the problems Jesus had with his family and what bearing this had on his liberating attitude toward women.

Then Peter spoke. "What about us?" he said to him. "We have left everything and followed you. What are we to have, then?" Jesus said to him, "I tell you solemnly, when all is made new and the Son of Man sits on his throne of glory, you will yourselves sit on twelve thrones to judge the twelve tribes of Israel. And everyone who has left houses, brothers, sisters, father, mother, children or land for the sake of my name will be repaid a hundred times over, and also inherit eternal life." (Mt 19:27–29; cf. Mk 10:28–30; Lk 18:28–30)

§210. Marriage and the Dignity of Women — II
See §122 for an analysis of Jesus' response to the question of some Sadducees about a woman married seven times—to whom would she belong in heaven? Jesus' answer presumed that she was a person and belonged to no one. (Mt 22:23–33; cf. Mk 12:18–27; Lk 20:27–40)

§211. Jesus' Concern for Women's Welfare
See §156 for a discussion of the concern for women's welfare at the final crisis that Jesus expressed.

"So when you see the disastrous abomination, of which the prophet Daniel spoke, set up in the Holy Place (let the reader understand), then those in Judaea must escape to the mountains; if a man is on the housetop, he must not come down to collect his belongings; if a man is in the fields, he must not turn back to fetch his cloak. Alas for those with child, or with babies at the breast, when those days come! Pray that you will not have to escape in winter or on a sabbath. For then there will be great distress such as, until now, since the world began, there never has been, nor ever will be again. And if that time had not been shortened, no one would have survived; but shortened that time shall be, for the sake of those who are chosen." (Mt 24:15–22; cf. Mk 13:14–20; Lk 21:20–24)

§212. Anointment of Jesus at Bethany

See §153 for an analysis of the account of Jesus' anointment by a woman while he was at table, his defense of her against grumbling men, and his promise that she would be remembered wherever the gospel was proclaimed. It is slightly ironic that in the Matthew and Mark accounts, which are almost identical, the women's name is not remembered, whereas in John's account where she is identified as Mary of Bethany, the sister of Martha and Lazarus, there is no mention made about her act "being remembered"—though of course it was.

Jesus was at Bethany in the house of Simon the leper, when a woman came to him with an alabaster jar of the most expensive ointment, and poured it on his head as he was at table. When they saw this, the disciples were indignant; "Why this waste?" they said. "This could have been sold at a high price and the money given to the poor." Jesus noticed this. "Why are you upsetting the woman?" he said to them. "What she has done for me is one of the good works indeed! You have the poor with you always, but you will not always have me. When she poured this ointment on my body, she did it to prepare me for burial. I tell you solemnly, wherever in all the world this Good News is proclaimed, what she has done will be told also, in remembrance of her." (Mt 26:6–13; cf. Mk 14:3–9; Jn 12:1–8)

§213. Women in Jesus' Passion and Resurrection

See pp. 198ff. for analyses of the extremely supportive involvement of women in the passion, death, and burial of Jesus and their presence at the empty tomb, their seeing the risen Jesus, and their reporting of all this to the male disciples.

(2) Passages Common to Matthew and Luke Alone

§214. The Virgin Conception of Jesus

Matthew's account of the virgin conception of Jesus, that is, by the Holy Spirit in the womb of Mary, does perforce focus on the woman Mary. But it focuses still more sharply on the man Joseph. Even though the couple were only betrothed, the legal force of their state was practically as strong as marriage—sexual intercourse by the betrothed woman with any other man would have been considered not fornication but adultery (though not so if the betrothed man did the same). Joseph was under obligation to divorce (necessary even though they were only betrothed) his apparently adulterous betrothed. He could have subjected her to the excruciatingly humiliating ordeal of Sotah (for a description of it, the only trial by ordeal in the Bible, see Num 5:11–31 and the Talmudic tractate Sotah; see §99), and possibly have had her executed. However, Joseph, "being a man of honor and wanting to spare her publicity, decided to divorce her informally" —a significant sensitivity toward women enacted at the beginning of Jesus' life. Luke's account of the virgin conception of Jesus is within a different context from Matthew's, namely, the "annunciation" to Mary (Lk 1:18–26), to be discussed below. It should be noted that whereas in Matthew's account here Joseph is the main focus of attention and the angel appears to him, in Luke's account Mary is the center of attention and the angel appears not to Joseph but to Mary.

This is how Jesus Christ came to be born. His mother Mary was betrothed to Joseph; but before they came to live together she was found to be with child through the Holy Spirit. Her husband Joseph, being a man of honour and wanting to spare her publicity, decided to divorce her informally. He had made up his mind to do this when the angel of the Lord appeared to him in a dream and said, "Joseph son of David, do not be afraid to take Mary home as your wife, because she has conceived what is in her by the Holy Spirit. She will give birth to a son and you must name him Jesus, because he is the one who is to save his people from their sins." Now all this took place to fulfil the words spoken by the Lord through the prophet: The virgin will conceive and give birth to a son and they will call him Emmanuel, a name which means "God-is-with-us." When Joseph woke up he did what the angel of the Lord had told him to do: he took his wife to his home and, though he had not had intercourse with her, she gave birth to a son; and he named him Jesus. (Mt 1:18–25; cf. Lk 1:26–38)

§215. Jesus' Problems with His Family — III

See §127 for an analysis of the problems Jesus had with his family and what bearing this had on his liberating attitude toward women.

"Do not suppose that I have come to bring peace to the earth: it is not peace I have come to bring, but a sword. For I have come to set a man against his father, a daughter against her mother, a daughter-in-law against her mother-in-law. A man's enemies will be those of his own household. Anyone who prefers father or mother to me is not worthy of me. Anyone who prefers son or daughter to me is not worthy of me." (Mt 10:34–37; cf. Lk 12:51–53)

§216. Female Imagery

Mark records relatively few stories and images used by Jesus, and of those he does record, none deal with women. Matthew, on the other hand, records a large number of stories and images used by Jesus. Five of them deal with women or female imagery, four in common with Luke. The four are as follows:

a. Heaven the Leaven in Dough

See §115 for an analysis of Jesus' use of the sexually parallel image likening the reign of heaven to leaven in a loaf, an image familiar to and clearly aimed at women listeners. (Mt 13:33; cf. Lk 13:20–21)

b. Jesus in a Female Image

See §118 for a discussion of Jesus' use of female imagery to describe himself.

"How often have I longed to gather your children, as a hen gathers her chicks under her wings." (Mt 23:37; cf. Lk 13:34)

c. Women at the "End of Days"

See §111 for an analysis of the sexually parallel image of the two women at the "end of days." (Mt 24:39–41; cf. Lk 17:34–37)

d. Queen of Sheba

Perhaps one of the most interesting passages of this group is the one referring to the Queen of the South, the Queen of Sheba. For a general analysis of it, see §113. The discussion here will be limited to a comparative analysis. In the earlier Marcan account there is simply a report of a demand for a sign, which Jesus rejects (Mk 8:11–12). Many scholars argue there was an earlier version of Matthew, written in Aramaic (now lost), and that often this earlier layer can be discerned in our present expanded Greek version. An example of the early Aramaic version of Matthew is said to be found in our present Greek version of Mt 16:1–4, where a sign is asked of Jesus, which request he rejects—except for the "sign of Jonah." However, in the second version, the Greek version, of Matthew the story is repeated in an expanded form which includes a reference not only to Jonah but also to the Queen of Sheba. A tradition including additional references to women was obviously known and used by the author of Greek Matthew, and of Luke, that was not known by the earlier authors of Aramaic Matthew and of Mark. This later tradition of Greek Matthew with the reference to the Queen of the South is found in our present Greek version of Mt 12:38–42.

Then some of the scribes and Pharisees spoke up. "Master," they said, "we should like to see a sign from you." He replied, "It is an evil and unfaithful generation that asks for a sign! The only sign it will be given is the sign of the prophet Jonah. For as Jonah was in the belly of the sea-monster for three days and three nights, so will the Son of Man be in the heart of the earth for three days and three nights. On Judgement day the men of Nineveh will stand up with this generation and condemn it, because when Jonah preached they repented; and there is something greater than Jonah here. On Judgement day the Queen of the South will rise up with this generation and condemn it, because she came from the ends of the earth to hear the wisdom of Solomon; and there is something greater than Solomon here." (Mt 12:38–42; cf. Mt 16:1–4; Mk 8:11–12; Lk 11:29–32)

§217. The Wedding Feast

The seventh account dealing with women which both Matthew and Luke alone record concerns women, albeit somewhat indirectly, only in Matthew's account. It is a story of Jesus' describing what the reign of heaven (reign of God in Luke—a synonymous expression) was like. Matthew described it as a wedding feast, whereas Luke made it simply a feast. Furthermore, Luke in the story makes getting married an excuse for not going to the banquet. In Matthew's account, that is not offered as an excuse. Hence, in comparison to Luke, in this case Matthew is more sympathetic, if not to women at least to marriage, in two points, one positive and one negative.

Jesus began to speak to them in parables once again, "The reign of heaven may be compared to a king who gave a feast for his son's wedding. He sent his servants to call those who had been invited, but they would not come. Next he sent some more servants. 'Tell those who have been invited,' he said, 'that I have my banquet all prepared, my oxen and fattened cattle have been slaughtered, everything is ready. Come to the wedding.' But they were not interested: one went off to his farm, another to his business, and the rest seized his servants, maltreated them and killed them. The king was furious. He despatched his troops, destroyed those murderers and burnt their town. Then he said to his servants, 'The wedding is ready; but as those who were invited proved to be unworthy, go to the crossroads in the town and invite everyone you can find to the wedding.' So these servants went out on the roads and collected together everyone they could find, bad and good alike; and the wedding hall was filled with guests. When the king came in to look at the guests he noticed one man who was not wearing a wedding garment, and said to him, 'How did you get in here, my friend, without a wedding garment?' And the man was silent. Then the king said to the attendants, 'Bind him hand and foot and throw him out into the dark, where there will be weeping and grinding of teeth.' For many are called, but few are chosen." (Mt 22:1–14; cf. Lk 14:16–24)

§218. The Genealogy of Jesus

The eighth and last account which Matthew and Luke have in common alone is like the seventh in that only Matthew's version deals with women. The account in each Gospel concerns Jesus' genealogy. At the beginning of Matthew's Gospel is a very interesting genealogy of Jesus which is supposed to establish him as the Messiah, as a "son of David," and a "son of Abraham." It is clearly intended to be artificial in that there are three sections with fourteen names each (two times the holy number of fullness, seven), though to make the structure symmetrical some generations listed in the Hebrew Bible were omitted by Matthew. It is, however, of interest here to note that the names of five women are included in the genealogy, an oddity since paternity alone was the source of legal rights. Moreover, each of the women had a "moral flaw" connected with sex: Tamar played a harlot and seduced Judah, her father-in-law; Rahab was a prostitute; Ruth sneaked into Boaz's bed and induced him to marry her; Bathsheba, Uriah's wife, committed adultery with David; and Mary was found with child before her marriage. The Christians claimed Jesus' virgin conception, and doubtless therefore detracting stories circulated about his "immoral," extramarital origin—how could such a one be the Messiah? Matthew's response was a messianic genealogy which listed four sexually "immoral" women (other women, such as the very popular "matriarchs" Sarah, Rebecca, and Rachel, are not mentioned) at key points in the Davidic line: Tamar was associated with the founding fathers of the twelve tribes of Israel, namely, "Judah and his brothers"; Rahab played a role in the gaining of the Promised Land; Ruth was remembered as founding mother of the House of David (see Ruth 4:17–22); Bathsheba was the wife of David the first real king of Israel, and the mother of its greatest king, Solomon. Matthew obviously saw this pattern of sexually "irregular" women playing crucial roles at the turning points in the history of the chosen people, reaching its climax in Mary, the mother of the Messiah. It is perhaps an indication of the relatively high status of women among the primitive Christian communities in Palestine, where (probably) and for whom Matthew's Gospel was written, that such a proud claim could be made to such women in Jesus' ancestry.

A genealogy of Jesus Christ, son of David, son of Abraham:
Abraham was the father of Isaac,
Isaac the father of Jacob,
Jacob the father of Judah and his brothers,
Judah was the father of Perez and Zerah, *Tamar being their mother,*
Perez was the father of Hezron,
Hezron the father of Ram,
Ram was the father of Amminadab,
Amminadab the father of Nahshon,
Nahshon the father of Salmon,
Salmon was the father of Boaz, *Rahab being his mother,*
Boaz was the father of Obed, *Ruth being his mother,*
Obed was the father of Jesse;
and Jesse was the father of King David.

David was the father of Solomon, *whose mother had been Uriah's wife,*
Solomon was the father of Rehoboam,
Rehoboam the father of Abijah,
Abijah the father of Asa,
Asa was the father of Jehoshaphat,
Jehoshaphat the father of Joram,
Joram the father of Azariah,
Azariah was the father of Jotham,
Jotham the father of Ahaz,
Ahaz the father of Hezekiah,
Hezekiah was the father of Manasseh,
Manasseh the father of Amon,
Amon the father of Josiah;
and Josiah was the father of Jechoniah and his brothers.
Then the deportation to Babylon took place.

After the deportation to Babylon;
Jechoniah was the father of Shealtiel,
Shealtiel the father of Zerubbabel,
Zerubbabel was the father of Abiud,
Abiud the father of Eliakim,
Eliakim the father of Azor,
Azor was the father of Zadok,
Zadok the father of Achim,
Achim the father of Eliud,
Eliud was the father of Eleazar,
Eleazar the father of Matthan,
Matthan the father of Jacob;

and Jacob was the father of Joseph the husband of *Mary;*
of her was born Jesus who is called Christ.

The sum of generations is therefore: fourteen from Abraham to
David; fourteen from David to the Babylonian deportation; and fourteen from the Babylonian deportation to Christ. (Mt 1:1–17; cf. Lk
3:23–38, where the genealogy is almost completely different and no
women are mentioned.)

(3) Passages Special to Matthew

As noted above, there are ten passages which deal with women that
are found in Matthew alone. Of these, three really reflect nothing as
far as the attitude toward women is concerned.

§219. Infancy Narratives

Three accounts surrounding the infancy of Jesus that deal with
women are peculiar to Matthew. The woman mainly involved was
Mary the mother of Jesus. The first account is about the coming of
the Magi. Matthew records that when the Magi found the house
they went in and "they saw the child with his mother Mary" (Mt
2:11). Later Joseph was told by an angel in a dream to "take the
child and his mother" (2:13) into Egypt; he did so (2:14). After
Herod's death Joseph was again told by an angel in a dream to
"take the child and his mother" (2:20) back to Israel; and he did so
(2:21). Following the pattern established in the earlier portion
about the virginal conception of Jesus, Matthew, in contrast to
Luke, continues to make Joseph the lead character in the story,
with the angel always appearing to him. Mary appears only as "his
mother," who is either with Jesus when the Magi find him or is
taken to or from Egypt by her husband. These passages reflect
nothing of Jesus' attitude toward women, and certainly indicate
nothing positive on the part of Matthew.

(1) After Jesus had been born at Bethlehem in Judaea during the reign of
King Herod, some wise men came to Jerusalem from the east. "Where is the
infant king of the Jews?" they asked. "We saw his star as it rose and have
come to do him homage." . . . The sight of the star filled them with delight,
and going into the house they saw the child with his mother Mary, and falling
to their knees they did him homage. (Mt 2:1–2, 10–11)

(2) After they had left, the angel of the Lord appeared to Joseph in a dream
and said, "Get up, take the child and his mother with you, and escape into
Egypt, and stay there until I tell you, because Herod intends to search for
the child and do away with him." So Joseph got up and, taking the child and

his mother with him, left that night for Egypt, where he stayed until Herod was dead. (Mt 2:13–15)

(3) After Herod's death, the angel of the Lord appeared in a dream to Joseph in Egypt and said, "Get up, take the child and his mother with you and go back to the land of Israel, for those who wanted to kill the child are dead." So Joseph got up and, taking the child and his mother with him, went back to the land of Israel. But when he learnt that Archelaus had succeeded his father Herod as ruler of Judaea he was afraid to go there, and being warned in a dream he left for the region of Galilee. There he settled in a town called Nazareth. (Mt 2:19–23)

§220. Adultery of the Heart

The saying attributed to Jesus that the man who lusts after a woman commits adultery with her in his heart does not reflect a great deal about Jesus' or Matthew's attitudes toward women. The primary point seems to be that moral evil lies in the will—even if the fulfillment of the act were prevented. In this, Jesus was not teaching something new, even concerning sexual morality. The sixth (or seventh) commandment says, you shall not commit adultery, and the ninth (tenth) goes on to the evil in the heart when it says, you shall not covet your neighbor's wife. Jesus' teaching is clearly traditional (see also Job 31:1, and the Testaments of the Twelve Patriarchs, written around 106 B.C.E.: "Do ye, therefore, my children, flee evildoing and cleave to goodness. For he that hath it looketh not on a woman with a view to fornication, and he beholdeth no defilement" —Testament of Benjamin 8:1–2; "I never committed fornication by the uplifting of my eyes"—Testament of Issachar 7:2; Charles, Vol. 2, pp. 358, 327.) The absence of any parallel statements in the Decalogue, in Job, in the Testaments of the Twelve Patriarchs, and here in Matthew forbidding the woman to covet the man does reflect patriarchal assumptions. Is this male bias by omission to be attributed to Jesus or Matthew and/or his sources? We cannot of course be certain, but given the many other sexually parallel statements, stories, and images used by Jesus, there is a stronger likelihood the imbalance comes from Matthew and/or his sources.

"You have learnt how it was said: You must not commit adultery. But I say this to you: if a man looks at a woman lustfully, he has already committed adultery with her in his heart." (Mt 5:27–28)

§221. The Mother of the Sons of Zebedee

In Matthew's Gospel, Salome, the wife of Zebedee and the mother of the apostles James and John, asked Jesus for places of honor for her sons; in Mark's earlier version the brothers asked for themselves (Mk 10:35–40). Matthew's account (Mt 20:20–23) is a bit awkward, for in verses 20 and 21 the exchange is between Jesus and the mother (the verbs are singular), but in 22 and 23, without any indication of a change in the conversation partners, Jesus addresses the brothers (the verbs are now plural). Is this because in changing the Marcan account Matthew neglected to add a phrase something like, "and turning to the brothers, Jesus said . . ."?

Why does Matthew's tradition make the mother ask rather than the sons? If it is because it reflects the historical fact, it would indicate that at least this woman wielded a strong influence with two apostles and presumably also with Jesus. She obviously did not approach Jesus unbeknownst to her sons; they were there and collaborated. It would seem she was the mediator because she was thought to have greater influence with Jesus than her two apostle sons—all the more extraordinary since these two men were not shy, being nicknamed by Jesus "sons of thunder," and along with Peter were regularly the inner circle of the apostles, being chosen to view the transfiguration, go apart with Jesus at the Garden of Gethsemane, etc. Her standing with Jesus must have been considerable! In return she remained by Jesus to the crushing end—and the resurrection: she stood by the cross (Mt 27:56; Mk 15:40), and was at the empty tomb (Mk 16:1).

Then the mother of Zebedee's sons came with her sons to make a request of him, and bowed low; and he said to her, "What is it you want?" She said to him, "Promise that these two sons of mine may sit one at your right hand and the other at your left in your kingdom." "You do not know what you are asking" Jesus answered. "Can you drink the cup that I am going to drink?" They replied, "We can." "Very well," he said, "you shall drink my cup, but as for seats at my right hand and my left, these are not mine to grant; they belong to those to whom they have been allotted by my Father." (Mt 20:20–23; cf. Mk 10:35–40)

§222. The Multiplication of Loaves

All four of the Gospels include the account of the multiplication of the loaves and fishes by Jesus to feed a multitude in the desert. Two of them, Mark and Matthew, record two such events; many scholars argue that these are simply two forms of the same account. However that may be, what should be especially noted here about Matthew's account is that it alone speaks of women; all the other Gospel writers speak of five thousand *men (andres)* being fed. Matthew in both his accounts says there were "five [or four] thousand men *(andres)*, besides women *(gynaikōn)* and children." From what we know from elsewhere in the Gospels there were many women among Jesus' listeners. Yet women are not mentioned in any version except Matthew's. All of the evangelists must have known that women would have been present at this teaching and miracle as well as men. But apparently the primitive form of the story of the five thousand which the earliest Gospel, Mark, has (Mk 6:31–44)—which refers only to men—was accepted by Luke and John without their reflecting that certainly women would also have been present, or if they did, without their thinking it important enough to allude to. (Mark's other account, of the feeding of four thousand—Mk 8:1–10—refers to the crowd, and not to men or women.)

With Matthew either there was additional information available about the presence of women, or there were some insistent voices among his sources which made it seem important to allude to the women and children, or Matthew himself decided it was important enough that they should be explicitly mentioned. Perhaps the desire to enhance the magnitude of the miracle played a role in inducing Matthew to mention the women. But besides the fact that the women and children were doubtless present, and the fact that mentioning them would magnify the miracle, it is also true that having compassion on the women and children fit perfectly with Jesus' extremely positive attitude toward both groups. This would seem to be a clear indication that Matthew was sensitive to this "feminist" attitude of Jesus.

When Jesus received this news he withdrew by boat to a lonely place where they could be by themselves. But the people heard of this and, leaving the towns, went after him on foot. So as he stepped ashore he saw a large crowd; and he took pity on them and healed their sick.

When evening came, the disciples went to him and said, "This is a lonely place, and the time has slipped by; so send the people away, and they can go to the villages to buy themselves some food." Jesus replied, "There is no need for them to go: give them something to eat yourselves." But they answered, "All we have with us is five loaves and two fish." "Bring them here to me," he said. He gave orders that the people were to sit down on the grass; then he took the five loaves and the two fish, raised his eyes to heaven and said the blessing. And breaking the loaves he handed them to his disciples who gave them to the crowds. They all ate as much as they wanted, and they collected the scraps remaining, twelve baskets full. Those who ate numbered about five thousand men, to say nothing of women and children. (Mt 14:13–21; cf. Mk 6:31–44; Lk 9:10–17; Jn 6:1–13)

Jesus went on from there and reached the shores of the Sea of Galilee, and he went up into the hills. He sat there, and large crowds came to him bringing the lame, the crippled, the blind, the dumb and many others; these they put down at his feet, and he cured them. The crowds were astonished to see the dumb speaking, the cripples whole again, the lame walking and the blind with their sight, and they praised the God of Israel.

But Jesus called his disciples to him and said, "I feel sorry for all these people; they have been with me for three days now and have nothing to eat. I do not want to send them off hungry, they might collapse on the way." The disciples said to him, "Where could we get enough bread in this deserted place to feed such a crowd?" Jesus said to them, "How many loaves have you?" "Seven," they said, "and a few small fish." Then he instructed the crowd to sit down on the ground, and he took the seven loaves and the fish, and he gave thanks and broke them and handed them to the disciples who gave them to the crowds. They all ate as much as they wanted, and they collected what was left of the scraps, seven baskets full. Now four thousand men had eaten, to say nothing of women and children. (Mt 15:29–38; cf. Mk 8:1–10)

§223. Prostitutes and the Reign of God

As noted in §145, it is very unlikely that Matthew can be credited in 21:31–32 with apparently substituting the term "prostitutes" *(pornai)* for "sinners" as a pair with "tax collectors" (the latter two are connected ten times with Jesus by the Gospels; this is the only time "prostitute" is mentioned in the Gospels other than in a parable); Jesus himself must have used the term deliberately, with all its pro-woman implications. Still, either the term and story were retained only in Matthew's special sources, or if they were also known by Mark or Luke, they either were not used by them or were used and later suppressed. This latter is just possible with Luke, given his general sympathy for women, his sole recording of the story of Jesus and the sinful woman (most likely a prostitute—Lk 7:38–50), and the possibility that the story of the adulterous woman now most often placed in Jn 8:2–11 was really torn loose from after Lk 21:38 (where some manuscripts locate it, and because the Greek language is quite Lucan—and certainly not Johannine). However, in view of the lack of any positive manuscript evidence that Luke had used the term in this connection, the most likely conclusion is that this story was known only to Matthew's special source. The fact that Matthew did not leave the story aside, or substitute the word "sinners" for "prostitutes," not only indicates Jesus as the ultimate source of the story and term but also that here again Matthew's sources favorable to women were at work in the tradition peculiar to Matthew which retained this story, and that Matthew himself was also sufficiently influenced by the pro-woman attitude of Jesus and the tradition that transmitted the evidence for it as to include this story and term here. (Mt 21:23, 31–32)

§224. Pilate's Wife

Only Matthew records the story about Pilate's wife speaking to Pilate in behalf of Jesus (see §155 for analysis). This is another example of the pro-woman element active in Matthew's sources and his sympathizing with it sufficiently to put it in his Gospel. Since the story does show at least this presumably Roman woman in a light sympathetic to Jesus, one might have expected to find it in Mark's Gospel if he knew of it, since he presumably was writing in Rome for Gentiles. Its absence in Mark, then, can only mean his sources did not contain it, again highlighting the strongly pro-woman element in Matthew's special sources. (Mt 27:19)

(4) Sexually Parallel Stories and Images

The several sexually parallel stories and images found in the Gospels were individually analyzed above. However, note should be taken here of their relationship to the several Gospel writers and the implications of those relationships.

These are either sets of stories or images in the Gospels which focus on a man and on a woman in parallel fashion. It is especially interesting that with a single possible exception they all are recorded only in either Matthew or Luke or in both; none are to be found in John, and perhaps only one in Mark. Both Matthew and Luke record the same three of the parallel sets; one set is peculiar to Matthew; four are peculiar to Luke. Did one simply copy the idea and three common sets from the other and then go on to put together another one or four pairs on his own? But then why did Luke not copy all four of Matthew's sets instead of just three, or, even more, why did Matthew not copy all seven of Luke's sets instead of just three? These omissions, among other evidence elsewhere, would argue against a copying of one from the other in either direction.

Moreover, scholars are not at all agreed on what the relationship in general is between Matthew and Luke. There are 230 verses which Matthew and Luke have in common that are not found in Mark (nor in John). Many scholars postulate a third document prior to either Matthew or Luke, now lost (usually called Q, perhaps for the German *Quelle*, "source"), which both had separately; Matthew and Luke each also had sources completely peculiar to themselves. It is also suggested by some scholars that not only prior common and independent written documents but also prior common and independent oral traditions are necessary to account for all the similarities and dissimilarities in the Gospels. It would seem that this latter combination is the most likely solution of this "synoptic" problem, though precisely what the documents and oral traditions were and their relationships has by no means been satisfactorily explained to date—if indeed it is completely possible at all.

In this matter of the sexually parallel images and stories it is clear that forces were at work in the sources of both Matthew and Luke which discerned a strongly affirming attitude toward women by Jesus, an attitude that saw them as equal to men. The images and stories about women were there in the sources of Matthew and Luke, whether written or oral. Hence a "balancing" of images and stories about women as well as men could not be attributed to Matthew and Luke but probably would have to be attributed to Jesus himself. However, it should be noted that (*a*) Mark records almost none of these female images or stories individually, let alone in sexually parallel pairs, and (*b*) all of the female images and stories used by Jesus (save the one where Jesus likens himself to a hen) are found only in these parallel sets in Matthew and Luke. This strongly suggests that these particular close pairings would have to be attributed to the sources of Matthew and Luke, written and/or oral. Jesus himself, however, may well have juxtaposed one or more of our present sets of sexually parallel images or stories. Since Jesus obviously told the original stories and used the images, at least in some form if not always exactly as we have them recorded in the Gospels, and hence must have consciously "balanced" male images and stories with female ones, it seems very likely that he also "paired" some of the stories, though which ones, etc., we cannot easily know. In any case, the presence of these eight sexually parallel images and stories in Matthew and Luke is a clear indication that forces sympathetic to women were strongly at work in the sources of both Matthew and Luke.

Further, from evidence elsewhere in both Matthew and Luke it is also clear that this positive attitude toward women not only was in the sources prior to the Gospels of Matthew and Luke but was also picked up by the Gospel writers themselves. Moreover, since the pro-woman attitude on the part of Jesus is expressed, both positively and negatively, in all four of the Gospels, and since we have absolutely no evidence of such a "feminist" movement in Palestinian Judaism of the time (in fact, just the opposite occurred with the development of Rabbinic Judaism), this "feminism" would have to be attributed ultimately and powerfully to Jesus.

In fact, one of the most fundamental criteria that scholars (e.g., Ernst Käsemann and Reginald H. Fuller) use to discover authentic sayings or actions of Jesus is to discern whether they are distinctive over against his environment. A Jewish scholar puts the principle into action when he writes: "The relation of Jesus to women seems unlike what would have been usual for a Rabbi. He seems to have definitely broken with orientalism in this particular. . . . But certainly the relations of Jesus towards women, and of theirs towards him, seem to strike a new note, and a higher note, and to be off the line of Rabbinic tradition" (Montefiore, *Rabbinic Literature and Gospel Teaching,* pp. 217f.).

The following are the texts involved:

Common to Luke and Perhaps Mark
Lk 8:16–17   Mk 4:21–22

Common to Matthew and Luke
Lk 17:34–37   Lk 11:29–32   Lk 13:20–21
Mt 24:39–41   Mt 12:38–42   Mt 13:33

Special to Luke
Lk 4:24–27   Lk 15:1–3   Lk 18:1–8

Special to Matthew
Mt 25:1–3

§225. Conclusions

As noted at the beginning of the section, Matthew's Gospel goes far beyond Mark's in its pro-woman attitude. This is true in terms of absolute quantity (36 passages dealing with women of 180 verses in length compared to Mark's 20 passages of 114 verses in length), proportion of "women passages" in comparison to overall length (Mark is 67 percent of the length of Matthew, but has only 55 percent of the number of women passages), and the uniquely positive attitude of a significant number of Matthew's passages.

One important point is the possibility of an intensification of a sensitivity toward women from the perhaps earliest written form of a Gospel, the Aramaic version of Matthew, of which Papias (A.D. 130) speaks when he refers to Matthew's composition of the discourses *(logia)* of Jesus in Aramaic. (Scholars do in fact find something of a flavor of a Greek translation of Aramaic in Jesus' discourses as recorded in the present Greek version of Matthew, but not in the narrative sections.) Many scholars contend that Mark had this Aramaic Matthew (or a very literal Greek translation of it) at his disposal when composing his Gospel, and that the canonical Greek Matthew Gospel writer in turn had both the Aramaic Matthew, and Mark, among other sources, at his disposal. Thus the chronological order of composition would have been: Aramaic Matthew; Mark; Greek Matthew.

When it is recalled that the later Greek Matthew (Mt 16:1–4) strand of the demand of a sign from Jesus adds the sexually parallel sign of the Queen of Sheba, not found in either the earlier Aramaic Matthew strand (Mt 12:38–42) or Mark (Mk 8:11–12), and that Greek Matthew strongly communicates a pro-woman message in his very structuring of the events and discourses of Jesus—of course not found in the Aramaic Matthew listing of Jesus' discourses—a movement of an ever-sharper focus on women in Jesus' life and gospel becomes at least dimly visible.

Besides the pro-woman accounts that Mark records (all but two of which Matthew also records) and the additional accounts that Matthew has in common with Luke, which at times are even more sympathetic toward women than Luke's (see §264), Matthew also records a number of unique, pro-women elements: the inclusion of women in Jesus' genealogy, likening the reign of heaven to a wedding feast, placing prostitutes in it before priests, listing women among those whom Jesus fed by the multiplication of loaves and fishes, and mentioning Pontius Pilate's wife among Jesus' sympathizers.

In sum, the present Gospel of Matthew is very strongly pro-woman in the image of Jesus it projects—considerably more so than either the putative Aramaic Matthew, or Mark, or John.

d. The Gospel According to Luke

Where John has eight passages dealing with women, Mark twenty, and Matthew thirty-six, Luke has forty-two. It should be noted that the number of passages dealing with women is not simply dependent on the overall relative lengths of the four Gospels. It is true that Luke is both the longest Gospel and the one with the most passages and verses dealing with women. However, the relative proportion of the overall lengths of the Gospels and the number of women passages in them and their length are quite irregular. Taking Luke as the standard in both cases, the relationships are as follows:

Length		Women Passages		Women Verses	
Luke	100%	(42)	100%	(220)	100%
Matthew	92%	(36)	85%	(180)	82%
John	75%	(8)	19%	(119)	54%
Mark	62%	(20)	47%	(114)	52%

As seen above, John has by far the smallest number of women passages, though the third in overall length (four of the passages, however, are very long, so that in total length John has more verses of women passages than Mark). Even Mark has dropped from 62 percent of the length of Luke to 47 percent of the number of women passages of Luke (52 percent in terms of verses of the same). Matthew and Luke both have a large number of women passages as compared to Mark and especially John; on the basis of the number of women passages, the two of them could be called strongly pro-woman; Mark moderately so, and John weakly, but John would have to be designated moderately strong in view of the number of women verses and the uniquely positive quality of some of his material. In comparing Matthew with Luke on the basis of number of women passages in comparison to overall length it is clear that Luke has pulled ahead of even Matthew in "feminism." Where Matthew was 92 percent of the length of Luke, he dropped to 85 percent in the number of women passages of Luke (82 percent in terms of verses of the same).

Of Luke's forty-two passages dealing with women or the "feminine," as noted above, three are common to all four evangelists and nine more are common to all three Synoptics, Luke, Matthew, and Mark; another five are common to just Luke and Matthew, and two are reported by only Luke and Mark. Luke has far and away the largest number of unique women passages, twenty-three, whereas Matthew has ten special to him, John three, and Mark none. Thus both on the basis of sheer quantity and the very large number of women passages special to Luke, it is clear that Luke exhibits the greatest stress on women by far, followed by Matthew, much farther back by Mark, and least of all by John.

The relationship of the forty-two women passages in Luke and the other Gospels is as follows:

(1) Passages Common to Luke and Mark Alone

§226. Oppression of Widows

See pp. 183ff. for a discussion of Jesus' biting condemnation of the oppression of the most defenseless group in that male-dominated society, widows.

While all the people were listening he said to the disciples, "Beware of the scribes who like to walk about in long robes and love to be greeted obsequiously in the market squares, to take the front seats in the synagogues and the places of honour at banquets, who swallow the property of widows, while making a show of lengthy prayers. The more severe will be the sentence they receive." (Lk 20:45–47; cf. Mk 12:38–40)

§227. The Widow's Mite

See §129, for an analysis of Jesus' lifting up of a widow as a model to be imitated.

As he looked up he saw rich people putting their offerings into the treasury; then he happened to notice a poverty-stricken widow putting in two small coins, and he said, "I tell you truly, this poor widow has put in more than any of them; for these have all contributed money they had over, but she from the little she had has put in all she had to live on." (Lk 21:1–4; cf. Mk 12:41–44)

(2) Passages Common to Luke and Matthew Alone

§228. Sexually Parallel Stories and Images

See pp. 164ff. for an analysis of the several sexually parallel stories and images used by Jesus. As noted, neither Mark nor John records any stories told by Jesus dealing with women—in fact, they record relatively few of Jesus' stories in general. Hence, the sexually parallel stories and images of Jesus are all recorded either by Luke or Matthew or both. Three are recorded by both Luke and Matthew. They are as follows:

a. The Queen of the South

See §113 for the discussion of Jesus' reference to the Queen of the South, i.e., the Queen of Sheba, playing a judgmental role at the Judgment Day, paralleling a similar role filled by Jonah.

The crowds got even bigger and he addressed them, "This is a wicked generation; it is asking for a sign. The only sign it will be given is the sign of Jonah. For just as Jonah became a sign to the Ninevites, so will the Son of Man be to this generation. On Judgement day the Queen of the South will rise up with the men of this generation and condemn them, because she came from the ends of the earth to hear the wisdom of Solomon; and there is something greater than Solomon here. On Judgement day the men of Nineveh will stand up with this generation and condemn it, because when Jonah preached they repented; and there is something greater than Jonah here." (Lk 11:29–32; cf. Mt 12:38–42; 16:1–4; Mk 8:11–12)

b. Heaven the Leaven in Dough

See §115 for an analysis of Jesus' image of the reign of heaven in the form of leaven in dough, an image clearly familiar to women and directed at them.

Another thing he said, "What shall I compare the reign of God with? It is like the yeast a *woman* took and mixed in with three measures of flour till it was leavened all through." (Lk 13:20–21; cf. Mt 13:33)

c. Women at the "End of Days"

See §111 for an analysis of the sexually parallel image of two women who are treated exactly the same as men at the "end of days." (Lk 17:34–37; cf. Mt 24:40–41)

§229. Jesus' Dismantling of Restrictive Family Bonds — I

See §127 for an analysis of Jesus' efforts at dismantling the restrictive family bonds that so often stifled people, especially women, in the culture in which he lived. (Lk 12:51–53; cf. Mt 10:34–37; also Lk 18:28–30; Mt 19:29)

§230. Jesus in a Female Image

See §118 for a discussion of Jesus' using female imagery to describe himself. (Lk 13:34; cf. Mt 23:37)

(3) Passages Common to Luke, Mark, and Matthew

The nine "women passages" that Luke has in common with both Mark and Matthew, in the opinion of most scholars, stem either from the earliest of the three Gospels, Mark, or the putative source, Q, prior to all of them.

§231. Jesus' First Cures: Men and Women

See §§184 and 201 for discussions on how Mark and Matthew placed accounts of the first two cures Jesus performed, of a man and a woman, at the beginning of Jesus' public life. Luke does the same. The man was from Capernaum and had an "unclean spirit" (Lk 4:33–37); the woman was Simon's (Peter's) mother-in-law. Hereby the earliest and subsequent Gospel traditions made it clear that the preaching and bringing of the good news of the reign of God was equally to women and men.

Leaving the synagogue he went to Simon's house. Now Simon's mother-in-law was suffering from a high fever and they asked him to do something for her. Leaning over her he rebuked the fever and it left her. And she immediately got up and began to wait on them. (Lk 4:38–39; cf. Mk 1:29–31; Mt 8:14–15)

§232. Lamp on a Lampstand

See §108 for an analysis of Luke's treatment of Jesus' image of placing a lamp on a lampstand as a sexually parallel story—which neither of the other two Synoptic Gospels does, though they do record the image of a lamp on a lampstand. This is one bit of evidence of a greater sensitivity to the cause of women's equality on the part of Luke and/or his sources. (Lk 8:16–18; cf. Mk 4:21–22; Mt 5:15; Lk 11:33–36)

§233. Jesus' Mother and Brothers

See §126 for a discussion of Jesus' attitude toward his family and how this reflected his concern for the lot of women. Here it should simply be noted that although Mark and Matthew refer to Jesus' sisters as well as to his mother and brothers, Luke does not. What significance this may have is not clear.

His mother and his brothers came looking for him, but they could not get to him because of the crowd. He was told, "Your mother and brothers are standing outside and want to see you." But he said in answer, "My mother and my brothers are those who hear the word of God and put it into practice." (Lk 8:19–21; cf. Mk 3:31–35; Mt 12:46–50)

§234. Jesus' Dismantling of Restrictive Family Bonds — II

See §127 for an analysis of Jesus' problems with his family and his attempt to dismantle the restrictive forces of the family—which particularly worked against women. All three of the Synoptics record something of this dismantling effort of Jesus, but there is a gradation in the recording: Mark has one such account (Mk 10:29–30), Matthew two (Mt 10:37–38; 19:29), and Luke three. In miniature this proportional relationship also reflects the intensity of the three evangelists' emphasizing the concern of Jesus for women. Luke again turns out to be the strongest "feminist"—after Jesus. (Lk 18:28–30; cf. Mk 10:28–30; Mt 19:27–29; see also Lk 12:51–53; 14:26–27; Mt 10:35–39)

§235. Jairus' Daughter and the Woman with a Flow of Blood

See §131 for analyses of Jesus' cures of two women, one with a long-term hemorrhage and one dead. In all three Synoptic accounts Jesus apparently violates or accepts the violation of two basic regulations of ritual purity in order to cure women. First, he touched what everyone thought was a ritually unclean object, a corpse, Jairus' twelve-year-old daughter; and second, he commended the ritually unclean hemorrhaging woman for having touched him in faith. Jesus' championing of children (Luke is the only Gospel writer who records that Jairus' daughter was a child of twelve) and women within the context of making light of ritual purity is reflected in a variant reading elsewhere in Luke (see §262), where Jesus is accused of leading astray children and women with the result that the latter do not observe the ritual purifications. (Lk 8:40–56; cf. Mk 5:21–43; Mt 9:18–26)

§236. Marriage and the Dignity of Women — I

See §120 for an analysis of Jesus' revolutionary egalitarian attitude toward women in marriage by eliminating the husband's—till then almost unlimited—right to divorce his wife.

"Everyone who divorces his wife and marries another is guilty of adultery, and the man who marries a woman divorced by her husband commits adultery." (Lk 16:18; cf. Mk 10:1–12; Mt 5:32; 19:9)

§237. Marriage and the Dignity of Women — II

See §122 for an analysis of Jesus' response to the question of some Sadducees about a woman married seven times—to whom would she belong? Jesus' answer presumed that she was a person and belonged to no one.

Some Sadducees—those who say that there is no resurrection—approached him and they put this question to him, "Master, we have it from Moses in writing, that if a man's married brother dies childless, the man must marry the widow to raise up children for his brother. Well then, there were seven brothers. The first, having married a wife, died childless. The second and then the third married the widow. And the same with all seven, they died leaving no children. Finally the woman herself died. Now, at the resurrection, to which of them will she be wife since she had been married to all seven?"

Jesus replied, "The children of this world take wives and husbands, but those who are judged worthy of a place in the other world and in the resurrection from the dead do not marry because they can no longer die, for they are the same as the angels, and being children of the resurrection they are sons of God. And Moses himself implies that the dead rise again, in the passage about the bush where he calls the Lord the God of Abraham, the God of Isaac and the God of Jacob. Now he is God, not of the dead, but of the living; all are alive for him." (Lk 20:27–38; cf. Mk 12:18–27; Mt 22:23–33)

§238. Jesus' Concern for Women's Welfare

See §197 for a discussion of the concern for women's welfare at the final crisis that Jesus expressed. Unlike Mark and Matthew, Luke does not have sexually parallel images here, pairing the men in the field and on the housetop with the women who are pregnant and nursing children. Rather, he refers to *only* the women. Thus Luke's version stresses Jesus' concern for women even more than the versions of Matthew and Mark.

"When you see Jerusalem surrounded by armies, you must realise that she will soon be laid desolate. Then those in Judaea must escape to the mountains, those inside the city must leave it, and those in country districts must not take refuge in it. For this is the time of vengeance when all that scripture says must be fulfilled. Alas for those with child, or with babies at the breast, when those days come!" (Lk 21:20–23; cf. Mk 13:14–20; Mt 24:15–22)

§239. Women in Jesus' Passion and Resurrection

See §§155–171 for analyses of the close connection of women with the passion, death, and burial of Jesus, their witnessing the empty tomb and reporting of the resurrection to the male disciples, on all of which all four of the evangelists agree almost unanimously. It is worthy of note here that Luke, unlike the other three evangelists, does not report any appearances of the risen Jesus to women. For a discussion of this, see §264.

§240. Women Witness the Burial of Jesus

See §158 for an analysis of the account of the women disciples watching the burial of Jesus. Luke here refers to them specifically as those who followed Jesus from Galilee. Mark and Matthew refer to the same group of women as being at the crucifixion and death of Jesus and then specify Mary Magdalene and others by name as observing the burial. Luke names Mary Magdalene and others only in connection with the later visit of the women to the tomb. It is clear that all three Synoptic Gospels are here dependent on basically the same tradition, that the women in question were Jesus' Galilean women disciples, including prominently Mary Magdalene.

Meanwhile the women who had come from Galilee with Jesus were following behind. They took note of the tomb and of the position of the body.
Then they returned and prepared spices and ointments. And on the sabbath day they rested, as the Law required. (Lk 23:55–56; cf. Mk 15:47; Mt 27:61)

(4) Passages Special to Luke

§241. A Woman "Evangelist"?

Of the forty-two passages in Luke dealing with women or the feminine, over half, twenty-three, are special to Luke. This compares to ten special to Matthew out of a total of thirty-six, three special to John (though all quite long) out of a total of eight, and none special to Mark out of a total of twenty. Here is further indication that Luke was most especially open to women in the writing of his Gospel.

It is interesting to note that of the twenty-three women passages special to Luke, sixteen of them occur within the sections of Luke's Gospel that are made up either totally of material special to Luke (1:1 to 2:52) or of material special to Luke plus material common to Luke and Matthew alone (9:51 to 18:14). Several scholars point out that although Luke clearly was not a Jew or a Palestinian or an eyewitness of Jesus, those sections have both such a strong unity and definitely Palestinian Jewish eyewitness character that they must have been either originally written or told by a Palestinian Jewish follower of Jesus (e.g., Karl Heinrich Rengstorf et al., *Das Neue Testament Deutsch*, Vol. 1, Pt. 3, p. 10; Göttingen, 1968). Given the strong presence of stories about women in this "proto-Gospel" within Luke and the strong prejudice against accepting the witness of women ("When the women returned from the tomb they told all this to the Eleven and to all the others. . . . But this story of theirs seemed pure nonsense, and they did not believe them"—Lk 24:9, 11), it is possible that this "proto-Gospel" was written or told by a woman disciple of Jesus and used by Luke without referring to her as his source, lest his Gospel be discredited and disbelieved. A woman "proto-Gospel" writer would certainly fit well with the central place women (Elizabeth and Mary) hold in Luke's narrative of events before Jesus' adult life (Luke 1 and 2), and the intimate sensitivity with which the inner feelings and thoughts of the women are dealt.

However, what is much easier to sustain than the formal notion of a woman writer of Luke's "proto-Gospel" is that one or more women disciples were responsible for the remembrance and handing on, either in oral or written form, of at least most of those passages which pertain in a special way to women. It is not likely that in a very male-oriented society men would have been particularly aware of the vital significance of many of the things Jesus said and did relating to women, whereas to sensitive women they would have seemed as loud as thunderclaps. These women then, having experienced or noticed these things, would have been the ones to remember them and pass them on and would have been the ultimate source for the women material in the "proto-Gospel" sections of Luke, and the seven other uniquely Lucan women passages. Thus, even if she, or they, might not be proved the proximate "evangelist" of the "proto-Gospel" material of Luke, they could certainly be called "proto-evangelists," in the sense of having communicated the good news of Jesus.

§242. Elizabeth Conceives John the Baptist

Immediately after his brief prologue Luke begins his Gospel with the story of a man and a woman who were married, but childless. This lack of children was thought to be a great "humiliation" for the wife, not for the man. In fact, a little later the rabbis legislated that "if a man took a wife and lived with her for ten years and she bore no child, he shall divorce her" (Talmud bYebamoth 64a; cf. Mishnah Yebamoth 6, 6). There is an interesting sort of parity between the man and the woman, Zechariah and Elizabeth, expressed here by Luke's "proto-Gospel" source, interesting in the light of the definite inferior social position women held in that society. But Luke's "proto-Gospel" source refers to both the woman and the man together and is careful to point out the purity of priestly lineage of Elizabeth as well as of Zechariah. Then the focus on Zechariah which immediately follows (Lk 1:8–22) is balanced by the shift to Elizabeth (Lk 1:23–25, 36–45, 57–62).

It should also be noted that there is a strong resemblance between the story of Elizabeth's barrenness and her finally bearing a son who was to become a leading figure in Israel on the one hand, and similar events with Sarah, who bore Isaac (cf. Gen 17:15ff.), with Samson's mother whose name we are not told (Judg 13:2–7), and with Hannah the mother of Samuel (1 Sam 1:5–6) on the other. The similar form of the Elizabeth-Zechariah story strongly suggests that the "proto-Gospel" writer was familiar with these earlier stories of the Hebrew Bible, reinforcing the likelihood of the Jewishness of Luke's "proto-Gospel" source.

In the days of King Herod of Judaea there lived a priest called Zechariah who belonged to the Abijah section of the priesthood, and he had a wife, Elizabeth by name, who was a descendant of Aaron. Both were worthy in the sight of God, and scrupulously observed all the commandments and observances of the Lord. But they were childless: Elizabeth was barren and they were both getting on in years.

Now it was the turn of Zechariah's section to serve, and he was exercising his priestly office before God when it fell to him by lot, as the ritual custom was, to enter the Lord's sanctuary and burn incense there. And at the hour of incense the whole congregation was outside, praying.

Then there appeared to him the angel of the Lord, standing on the right of the altar of incense. The sight disturbed Zechariah and he was overcome with fear. But the angel said to him, "Zechariah, do not be afraid, your prayer has been heard. Your wife Elizabeth is to bear you a son and you must name him John. He will be your joy and delight and many will rejoice at his birth, for he will be great in the sight of the Lord; he must drink no wine, no strong drink. Even from his mother's womb he will be filled with the Holy Spirit, and he will bring back many of the sons of Israel to the Lord their God. With the spirit and power of Elijah, he will go before him to turn the hearts of fathers towards their children and the disobedient back to the wisdom that the virtuous have, preparing for the Lord a people fit for him." Zechariah said to the angel, "How can I be sure of this? I am an old man and my wife is getting on in years." The angel replied, "I am Gabriel who stands in God's presence, and I have been sent to speak to you and bring you this good news. Listen! Since you have not believed my words, which will come true at their appointed time, you will be silenced and have no power of speech until this has happened." Meanwhile the people were waiting for Zechariah and were surprised that he stayed in the sanctuary so long. When he came out he could not speak to them, and they realised that he had received a vision in the sanctuary. But he could only make signs to them, and remained dumb.

When his time of service came to an end he returned home. Some time later his wife Elizabeth conceived, and for five months she kept to herself. "The Lord has done this for me," she said, "now that it has pleased him to take away the humiliation I suffered among people." (Lk 1:5–25)

§243. The Annunciation

There are striking similarities between the announcement of the coming birth of John the Baptist and his kinsman Jesus: both sons were to be leading figures in Judaism; their conceptions were to be extraordinary—John conceived in old age and "even from his mother's womb he will be filled with the Holy Spirit," and Jesus conceived without an earthly father, but "the Holy Spirit will come upon you and the power of the Most High will cover you with its shadow"; the announcements were delivered by angels. There are also at least two significant differences: Zechariah was somewhat resistant to the announcement and was consequently punished with temporary dumbness, whereas Mary was fully open and hence suffered no punishment; most important, in the case of John the angelic announcement was made to the man, in Jesus' case it was made to the woman. The importance of this latter difference would not be neutralized simply by noting that any angelic announcement made about the virgin conception of Jesus would have to be made to the prospective mother because there was no prospective father, for as a matter of fact Matthew's Gospel does do just about that: in Matthew there is a single angelic announcement of the virgin conception recorded, and it is made to Joseph, Mary's betrothed (cf. Mt 1: 18–25).

In the sixth month the angel Gabriel was sent by God to a town in Galilee called Nazareth, to a virgin betrothed to a man named Joseph, of the House of David; and the virgin's name was Mary. He went in and said to her, "Rejoice, so highly favoured! The Lord is with you." She was deeply disturbed by these words and asked herself what this greeting could mean, but the angel said to her, "Mary, do not be afraid; you have won God's favor. Listen! You are to conceive and bear a son, and you must name him Jesus. He will be great and will be called Son of the Most High. The Lord God will give him the throne of his ancestor David; he will rule over the House of Jacob for ever and his reign will have no end." Mary said to the angel, "But how can this come about, since I am a virgin?" "The Holy Spirit will come upon you," the angel answered, "and the power of the Most High will cover you with its shadow. And so the child will be holy and will be called Son of God. Know this too: your kinswoman Elizabeth has, in her old age, herself conceived a son, and she whom people called barren is now in her sixth month, for nothing is impossible to God." "I am the handmaid of the Lord," said Mary, "let what you have said be done to me." (Lk 1:26–38)

§244. The Visitation

In this scene Luke describes Mary's visit to her kinswoman Elizabeth. The focus is entirely on the two women, the two expectant mothers of leading figures of Israel. What is especially to be noted here is that according to Luke the first person, besides Mary, to whom Jesus' messiahship is revealed is a woman, Elizabeth: "Elizabeth was filled with the Holy Spirit . . . and said, . . . 'Why should I be honoured with a visit from the mother of my Lord [i.e., of Messiah]?' " (Lk 1:41–43). Where Zechariah reacted in a resistant fashion in the face of the "divine," and was punished, Elizabeth reacted positively and was rewarded by a visit from the Messiah *in utero* and by being informed that her son was to be named John (cf. Lk 1: 60: "But his mother spoke up. 'No,' she said, 'he is to be called John' ").

Mary set out at that time and went as quickly as she could to a town in the hill country of Judah. She went into Zechariah's house and greeted Elizabeth. Now as soon as Elizabeth heard Mary's greeting, the child leapt in her womb and Elizabeth was filled with the Holy Spirit. She gave a loud cry and said, "Of all women you are the most blessed, and blessed is the fruit of your womb. Why should I be honoured with a visit from the mother of my Lord? For the moment your greeting reached my ears, the child in my womb leapt for joy. Yes, blessed is she who believed that the promise made her by the Lord would be fulfilled." (Lk 1:39–45)

§245. The Magnificat

The song of joy uttered by Mary when she met Elizabeth starts with the words, "My soul *magnifies* the Lord," in the Western traditional Latin Vulgate, *"Magnificat* anima mea Dominum." Hence the customary title.

The great majority of early manuscripts state in verse 46 that Mary said the Magnificat, but a few attribute it to Elizabeth. Some scholars —e.g., John Martin Creed, *The Gospel According to St. Luke* (London, 1930); J. B. Phillips in his 1952 (1st ed.) translation of the Gospels; and John Drury, *Luke* (Macmillan Publishing Co., 1973)— follow this minority tradition of attributing the Magnificat to Elizabeth because they are convinced the text makes more sense in Elizabeth's mouth than in Mary's. If that were the case, then the balancing of the focus between Zechariah and Elizabeth would be still more clearly parallel (the Magnificat in Elizabeth's mouth matching the song, the Benedictus—Lk 1:68–79—in Zechariah's), and even tip in

Elizabeth's favor (she was believing and rewarded rather than disbelieving and punished).

Whomever the Magnificat is attributed to, it is clear that it very closely resembles the Song of Hannah the mother of Samuel (1 Sam 2:1–10), mentioned above. In both the Magnificat and the Song of Hannah there is a stress on praising God for lifting up the lowly and the humble, and feeding the hungry. Who are the lowliest of Near Eastern society? Women. Who are the first to go hungry? Widows. There is a clear sense of solidarity, even almost identity, of women with the lowliest and hungriest expressed by placing these two songs in the mouths of women (who were lifted up in the only way possible for women in that society—by bearing a son). Both songs contain cries of joy that the lowly (read: women) were finally raised up. Whoever may have composed the two songs (it is not likely that Mary, or Elizabeth, composed on the spot the Magnificat with its extraordinary parallels to the Song of Hannah) and in whatever context, it is apparent that the editor of 1 Samuel and Luke's source for the Magnificat (his possibly woman evangelist) both realized that women—especially those who had not borne a son—would be recognized by all as lowly and poor. They expressed this realization simply by attributing these songs, whether composed by women or not, to women.

Magnificat

And Mary said:
"My soul proclaims the greatness of the Lord
and my spirit exults in God the saviour;
because he has looked upon his lowly handmaid.
Yes, from this day forward all generations will call me blessed,
for the Almighty has done great things for me.
Holy is his name,
and his mercy reaches from age to age for those who fear him.
He has shown the power of his arm,
he has routed the proud of heart.
He has pulled down princes from their thrones and exalted the lowly.
The hungry he has filled with good things, the rich sent empty away.
He has come to the help of Israel his servant, mindful of his mercy
—according to the promise he made to our ancestors—
of his mercy to Abraham and to his descendants for ever."

Mary stayed with Elizabeth about three months and then went back home. (Lk 1:46–56)

Song of Hannah

Then Hannah said this prayer:
"My heart exults in Yahweh

my horn is exalted in my God,
my mouth derides my foes,
for I rejoice in your power of saving.

There is none as holy as Yahweh,
(indeed, there is no one but you)
no rock like our God.

Do not speak and speak with haughty words,
let not arrogance come from your mouth.
For Yahweh is an all-knowing God
and his is the weighing of deeds.

The bow of the mighty is broken
but the feeble have girded themselves with strength.
The sated hire themselves out for bread
but the famished cease from labour;
the barren woman bears sevenfold,
but the mother of many is desolate.

Yahweh gives death and life,
brings down to Sheol and draws up;
Yahweh makes poor and rich,
he humbles and also exalts.

He raises the poor from the dust,
he lifts the needy from the dunghill
to give them a place with princes,
and to assign them a seat of honour;
for to Yahweh the props of the earth belong,
on these he has posed the world.

He safeguards the steps of his faithful
but the wicked vanish in darkness
(for it is not by strength that man triumphs).
The enemies of Yahweh are shattered,
the Most High thunders in the heavens.

Yahweh judges the ends of the earth,
he endows his king with power,
he exalts the horn of his Anointed." (1 Sam 2:1–10)

§246. Birth and Circumcision of John the Baptist

In Luke's next scene Elizabeth is the center of focus as the birth of John is briefly related. She is also the center of attention in the first part of Luke's narration of the circumcision and naming of John. It appears that Elizabeth had the name of John revealed to her. In typical Palestinian fashion she was not even going to be consulted—"they were going to call him Zechariah after his father"—but she interposed a no and insisted on John. In typical fashion her authority counted for nothing and the crowd insisted on going to the "real" authority, the man: "they made signs to his father [who was still struck dumb by the angel] to find out what he wanted him called" (Lk 1:62). But Elizabeth's decision was vindicated by Zechariah and, as was to be expected, "they were all astonished." Thus Zechariah supported his wife in the naming of the child John. (There is no indication in the Gospel that the name John came from anyone except through Elizabeth, though it is possible that Zechariah could have written to Elizabeth that the angel said the boy's name was to be John; however, if that were the case, one would have expected that the Gospel might have recorded that Elizabeth said that Zechariah had told her the boy's name was to be John.) Zechariah now received his power of speech again and praised God with his song, the Benedictus (from the first word of the Latin Vulgate translation: "Blessed be the Lord, the God of Israel," "Benedictus Dominus Deus Israel").

Meanwhile the time came for Elizabeth to have her child, and she gave birth to a son; and when her neighbours and relations heard that the Lord had shown her so great a kindness, they shared her joy.

Now on the eighth day they came to circumcise the child; they were going to call him Zechariah after his father, but his mother spoke up. "No," she said, "he is to be called John." They said to her, "But no one in your family has that name," and made signs to his father to find out what he wanted him called. The father asked for a writing-tablet and wrote, "His name is John." And they were all astonished. At that instant his power of speech returned and he spoke and praised God. (Lk 1:57–64)

§247. The Birth of Jesus

Only Luke records the birth of Jesus in any detail. Matthew merely says that Jesus was "born at Bethlehem in Judaea during the reign of King Herod" (Mt 2:1). Luke's is the familiar story of Joseph and Mary traveling from Nazareth to Bethlehem to register in a Roman census, and of Jesus' being born there; angels announce the event to shepherds in the area. Of course nothing here indicates anything of Jesus' attitude toward women, but there are two small hints of Luke's positive attitude in his references to Mary. When recording that the shepherds came to Bethlehem to find the Messiah, Luke mentions Mary first, not a usual order in a patriarchal society: "So they hurried away and found Mary and Joseph, and the baby lying in the manger." Secondly, Luke then speaks of Mary, not Joseph, keeping and pondering all these things in her heart. This would seem to indicate that Luke had access to Mary, or an intimate tradition stemming from Mary. Joseph apparently had died before Jesus' public life, but Mary lived through it and clearly became an important figure in the early Christian community, although not in the circles Paul traveled in, for he never refers to her. Luke is especially sensitive to Mary—he has twenty references to Mary or Jesus' mother, as compared to eleven in Matthew, seven in John, three in Mark, and none in Paul. This sensitivity in Luke toward Mary parallels his sensitivity toward women in general.

Now when the angels had gone from them into heaven, the shepherds said to one another, "Let us go to Bethlehem and see this thing that has happened which the Lord has made known to us." So they hurried away and found Mary and Joseph, and the baby lying in the manger. When they saw the child they repeated what they had been told about him, and everyone who heard it was astonished at what the shepherds had to say. As for Mary, she treasured all these things and pondered them in her heart. And the shepherds went back glorifying and praising God for all they had heard and seen; it was exactly as they had been told. (Lk 2:15–20)

§248. Prophecy of Simeon
When Mary and Joseph took the infant Jesus to the Temple at Jerusalem for the ritual redemption of the firstborn son, they were met by a devout man, Simeon, who prophesied concerning Jesus as the Messiah. Then Simeon addressed not Joseph or both parents, but rather Mary alone, reinforcing the above-discussed pattern of focusing on Mary. He spoke not only of Jesus, but also of what would happen to Mary because of him: "A sword will pierce your own soul."

As the child's father and mother stood there wondering at the things that were being said about him, Simeon blessed them and said to Mary his mother, "You see this child: he is destined for the fall and for the rising of many in Israel, destined to be a sign that is rejected—and a sword will pierce your own soul too—so that the secret thoughts of many may be laid bare." (Lk 2:33–35)

§249. Prophecy of Anna
As noted above (§149), we have here another instance of sexually parallel passages. Normally at least two witnesses are required in Jewish law to authenticate something; Luke records both a male and a female witness, indicating again that he understands Jesus' gospel, his messiahship, to be for both women and men. Both Simeon and the woman, Anna, are prophets. In fact, only she of the two is explicitly named a prophet *(prophētis)*. She too prophesied and spoke publicly of the messianic child. Thus in Luke, for every man playing

a significant role in the early and "pre" life of Jesus there is also an equally or more significant woman: Elizabeth and Zechariah, Mary and Joseph, Anna and Simeon.

There was a woman prophet also, Anna the daughter of Phanuel, of the tribe of Asher. She was well on in years. Her days of girlhood over, she had been married for seven years before becoming a widow. She was now eighty-four years old and never left the Temple, serving God night and day with fasting and prayer. She came by just at that moment and began to praise God; and she spoke of the child to all who looked forward to the deliverance of Jerusalem. (Lk 2:36–38)

§250. Jesus "Lost" in the Temple

In the sole Gospel account of an event of Jesus' life between his infancy and his public life, Luke reflects two elements which bear on the status of women. The first is indirect and remote. Elsewhere (§127) it has been pointed out how Jesus made a strenuous effort to dismantle the restrictive bonds of the family and that this dismantling would have by far the greatest liberating effects on women. Already here, at the pre-adult age of twelve (Jewish males took on adult responsibility with the rite of *bar mitzvah* at thirteen), Jesus began his efforts at loosening family bonds. When his parents chide him for going off on his own, he responds that they need not be so overly concerned about him, that he had other matters beyond their scope to attend to—an intimation of much stronger words ahead, coupled, nevertheless, with his obeying his parents after this twelve-year-old foreshadowing experience.

Secondly, it should also be noted that again in this story Luke focuses not on Joseph, but on Mary. It is her exchange with Jesus that Luke records, again pointing to a tradition that goes back to the personal recollections of Mary.

Every year his parents used to go to Jerusalem for the feast of the Passover. When he was twelve years old, they went up for the feast as usual. When they were on their way home after the feast, the boy Jesus stayed behind in Jerusalem without his parents knowing it. They assumed he was with the caravan, and it was only after a day's journey that they went to look for him among their relations and acquaintances. When they failed to find him they went back to Jerusalem looking for him everywhere.

Three days later, they found him in the Temple, sitting among the doctors, listening to them, and asking them questions; and all those who heard him were astounded at his intelligence and his replies. They were overcome when they saw him, and his mother said to him, "My child, why have you done this to us? See how worried your father and I have been, looking for you." "Why were you looking for me?" he replied. "Did you not know that

I must be busy with my Father's affairs?" But they did not understand what he meant. (Lk 2:41–50)

§251. Mary's Memoirs

Luke closes the introductory part of his Gospel by noting that Jesus obeyed his parents and matured, and that "his mother stored up all these things in her heart," rather pointedly implying that much of the foregoing was based, at least ultimately, on her remembrances. But one is given the impression that the significance of the events was by no means always so clear at the moment, but became so only in Mary's later reflections: "As the child's father and mother stood there wondering at the things that were being said about him" (Lk 2:33); "But they did not understand what they meant" (2:50); "As for Mary, she treasured all these things and pondered them in her heart" (2:19); "His mother stored up all these things in her heart" (2:51). Thus, as no other New Testament writer, Luke was concerned to gather into his Gospel the tradition of not just Mary's recollections, but her remembrances reflected on—Mary's memoirs.

He then went down with them and came to Nazareth and lived under their authority. His mother stored up all these things in her heart. And Jesus increased in wisdom, in stature, and in favour with God and humanity. (Lk 2:51–52)

§252. Luke's Introduction—A Woman "Evangelist"?

In Luke's introductory section, just reviewed, scholars often note the close parallelism and, at the same time, tightly interwoven quality of the John the Baptist and Jesus stories. But it is equally valid to note the sexual parallelism and, at the same time, integrated quality of the female and the male elements all throughout the introduction. This sexual balance is clearly deliberate on the evangelist's part and reinforces the possibility that this portion of Luke's Gospel, plus Lk 9:51 to 18:14, originally stemmed from a woman disiciple of Jesus, as discussed above.

§253. Jesus' Concern for Widows

Jesus' special concern for widows was analyzed above, pp. 183ff., and each of the events or stories about widows has been treated separately. But here it should again be noted that of the eight stories about widows found in the Gospels, seven of them are found in Luke's Gospel, four of them exclusively so. One is the sexually parallel story of the widow Anna, analyzed just above ·as part of Luke's introductory section. The second widow story found in Luke alone is the sexually parallel reference to the widow of Zarephath (Lk 4:25–27). The third, also sexually paired, is the touching story of the widow of Nain (Lk 7:11–17), and the fourth, again sexually paralleled, is Jesus' story of the widow and the wicked judge (Lk 18:1–8). It is apparent that Jesus was especially concerned about the plight of widows. But it is also clear that of all the evangelists Luke was by far the most sensitive to Jesus' concern about the burdens of widows since he exclusively recorded half the stories about widows, plus three quarters of the rest. Might this suggest that the possibly female "evangelist" of the "proto-Gospel" was herself a widow, or at least closely identified with widows?

§254. Jesus and the Penitent Woman

See §144 for a discussion of Jesus' deliberate breach of several social and religious customs in permitting a woman—of ill-repute!— to touch him in public, and in treating her as a full human being, whose primary quality is personhood. (Lk 7:36–50)

§255. Women Disciples of Jesus

See §150 for an analysis of the report that women also were openly among Jesus' followers—most extraordinary for that time and place. Was it from among them that Luke's possible woman "proto-evangelist" came? The woman mentioned most often by all the Gospel writers and to whom the risen Jesus first appeared—Mary Magdalene? Or the committed, intellectual disciple of Jesus who sat at his feet, Mary of Bethany? Possibly. But we have no documentary means of knowing. (Lk 8:1–3)

§256. The Intellectual Life for Women

See §147 for an analysis of Jesus' visit to the house of his friends Martha and Mary, of how Jesus made it abundantly clear that the supposedly exclusively male role of the intellectual, of the "theologian," was for women as well as for men, of how he explicitly rejected the housekeeper role as *the* female role. How this story must have buoyed up those Jewish women whose horizons and desires stretched beyond the kitchen threshold. It is, consequently, not at all surprising to find this story in the "proto-Gospel" section of Luke (Lk 1:1 to 2:52; 9:51 to 18:14) that many scholars attribute originally to a Jewish eyewitness follower of Jesus, who we have suggested might have been a woman disciple. One might ask who would have particularly noticed or have bothered to remember such a small event as the Martha and Mary story except a woman. It would have meant little to a man, but to a woman it would have been a door to a whole new world. Hence, it is quite likely that a woman (or women) was responsible for the preservation of this episode in Jesus' life. It also is likely that the woman originally responsible for remembering this event was the one who was there and was deeply impressed by it, namely, Mary of Bethany. Again, the question naturally arises, was this deeply religious intellectual woman disciple of Jesus the "evangelist" of Luke's "proto-Gospel"? In any case, Luke's sensitivity to women ultimately preserved this Magna Charta for women. (Lk 10:38–42)

§257. Rejection of the Baby-Machine Image
See §148 for an analysis of the brief passage wherein Jesus explicitly rejected the sexually reductionist baby-machine image of women in favor of a personal, spiritual one. Again, one wonders why this very tiny event was remembered and recorded. And more, who would have even noticed it and striven to preserve it except one to whom it meant a great deal, namely, a woman? This passage too is in the "proto-Gospel" (of the woman "evangelist"?) section of Luke. (Lk 11:27–28)

§258. Healing of a Woman on the Sabbath
See §132 for a discussion of Jesus' healing on the Sabbath of a woman ill for eighteen years, and the uproar it caused. It should be recalled that John recorded no healings by Jesus on the Sabbath and Matthew and Mark each recorded one healing—of a man—while Luke recorded three Sabbath healings, two of men and one of a woman. This single recollection of the healing of a woman is recorded (by the "woman evangelist"?) in the "proto-Gospel" section of Luke, again reinforcing the likelihood of its originally stemming from a woman. In the passage Jesus also referred to the cured woman in unheard-of fashion as a *daughter* of Abraham—a detail a woman was much more likely to notice and preserve, since it would mean so much more to her. (Lk 13:10–17)

§259. Jesus' Dismantling of Restrictive Family Bonds — III
Several times above (see §127) it has been noted that Jesus deliberately set about the task of dismantling the restrictive family bonds that often were overwhelmingly stifling in that culture, and most especially for women. It was also noted that Mark records one such

explicit passage, Matthew two (in common with Luke), and Luke three. It is interesting that two of these passages in Luke occur in the "proto-Gospel" section. Though there is a certain sexual asceticism expressed in two of these Lucan passages—or perhaps rather because there is—the fact that two of the three are found in the "proto-Gospel" section adds another argument for seeing a woman "evangelist" as Luke's source here.

> Great crowds accompanied him on his way and he turned and spoke to them. "If any one comes to me without hating his father, mother, wife, children, brothers, sisters, yes and his own life too, he cannot be my disciple." (Lk 14:25–26; cf. Lk 12:51–53; 18:28–30)

§260. God in the Image of a Woman

See §116 for a discussion of Jesus' use of a woman as an image of God, a usage vigorously resisted by the Hebrew prophets and other Hebrew devotees of the one true God, Yahweh (e.g., Judg 3:7; see Patai, *Hebrew Goddess,* for details). As noted above, because of their unique qualities, the three stories about how God is concerned about the "lost" were doubtless told originally by Jesus. It is also likely that they were told in response to complaints that Jesus was consorting with sinners; each one makes a most apt reply to such a charge. We cannot, however, be sure that they were all told at one time, as they are recorded in Luke. In fact, since each of them is quite effective in itself, it seems more likely that they were related by Jesus on similar but different occasions. Still, the inclusion of a story of God's concern for the "lost" which projected God in a female image doubtless must be attributed to Jesus, along with the rest of the stories and images. Jesus clearly was concerned to maintain a sexual balance in this category of parables, as in others. This, of course, makes very special sense since the complaint was that Jesus welcomed "sinners" (*hamartōlous,* Lk 15:2), which term included the sort of women who followed Jesus (e.g., *hamartōlos,* Lk 7:37). However, the bringing together of these three stories of Jesus in one place probably should be attributed to Luke, or perhaps more aptly, Luke's source, where Luke may well have found the three parables already successively arranged. This is particularly likely since the stories are located in the "proto-Gospel" section which is largely unique to Luke and has a specially cohesive quality. The fact that none of the other Gospels record the story projecting God in a female image—though Matthew does record one of these three stories of God's concern for the lost (Mt 18:12–14)—and that nowhere else in the New Testament is God portrayed in a female image also enhances the likelihood of a female "evangelist" for this "proto-Gospel" section of Luke. A woman would have been especially keen to recall and record such imagery coming from the lips of the Messiah. (Lk 15:8–10)

§261. Jesus and the Adulterous Woman

See §143 for an analysis of the extraordinary story of the woman caught in the act of adultery being used to set a trap for Jesus, his avoiding it and his refusal to condemn the woman—which act was probably responsible for the long resistance in early Christian history to receiving the story as authentic. As noted in §179, scholars generally agree on linguistic grounds that the story surely was not written by John, though it is usually printed there in most Bibles, but rather, as a note in the Jerusalem Bible states at Lk 21:38: "The adulterous woman passage of Jn 7:53–8:11, for the Lucan authorship of which there are many good arguments, would fit into this context admirably." For example, the strong similarity of the wording of Lk 21:37–38 to Jn 8:1–2 suggests that the latter is simply a modification of the former after the story was cut out of Luke:

In the daytime he would be in the Temple teaching [1. *didaskōn*], but would spend the night on the hill called the Mount of Olives [2. *eis to oros . . . elaiōn*]. And from early morning all the people [3. *kai pas ho laos*] would gather round him in the Temple [4. *en tō hierō*] to listen to him [5. *pros auton*]. (Lk 21:37–38)
And Jesus went to the Mount of Olives [2. *eis to oros tōn elaiōn*]. At daybreak he appeared in the Temple [4. *eis to hieron*] again; and as all the people [3. *kai pas ho laos*] came to him [5. *pros auton*], he sat down and began to teach [1. *edidasken*] them. (Jn 8:1–2)

The story depicts Jesus as taking an extremely sensitive and courageous stand, but one, as noted in the earlier analysis, which apparently scandalized many early Christians, leading to the story's deletion from all early manuscripts. But it did already have a partial precedent in the other Lucan story of Jesus and the penitent "prostitute" (Lk 7:36–50). It thus fits well into the strongly pro-woman spirit of Luke's Gospel. Because of that general "feminist" kinship, and because of the special kinship of the putatively Lucan story of the adulterous woman with the definitely Lucan story of the penitent "prostitute" (here are represented the amateur and the professional violators of sexual mores), it is quite possible that the wandering story of the adulterous woman also came from the suggested woman "evangelist" of the "proto-Gospel" of Luke. Again, a woman follower of

Jesus would be especially impressed with this event and especially eager to preserve it. Was this unknown woman among those earliest Christians driven into the Syrian Diaspora ("both men and *women*"—Acts 8:3; "men or *women*"—Acts 9:2), where she composed her "Gospel" (*euaggelizomenoi*—Acts 8:4)? Indeed, the solely Lucan passages, i.e., the "proto-Gospel," where this story might earlier have been located, not only betrays an intimate knowledge of Palestinian Judaism but is also clearly aimed at non-Jewish readers. Further, the earliest documentary evidence of the story of the adulterous woman is the reference in the third-century Didascalia, which originated in Syria (and which also refers to deaconesses as an image of the Holy Spirit! See §312).

§262. Jesus "Leads Women Astray"

Not only are the Gospels full of incidents wherein Jesus championed the cause of women and of children (e.g., Lk 9:46–48 and parallels, Lk 18:15–17 and parallels, where Jesus draws children to himself and says that all must become like them), but his reputation for this behavior was widespread enough that he may well have been denounced to Pilate for having "led women and children astray." There are at least three variant readings in Luke's Gospel, two of which are very early, which witness to this tradition. The oldest one, stemming from Marcion, who lived in the first half of the second century when some of the canonical Apostolic Writings (New Testament) were still being written, simply says that Jesus was accused of "leading astray both the women and the children." The second ancient variant reading comes from the fourth-century Palestinian-born church father Epiphanius, whose text stated that Jesus' accusers charged: "and he has turned our children and wives away from us for they are not bathed as we are, nor do they purify themselves."

It is not at all surprising that these very early pro-woman traditions turn up in Luke's Gospel, given the strongly pro-woman character of that Gospel. They support the notion that Jesus was a feminist, was widely known to be a feminist, was despised by many for being a feminist, and was politically denounced as a feminist.

It would appear from the second tradition that Jesus' lesson of the relative unimportance (vis-à-vis the woman's person) of regular female ritual impurity from the issuance of blood, as taught in the episode of the woman with the twelve-year hemorrhage (see §131), was widely learned and applied. To generate the remembrance of this tradition many women followers of Jesus must have had a high opinion of their experience of a new attitude toward the purity, or impurity, of their own bodies, and the fact that so many men perceived it as "turning their wives away from them." This so infuriated the men that they publicly denounced Jesus for it to the Roman governor and demanded that he be executed. These extremely early traditions attached to Luke (were they "suppressed" as was the wandering Lucan story of the adulterous woman?) reflect the notion that Jesus' feminism was perceived as a capital crime! (similar to that other Jewish feminist, Beruria—see §85).

They began their accusation by saying, "We found this man inciting our people to a revolt, opposing payment of the tribute to Caesar, [leading astray the women and the children *(kai apostrephonta tas gynaikas kai ta tekna)*— Marcion], and claiming to be Christ, a king. : . . He is inflaming the people with his teaching all over Judaea; it has come all the way from Galilee, where he started, down to here, [and he has turned our children and wives away from us for they are not bathed as we are, nor do they purify themselves (*et filios nostros et uxores avertit a nobis, non enim baptizantur sicut nos nec se mundant*—Epiphanius)]." (Lk 23:2, 5)
[For variant texts and references, see Eberhard Nestle, ed., *Novum Testamentum Graece et Latine*, p. 221; Stuttgart, 1954; and Roger Gryson, *The Ministry of Women in the Early Church*, p. 126; Liturgical Press, 1976.]

§263. Jerusalem Women on the Via Dolorosa
See §156 for a discussion of the unique Lucan recording of the exchange between the mourning women of Jerusalem and Jesus on the way to his execution. As noted, these women must have been strongly committed followers of Jesus to have risked their safety publicly to mourn and attempt to comfort a condemned prisoner, something the male followers of Jesus failed to do, and consequently it is to women alone that Jesus addressed himself on his Via Dolorosa. Clearly Jesus did what apparently no other rabbi was even concerned to do—he reached out and deeply touched the hearts of many Jewish women, and they responded to him here with reckless abandon. A male disciple of Jesus might well have recalled this incident with shame, though there is no hint of such shame in the text as we now have it. But how much more likely is it that a woman follower of Jesus would have had burned on her memory how the women—perhaps she too—rushed out to meet Jesus on the way to his agonizing and humiliating death, only to have him speak to their need alone, as he reached out to them one last time to show his concern for them in his last minutes: "But Jesus turned to them and said, 'Daughters of

Jerusalem, do not weep for me; weep rather for yourselves and for your children.' "

As they were leading him away . . . large numbers of people followed him, and of women too, who mourned and lamented for him. But Jesus turned to them and said, "Daughters of Jerusalem, do not weep for me; weep rather for yourselves and for your children. For the days will surely come when people will say, 'Happy are those who are barren, the wombs that have never borne, the breasts that have never suckled!' Then they will begin to say to the mountains, 'Fall on us!'; to the hills, 'Cover us!' For if men use the green wood like this, what will happen when it is dry?" (Lk 23:26–31)

§264. Was Luke Pro-Woman or Anti-Woman?

Almost everything that has been analyzed up to now has reflected a positive attitude toward women on the part of Luke and/or his sources. However, there are some items that can be seen as perhaps reflecting a somewhat negative attitude when compared with similar passages in Matthew and/or Mark. It would be well to list them, analyze them individually, and evaluate their overall implications. Perhaps ten such passages can be discerned.

(1) Lk 3:23–38. Luke here presents an ancestral genealogy of Jesus, listing only male ancestors, whereas Matthew includes four women in his genealogy of Jesus (Mt 1:1–17; see §218). However, it was not at all customary to include women in genealogies, so one would have to say not that Luke is thereby negative in his attitude toward women, but rather that Matthew is especially positive in this instance.

(2) Lk 4:22. "They said, 'This is Joseph's son, surely?' " Again, nothing negative toward women here. But the corresponding description of Jesus in Mark is as follows: "This is the carpenter, surely, the son of Mary, the brother of James and Joset and Jude and Simon? His sisters, too, are they not here with us?" (Mk 6:3). And in Matthew: "This is the carpenter's son, surely? Is not his mother the one called Mary, and his brothers James and Joseph and Simon and Jude? His sisters, too, are they not all here with us?" (Mt 13:55). There does seem to be a greater awareness of women relatives in Mark and Matthew here than in Luke and/or his sources.

(3) Lk 8:19 (see §233). Luke records that Jesus' mother and brothers came to see him and Jesus responded that those who act on the word of God are his mother and his brothers. Matthew (Mt 12:46–50) and Mark (even more—Mk 3:31–35) add "sisters" to the account. Again, this indicates nothing of a negative attitude toward women, especially since Luke does include "mother," but it does

perhaps indicate a slightly greater awareness of women on Matthew's and Mark's part than Luke's in this instance.

(4) Lk 9:10–17 (see §222). All four evangelists record the accounts of the multiplication of the loaves and fishes (Mk 6:31–44; 8:1–10; Mt 14:13–21; 15:29–38; Jn 6:1–13; Lk 9:10–17). Three, including Luke, refer only to thousands of men being fed (or to a crowd of thousands), whereas Matthew adds women and children besides. Again, nothing negative on Luke's—or Mark's or John's—part in this account, but rather a greater awareness of women on Matthew's part.

(5) Lk 12:35–37. Luke records a saying of Jesus about men waiting for their master to return from the wedding feast—nothing negative. However, Matthew's version (Mt 25:1–13; see §114) tells of ten bridesmaids waiting. Again, a stronger emphasis on women in Matthew than in Luke.

(6) Lk 14:15–24. Luke records a parable in which the realm of God is likened to people invited to a banquet. However, in Matthew's version (Mt 22:2–10; see §217) it is a wedding banquet, perhaps adding thereby a further "feminine" element. Further, in Luke's version one excuse offered for not accepting the banquet invitation is, "I have married a wife," suggesting that marriage might be an obstacle to responding to God's call.

(7) Lk 14:26 (see §128). In quoting Jesus' listing of those relatives who must give way to the demands of discipleship, Luke records not only father, mother, brothers, sisters, and children—as does Matthew (Mt 10:37–38 does not mention siblings, but see Mt 19:29)—but also "wife," perhaps again reflecting an attitude that views marriage as an obstacle to the full following of God's call.

(8) Lk 18:29. A similar listing of relatives left for the "sake of the reign of God" includes "wife" in Luke's version, but not in either Mark's (Mk 10:28–30) or Matthew's (Mt 19:29).

(9) Lk 23:49 (see §157). Luke mentions Jesus' women disciples as present at the crucifixion; so do Mark (Mk 15:41) and Matthew (Mt 27:56). However, the latter two mention only the women as being present, but Luke includes in addition "all his [Jesus'] friends," perhaps slightly diluting the focus on the loyalty of the women.

(10) Lk 24:1–11 (see §162). In Luke's Gospel several women are the first witnesses to the empty tomb, but no appearances of Jesus to women are recorded, whereas in Matthew (Mt 28:9–10), John (Jn 20:11–18), and the later added ending of Mark (Mk 16:9–11) they are.

It should be noted first that numbers 1–5 and 9 in no way indicate in themselves anything negative in Luke's attitude toward women, but rather evidence a somewhat sharper focus on women on the part of Matthew and/or Mark. Secondly, numbers 6–8 indicate an attitude that marriage was a burden in seeking the reign of God. Moreover, these three statements are written solely from the man's point of view, i.e., *wives* must be given up, or, "I have married a *wife*, and so I cannot come." No mention is made of marrying or giving up *husbands*. This sexually ascetic perspective reflects very well Paul's attitude toward marriage—i.e., best to avoid it if at all possible; his attitude was doubtless influenced by his expectation of the second coming of Christ imminently, which made worldly matters like marriage, slavery, etc., of relatively little significance—as expressed in his First Letter to the Corinthians, ch. 7; Luke, according to deutero-Pauline sources (Col 4:14; 2 Tim 4:11; Philem 24), was a long-time companion and fellow worker of Paul. Perhaps a second influence of Paul on Luke here can also be seen in number 10. According to Paul's writings Jesus did not appear first to the women, as in the three Gospels other than Luke; indeed, he did not appear to them at all, unless they were among "the five hundred" (1 Cor 15:3–7). It appears that Luke followed his teacher Paul in this regard also. But perhaps the most interesting, and obvious, point to be noted about all this "negative" evidence of Luke's is that it can be construed negatively only on a basis of comparison with other Gospel accounts of the same event, i.e., none of these passages comes from sections of Luke that are unique to him. That means their source is not the "proto-Gospel" by the possibly woman "evangelist" embedded within Luke. This would indicate that the "proto-Gospel" source was more consciously and strongly pro-woman than Luke's other sources, and Luke himself—another fact that points toward at least the possibility of a woman "evangelist."

§265. Conclusion

In sum it can be said that beyond the evidence that clearly points to the fact that Jesus himself was a vigorous feminist, Luke's Gospel reflects this feminism most intensely of all the Gospels. In choosing to record all this pro-woman material, Luke himself also clearly indicates a very sympathetic attitude toward women. However, his pro-woman material falls into two categories: that which is recorded in common with other Gospels and that which is unique to Luke. The former is almost as large (19 passages—17 of them in common with

Matthew) as the latter (23 passages). In the commonly recorded passages sometimes Luke's version highlights women more than the other version(s); sometimes the other way around. It would have to be judged that in regard to this commonly recorded material Matthew and Luke exhibit an attitude that is about equally sympathetic toward the cause of women. But in the material special to each Gospel, Luke is giant strides ahead of all the others in pro-woman passages. Simply in terms of numbers of passages dealing with women, Luke has 23 (practically all actively pro-woman) special to him; Matthew 10 (though half of these do not reflect an attitude toward women); John 3; and Mark none. Again, it is in that "proto-Gospel" section of Luke that the feminism of his Gospel really stands out. Thus it is clear that a strongly feminist "evangelist" was the source of the "proto-Gospel," again enhancing the possibility that it was a woman "evangelist," who perforce had to remain anonymous, at least in Luke's judgment, for the sake of the credibility of the Gospel in that male-dominated society.

3. "Androgynous" Jesus

The preceding pages have analyzed the Gospel texts that deal somehow with women, showing the attitude toward women on the part of Jesus and the Gospel writers and/or sources. But there is another message about Jesus' attitude toward women and men to be found in the psychological image of Jesus that is projected by the Gospels. That image is of an androgynous person—not in the sense of having a combination of male and female physical characteristics, but rather having a fusion and balance of so-called masculine and feminine psychological traits.

The notion that the significance of Jesus lay in his humanity rather than specifically in his maleness is one that was stated clearly and officially already in early Christianity. In the Nicene Creed (A.D. 325), ancient Christians said of Jesus, "et *homo* factus est," "and he became *human.*" They did *not* say, "et *vir* factus est," "and he became *male* (*vir*ile)." There was even a limited amount of Christian painting of Jesus as physically androgynous (see Leipoldt, *Die Frau in der antiken Welt und im Urchristentum*), but it was not very fully developed. However, if the question is asked whether the image of Jesus found in the Gospels is psychologically masculine or feminine, abundant material for an answer is at hand.

Certain ways of acting, thinking, speaking, etc., are popularly said to be specifically manly and their opposites womanly. (1) Men are supposed to be reasonable and cool—women are to be persons of feeling and emotion; (2) men are to be firm, aggressive—women, gentle, peaceful; (3) men should be advocates of justice—women, of mercy; (4) men should have pride and self-confidence—women should have humility and reserve; (5) men are said to be the providers of security (food, clothing, shelter)—women, the ones who need security; (6) men are supposed to be concerned with organization and structure—women with persons, especially children.

Analyzing the Gospel image of Jesus, we will ask: in which of these divisions did he fit?

§266. Jesus: Reasonable and Cool—Feeling and Emotion

Jesus had a large number of vigorous, at times even extremely vicious, enemies, both in debate and in life-and-death situations. In debate: After Jesus criticized the chief priest and scribes, "they waited their opportunity and sent agents to pose as men devoted to the Law, and to fasten on something he might say and so enable them to hand him over to the jurisdiction and authority of the governor. They put to him this question: 'Master, we know that you say and teach what is right; you favour no one, but teach the way of God in all honesty. Is it permissible for us to pay taxes to Caesar or not?' " They were a clever lot, for Israel was occupied by Roman troops and the Jews in general consequently hated everything Roman with a passion, and especially the publicans (native tax collectors for Rome). If Jesus had said straight out to pay Roman taxes, he would have immediately lost his influence with the people, which would have suited his enemies. But if he had said not to pay taxes, he would have immediately ended up in a Roman jail, or perhaps worse, which also would have suited his enemies.

"But he was aware of their cunning and said, 'Show me a denarius. Whose head and name are on it?' 'Caesar's,' they said. 'Well, then,' he said to them, 'give back to Caesar what belongs to Caesar—and to God what belongs to God.' " A most *reasonable* response: "As a result, they were unable to find fault with anything he had to say in public; his answer took them by surprise and they were silenced" (Lk 20:20–26).

In life-and-death situations: "When they heard this everyone in the synagogue was enraged. They sprang to their feet and hustled him out of the town; and they took him up to the brow of the hill their town was built on, intending to throw him down the cliff." Jesus' reaction? "But he slipped through the crowd and walked away" (Lk 4:28–30). Real *cool.*

More examples could be given, but these would seem sufficient to place Jesus in the "masculine" camp for this category.

On the other hand, once when Jesus came to the little town of Nain he saw a funeral procession for a young man, "the only son of his mother, and she was a widow." The widow was in a desperate situation, for in that culture women had almost no legal or economic standing except through a man—father, husband, son. Understandably the woman was weeping. A pitiable sight. But here Jesus' reaction wasn't cool: "When the Lord saw her he *felt* sorry for her. 'Do not cry,' he said. Then he went up and put his hand on the bier and the bearers stood still, and he said, 'Young man, I tell you to get up.' And the dead man sat up and began to talk, and Jesus gave him to his mother" (Lk 7:11–15). Jesus responded with *feeling.*

Another time when Jesus visited his friends Martha and Mary, two sisters, he learned that their brother Lazarus had died. Mary came to Jesus and "when Jesus saw her weeping, and the Jews who had accompanied her also weeping, he was troubled in spirit, *moved by the deepest emotions.* 'Where have you laid him?' he asked. 'Lord, come and see,' they said. *Jesus began to weep,* which caused the Jews to remark, 'See how much *he loved* him!' " (Jn 11:33–36). Jesus was clearly a person with deep emotions, and he showed them publicly.

Hence, it would seem that in this category Jesus had not only the so-called "masculine" characteristics but also the so-called "feminine" ones.

§267. Jesus: Firm and Aggressive—Gentle and Peaceful

There is no question but that Jesus was *firm.* He certainly was firm when he said to his chief follower Peter—in front of the rest of his followers(!): "Get behind me, Satan!" (Mk 8:33).

Jesus' *aggressiveness* was expressed in several inflammatory statements: "I have come to bring fire to the earth, and how I wish it were blazing already!" (Lk 12:49). "Do not suppose that I have come to bring peace to the earth: it is not peace I have come to bring, but a sword" (Mt 10:34). "From John the Baptist's time until now the reign of God has suffered violence, and the violent take it by force" (Mt 11:12). Jesus was most aggressive in his verbal attack on his enemies among the scribes and Pharisees. *Six times* in a row he denounced them to their faces as frauds: "Alas for you, scribes and Pharisees, you frauds!" And he went on: "Alas for you, blind guides!

... You blind men! ... You blind guides! Straining out gnats and swallowing camels! ... Alas for you, scribes and Pharisees, you hypocrites! You are like whitewashed tombs that look handsome on the outside, but inside are full of dead men's bones and every kind of corruption. In the same way you appear to people from the outside like good honest men, but inside you are full of hypocrisy and lawlessness. ... Serpents, brood of vipers!" (Mt 23:23–33).

Jesus' firmness and aggressiveness was not simply in his words, but in his actions as well: "So they reached Jerusalem and he went into the Temple and began driving out those who were selling and buying there; he upset the tables of the money changers and the chairs of those who were selling pigeons. Nor would he allow anyone to carry anything through the Temple. And he taught them and said, 'Does not scripture say: My house will be called a house of prayer for all the peoples? But you have turned it into a robbers' den.'" (Mk 11:15–17.)

On the other hand Jesus spoke of *gentleness.* He described himself in an image that was the epitome of gentleness: "Jerusalem, Jerusalem, you that kill the prophets and stone those who are sent to you! How often have I longed to gather your children, as a hen gathers her brood under her wings." Note that Jesus doesn't hesitate to use the feminine image of the hen to describe himself (Lk 13:34). In the Sermon on the Mount he said, "Blessed are the *gentle:* they shall have the earth for their heritage" (Mt 5:4). With extraordinary gentleness Jesus spoke to the weary and weighted: "Come to me, all you who labour and are overburdened, and I will give you rest. Shoulder my yoke and learn from me, for I am *gentle* and humble in heart, and you will find rest for your souls. Yes, my yoke is easy and my burden light" (Mt 11:28–31).

If one word could sum up the life and message of Jesus, that word might be peace, *shalom.* In fact, at his birth angels sang, "Glory to God in high heaven, *peace* on earth to those on whom his favor rests" (Lk 2:14). Time and again when Jesus healed someone he said, "Your faith has saved you, go in *peace"* (Lk 7:50). He instructed his disciples in peace: "Whatever house you go into, let your first words be, *'Peace* to this house!' And if a person of *peace* lives there, your *peace* will go and rest thereon" (Lk 10:5–6). Jesus went "far out" on peace; he taught, "When someone slaps you on one cheek, turn the other!" (Lk 6:29). He promised much to the peacemakers: "Blessed are the *peacemakers:* They shall be called the sons of God" (Mt 5:9). To his followers he gives more: "I have told you this so that you may find *peace* in me" (Jn 16:33). *"Peace* I bequeath to you, my own *peace* I give you, a *peace* the world cannot give, this is my gift to you" (Jn 14:27).

Obviously Jesus was firm, aggressive *and* gentle, peace-loving; in this second category he was both "masculine" and "feminine."

§268. Jesus: Justice—Mercy

Jesus was a strong advocate of justice. To be just is to do what is right, and in society it means to follow the law. Jesus insisted on scrupulously following the law: "Do not imagine that I have come to abolish the Law or the Prophets. I have come not to abolish but to complete them. I tell you solemnly, till heaven and earth disappear, not one dot, not one little stroke, shall disappear from the Law until its purpose is achieved. Therefore, whoever infringes even one of the least of these commandments and teaches others to do the same will be considered the least in the reign of heaven; but whoever keeps them and teaches them will be considered great in the reign of heaven" (Mt 5:17–19). In the Beatitudes, Jesus promised, "Blessed are those who hunger and thirst for *justice;* they shall have their fill" (Mt 5:6). Several times Jesus spoke of the last judgment—where final justice would be meted out: "So will it be at the end of time. The Son of Man [Jesus] will send his angels and they will gather out of his realm all things that provoke offences and all who do evil, and throw them into the blazing furnace, where there will be weeping and grinding of teeth. Then the *just* will shine like the sun in the realm of their Father" (Mt 13:41–43). Again: "This is how it will be at the end of time: the angels will appear and separate the wicked from the *just* to throw them into the blazing furnace where there will be weeping and grinding of teeth" (Mt 13:49–50). And still again: "When the Son of Man comes in his glory . . . all the nations will be assembled before him. Then he will separate them into two groups, as a shepherd separates sheep from goats. The sheep he will place on his right hand, the goats on his left. . . . These will go off to eternal punishment and the *just* to eternal life" (Mt 25:31–33, 46). The epitaph on Jesus' life, spoken by the Roman centurion as Jesus hung dead on the cross, was: "Certainly this was a *just* man" (Lk 23:47).

Nevertheless, Jesus also said: "It is not the healthy who need the doctor, but the sick. Go and learn the meaning of the words: What I want is *mercy,* not sacrifice. And indeed I did not come to call the *just,* but sinners" (Mt 9:13). Jesus carried out these words many times, just as he did with the woman who was caught in the act of adultery, an act punishable by death (Deut 22:22–24). He said, "Let him who is without sin among you be the first to throw a stone at her." After all had left but Jesus and the woman he asked her, "Has no one condemned you?" She said, "No one, Lord." And Jesus said, "Neither do I condemn you; go, and do not sin again" (Jn 8:7–11). In the Beatitudes, Jesus promised, "Blessed are the *merciful:* They shall have *mercy* shown them" (Mt 5:7). In a similar vein he also taught: "Be *merciful,* even as your Father is merciful. Judge not, and you will not be judged; condemn not, and you will not be condemned; *forgive,* and you will be forgiven" (Lk 6:36–37). And how often should we forgive? That's what Peter wanted to know: " 'Lord, how often shall my brother sin against me, and I *forgive* him? As many as seven times?' Jesus said to him, 'I do not say to you seven times, but seventy times seven' " (Mt 18:21–22).

Jesus told many powerful parables, but perhaps his most moving was that of the prodigal son who took his inheritance while his father was still alive, wasted it on wild living, and then finally crawled home in shame: "While he was still a long way off, his father caught sight of him and was deeply moved with *mercy.* He ran out to meet him, threw his arms around his neck, and kissed him. The son said to him, 'Father, I have sinned against God and against you. I no longer deserve to be called your son.' The father said, . . . 'Let us eat and celebrate, because this son of mine was dead and has come back to life. He was lost and is found' " (Lk 15:20–22, 24).

But in this matter of mercy and forgiveness Jesus went beyond all his predecessors—and successors. He preached the doctrine of loving one's enemies: "You have learnt how it was said: You must love your neighbour and hate your enemy. But I say this to you: Love your enemies and pray for those who persecute you" (Mt 5:43–44). Incredible *words.* But Jesus *did* just that at the most critical moment of his life—his death: "When they reached the place called The Skull, they crucified him there and the two criminals also, one on the right, the other on the left. Jesus said, 'Father, *forgive them;* they do not know what they are doing' " (Lk 23:33–34). To the bitter end, Jesus was a man of mercy.

As in the first two categories, so also in this, Jesus strongly exemplified both the "masculine" and the "feminine" traits. Jesus was a person of both justice and mercy, forgiveness.

§269. Jesus: Pride and Self-Confidence—Humility and Reserve

It might be thought that pride was foreign to Jesus. But there is a kind of pride which, like its counterpart, humility, is simply truthfulness, affirming the good seen in oneself. A striking example of this pride occurred when a woman anointed Jesus with some expensive perfumed ointment; there were complaints among his followers that the ointment should rather have been sold and the money given to the poor. "But Jesus said, 'Leave her alone. Why are you upsetting her? What she has done for me is one of the good works. You have the poor with you always, and you can be kind to them whenever you wish, but you will not always have me'" (Mk 14:6–9).

A perhaps even clearer example of this pride appeared when Jesus made his triumphant entry into Jerusalem: "Great crowds of people spread their cloaks on the road, while others were cutting branches from the trees and spreading them in his path. The crowds who went in front of him and those who followed were all shouting: 'Hosanna to the Son of David! Blessings on him who comes in the name of the Lord! Hosanna in the highest heavens!' And when he entered Jerusalem, the whole city was in turmoil" (Mt 21:8–10). "Some Pharisees in the crowd said to him, 'Teacher, rebuke your disciples.' He replied, 'If they were to keep silence, I tell you the very stones would cry out'" (Lk 19:39–40).

The self-assurance and self-confidence that Jesus exhibited when dragged before the chief council of Israel was extraordinary. Only in someone who had a very deep grasp on himself could it be found; despite the violence and threats involved, Jesus was clearly in control, in a way that usually happens only in spy thrillers: After being beaten, "he was brought before their council and they said to him, 'If you are the Messiah, tell us.' 'If I tell you,' he replied, 'you will not believe me, and if *I* question *you*, you will not answer. But from now on, the Son of Man will be seated at the right hand of the Power of God' [a quotation from Ps 110:1]. Then they all said, 'So, you are the Son of God then?' He answered, 'It is you who say I am'" (Lk 22:67–70).

If possible, even more self-assured was Jesus' attitude later before Pilate, the notoriously cruel and bloodthirsty Roman governor of the area. The man had the power of granting release and of sentencing to a vicious death, and yet Jesus had a steel control over himself—and his judge: "Pilate . . . called Jesus to him, 'Are you the king of the Jews?' Jesus replied, 'Do you ask this of your own accord, or have others spoken to you about me?' Pilate answered, 'Am I a Jew? It is your own people and the chief priests who have handed you over to me: what have you done?' Jesus replied, 'Mine is not a kingdom of this world; if my kingdom were of this world, my men would have fought to prevent my being surrendered to the Jewish authorities. But my kingdom is not of this kind.' 'So you are a king then?' said Pilate. 'It is you who say it,' answered Jesus. 'Yes, I am a king. I was born for this, I came into the world for this: to bear witness to the truth; and all who are on the side of truth listen to my voice.' . . . 'Surely you know I have power to release you and I have power to crucify you?' 'You would have no power over me,' replied Jesus, 'if it had not been given you from above' " (Jn 18:33–37; 19:10).

And yet, Jesus is, rightly, known for teaching humility. As noted above, he said, "Learn from me, for I am gentle and *humble* in heart" (Mt 11:29). He put flesh on this teaching with a story: "When someone invites you to a wedding feast, do not take your seat in the place of honour. A more distinguished person than you may have been invited, and the person who invited you both may come and say, 'Give up your place to this person.' And then, to your embarrassment, you would have to go and take the lowest place. No; when you are a guest, make your way to the lowest place and sit there, so that, when your host comes, he may say, 'My friend, move up higher.' In that way, everyone with you at the table will see you honoured. For everyone who exalts himself will be humbled, and the one who *humbles* himself will be exalted" (Lk 14:7–11).

Another story Jesus told had much the same message. He spoke of a Pharisee in the Temple who bragged to God about all his virtues, and of a hated tax collector who beat his breast and said, "God, be merciful to me, a sinner." Jesus concluded: "This man, I tell you, went home again at rights with God; the other did not. For everyone who exalts himself will be humbled, but the one who *humbles* himself will be exalted" (Lk 18:9–14).

Jesus paradoxically also often taught his followers *reserve*. For example, he said: "Be careful not to parade your good deeds before people to attract their notice." Or, "When you give alms, do not have it trumpeted before you. . . . But when you give alms, your left hand must not know what your right is doing; your almsgiving must be secret." And further, "When you pray, do not imitate the hypocrites; they love to say their prayers standing up in the synagogues. . . . But when you pray, go to your private room and, when you have shut your door, pray to your Father who is in that secret place" (Mt 6:1–6).

From this evidence, and still more in the Gospels, we would have to conclude that Jesus combined the so-called "masculine" traits of pride and self-confidence with the supposedly "feminine" characteristics of humility and reserve.

§270. Jesus: Provider of Security—Need for Security

The pattern that has emerged by now is so clear it hardly seems necessary to continue with a thorough analysis. A brief one will suffice.

It was to Jesus that his many followers flocked to find the *security* of the meaning of human life; of whom Peter said, "Lord, to whom shall we go? You have the words of eternal life" (Jn 6:67); who said of himself, "I am the bread of life. He who comes to me will never be hungry" (Jn 6:35). Yet it was also the same Jesus who sent his disciples out with "no purse, no haversack, no sandals" (Lk 10:4); who said to them, "That is why I am telling you not to worry about your life and what you are to eat, nor about your body and how you are to clothe it" (Lk 12:22); who said of himself, "Foxes have holes and the birds of the air have nests, but the Son of Man has nowhere to lay his head" (Lk 9:58); and who in the end felt a crushing need for security in his God: "My God, my God, why have you forsaken me?" (Mk 15:34). Jesus provided—and needed—security.

§271. Jesus: Organization—People

Briefly, in the final category, note Jesus' concern with *organization and structure* by recalling his carefully choosing his followers, his apostles—twelve, to match symbolically the twelve tribes of Israel ("You will sit on thrones to judge the twelve tribes of Israel"—Lk 22:30); the painful and painstaking instruction of his followers; and his sending out of the seventy disciples like lead men in a campaign today "to all the towns and places he himself was to visit" (Lk 10:1). But note also Jesus' intense concern with individual *persons*—his healing of numerous miserable people including lepers, blind, lame, paralytics; and his raising of the dead. Note his affection for despised individuals, such as the tax collector Zacchaeus (Lk 19:1–6), the "sinful" woman (Lk 7:36–50), and the adulterous woman (Jn 8:1–11). There is also Jesus' special concern for *children*—in fact, his holding them up as a model: "People were bringing little children to him, for him to touch them. The disciples turned them away, but when Jesus saw this he was indignant and said to them, 'Let the little children come to me; do not stop them; for it is to such as these that the reign of God belongs. I tell you solemnly, anyone who does not welcome the reign of God like a child will never enter it.' Then *he put his arms around them,* laid his hands on them and gave them his blessing" (Mk 10:13–16).

§272. Conclusion

Thus in all the traditional categories of so-called feminine and masculine traits the image of Jesus that is projected is very strongly both; it is emphatically androgynous. The model of how to live an authentically human life that Jesus of the Gospels presents is not one that fits the masculine stereotype, which automatically relegates the "softer," "feminine" traits to women as being beneath the male— nor indeed is it the opposite stereotype. Rather, it is an egalitarian model. Thus the same message that Jesus (and the Gospel writers and their sources) taught in his words and dealings with women, namely, egalitarianism between women and men, was also taught by his own androgynous life-style.

B. THE APOSTOLIC WRITINGS (NEW TESTAMENT)— OTHER THAN THE GOSPELS

Besides the four Gospels, the Apostolic Writings (New Testament) are made up of a variety of writings, mainly the Acts of the Apostles, the lengthy account of the early missionary years of the spread of the belief in Jesus as the Messiah or Christ (it is largely about the efforts of Peter and Paul); and letters written to the early Christian communities (these were mostly, but not exclusively, written by Paul and his followers). As noted above, this section of the Apostolic Writings is not directly about Jesus, but about the followers of Jesus, their beliefs and lives.

Perhaps the first difference between the Gospels and the rest of the Apostolic Writings to be noticed in this study is the attitude toward women. There is not only a large amount of evidence of a positive attitude by Jesus toward women exhibited in the Gospels; there is also a complete lack of any evidence of a negative attitude toward women by Jesus. The same cannot be said of the followers of Jesus in the rest of the Apostolic Writings. There are a number of negative statements about women to be found in the Apostolic Writings outside of the Gospels. These generally are very familiar to hundreds of millions of people, having been read and preached on in churches for millennia, having had hundreds of books written on them, and having been incarnated in church laws, structures, and customs. For the sake of completeness they will be quoted and briefly commented on elsewhere in this book.

However, the positive attitudes toward women held by the early followers of Jesus are much less often focused on—in fact, they are often almost totally overlooked. Hence, in an attempt to right that imbalance somewhat, we will gather them together here and briefly comment on them.

1. WOMEN CONVERTS TO CHRISTIANITY

Despite the restrictions women experienced in religion in the Semitic world, from the very beginning women were not only followers of Jesus but also formal adherents of the religion that sprang up in response to his life—Christianity. Women converts everywhere permeated the beginnings of Christianity, apparently riding on the momentum of the liberating experience they underwent during the lifetime of Jesus.

It should be noticed that all the quotations documenting this initial involvement of women in primitive Christianity come from the Acts of the Apostles—which was written by Luke, whose Gospel was by far the most sympathetic to women and very likely incorporated many elements that stemmed from women, whether in the role of "proto-evangelist" or otherwise, as sources. The influence of women in this second writing of Luke's will be apparent throughout many of the sections that follow.

§273. Women in the Upper Room

After the ascension of Jesus, Jewish-Christian women were part of the praying community in the upper room in Jerusalem:

All these joined in continuous prayer, together with *several women, including Mary* the mother of Jesus, and with his brothers. (Acts 1:14)

§274. Women Receive the Holy Spirit

The women as well as the men received the Holy Spirit and the gift of tongues:

When Pentecost day came round, they [the group previously mentioned in Acts 1:14] had all met in one room, when suddenly they heard what sounded like a powerful wind from heaven, the noise of which filled the entire house in which they were sitting; and something appeared to them that seemed like tongues of fire; these separated and came to rest on the head of *each of them.* They were *all* filled with the Holy Spirit, and began to speak foreign languages as the Spirit gave them the gift of speech. (Acts 2:1–4)

§275. Women Among First Converts
Women were among the first converts to Christianity:

And the numbers of men and *women* who came to believe in the Lord increased steadily. (Acts 5:14)

§276. Saul Persecutes Women Converts — I
That there were a large number of women converts to Christianity in Palestine is reflected in the accounts of their persecution by Saul (Paul). Normally in that society women would hardly have been mentioned in religious matters. But they are specifically referred to here:

Saul then worked for the total destruction of the Church; he went from house to house arresting both men and *women* and sending them to prison. (Acts 8:3)

§277. Saul Persecutes Women Converts — II
In two different accounts of Saul's traveling as far as Syria to arrest Christians, women as well as men are again specifically mentioned:

Meanwhile Saul was still breathing threats to slaughter the Lord's disciples. He had gone to the high priest and asked for letters addressed to the synagogues in Damascus, that would authorise him to arrest and take to Jerusalem any followers of the Way, men *or women,* that he could find. (Acts 9:1–2)

Paul said, . . . "I even persecuted this Way to the death, and sent *women* as well as men to prison in chains, as the high priest and the whole council of elders can testify." (Acts 22:4–5)

§278. Paul Preaches to Women
Once converted to Christianity, Paul preached the gospel just as eagerly to women as to men. At the Roman colony of Philippi he gladly preached to a prayer group made up only of women—probably a combination of born Jews, converts to Judaism (proselytes), and Gentiles who largely followed Jewish belief and practice ("God-fearers"):

sat down and preached to the *women* who had come to the meeting. (Acts 16:13)

§279. Women Resist Paul

However, in Antioch in Pisidia (Asia Minor), Paul met with stiff resistance, and here too women played a key role, so much so that they are mentioned first by the author of the Acts of the Apostles:

But the Jews worked upon some of the devout women of the upper classes and the leading men of the city and persuaded them to turn against Paul and Barnabas and expel them from their territory. (Acts 13:50)

§280. Lydia, First "European" Christian

The first "European" convert to Christianity was a woman, Lydia (living in Philippi), who, it seems, was also a head of a household, a person of some means and strong initiative:

One of these women was called Lydia, a God-worshipper, who was from the town of Thyatira and was in the purple-dye trade. She listened to us, and the Lord opened her heart to accept what Paul was saying. After she and her household had been baptised she sent us an invitation: "If you really think me a true believer in the Lord," she said, "come and stay with us"; and she would take no refusal. (Acts 16:14f.)

§281. Upper-Class Greek Women Become Christian

Many important women of Greek society actively joined the Christian church. So it was in Thessalonica:

And some of them were persuaded, and joined Paul and Silas; as did a great many of the devout Greeks and *not a few of the leading women*. (Acts 17:4)

So also in Beroea (again note that the women's importance is reflected by their being listed first):

Many of them therefore believed, with *not a few Greek women of high standing* as well as men. (Acts 17:12)

And in Athens:

But some men joined him and believed, among them Dionysius the Areopagite and *a woman* named Damaris and others with them. (Acts 17:34)

2. Women Co-Workers in the Gospel

Women were not merely converts to Christianity in its earliest phase but also critical workers in the spread and administration of Christianity. Paul, the chief missionary of Christianity to the Jews scattered throughout the Roman empire and to the Gentiles, refers to many such co-workers in the spread of the gospel, both in his earlier letters to the Philippians (c. A.D. 56) and to the Romans (c. A.D. 57) and in the latest letter, the Second Epistle to Timothy (perhaps largely written by a disciple of Paul's late in the first century). The spread of Christianity took place not only because women were accepted into the church but also because they worked to promote it, to spread the gospel, the *evangelium*—that is, they were "evangelists." The names of some of these women workers in the gospel have been preserved in the Apostolic Writings (New Testament) documents:

(1) Paul is said to have exchanged greetings between two women collaborators, Prisca and Claudia, among others:

Greetings to Prisca and Aquila. . . . Greetings to you from Eubulus, Pudens, Linus, Claudia and all the brethren. (2 Tim 4:19, 21)

(2) At the end of his long epistle to the church at Rome, Paul sent greetings to twenty-eight persons, ten of them women, including Julia; Nereus' sister; and Olympas:

Greetings . . . to Philologus and Julia, Nereus and sister, and Olympas. (Rom 16:15)

(3) One woman Paul called his "mother":

Greetings . . . to Rufus, a chosen servant of the Lord, and to his mother who has been a mother to me too. (Rom 16:13)

(4) Prisca is specifically called a co-worker in the Lord:

My greetings to Prisca and Aquila, my co-workers in Christ Jesus. (Rom 16:3)

(5) Four women worked very hard "for the Lord," obviously in spreading the gospel and building up the church:

Greetings to Mary who worked so hard among you. . . . Greet those workers in the Lord Tryphaena and Tryphosa. Greet the beloved Persis, who has worked hard in the Lord. (Rom 16:6, 12)

(6) John Chrysostom, usually very critical of women as such (see §343), wrote a series of homilies commenting on Paul's letter to the Romans. In reference to Paul's greeting of Mary he said:

How is this? A woman again is honored and proclaimed victorious! Again are we men put to shame. Or rather, we are not put to shame only, but have even an honor conferred upon us. For an honor we have, in that there are such women among us, but we are put to shame, in that we men are left so far behind by them. . . . For the women of those days were more spirited than lions. (Migne, *Patrologia Graeca,* Vol. 51, cols. 668f.)

(7) The woman Junia, called a compatriot by Paul, and an outstanding apostle(!), apparently also suffered imprisonment for the gospel:

Greetings . . . to those outstanding apostles Andronicus and Junia, my compatriots and fellow prisoners who became Christians before me. (Rom 16:7)

(8) Phoebe, deacon and ruler of the church at Cenchreae is thought by many scholars to be the bearer of Paul's epistle to the Romans, and is commended to their hospitality:

I commend to you our sister Phoebe, a deacon of the church at Cenchreae. Give her, in union with the Lord, a welcome worthy of saints, and help her with anything she needs: for she has been a ruler over many, indeed over me. (Rom 16:1-2)

(9) Paul speaks of Euodia and Syntyche "struggling" (*syn-ethlesan,* the same root as in "athletics") along with him and other fellow missionaries in the "gospel." Clearly, if Paul used such a strong verb, these women did not simply supply material support for Paul and the other men but preached, taught, and spread the gospel as vigorously as they. In fact, Paul thought Euodia and Syntyche were so important to the life of the church at Philippi that he bade them by name to overcome their differences:

I plead with Euodia just as I do with Syntyche: come to some mutual understanding in the Lord. Yes, and I ask you, too, my dependable fellow worker, to go their aid; they have struggled at my side in promoting the gospel, along with Clement and the others who have labored with me, whose names are in the book of life. (Phil 4:2-3)

3. WOMEN'S HOUSE CHURCHES

(1) Not only did many women embrace and work to spread the gospel; their houses were often the first Christian "churches." Perhaps the earliest such reference is to the house of Mary the mother of John Mark (traditionally, but not necessarily, the writer of the Gospel of Mark), which was in Jerusalem:

[Peter, when he had escaped from prison,] went straight to the house of Mary the mother of John Mark, where a number of people had assembled and were praying. (Acts 12:12)

(2) Some scholars see a house church in Paul's reference to the woman Chloe; it is possible, though questionable:

For it has been reported to me by Chloe's people that there is quarreling among you. (1 Cor 1:11)

(3) A clearer example is that of Lydia, Paul's convert:

One of these women was called Lydia. . . . After she and her household had been baptised she sent us an invitation: "If you really think me a true believer in the Lord," she said, "come and stay with us"; and she would take no refusal. . . . From prison they went to Lydia's house where they saw all the brethren and gave them some encouragement. (Acts 16:14–15, 40)

(4) Not an absolutely certain reference to a house church, but very likely so, is that concerning the woman deacon Phoebe:

I commend to you our sister Phoebe, a deacon of the church at Cenchreae, . . . for she has been a ruler over many, indeed over me. (Rom 16:1–2)

(5) An unquestionable example of a church at the house of a woman is that of Nympha (though even here because of an *inferior* Greek manuscript tradition some try to make the unlikely case that Nympha is a man's name). Paul writes:

Please give my greetings to the brethren at Laodicea and to Nympha and the church which meets at her house. (Col 4:15)

(6) Although one house church at Colossae was in a woman's house (Nympha's), a second was not. Nevertheless, even in that one a woman, Apphia, was singled out by Paul apparently as a leader in that house church:

From Paul, a prisoner of Christ Jesus and from our brother Timothy; to our dear fellow worker Philemon, our sister Apphia, our fellow soldier Archippus and the church that meets at your [singular] house. (Philem 1–2)

(7) A final example of a church at the house of a woman (Prisca) and her husband is clearly documented twice:

> My greetings to Prisca and Aquila. . . . My greetings also to the church that meets at their house. (Rom 16:3, 5)

> Aquila and Prisca, with the church that meets at their house, send you their warmest wishes, in the Lord. (1 Cor 16:19)

4. Priscilla (Prisca)

(1) One of Paul's staunchest supporters and most able collaborators in teaching and spreading the gospel was Priscilla (Prisca). She, along with her husband Aquila, is mentioned six times in the New Testament. Four of the six times she is named first. Paul met them in Corinth:

> After this Paul left Athens and went to Corinth, where he met a Jew called Aquila whose family came from Pontus. He and his wife Priscilla had recently left Italy because an edict of Claudius had expelled all the Jews from Rome. Paul went to visit them, and when he found they were tentmakers, of the same trade as himself, he lodged with them, and they worked together. (Acts 18:1–3)

(2) The three then traveled together toward the east:

> After staying on for some time, Paul took leave of the brothers and sailed for Syria, accompanied by Priscilla and Aquila. . . . When they reached Ephesus, he left them. (Acts 18:18–19)

(3) Paul sent greetings to and from Priscilla by name in three of the "Pauline" epistles, an indication of her prominence in Paul's work and the early Christian church:

> My greetings to Prisca and Aquila . . . (Rom 16:3)

> Aquila and Prisca, with the church that meets at their house, send you their warmest wishes, in the Lord. (1 Cor 16:19)

> Greetings to Prisca and Aquila . . . (2 Tim 4:19)

(4) On one occasion Paul not only acknowledged Priscilla and Aquila's saving of his life at the risk of their own, he referred to them as co-workers *(syn-ergous)* in Christ and indicated that the whole Gentile Christian church lay within the scope of their work:

> My greetings to Prisca and Aquila, my co-workers in Christ Jesus, who risked death to save my life: I am not the only one to owe them a debt of

gratitude, all the churches among the pagans do as well. My greetings also
to the church that meets at their house. (Rom 16:3–5)

(5) Priscilla's teaching the gospel, along with her husband Aquila,
to the brilliant preacher Apollos reveals something of the range of
women's involvement in early Christianity. It has even been thought
by a number of scholars, e.g., Adolf Harnack (see Ruth Hoppin,
Priscilla, Author of the Epistle to the Hebrews; Exposition Press,
1969), that Priscilla is the anonymous author of the Letter to the
Hebrews in the New Testament.

An Alexandrian Jew named Apollos now arrived in Ephesus. He was an
eloquent man, with a sound knowledge of the scriptures, and yet, though he
had been given instruction in the Way of the Lord and preached with great
spiritual earnestness and was accurate in all the details he taught about Jesus,
he had only experienced the baptism of John. When Priscilla and Aquila
heard him speak boldly in the synagogue, they took him and expounded to
him the Way of God more accurately. (Acts 18:24–26)

(6) John Chrysostom (A.D. 337–407), who often spoke very negatively of women (see §343), was clearly very impressed with Priscilla
and the fact that she was greeted by Paul first, before her husband
Aquila. He referred to the significance of this fact when preaching
on the second letter to Timothy (2 Tim 4:19). However, when he
wrote his homilies commenting on the text of Paul's letter to the
Romans he was so struck by Priscilla's precedence that he wrote two
separate homilies on the topic and delivered them within a few days
of each other! A brief excerpt follows:

It is worth examining Paul's motive, when he greets them, for putting
Priscilla before her husband. Indeed, he did not say: "Salute Aquila and
Priscilla," but rather, "Salute Priscilla and Aquila" [Rom 16:3]. He did not
do so without reason: the wife must have had, I think, greater piety than her
husband. This is not a simple conjecture; its confirmation is evident in the
Acts. Apollos was an eloquent man, well versed in Scripture, but he knew
only the baptism of John; this woman took him, instructed him in the way
of God, and made of him an accomplished teacher. (Migne, *Patrologia
Graeca,* Vol. 51, cols. 191f.)

5. WOMAN AS A DISCIPLE

In the early Palestinian church there was a woman called a disciple
(*mathētria,* the feminine form of *mathētēs,* the Greek word for "disciple"—could she perhaps have been one of the "seventy-two" sent
out by Jesus in Lk 10:1?). Again, a woman is centrally involved in a
resurrection story:

At Jaffa there was a woman *disciple* called Tabitha, or Dorcas in Greek, who never tired of doing good or giving in charity. But the time came when she got ill and died, and they washed her and laid her out in a room upstairs. Lydda is not far from Jaffa, so when the disciples heard that Peter was there, they sent two men with an urgent message for him, "Come and visit us as soon as possible." Peter went back with them straightaway, and on his arrival they took him to the upstairs room, where all the widows stood around him in tears, showing him tunics and other clothes Dorcas had made when she was with them. Peter sent them all out of the room and knelt down and prayed. Then he turned to the dead woman and said, "Tabitha, stand up." She opened her eyes, looked at Peter and sat up. Peter helped her to her feet, then he called in the saints and widows and showed them she was alive. The whole of Jaffa heard about it and many believed in the Lord. (Acts 9:36–42)

6. Woman as an Apostle

Paul refers to a woman, Junia, as an "outstanding *apostle*" *(apostolos)*. Some scholars, unwarrantedly, argue that Junia is a contraction of a much less common male name; but even the virulently misogynist fourth-century bishop of Constantinople, John Chrysostom, noted: "Oh, how great is the devotion of this woman that she should be counted worthy of the appellation of apostle!" (*The Homilies of St. John Chrysostom, Nicene and Post-Nicene Fathers,* Series I, 11:555; Wm. B. Eerdmans Publishing Co., 1956). "John Chrysostom was not alone in the ancient church in taking the name [*Jounian*] to be feminine. The earliest commentator on Romans 16:7, Origen of Alexandria (c. 185–253), took the name to be feminine (*Junia* or *Julia,* which is a textual variant), as did Jerome (340/50–419/20), Hatto of Vercelli (924–961), Theophylact (c. 1050-c. 1108), and Peter Abelard (1079–1142). In fact, to the best of my knowledge, no commentator on the text until Aegidus of Rome (1245–1316) took the name to be masculine" (see Bernadette Brooten, " 'Junia . . . Outstanding Among the Apostles' (Romans 16:7)," in Swidler and Swidler, *Women Priests: A Catholic Commentary on the Vatican Declaration,* p. 141, for a totally convincing scholarly analysis which argues that Junia was a woman apostle). It is odd that it is only in more modern times that Christian writers have strained to make Junia into a male name; misogynism apparently still persists:

Greetings . . . to those outstanding *apostles* Andronicus and *Junia,* my compatriots and fellow prisoners who became Christians before me. (Rom 16:6–8)

7. WOMEN PROPHETS

§282. Anna the Prophet

Although women prophets (persons through whom God spoke) were not as prominent as men prophets in the Hebraic tradition, as seen above in §78, they were clearly there. This female prophetic tradition also passed over into the Christian tradition, and it is by way of the bridge woman prophet *(prophētis)* Anna who stands in the Hebraic tradition and reaches out to Jesus as Messiah:

> There was a woman prophet *(prophētis)* also, Anna the daughter of Phanuel, of the tribe of Asher. She was well on in years. Her days of girlhood over, she had been married for seven years before becoming a widow. She was now eighty-four years old and never left the Temple, serving God night and day with fasting and prayer. She came by just at that moment and began to praise God; and she spoke of the child to all who looked forward to the deliverance of Jerusalem. (Lk 2:36–38)

§283. Elizabeth the Prophet

Another Jewish woman who is a bridge figure in the prophetic tradition from the Hebraic to the Christian tradition is Elizabeth, Jesus' aunt; she stands in the prophetic line because she spoke upon being filled with the Holy Spirit of God, that is, she became God's mouthpiece:

> Elizabeth was filled with the Holy Spirit. She gave a loud cry and said, "Of all women you are the most blessed, and blessed is the fruit of your womb. Why should I be honoured with a visit from the mother of my Lord? For the moment your greeting reached my ears, the child in my womb leapt for joy. Yes, blessed is she who believed that the promise made her by the Lord would be fulfilled." (Lk 1:41–45)

§284. Mary the Prophet

Mary likewise has been seen by Christians as standing in this same prophetic tradition when she responded to her cousin Elizabeth with her "Magnificat," concerning which Pope Paul VI said: "She was a woman who did not hesitate to proclaim that God vindicates the humble and the oppressed and removes the powerful people of this world from their privileged positions" *(Marialis Cultus,* 37). See §245 for an analysis of and the text of the Magnificat: Lk 1:46–55.

§285. Women Pentecostal Prophets

"Christian" prophets (persons who were filled with God's Spirit and through whom God spoke) appeared on the first Christian Pentecost, and *women* were among them:

They went to the upper room. . . . All these joined in continuous prayer, together with several women, including Mary the mother of Jesus. . . . When Pentecost day came round, they had all met in one room, when suddenly they heard what sounded like a powerful wind from heaven, the noise of which filled the entire house in which they were sitting; and something appeared to them that seemed like tongues of fire; these separated and came to rest on the head of each of them. They were *all* filled with the *Holy Spirit, and began to speak* foreign languages as the *Spirit* gave them the gift of speech. (Acts 1:13–14; 2:1–4)

§286. Joel and Women Prophets

In keeping with the tradition of women prophets in the Hebrew Scriptures (and the Gospels), Peter quoted, on that first Christian Pentecost, from the prophet Joel (Joel 3:15), who twice spoke of women prophesying:

But Peter standing with the Eleven, lifted his voice and addressed them. . . . "This is what was spoken by the prophet Joel:

And in the last days it shall be, God declares,
that I will pour out my Spirit upon all flesh,
and your sons and daughters shall prophesy,
and your young men shall see visions,
and your old men shall dream dreams;
yea, and on my menservants and my maidservants in those days
I will pour out my Spirit; and they shall prophesy." (Acts 2:14, 16–18)

§287. Philip's Daughters, Prophets — I

Not only did the Jewish-Christian women who were gathered in the upper room in Jerusalem at the descent of the Holy Spirit "prophesy," but so also did the Jewish-Christian daughters of the "deacon" Philip:

The end of our voyage from Tyre came when we landed at Ptolemais, where we greeted the brethren and stayed one day with them. The next day we left and came to Caesarea. Here we called on Philip the evangelist, one of the Seven, and stayed with him. He had four virgin daughters who were prophets. (Acts 21:7–9)

§288. Philip's Daughters, Prophets — II

The reputation of Philip's daughters as prophets was so significant and long-lasting in its influence that their burial place was used (along with that of the apostles John and Philip, among others; the latter was mistakenly thought to be the same as Philip the evangelist of Acts 21:8–9 by Eusebius, and probably also by Polycrates, whom he quotes) to back the claim of apostolicity of a particular tradition by Bishop Polycrates of Ephesus (present-day Turkey) against Pope Victor I (A.D. 189–198). The second document referring to these four women prophets stems from Gaius in the years 198–217. Both documents are found only as excerpts in the *Ecclesiastical History* of Eusebius of Caesarea (A.D. 260–340), written before 303:

> The date of John's death has also been roughly fixed: the place where his mortal remains lie can be gathered from a letter of Polycrates, Bishop of Ephesus, to Victor, Bishop of Rome. In it he refers not only to John but to Philip the apostle and Philip's daughters as well: "In Asia great luminaries sleep who shall rise again on the last day, the day of the Lord's advent, when He is coming with glory from heaven and shall search out all His saints— such as Philip, one of the twelve apostles, who sleeps in Hierapolis with two of his daughters, who remained unmarried to the end of their days, while his other daughter lived in the Holy Spirit and rests in Ephesus." So much Polycrates tells us about their deaths. And in the *Dialogue* of Gaius of whom I spoke a little while ago, Proclus, with whom he was disputing, speaks thus about the deaths of Philip and his daughters, in agreement with the foregoing account: "After him there were four women prophets at Hierapolis in Asia, daughters of Philip. Their grave is there, as is their father's." That is Gaius's account. Luke in the Acts of the Apostles refers to Philip's daughters as then living with their father at Caesarea in Judaea and endowed with the prophetic gift. (Eusebius, *Ecclesiastical History* III.31)

§289. Veiled Women Prophets

In a "left-handed" way Paul documents the spread of prophecy among Greek-Christian women:

> For a woman, however, it is a sign of disrespect to her head if she prays or prophesies unveiled. (1 Cor 11:5)

§290. A Woman Prophet Leader of a Church

In the latter part of the first century, John the author of the Apocalypse wrote in a prophetic fashion to the church in Thyatira (present-day Turkey) complaining about a "Jezebel" of a woman prophet, apparently the leader of a whole group of Christians who advocated a coexistence with pagan culture that permitted them the "immorality" of eating food offered to idols; John insisted on a radical break. Obviously this "woman prophet" exercised her gifts of prophecy and teaching *(didaskein)* within the Christian church, for she was "encouraged" *(apheis)* by the local church and "given time to reform" even by her apocalyptic opponent John. She clearly had many followers, as the reference to her so-called "children" *(tekna)* and John's great concern indicate. Whether she was too lax or John too rigoristic is not at issue here; her exercising "prophecy" and wide influence within the Christian church is substantiated by the text. It should also be noted that Thyatira became the center of the Montanist movement, in which women prophets played a prominent role, in the middle of the next (the second) century. The influence of our woman prophet apparently was long-lasting. It is unfortunate that the burgeoning antifeminism of the Christian church forced Montanism, and women prophets, into sectarianism:

> Nevertheless, I have a complaint to make: you are encouraging the woman Jezebel who claims to be a prophet, and by her teaching she is luring my servants away to commit the immorality of eating food which has been sacrificed to idols. I have given her time to reform but she is not willing to change her immoral life. Now I am consigning her to bed, and all her partners in immorality to troubles that will test them severely, unless they repent of their practices; and I will see that her children die. (Rev 2:20–23)

§291. Women Prophets Attacked by Apocryphal Peter

Leadership roles exercised by women in Christianity, including that of prophecy, were frequently attacked by many church fathers and in other writings. Here is partially cited one early, second-century, apocryphal document, the Kerygmata Petrou, in which Peter is made to say extremely vicious things about women prophets. They are seen as aping men prophets, as having tendencies toward polytheism and seeing the female element in the divine. The latter is doubtless a reference to the echoes of the Goddess worship that could be heard in the Hebraic-Judaic feminine Wisdom tradition that entered into the Christian, both orthodox catholic and Gnostic, tradition. Apocryphal Peter's protest here is a continuation of the patriarchal Yahwist protest against women leaders and the Goddess—it is quite alien to the Jewish and Christian Wisdom and the Jesus traditions.

> "Along with the true prophet there has been created as a companion a female being who is as far inferior to him as *metousia* is to *ousia,* as the moon is to the sun, as fire is to light. . . .
> "There are two kinds of prophecy, the one is male . . . the other is found

amongst those who are born of women. Proclaiming what pertains to the present world, female prophecy desires to be considered male. On this account she steals the seed of the male, envelops them with her own seed of the flesh and lets them—that is, her words—come forth as her own creations. She promises to give earthly riches gratuitously in the present world and wishes to exchange (the slow) for the swift, the small for the greater. She not only ventures to speak and hear of many gods, but also believes that she herself will be deified; and because she hopes to become something that contradicts her nature, she destroys what she has. Pretending to make sacrifice, she stains herself with blood at the time of her menses and thus pollutes those who touch her." (Kerygmata Petrou, *New Testament Apocrypha*, Vol. 2, p. 117)

8. WOMEN AS TEACHERS

§292. Priscilla the Teacher

The author of the Pauline epistle to Timothy did "not permit a woman to teach or exercise supreme authority over a man" (see §334). But Priscilla taught the great Apollos the gospel:

> But when Priscilla and Aquila heard him, they took him and *expounded (exethento)* to him the Way of God *more accurately.* (Acts 18:26)

§293. "Gray Panther" Women Teachers

The author of the Pauline epistle to Titus also bade the older women *(presbytidas)* to teach what is good:

> Bid the older women . . . to *teach (kalodidaskalous)* what is good. (Titus 2:3)

9. THE ECCLESIAL ORDER OF WIDOWS

§294. The Widow Anna

In the Christian tradition widowhood was not only the object of charity but also one of the earliest "orders" of women in the church, analogous to that of priests and bishops. A bridge person, a Hebrew widow who spent her life in a search for holiness and who was connected to Jesus as Messiah, was Anna. See §249 for an analysis of the text: Lk 2:36–38.

§295. Widows Follow Jesus and a Woman Disciple

Later, many other Hebrew women followed Jesus. Often scholars suggest that many of the women who "ministered" (*diēkonoun,* Lk

8:1–3; Mk 15:40–41) were of necessity widows, devoting their lives to a search for holiness. That these women formed a society or "order" after the time of Jesus can be seen by the distinction Peter makes between ordinary Christians ("saints") and widows, who apparently were banded together around their leader Tabitha; she also obviously enjoyed a great prominence in the Palestinian Christian church. See above, p. 299, for the complete text:

> At Jaffa there was a women disciple called Tabitha. . . . Peter went back with them straightaway, and on his arrival they took him to the upstairs room, where *all the widows* stood round him in tears. . . . Peter helped her to her feet, then he called in the *saints and widows* and showed them she was alive. (Acts 9:36, 39–40, 41)

§296. Widows Ministered To — I

The widows, who had ministered *(diēkonoun)* to Jesus and his disciples, in turn became the object of special physical service *(diakonia)* instituted by the Twelve—the beginning of the special "office" of the diaconate. Since all church "members who might be in need" (Acts 4:35) received whatever food and shelter they needed, the reference to distributions to widows indicates their special quality. This "order of widows" was provided such "logistical support" already in the Jerusalem church in both Hebrew- and Greek-speaking cultural forms:

> About this time, when the number of disciples was increasing, the Hellenists made a complaint against the Hebrews: in the daily distribution their own *widows* were being overlooked. So the Twelve called a full meeting of the disciples and addressed them, "It would not be right for us to neglect the word of God so as to give out food; you, brethren, must select from among yourselves seven men of good reputation, filled with the Spirit and with wisdom; we will hand over this duty to them." (Acts 6:1–3)

§297. Widows Ministered To — II

But it was clear that these "deacons" were to supply more than material goods, for we know from elsewhere that at least two of them, Stephen and Philip, were also teachers of the good news:

> "You, brethren, must select from among yourselves seven men of good reputation, filled with the Spirit and with wisdom; we will hand over this duty to them.". . . The whole community approved of this proposal and elected Stephen, a man full of faith and of the Holy Spirit, together with Philip. . . . They presented these to the apostles, who prayed and laid their hands on them.* (Acts 6:3–6)
>
> *[Greek *epethekai autois tas cheiras;* this laying on of hands often signified

an "ordination" in the Christian church; it is often thought to be so intended here. It, and variations, often appeared in the ordination of deaconesses, and even widows.]

§298. Widows Ministering and Ministered To

The author of the Pauline epistle to Timothy distinguished between widows who were simply women whose husbands had died and those who belonged to the "order" of widows who devoted their lives to the service of the Christian community and who in turn were supported by it:

Enrolment as a widow is permissible only for a woman at least sixty years old who has had only one husband. She must be a woman known for her good works and for the way in which she has brought up her children, shown hospitality to strangers and washed the saints' feet, helped people who are in trouble and been active in all kinds of good work. (1 Tim 5:9–10)

§299. The "Order" of Widows

a. "Virginal" Widows in the East

At the end of the first century or the beginning of the second we find a reference to Christian widows that clearly must be meant as a church "order," for they are referred to as virgins! Ignatius of Antioch (A.D. 35–107) wrote to the Smyrnians:

Greetings to the families of my brethren including their wives and children, and to the virgins who are enrolled among the widows. (Ignatius, *Letter to the Smyrnians* XIII.1)

b. "Virginal" Widows in the West

In the West, Tertullian (A.D. 160–225) confirmed Christian widowhood as an "order" that had virgins as members. Even the Pauline age requirement of sixty years was no longer observed, for Tertullian speaks of teen-age members!

I know for sure places where virgins not yet twenty years of age are established in the state of widowhood. (Tertullian, *De virginibus velandis* C.9)

c. Wise Widows

Ignatius of Antioch was taught by the apostles, and it was his disciple Polycarp (d. A.D. 155) who wrote that this Christian teaching was to be passed on in its fullness to the order of widows:

Let us teach the widows to be wise, intelligent about the faith of the Lord. (Polycarp, Letter to the Philippians IV.3)

d. Widows Teach Women

The fifth-century *Statuta ecclesiae antiqua* (from southern France) indicates that this instruction in the gospel was given so that the widows could further teach, albeit just other women:

> Widows, or virgins, who are chosen for the ministry of the baptism of women ... should be instructed for this office, so that they can teach ignorant and backward women with apt and sound words, so that at the time of baptism they can answer the questions of the baptizer and about how they should live once they are baptized. (*Statuta ecclesiae antiqua* C.12)

e. "Pastoral" Widows Are Ordained

In another fifth-century document, this one from Syria, the *Testamentum Domini Nostri Jesu Christi,* the order of widows attained their highest status. This document, originally written in Greek, unfortunately is extant only in various ancient translations, preeminently the Syriac, which was critically edited and published with a Latin translation by I. E. Rahmani, Mainz, 1899. The widows in this document are distinguished from ordinary widows by the designation "widows who sit in front" *(viduae habentes praecedentiam sessionis),* which term is used six times. Once, in a litany chanted by the deacon, she is referred to as a "female priest" *(pro presbyteris [feminis] supplicemus,* after similar petitions for the *episcopo, presbyteris, diaconis*). Unlike all other documents, which speak of "appointing" widows, the *Testamentum Domini* speaks of "ordaining" *(ordinetur)* them. They are instructed to receive communion with the rest of the clergy, after the deacons and before the readers and subdeacons. Moreover, they are placed within the veil around the altar during the Eucharist (much like the iconostasis in later Orthodox Christianity and the rood screen in Western Christianity— behind which today women are not allowed during the Eucharist), along with the other clergy. As Gryson notes, "undeniably they were considered a part of the clergy. Indeed, no other document attributes to women a rank as high in the ecclesiastical hierarchy as that of widows who sat in front" (p. 66).

In the democratic twentieth century it is interesting to note that the widows—in exact parallel to the instructions concerning the ordination of the bishop, priests, and deacons—are to be ordained from among "those who are chosen" *(quae eligitur)* by the congregation, that is, *all* the clergy were elected by the people.

Once ordained, the widow had a wide range of pastoral duties oriented toward women. She was to teach the women catechumens *(quae introeunt, efficiat ut sciant . . .),* instruct the ignorant, teach women prisoners *(doceat reas),* encourage and lead in prayer the virgins, admonish and try to win back those women who have gone astray, visit sick women, anoint women being baptized and supervise the deaconesses. (It is clear that in this document the "widows who sit in front" have the status that in other documents the deaconesses do, and vice versa.)

Let her who is chosen be *ordained* a widow *(Ordinetur in viduam illa, quae eligitur).* . . . Let her *instruct* the ignorant *(erudiat ignorantes),* convert and *teach* the prisoners *(doceat reas)* . . . and she should supervise the deaconesses. *(Testamentum Domini* I.40; I. E. Rahmani, ed., *Testamentum Domini,* Syriac text with Latin trans., pp. 95f.; Mainz, 1899)

f. Widows Administer "Extreme Unction" to Men

Still, in the early third-century Didascalia (Syria) it is clear that at least some of the ministrations of the widow, other than teaching, were directed at men as well as women, for the extant Syriac and ancient Latin manuscripts clearly say brothers, *fratres.* Also, many scholars, e.g., Cardinal Jean Daniélou, see in this praying and laying on of hands the administration of the Sacrament of the Dying, Extreme Unction:

Why, O undisciplined widow, when you see your fellow widows or brothers *(conviduas . . . fratres)* lying in infirmity, do you not hasten to your members, that you may fast and pray over them and impose hands? (Didascalia III.8.3)

g. Widows Likened to Altars, Virgins to Priestesses of Christ

In fourth-century letters written by Pseudo-Ignatius, widows are likened to altars. But what is quite startling is that virgins are said to be like priestesses of Christ. The term used is not *presbytera* but rather *hiereia* (same root as in "hierarchy"). In the whole of the Apostolic Writings (New Testament) no individual Christian is ever specifically identified as a priest *(hiereus),* only pagan and Jewish priests are. Christians as a whole might be called a "royal priesthood" *(basileion hierateuma—*1 Pet 2:9), but Christian "priests" are called "presbyters" *(presbyteros). Hiereus* designated a cultic leader, which the early Christians claimed not to have; only with the passage of time did Christians associate church leadership with cultic leadership and the term "priest" (*hiereus* in Greek, *sacerdos* in Latin). Thus it is striking that a Christian woman would be called a *hiereia* of Christ.

Honor those who continue in virginity, as the priestesses of Christ *(hiereias Christou);* and the widows that persevere in gravity of behavior, as the altar of God. (F. Funk and F. Diekamp, *Patres apostolici,* Vol. 2, p. 142; Tübingen, 1913)

10. Women Deacons

§300. Women and Men Deacons Given Pauline Instructions

Already in the lifetime of Paul (d. A.D. 63), the office of deacon was established (see Phil 1:1). Women as well as men served in this *"ordained"* office. Later when the Pauline First Epistle to Timothy was written (probably toward the end of the first century) men and women deacons were both required to have parallel qualities:

Deacons likewise must be serious, not double-tongued, not addicted to much wine, not greedy for gain; they must hold the mystery of the faith with a clear conscience. And let them also be tested first; then if they prove themselves blameless let them serve as deacons. In the same way the women deacons must be serious, no slanderers, but temperate, faithful in all things. (1 Tim 3:8–11) [Though the Greek word here translated "women deacons" is *gynaikas,* women, most scholars, as well as most Greek fathers of the church, e.g., John Chrysostom, Theodore of Mopsuestia, and Theodoret of Cyrrhus (see Gryson, *Ministry of Women in the Early Church,* p. 87), agree that in this context—the necessary characteristics for bishops, deacons, and women deacons are being listed—it has the meaning of women deacons; those who argue it refers to the deacons' wives overlook the lack of a parallel with bishops' wives—ch. 3:1–7—whereas in every other regard there are matching parallels.]

§301. Phoebe a Deacon

Paul also names, and honors, a specific woman deacon. Here Paul refers to Phoebe as a deacon *(diakonos),* not as a deaconness (*diakonissa,* a Greek word that appears only in the late fourth-century Syrian document, the Apostolic Constitutions. This document incorporates most of the text of the early third-century Syrian Didascalia, whose original Greek text is lost. However, wherever the Apostolic Constitutions quotes the Didascalia it uses the term "woman deacon," that is, the feminine article with the regular noun "deacon"— *"hē diakonos."* Otherwise it uses the neologism *"diakonissa."* See Gryson, *Ministry of Women in the Early Church,* p. 138). Though the term "deacon" may not have had the formalized official quality during Paul's lifetime (d. A.D. 67) that is acquired later, as in the perhaps late first-century letters to Timothy (see below, pp. 314f.), Paul does address his letter to the Philippians to the *episkopois kai diakonois* (Gryson, p. 121). Since the latter term is usually translated "deacon," it is appropriate to translate Phoebe's *diakonos* as "deacon" as well. Clement of Alexandria, who wrote during the latter part of the second century, perhaps only decades after the letters to Timothy were composed, clearly refers to women deacons (*diakanōn gynaikōn*—in Stromata 3, 6, 53, 3–4; see Gryson, p. 30). Clement's student Origen, in commenting on Paul's letter to the Romans and its reference to Phoebe, states: "This text teaches with the authority of the Apostle that even women are instituted deacons in the Church [*feminas in ministeris Ecclesiae constitui,* in the extant Latin translation; in the original Greek as reconstructed by Gryson, p. 134: *kai gynaikas diakonous tēs Ekklēsias kathistasthai*]. . . . And thus this text teaches at the same time two things: that there are, as we have already said, women deacons in the Church [*et haberi, ut diximus, feminas ministras in Ecclesia,* in Latin; *kai einai, hōs eipamen, gynaikas diakonous en tē Ekklēsia,* in reconstructed Greek, ibid.], and that women, who have given assistance to so many people and who by their good works deserve to be praised by the Apostle, ought to be accepted in the diaconate [*in ministerium,* Latin; *eis diakonian,* reconstructed Greek]":

> I commend to you our sister Phoebe, a deacon of the church at Cenchreae. (Rom 16:1)

§302. Phoebe a Ruler Over Paul

Paul also refers to Phoebe as a "ruler" *(prostatis),* not as a "helper," as it is usually, and unwarrantedly, translated; the word appears nowhere else in the New Testament and always means ruler, leader, or protector in all Greek literature. Paul uses a verb form of the word in 1 Thess 5:12 *(proistamenous),* and it is translated as "rule over," as are also similar verb forms in 1 Tim 3:4, 5; 5:17, where the references are to bishops, priests, and deacons! (See J. Massyngberde Ford, "Biblical Material Relevant to the Ordination of Women," *Journal of Ecumenical Studies,* Vol. 10, No. 4, Fall 1973, pp. 676f.):

> Give her [Phoebe], in union with the Lord, a welcome worthy of saints, and help her with anything she needs, for she has been a ruler *(prostatis)* over many, indeed over me.

[*gar aute prostatis pollon egenethe, kai emou autou*
for she ruler of many has been and of me myself] (Rom 16:2)

§303. Martha a "Deacon"

In John's account of Jesus' attending a dinner in Bethany (Jn 12:2), Martha is said to have served at the table *(diekonei)*—the same work assigned to the early "deacons" (Acts 6:1–6). As Raymond E. Brown points out ("Roles of Women in the Fourth Gospel," p. 690), John was "writing in the 90's, when the office of *diakonos* already existed in the post-Pauline churches (see the Pastoral epistles) and when the task of waiting on tables was a specific function to which the community or its leaders appointed individuals by laying on hands. In the Johannine community a woman could be described as exercising a function which in other churches was the function of an 'ordained' person." In a different story, Luke 10:40–41, Martha again is described as serving at table *(diakonian . . . diakonein)*. It is perhaps almost as possible that Luke, here writing ten or twenty years before John, may have had a similar awareness of the ecclesial connotation the word *diakonia* acquired early in Christianity, especially since it was the same Luke who shortly thereafter wrote of the first "deacons" in the Acts of the Apostles, that they were "to serve at table *(diakonein)* . . . and that they laid hands *(cheiras)* on them." (Acts 6:2–6)

Six days before the Passover, Jesus went to Bethany, where Lazarus was, whom he raised from the dead. They gave a dinner for him there; Martha served *(diekonei)*. (Jn 12:1–2)

Now Martha who was distracted with all the serving [*diakonian*] said, "Lord, do you not care that my sister is leaving me to do all the serving *(diakonein)* myself?" (Lk 10:40)

§304. Deaconesses Are Ordained

Although the status of women in the Christian church gradually deteriorated after the first generation of the church (e.g., from Jesus, to Paul, to the late pastoral epistles, to Timothy, etc.), there are records of the ordination of deaconesses *(diako-nisses)* in the fourth century in the East and perhaps in the second century in the West. In the fourth-century Apostolic Constitutions (probably from Syria) the bishops were charged to *ordain* deaconesses:

Ordain *(procheirisai)* also a woman deacon *(diakonon)* who is faithful and holy. (Apostolic Constitutions III.16.1, Alexander Roberts and James Donaldson, eds., *The Ante-Nicene Fathers,* Vol. 7, p. 431; Wm. B. Eerdmans Publishing Co., 1951)

§305. Ordination Prayer for Deaconesses

Also in the Apostolic Constitutions the prayers are given for the ordination of a bishop, then a priest, a deacon, a deaconess, a subdeacon, and a lector, followed by regulations concerning confessors, widows, virgins, and exorcists; concerning all the latter it is explicitly stated that they are *not* ordained, clearly implying that the former six were. Precisely the same terms, prayers, and actions (laying on of hands, etc.) were used for the deaconess as for the bishop, priest, and deacon. If these were sacramentally ordained, so was the deaconess:

Concerning a deaconess *(diakonissa),* I Bartholomew make this constitution: O bishop, thou shalt lay thy hands upon her *(epitheseis autē tas cheiras)* in the presence of the presbytery, and of the deacons and deaconesses, and shalt say: O Eternal God, the Father of our Lord Jesus Christ, the Creator of man and of woman, who didst replenish with the Spirit Miriam, and Deborah, and Anna, and Huldah; who didst not disdain that Thy only begotten Son should be born of a woman; who also in the tabernacle of the testimony, and in the temple, didst ordain women to be keepers of Thy holy gates, do Thou now also look down upon this Thy servant, who is to be ordained *(procheirizomenēn)* to the office of a woman deacon *(diakonian),* and grant her Thy Holy Spirit, and "cleanse her from all filthiness of flesh and spirit," that she may worthily discharge the work which is committed to her to Thy glory, and the praise of Thy Christ, with whom glory and adoration be to Thee and the Holy Spirit for ever. Amen. (Roberts and Donaldson, *Ante-Nicene Fathers,* Vol. 7, p. 492)

§306. Women Clerics

The Council of Nicea (325) somewhat earlier referred to deaconesses as *clerics:*

Likewise, however, both deaconesses *(diakonissōn)* and in general all those who are numbered among the clergy [*kanoni* in the Greek, *clericos* in the Latin] should retain the same form. (J. D. Mansi, *Sacrorum conciliorum nova et amplissa collectio,* Vol. 2, pp. 676ff.; Florence, 1757–1798)

§307. Deaconesses at Chalcedon

Somewhat later the Council of Chalcedon (451) stated a regulation concerning the *ordination* of deaconesses and spoke of the deaconess's ministry, her "liturgy" *(leitourgia):*

A woman should not be ordained (*cheirotonēsthai* in the Greek, *ordinandam* in the Latin) a deaconess before she is forty. And if after receiving ordination *(cheirothesian)* she continued in her ministry *(leitourgia)*. . . . (Mansi, *Sacrorum conciliorum nova et amplissa collectio,* Vol. 7, p. 364)

§308. Women in "Orders"

In the West the misogynist church father Tertullian (160–225) wrote:

How many men and women there are whose chastity has obtained for them the honor of ecclesiastical orders! *(in ecclesiasticis ordinibus).* (Migne, *Patrologia Latina,* Vol. 2, col. 978)

§309. Second-Century Women Deacons

A very early second-century letter from Pliny to the emperor Trajan (reign A.D. 98–117) refers to two women deacons *(ministrae,* the Latin translation then for *diakones),* who were apparently the leaders and most knowledgeable persons in their local church, which was then being persecuted:

I judged it so much the more necessary to extract the real truth with the assistance of torture, from two maidservants [*ancillis*], who were called deacons [*ministrae*]: but I could discover nothing more than depraved and excessive superstition. (Pliny, *Letters,* ed. by William Melmoth, Vol. 2, p. 405; Cambridge, Mass., 1963)

§310. Deaconesses Teach

Although after New Testament times the deaconess was authentically ordained as part of the clerical hierarchy, her official ministry was normally limited to women, surely a regression from the time of Phoebe and Priscilla. Nevertheless, her responsibilities did include religious teaching, as is seen in the early third-century Didascalia (it is perhaps indicative of still further slippage that in the parallel passage of the fourth-century Apostolic Constitutions the words "instructs and teaches" are missing):

And when she who is being baptized has come up from the water, let the deaconess receive her, and *teach and instruct* her how the seal of baptism ought to be kept unbroken in purity and holiness. For this cause we say that the ministry of a woman deacon is especially needful and important. For our Lord and Savior also was ministered unto by women *ministers.* . . . And thou also hast need of the ministry of a deaconess for many things. (Didascalia III.12)

§311. Sixth-Century Deaconesses

A sixth-century Western church father, Pseudo-Jerome, gives testimony of the continuing teaching office of the Eastern deaconesses in his commentary on Rom 16:1–2, where he states that Phoebe "is a deacon *(in ministerio)* of the church in Cenchreae":

As even now among Orientals deaconesses may be seen to minister *(ministrare)* to their own sex in Baptism, we have found some early women who have privately taught in the ministry of the word *(ministerio verbi)*, e.g., Priscilla whose husband was called Aquila. (Migne, *Patrologia Latina,* Vol. 30, col. 743)

§312. Deaconess Likened to the Holy Spirit

Perhaps the highest praise of the deaconess in Christian documents comes from the Didascalia, where she is likened to the Holy Spirit! In this passage she is also listed before the priest:

Let him be honored by you as God, for the bishop sits for you in the place of God Almighty. But the deacon stands in the place of Christ; therefore he should be loved by you. And the deaconess shall be honored by you as a type of the Holy Spirit *(eis typon hagiou pneumatos*—as translated in the fourth-century Apostolic Constitutions); and the presbyters shall be to you in the likeness of the Apostles; and the orphans and widows shall be reckoned by you in the likeness of the altar. (Didascalia II.26.5–8)

§313. Decline of Deaconesses

Thus, at the time of the New Testament women were deacons, just as men were (Rom 16:1–2; 1 Tim 3:12). By the late fourth century the women deacons were called deaconesses, coming after deacons in status; nevertheless they were truly ordained and were classified as clerics. This was true mostly in the East; in the West the development of the "order" was much weaker. Still, even though the deaconess was largely expected to minister to other women, that restriction, as seen above (see §299), was not always maintained.

However, with the decline of the Roman empire sociological changes set off a decline in the order of deaconess, as reflected in the following Council statements:

Let no one proceed to the ordination of deaconesses anymore.
Council of Orange (A.D. 441), Canon 26

We abrogate completely in the entire kingdom the consecration of widows who are named deaconesses.
Council of Epaon (A.D. 517), Canon 21

No longer shall the blessing of women deaconesses be given, because of the weakness of the sex.
Council of Orleans II (A.D. 533)

By the twelfth century the order of deaconess almost totally disappeared from the church, both East and West. (For an excellent history of ecclesial women in the early centuries of Christianity, see Mary Lawrence McKenna, *Women of the Church: Role and Renewal;* P. J. Kenedy & Sons, 1967. For a collection of all the pertinent Greek and Latin texts, see Josephine Mayer, ed., *Monumenta de viduis diaconissio virginibusque tractantia,* 1938, in series *Florilegium Patristicum,* ed. by B. Geyer and J. Zellinger, 71ff.; Bonn: Peter Hanstein, 1904–.)

11. Women as Presbyters (Priests)?

The presbyters (Greek *presbyteros,* elder, whence English "priest" is derived) of the New Testament were the leaders of the Christian churches, as, for example, in Ephesus. The writer of the deutero-Pauline First Epistle to Timothy spoke a great deal about "bishops" (1 Tim 3:1–7), men deacons (3:8–13), women deacons (3:11), widows as a category of church "officers" (5:9–10), men presbyters (4:14; 5:1–2, 17–22), and women presbyters (5:2)! The author notes that Timothy was "ordained" by the elderhood, or presbyterate (*presbyteriou*—4:14, just four verses before the reference to the women presbyters, *presbyteras,* in 5:2), and a little later speaks of the honor and criticism of male presbyters (5:17–19). It is right in the middle of this discussion of presbyters that the author speaks of how Timothy, probably a leader set above the rest of the presbyterate, possibly even a "bishop" (*episkopos*—3:1), should deal with a man presbyter *(presbyterō)* and women presbyters *(presbyteras).* Thus, in 5:1–2 the words *presbyterō* and *presbyteras* are usually translated as "an older man" and "older women," but in this context of a discussion of the various "officers" of the church, a perfectly proper translation— which, if not more likely, is at least possible—would be "male presbyter" and "woman presbyters":

Do not rebuke a male presbyter *(presbyterō)* but exhort him as you would a father; treat younger men like brethren, women presbyters *(presbyteras)* like mothers, younger women like sisters. (1 Tim 5:1–2)

12. Episcopal Women?

(1) Though in New Testament times there was no "monarchical episcopacy," *episkopoi* (literally "overseers") did appear late in the period as sort of chairpersons of committees of presbyters. Many

scholars argue that the "elect lady" (lady—*kyria*, as parallel to lord, *kyrios*) to whom the Second Epistle of John is addressed, and her "elect sister," whose children send greetings, must be "symbols" of churches. But they are perhaps just as properly understood as real persons. (For a similar view, see Ernst Gaugler, *Die Johannesbriefe*, p. 283; Zurich: EVZ-Verlag, 1964.) Judging from the content of the letter, the elect lady is responsible not only for her natural children but also for the Christians in her charge (a house church as with Priscilla, Nympha, etc.?); does she not then have the function of an "overseer," *episkopa*, even though the title is not mentioned, but rather *kyria* is? Her sister also?

> The elder to the elect lady *(eklektē kyria)* and her children, whom I love in the truth, and not only I but also all who know the truth. . . . I rejoiced greatly to find some of your children following the truth, just as we have been commanded by the Father. And now I beg you, lady, *(kyria)*, not as though I were writing you a new commandment, but the one we have had from the beginning, that we love one another. . . . For many deceivers have gone out into the world, men who will not acknowledge the coming of Jesus Christ in the flesh: such a one is the deceiver and the antichrist. Look to yourselves, that you may not lose what you have worked for, but may win a full reward. Any one who goes ahead and does not abide in the doctrine of Christ does not have God; he who abides in the doctrine has both the Father and the Son. If any one comes to you and does not bring this doctrine, do not receive him into the house. . . . Though I have much to write to you, I would rather not use paper and ink, but I hope to come to see you and talk with you face to face, so that our joy may be complete. The children of your *elect sister* greet you. (2 Jn 1, 4–5, 7–10, 12–13)

(2) Already within the same century when John's epistle was probably written, i.e., the second century, church father Clement of Alexandria spoke of "elect persons" as a designation for officers of the church—which included not only bishops but also widows—supporting the contention that the "elect" lady of 2 John could properly be understood as a generic term for church officers:

> However, there are many other precepts written in the sacred books which pertain to elect persons *(prosōpa eklekta):* certain of these are for priests *(presbyterois)*, others indeed for bishops *(episkopois)*, others for deacons, still others for widows *(kērais)*, all of which should be discussed at another time. (Migne, *Patrologia Graeca*, Vol. 8, 675)

13. Women Authors of "Scripture"

As noted above (p. 298), a number of reputable scholars have presented strong cases in favor of Priscilla being the author of the canonical Letter to the Hebrews. But, barring the discovery of new documentary evidence, Priscilla can never be more than a strong candidate among other strong candidates for the authorship of the Letter to the Hebrews. However, the case is not nearly so tentative with some other "scriptural" documents, namely, the several apocryphal New Testament Acts of apostles, i.e., the Acts of "John," "Peter," "Paul," "Andrew," "Thomas," and the "Acts of Xanthippe and Polyxeus." No thought was given to the possibility of female authorship for these documents until the 1978 doctoral dissertation of Stevan Davies in the Religion Department of Temple University: "The Social World of the Apocryphal Acts." In a most persuasive marshaling of evidence and development of argumentation Davies shows that these documents give every indication of having been written both for women and by women.

§314. The Apocryphal Acts of the Apostles

To begin with, these Apocryphal Acts were all written between A.D. 160 and 225 in Greek in Greece or Asia Minor, except for the Acts of Thomas, which was written in Syriac in Roman Syria, immediately adjacent to Asia Minor. They all breathe deeply a spirit of sexual asceticism, that is, they assume that being Christian entails being celibate—the sexual act being described as abominable, filthy, unspeakable, etc. This anti-sex attitude, of course, permeates much of the history of Christianity. The form it takes in the Apocryphal Acts is doubtless more intensive than that found in Paul's epistles, but it surely is matched by some of the writings of the Desert Fathers, Jerome, Augustine (who in the *Confessions* set up his mutually exclusive choice between the joys of sex and Christ), and others. But in a society that tended to make married women subordinate to their husbands, being celibate allowed women to become their own mistresses as men were their own masters. Hence, in this regard sexual continence was a force of both liberation and egalitarianism for these Christian women.

The Apocryphal Acts . . . were written from within a particular community of Christians, a community somewhat outside the normal boundaries of society in the ancient world, a community which placed an exceptionally high value on sexual continence. It is our contention that the Acts derive from communities of continent Christian women, the Widows of their church, who were both adherents of apostles and participants in a stable church structure. (Stevan Davies, "The Social World of the Apocryphal Acts," unpublished dissertation, p. 73; Temple University, 1978)

§315. Women Models in the Apocryphal Acts

Throughout the Apocryphal Acts women are often central figures, outside of the apostles themselves clearly the most striking and praiseworthy. They usually are not the stereotypically weak woman, but rather are strong, stereotypically "male," vir-ile, exercising great vir-tue, even disguising themselves as males, as Thecla in the Acts of Paul (a portion of which is sometimes referred to as the Acts of Paul and Thecla, or even Martyrdom of the Holy Proto-Martyr Thecla). Women perform various miracles, even raising dead men—which is done by no male other than the apostles, making those women female quasi or equivalent apostles.

The figures of Drusiana, Cleopatra, Maximilla, Mygdonia, and Thecla are all impressive models of piety intended to be suitable for the emulation of Christians and, in particular, Christian women. There are no comparable role models in the Apocryphal Acts for Christian men. Stratocles, Marcellus, Lycomedes, the various men converted by Paul before his death, etc., are either flawed or of secondary importance in the narrative, or are not developed as narrative characters to any substantial extent. The great difficulty in Christian life is time and time again said to be the problem of continent living. This problem is always viewed from the standpoint of a woman who must leave her husband. At no time in the Apocryphal Acts does a man encounter substantial difficulties in leaving his wife. Married men are converted to the faith, if at all, either after their wives have converted or simultaneously with their wives. (Davies, "The Social World of the Apocryphal Acts," p. 92)

§316. Thecla Popular with Christian Women

The Acts of Paul and Thecla, in which some scholars argue is a historical core, were extremely popular in the early church, as is evidenced by the existence of not only the original Greek but also five different Latin translations plus Syriac, Armenian, Slavonic, and Arabic translations. In a manner typical of the Apocryphal Acts, Thecla was converted to Christianity by a wandering apostle, (St.) Paul. She and he assumed that her conversion meant her refusing to marry her fiancé. Eventually this precipitated all sorts of tortures and attempted executions of Thecla. Throughout these many trials, it is interesting to note, the women of the city were vocally in support of her. Once the various trials and tortures began, on no less than seven occasions the women as a group cried out for Thecla:

(1) But the women were panic-stricken, and cried out before the judgment-seat: "An evil judgment! A godless judgment!" . . . (2) But the women with their children cried out from above, saying: "O God, an impious judgment is come to pass in this city!" . . . (3) The women said: "May the city perish for this lawlessness! Slay us all, Proconsul! A bitter sight, an evil judgment!" . . . (4) And the crowd of the women raised a great shout. . . . (5) And the women mourned the more, since the lioness which helped her was dead. . . . (6) But as other more terrible beasts were let loose, the women cried aloud, and some threw petals, others nard, others cassia, others amomum, so that there was an abundance of perfumes. And all the beasts let loose were overpowered as if by sleep, and did not touch her. . . . (7) But all the women cried out with a loud voice, and as with one mouth gave praise to God, saying: "One is God, who has delivered Thecla!", so that all the city was shaken by the sound. (Acts of Paul and Thecla, *New Testament Apocrypha*, Vol. 2, pp. 360–363)

§317. Thecla Baptizes Herself

Besides having shown extraordinary courage and been the object of many saving miracles, Thecla did two other things which are worthy of note here. First, she baptized *herself*. Most documents indicate that only men baptized, although deaconesses assisted in the East in the early centuries of Christianity. The protest against this restriction is most obvious in the Acts of Paul and Thecla, where it is told of Thecla that in the midst of her trials,

when she had finished her prayer, she turned and saw a great pit full of water, and said: "Now is the time for me to wash." And she threw herself in, saying: "In the name of Jesus Christ I baptize myself on the last day!" (Acts of Paul and Thecla, *New Testament Apocrypha*, Vol. 2, p. 362)

§318. Thecla Teaches Christian Doctrine

Second, although beginning already in the later New Testament period women were increasingly restricted from teaching Christian doctrine (cf. 1 Tim 2:11–12; see §334), apparently many Christian women were aware of women's earlier freer involvement in Christian teaching (see §310), and in the Acts of Paul and Thecla registered a strong protest. Thecla not only instructs non-Christians in Christian doctrine and converts them but even does so at the behest of St. Paul.

So Thecla went in with her and rested in her house for eight days, instructing her in the word of God, so that the majority of the maidservants also believed; and there was great joy in the house. . . . And Thecla arose and said to Paul: "I am going to Iconium." But Paul said: "Go and teach the word of God!" . . . After enlightening many with the word of God she slept with a noble sleep. (Acts of Paul and Thecla, *New Testament Apocrypha*, Vol. 2, pp. 363–364)

§319. Thecla a Model for Christian Women

This baptizing and teaching by Thecla (who was listed as a saint by the Roman Catholic Church until 1969!), coupled with the great popularity of the Acts of Paul and Thecla, obviously provided a model for other Christian women to follow, as can be seen by the great disturbance of the late second-century North African Christian writer Tertullian.

But the impudence of that woman who assumed the right to teach is evidently not going to arrogate to her the right to baptize as well—unless perhaps some new serpent appears, like that original one, so that as the woman abolished baptism, some other should of her own authority confer it. But . . . certain Acts of Paul, which are falsely so named, claim the example of Thecla for allowing women to teach and to baptize. . . . How could we believe that Paul should give a female power to teach and to baptize, when he did not allow a woman even to learn by her own right? (Tertullian, *De Baptismo* 17.4)

§320. Women Authors of the Apocryphal Acts

After a lengthy and penetrating analysis, Stevan Davies concludes in his dissertation referred to above that because so many factors point to female rather than male authorship of the Apocryphal Acts,

Occam's Razor ought henceforth to cut the other way, that female authorship of the Apocryphal Acts ought to be assumed in the absence of any convincing arguments to the contrary. Were the Acts authored by men they would be men without high official position in the church, devoted to the lifestyle of sexual chastity but eager to associate with women, determined to promulgate a positive view of the female sex and to create models of exemplary women, greatly concerned with the financial well-being of Widows and Virgins of the Lord, devoted to wandering charismatic apostles, willing to hide their own identities while putting words in the mouths of Apostles of the first century, and prone to adopt the ancient love romance as the model for their own literary efforts. For women these traits are characteristic.

If anyone can bring evidence for the existence of men of this sort and argue that they, and not literate Widows or Deaconesses, composed the Acts, then the hypothesis of female authorship will be refuted. Until that time Christian women should be given credit for the creativity which remains embodied in their compositions, the Apocryphal Acts of the Apostles. . . .

Just as women of the present day seek to obtain fully equal standing with men in Christian churches, so did the Christian women of the second century. If our argument that the Apocryphal Acts originated in communities of continent Christian women can achieve general acceptance, Matristics will become a possibility. (Stevan Davies, "The Social World of the Apocryphal Acts," pp. 154f., appendix)

14. AUTHENTIC PAUL'S POSITIVE ATTITUDE TOWARD WOMEN

In attempting to assess Paul's attitude toward women, one must note the distinction between those Pauline letters which are universally accepted as Paul's and those which are generally or widely held by scholars not to be attributable directly to Paul. Those letters which are indisputably Paul's and which have something significant to say about women are: Romans, 1 Corinthians, Galatians, and, to a much lesser extent, 1 Thessalonians. Those letters which are very generally held by scholars to have been written after Paul's death (in 67?) by a disciple of his and which also speak of women are the so-called pastoral letters: 1 Timothy, 2 Timothy, Titus. The authorship of two other Pauline letters that speak of women, Ephesians and Colossians, is disputed. Whatever the relative merits of the various arguments for or against Paul's authorship, it seems clear that, as we have them, these two letters cannot be attributed to Paul in the same direct sense as the undisputed letters are: either Paul gave much more freedom to his amanuensis—he never directly wrote his own letters—than was his usual custom, or disciples pieced together fragments of lost Pauline letters, or some other like theory.

Hence, the attitudes toward women exhibited in the pastoral letters almost certainly provide no evidence for Paul's attitude, and those in Ephesians and Colossians probably do not. Those in Romans, 1 Corinthians, and Galatians do—with one important exception in Corinthians to be discussed below. The first two groups of letters, the so-called deutero-Pauline letters, even though not penned by Paul, of course still are part of the canon of the New Testament and hence will also be considered later.

The passages listed above wherein Paul teaches women as freely as men, treats them as co-workers in the spreading of the gospel, and refers to them as apostle, deacon, and ruler are all evidence of a positive attitude toward women. The pertinent passages in four of the undisputed letters of Paul and perhaps also Colossians, as well as a speech attributed to Paul in Luke's Acts of the Apostles, also add further evidence of a positive attitude. The oldest of the letters is 1 Thessalonians (c. 50), then Galatians (c. 54), 1 Corinthians (c. 56), Romans (c. 57), and Colossians (c. 62?).

§321. 1 Thessalonians 2:7

The first point is a small one, Paul's use of feminine imagery to describe himself. He does so in at least three instances. In the letter to the Thessalonians he refers to himself as a nursing mother (*trophos* —used in feminine form here).

But we were gentle when we were with you, like a nursing mother *(trophos)* taking care of her children. (1 Thess 2:7)

§322. 1 Corinthians 3:2

In the second instance Paul repeats the image of the nursing mother feeding her child milk rather than solid food, though the term *trophos* is not used here.

I treated you as sensual men, still infants in Christ. What I fed you with was milk, not solid food, for you were not ready for it. (1 Cor 3:1–2)

§323. Galatians 4:19

In the third instance Paul uses the imagery of giving birth to refer to himself, a clear indication that the most female of activities was not something he felt he as a male should disdain as alien to him— quite the contrary.

I must go through the pain of giving birth to you all over again, until Christ is formed in you. (Gal 4:19)

§324. Galatians 3:27–28

The next point is vastly more significant. Paul states that in the Christian sphere the religious distinction between male and female, along with the religious distinctions which existed between Jew and Gentile (or Greek, as he puts it here) and slave and free, all of which existed in Judaism, no longer exist. All are equal!

Paul, who here is said by many scholars to be using the phraseology common in the early Christian baptism liturgy, obviously made his own its explicit rejection of the threefold daily rabbinic prayer, discussed above (see §106), thanking God for not having made the man praying a Gentile, a woman, or a slave. As noted, the rabbinic prayer is recorded, in somewhat varying form, in three ancient sources. They are the Tosephta, a collection of rabbinic teachings from 200 B.C.E. to 200 C.E.; the Palestinian Talmud; and the Babylonian Talmud; both of the latter containing similarly early material and other teachings down to 400–500 C.E. In the Babylonian Talmud the prayer is attributed to Rabbi Meir (early second century C.E.), who claimed he faithfully passed on what he learned from his teacher Rabbi Akiba (50–135 C.E.). Given the tendency of the disciples of rabbis to memorize and pass on huge amounts of previous traditions, it is highly likely this threefold prayer was in one or several of its variant forms in use in Paul's lifetime (which even overlaps Akiba's by seventeen years). The striking similarity of Paul's (and the early Christian formulary's) inversion in Gal 3:28 is so close as to constitute a final proof that the threefold rabbinic prayer was well known in the middle of the first century of the Christian Era.

Praised be God that he has not created me a Gentile! Praised be God that he has not created me a woman! Praised be God that he has not created me a slave! (Tosephta Berakhoth 7, 18)

All [are] baptised in Christ, you have all clothed yourselves in Christ, and there are no more distinctions between Jew and Greek, slave and free, male and female, but all of you are one in Christ Jesus. (Gal 3:27–28)

§325. Colossians 3:11

This rejection of distinction "in Christ Jesus" is repeated in three other Pauline passages, once referring only to the distinction between Greek and Jew (Rom 10:12), once to Greeks-Jews and slaves-free (1 Cor 12:13), and once to an even longer list (Col 3:11), which normally is not translated with the reference to male and female. However, there are a number of ancient Greek and Latin manuscripts, including the first-century "Clermont" manuscript, which do contain the words male and female, and at the head of the list. (See Augustinus Merk, ed., *Novum Testamentum Graece et Latine*, Rome, 1959, and Joan Morris, *The Lady Was a Bishop*, pp. 122f.; Macmillan Publishing Co., 1973.)

Here there cannot be [male and female,] Greek and Jew, circumcised and uncircumcised, barbarian, Sythian, slave, free person, but Christ is all, and in all. (Col 3:11)

§326. Romans 5:12–14 and 1 Corinthians 15:21–22

A small but interesting point should be noted about Rom 5:12–14 and 1 Cor 15:21–22. In both instances Paul refers to the first sin in Eden. In doing so he attributes the sin to Adam, only to balance the sin by a single man with redemption by Christ. This is understandable since Adam in the Genesis story is the "first" man (see above, pp. 76ff., for a discussion of sexual differentiation in Genesis 2).

However, such an explanation is quite different from much of the interpretation prevalent just before and during Paul's time, which made not Adam but Eve the source of sin and death (see the second century B.C.E. Ben Sira 25:24: "Sin began with a woman, and thanks to her we all must die"; the first century B.C.E. Book of Adam and Eve: "And Adam said to Eve: 'Eve what have you wrought in us? You have brought upon us great wrath which is death' "; the first century B.C.E. Book of the Secrets of Enoch: "And I took from him a rib, and created him a wife, that death should come to him by his wife"; and the Tannaitic work, i.e., from 200 B.C.E. to 200 C.E., the Tosephta, Shabbath 2, 10(112): "The first man was the blood and life of the world . . . and Eve was the cause of his death"). It is also different from the deutero-Pauline 1 Tim 2:14, where it is said: "It was not Adam who was led astray but the woman who was led astray and fell into sin." The authentic Paul is clearly aware of Eve's having been "seduced" by the serpent (2 Cor 11:3), but he does not make her the source of sin and death; that responsibility he lays on Adam.

> Well then, sin entered the world through one man, and through sin death, and thus death has spread through the whole human race because everyone has sinned. Sin existed in the world long before the Law was given. There was no law and so no one could be accused of the sin of "law-breaking," yet death reigned over all from Adam to Moses, even though their sin, unlike that of Adam, was not a matter of breaking a law. (Rom 5:12–14)

> Death came through one man and in the same way the resurrection of the dead has come through one man. Just as all men die in Adam, so all men will be brought to life in Christ. (1 Cor 15:21–22)

§327. 1 Corinthians 7:1–9

The last passages positive toward women to be treated are found in the indisputably Pauline letter, 1 Corinthians; it contains four significant passages. One (1 Cor 3:2) has been treated above; a second (11:2–16) will be analyzed below (§335) along with other ambivalent passages. The third (1 Cor 14:33b–35), which prohibits women from speaking in assemblies and is clearly negative in its attitude toward women, is widely held, however, not to be authentically part of Paul's letter, but an insertion by an early scribe paraphrasing 1 Tim 2:11–12. Briefly, the major evidence is as follows: (1) This passage directly contradicts Paul's earlier statement (1 Cor 11:2–16) that women may speak in assembly; (2) this passage is obviously out of place, having nothing to do with what immediately precedes and follows it, though when it is removed the text reads logically and smoothly; (3) Paul would never base a Christian argument on the Law, as does 1 Cor 14:34; and (4) the thought of this passage is very similar to that of the deutero-Pauline 1 Tim 2:11–12—that it is a gloss from the deutero-Pauline circles inserted into the 1 Corinthians manuscript is quite likely. (See Robin A. Scroggs, "Paul and the Eschatological Woman," *Journal of the American Academy of Religion,* September 1972, p. 284.) Since this passage is almost certainly not Paul's, it too will not be treated here, but below with the other deutero-Pauline material (§334).

The fourth passage in 1 Corinthians is basically positive in its attitude toward women. In it Paul is saying yes to the legitimacy of marriage and sexuality within marriage (there were encratic groups at the time who opposed marriage and the use of sex). Paul emphasizes the equal sexual rights and responsibilities of the husband and wife in marriage, and stresses that he personally prefers, not commands, celibacy. Because the section is long, the whole of ch. 7, it will be quoted and commented on briefly in sections.

In the first section Paul is answering a man who apparently has a strong sexually ascetic bent. Paul's insistence on the propriety of marriage and the equal sexual rights of both wife and husband stems from rabbinic Judaism. The notion of sexual continence for the sake of prayer, however, is found already in the second century B.C.E. Testament of Naphtali (8.8): "There is a season for a man to embrace his wife, and a season to abstain therefrom for his prayer." However, Paul's stress on the mutuality of the consent goes beyond the early rabbinic rules, which, although generally stressing marital sexual mutuality, allowed rabbinic students to absent themselves for thirty days against their wives' will to study the Law (Mishnah Kethuboth 5, 6)—the later (fifth century C.E.) Talmud extended the time to three years (bKethuboth 62b).

Now for the questions about which you wrote. Yes, it is a good thing for a man not to touch a woman; but since sex is always a danger, let each man have his own wife and each woman her own husband. The husband must give his wife what she has the right to expect, and so too the wife to the husband. The wife has no rights over her own body; it is the husband who has them. In the same way, the husband has no rights over his body; the wife has them. Do not refuse each other except by mutual consent, and then only for an agreed time, to leave yourselves free for prayer; them come together again in case Satan should take advantage of your weakness to tempt you. This is a suggestion, not a rule: I should like everyone to be like me, but everybody has his own particular gifts from God, one with a gift for one thing and another with a gift for the opposite.

There is something I want to add for the sake of widows and those who are not married: it is a good thing for them to stay as they are, like me, but if they cannot control the sexual urges, they should get married, since it is better to be married than to be tortured. (1 Cor 7:1–9)

§328. 1 Corinthians 7:10–16

The next section of 1 Corinthians 7 concerns divorce. Paul repeats Jesus' novel (to Judaism) egalitarian prohibition of divorce and remarriage. He then proceeds on his own account to emend it to allow divorce and remarriage to save the Christian faith of the Christian partner of a mixed marriage; Paul too is evenhanded in his allowances and expectations for both the wife and husband.

For the married I have something to say, and this is not from me but from the Lord: a wife must not leave her husband—or if she does leave him, she must either remain unmarried or else make it up with her husband—nor must a husband send his wife away.

The rest is from me and not from the Lord. If a brother has a wife who is an unbeliever, and she is content to live with him, he must not send her away; and if a woman has an unbeliever for her husband, and he is content to live with her, she must not leave him. This is because the unbelieving husband is made one with the saints through his wife, and the unbelieving wife is made one with the saints through her husband. If this were not so, your children would be unclean, whereas in fact they are holy. However, if the unbelieving partner does not consent, they may separate; in these circumstances, the brother or sister is not tied: God has called you to a life of peace. If you are a wife, it may be your part to save your husband, for all you know; if a husband, for all you know, it may be your part to save your wife. (1 Cor 7:10–16)

§329. 1 Corinthians 7:25–40

The final portion of 1 Corinthians 7 is an extended discussion of Paul's personal—he distinctly says his own and not Jesus'—opinion on the advantages of celibacy. There seem to be two main reasons: first, the Second Coming of Christ is imminent (in his later letters Paul sees it to be postponed); second, and closely connected, the unmarried can devote more time and attention to "the things of the Lord," prayer and good works. Nevertheless, Paul is firm in his rejection of any condemnation of marriage, which apparently some in the Corinthian Christian community were looking for.

In this section on celibacy Paul maintains a relative evenhandedness for the most part. Verses 29–31 are addressed to men alone; there is no parallel addressed to women. Verses 36–38 are addressed to men, but they are more or less paralleled by vs. 39–40, which are addressed to women. The Greek for vs. 36–38 is so ambiguous that they could refer to a man giving his daughter in marriage, or a man marrying a maiden (both possibilities are provided below). In either case it is apparently the man who decides whether the woman is to marry or not. Of course the widowed woman in vs. 39–40 also makes the parallel decision about whether to marry or not. Though the situations are not exactly the same and the tilt is in fact in favor of the man, there is nevertheless a relative evenhandedness.

About remaining celibate, I have no directions from the Lord but give my own opinion as one who, by the Lord's mercy, has stayed faithful. Well then, I believe that in these present times of stress this is right: that it is good for a man to stay as he is. If you are tied to a wife, do not look for freedom; if you are free of a wife, then do not look for one. But if you marry, it is no sin, and it is not a sin for a young girl to get married. They will have their troubles, though, in their married life, and I should like to spare you that.

Brothers, this is what I mean: our time is growing short. Those who have wives should live as though they had none, and those who mourn should live as though they had nothing to mourn for; those who are enjoying life should live as though there were nothing to laugh about; those whose life is buying things should live as though they had nothing of their own; and those who have to deal with the world should not become engrossed in it. I say this because the world as we know it is passing away.

I would like to see you free from all worry. An unmarried man can devote himself to the Lord's affairs, all he need worry about is pleasing the Lord; but a married man has to bother about the world's affairs and devote himself to pleasing his wife; he is torn two ways. In the same way an unmarried woman, like a young girl, can devote herself to the Lord's affairs; all she need worry about is being holy in body and spirit. The married woman, on the other hand, has to worry about the world's affairs and devote herself to pleasing her husband. I say this only to help you, not to put a halter round your necks, but simply to make sure that everything is as it should be, and that you give your undivided attention to the Lord.

Still, if there is anyone who feels that it would not be fair to his daughter to let her grow too old for marriage, and that he should do something about it, he is free to do as he likes: he is not sinning if there is a marriage. On the other hand, if someone has firmly made his mind up, without any compulsion and in complete freedom of choice, to keep his daughter as she is, he will be doing a good thing. In other words, the man who sees that his daughter is married has done a good thing but the man who keeps his daughter unmarried has done something even better.

[An alternate reading of the above paragraph is as follows:

In the case of an engaged couple who have decided not to marry: if the man feels that he is acting properly toward the girl and if his passions are too strong and he feels that they ought to marry, then they should get married, as he wants to. There is no sin in this. But if a man, without being forced to do so, has firmly made up his mind not to marry, and if he has his will under complete control and has already decided in his mind what to do

—then he does well not to marry the girl. So that man who marries does well, but the one who doesn't marry does even better.]

A wife is tied as long as her husband is alive. But if the husband dies, she is free to marry anybody she likes, only it must be in the Lord. She would be happier, in my opinion, if she stayed as she is—and I too have the Spirit of God, I think. (1 Cor 7:25–40)

§330. Acts 17:28–29: Humanity in God's Womb

In the speech Paul made before Greek Gentiles in Athens he used paraphrases of Greek poetry, the first of which projects God in as feminine an image as possible, that of a pregnant woman. Paul speaks of all humanity as existing within God as does a fetus within its mother's womb, since "it is in him [God] that we live, and move, and exist" (this is said by Clement of Alexandria to be a paraphrase of the sixth-century B.C. Greek poet Epimenides). It is difficult to see how this image is not that of a fetus in a womb, especially since Paul then immediately paraphrases another Greek poet (perhaps Aratus, third century B.C.), by saying, "We are all his [God's] children." It would appear that Paul deliberately used the imagery of God as mother (not at all strange to Greeks) but retained masculine genders in the pronouns referring to God, giving an androgynous cast to the image of God here.

"Yet in fact God is not far from any of us, since it is in him that we live, and move, and exist, as indeed some of your own poets have said: 'We are all his children.' Since we are all the children of God . . ." (Acts 17:28–29)

§331. Conclusion

All told, one would have to describe Paul's attitude toward women expressed in this section as basically positive, evenhanded toward women and men. At the same time, his attitude toward sex and marriage in general is moderately negative, the sources of which would include the following: (1) the anticipated imminent Second Coming of Christ, already mentioned; (2) an anti-sex and marriage attitude in a limited part of contemporary Judaism, as reflected in the Essenes (who saw sex as a source of religious uncleanness); (3) ascetic attitudes in contemporary Hellenism—Paul himself indicates that Jesus was definitely not a source, suggesting that those later Gospel sayings stressing celibacy were placed on Jesus' lips by later church tradition.

IX. Ambivalent Elements in Christian Tradition

A. AUTHENTIC PAUL'S AMBIVALENT ATTITUDE TOWARD WOMEN

§332. 1 Corinthians 11:2–16

The last authentic Pauline passage dealing with women is 1 Cor 11:2–16. This is a notoriously difficult passage to understand, so much so that scholars often debate what is even a correct translation. Verse 3 is a case in point. Professor Robin A. Scroggs ("Paul and the Eschatological Woman Revisited," *Journal of the American Academy of Religion*, September 1974, pp. 543f.) argues, persuasively, that the Greek word used here for "head," *kephalē*, is not used in the metaphorical sense of chief or authority, but rather in the sense of "source," like the head waters of a river (ample statistics of the Greek usage are provided by Scroggs). Hence, when Paul writes that man is the *kephalē* of woman he is alluding to the Genesis 2 story of Eve being made from the rib of Adam, that Adam was her "source." This understanding is reinforced by v. 8, where Paul writes that "woman came from man." (It is interesting to note that Jesus refers only to the Genesis 1 account of creation, where the creation of male and female is described in a totally egalitarian manner, whereas Paul uses only the Genesis 2 account, which has traditionally, though incorrectly, been interpreted in a woman-subordinating manner.)

Paul appears extraordinarily preoccupied with an attempt to maintain visible distinctions between women and men. The women's liberation movement moving through the Greco-Roman world (see pp. 15ff.) would of course have the tendency to blur many of the traditional distinctions. Such developments would allow subterranean homosexuality more public scope; homosexuality, moreover, had al-

329

ready played a significant role in earlier Greek culture. Paul, as a devout Jew, was absolutely opposed to homosexuality; he rails against it elsewhere, e.g., Rom 1:26–27; 1 Cor 6:9–10. Paul's insistence on the one hand on women retaining long hair and having their heads covered—or shaving their heads!—and on the other hand on long hair on men being contrary to nature sounds very much like the voice of the frustrated older generation in the face of the 1960's generation gap. His final statement epitomizes his exasperation at "not being able to tell them apart": "To anyone who might still want to argue: it is not the custom with us, nor in the churches of God." If this understanding of this portion of the passage is not off the mark, then Paul is not trying to make women subordinate, but is resisting what he sees as an open door to homosexuality—which is another problem entirely. Thus, this whole passage is largely an attempt by Paul to maintain this visible distinction of long hair and covered heads for women and the opposite for men by means of a rather abstruse paraphrase of, or midrash on, the Genesis 2 story of the creation of Adam and Eve, plus some self-admittedly ineffectual arguments from "nature."

Two other points should also be noted about this very difficult passage. One, Paul says man is the image and manifestation or glory *(doxa)* of God, but woman is the manifestation or glory *(doxa)* of man, meaning woman was made from the side of man according to Genesis 2. Paul does *not* say woman is the image of man, for according to Genesis 1 she is the image of God. Paul here is still straining to find some scriptural basis for insisting on the head covering for women. His continuing with weak arguments and his final gasp of exasperation show he is aware he is not being very clear or persuasive. This unclarity reaches its peak in 1 Cor 11: 10 with its reference to angels. Though there have been many proffered explanations of the meaning of this text, no one is completely satisfied with any of them.

There are at least two particularly troublesome areas in verse 10. One concerns the word *exousia*. It often is translated as meaning "the woman ought to have a sign of 'submission' on her head" *(New American Bible)*. Another interpretation is, however, possible. Jean-Marie Aubert states: "But the word 'exousia' has the basic meaning of freedom of action, of power, which would give the exact opposite meaning to St. Paul's phrase: 'the woman ought to have a sign of power on her head. . . .' Therefore, far from being a symbol of power submitted to by the woman (= submission), the veil would be a symbol of her spiritual power exercised in the assembly." (Jean-Marie

Aubert, *La Femme antiféminisme et christianisme,* p. 39; Paris: Cerf/
Desclee, 1975.) Concerning the second problem area, the phrase
"because of the angels" *(dia tous angelous),* André Feuillet suggests
that the angels in the context refer to the male clergy gathered
around, who should not be distracted by the woman's uncovered hair.
He adds, "When the woman prays and prophesies she finds herself
associated with the angels. . . . She finds herself thus placed in a
privileged position which morally obliges her . . . to have on her head
a sign of the power she received from Christ." (André Feuillet, "Le
signe de puissance sur la tête de la femme, 1 Cor 11, 10," *Nouvelle
Revue Théologique* 95, 1973, p. 950.)

Lastly, as noted above (§289), Paul, when speaking of women
being veiled when prophesying (clearly, from the context, in church),
obviously presumes that women do properly pray and prophesy out
loud in church (providing one of the strong arguments below (§335)
against 1 Cor 14:33b–35 being authentically Paul's).

Thus, upon analysis this obscure passage may not express as strong
a negative attitude toward women as a superficial reading might lead
one to think. On the other hand it could hardly be described as
promoting the liberation of women. Still, there is an evenhandedness
in 1 Cor 11:11–12, which speaks about women and men needing
each other and coming from and being born from one another. But
Paul's concern to maintain the visible distinction between women
and men—no unisex!—has, perhaps unwarrantedly, beclouded his
reputation of having a positive attitude toward women.

You have done well in remembering me so constantly and in maintaining
the traditions just as I passed them on to you. However, what I want you
to understand is that Christ is the source *(kephalē)* of every man, man is the
source of woman, and God is the source of Christ. For a man to pray or
prophesy with his head covered is a sign of disrespect to his source. For a
woman, however, it is a sign of disrespect to her source if she prays or
prophesies unveiled; she might as well have her hair shaved off. In fact, a
woman who will not wear a veil ought to have her hair cut off. If a woman
is ashamed to have her hair cut off or shaved, she ought to wear a veil.

A man should certainly not cover his head, since he is the image of God
and reflects God's glory *(doxa);* but woman is the reflection of man's glory
(doxa). For man did not come from woman; no, woman came from man;
and man was not created for the sake of woman, but woman was created for
the sake of man. That is the argument for women's covering their heads with
a symbol of the authority over them, out of respect for the angels. However,
though woman cannot do without man, neither can man do without woman,
in the Lord; woman may come from man, but man is born of woman—both
come from God.

Ask yourselves if it is fitting for a woman to pray to God without a veil; and whether nature itself does not tell you that long hair on a man is nothing to be admired, while a woman, who was given her hair as a covering, thinks long hair her glory?

To anyone who might still want to argue: it is not the custom with us, nor in the churches of God. (1 Cor 11:2–16)

Thus the undisputedly Pauline materials yield a number of positive actions and attitudes toward women, plus a very confused passage which, depending on the translation, at worst is quite negative toward women, and at best is perhaps best described as not really negative toward women, but not positive either.

B. DEUTERO-PAULINE (AND OTHER) AMBIVALENT (AND SOME NEGATIVE) ATTITUDES TOWARD WOMEN

As noted above, the Pauline authorship of the letter to the Ephesians is strongly disputed by scholars and the letter to the Colossians even more so; further, the two letters to Timothy and the one to Titus are almost unanimously considered not to have been written by Paul, but by some later disciples of his. None of the statements about women in this deutero-Pauline material is positive in its attitude; at most some of them are ambivalent, several are quite negative.

§333. Household Tables

Both the statements about women in Ephesians (Eph 5:21–33) and Colossians (Col 3:18–25), as well as those in Titus (Tit 2:3–9) and the First Letter of Peter (1 Pet 3:1–7, which was clearly not written by Peter, but perhaps by Silvanus, or Silas, mentioned in 1 Pet 5:12, a frequent companion of Paul), have a basic similarity: they give expression to the "household tables." This was a set of rules governing "proper" duties of the various strata in a household. It was said to have originated with Zeno the founder of Stoicism at the end of the fourth century B.C. and had in the ensuing period become the common property of all the schools of Hellenistic ethics, including Hellenistic Judaism. The various "strata" with superordinate and subordinate responsibilities vis-à-vis each other included husbands and wives, parents and children, masters and slaves. In each of the four instances listed dealing with women, slaves being subordinate to their masters is also mandated; three times children are also charged with obedience to parents; twice (Titus and 1 Peter) submission to civil authorities is likewise exhorted. Although the undisputed Pauline writings required respect for civil authority (Rom 13:1–7) and a sort of good order in general, they nowhere adopt the "household tables," which figure so prominently in these later extra-Pauline New Testament writings. In general these later writings reflect a settling down of Christianity, a growing more conservative and organized for the "long haul." That shift from Jesus' radicalness in his attitude toward women, and Paul's openness to them, to the late New Testament uncritical acceptance of one popular (probably largely middle and lower class) Hellenistic morality places women—or to be more precise, wives, for unmarried women are not discussed here—in a clearly unequal, subordinate position.

a. Ephesians 5:21–33

The author follows the Stoic household tables but provides Christian symbolism, motivations, or scriptural quotations for each pair: wives-husbands (Eph 5:21–33), children-parents (Eph 6:1–4), slaves-masters (Eph 6:5–9). The husband-wife relationship is compared with the relationship of Christ and the church, with the requisite love of the husband for his subordinate wife being enjoined—a sublime comparison for a married couple, but one that only reinforced the subordination of the wife.

Wives should regard their husbands as they regard the Lord, since as Christ is the head of the Church and saves the whole body, so is a husband the head of his wife; and as the Church submits to Christ, so should wives to their husbands, in everything. Husbands should love their wives just as Christ loved the Church and sacrificed himself for her to make her holy. He made her clean by washing her in water with a form of words, so that when he took her to himself she would be glorious, with no speck or wrinkle or anything like that, but holy and faultless. In the same way, husbands must love their wives as they love their own bodies; for a man to love his wife is for him to love himself. A man never hates his own body, but he feeds it and looks after it; and that is the way Christ treats the Church, because it is his body—and we are its living parts. For this reason, a man must leave his father and mother and be joined to his wife, and the two will become one body. This mystery has many implications; but I am saying it applies to Christ and the Church. To sum up; you, too, each of you, must love his wife as he loves himself; and let every wife respect her husband. (Eph 5:21–33)

b. Colossians 3:18 to 4:1

Though the author has just declared (Col 3:11) that in the "religious sphere," that is, "in Christ," there is no distinction between slave and free (and in some manuscripts also between male and female—cf. §325), he is unwilling to translate that into immediate social action, for he then uncritically accepts the Stoic household tables and admonishes wives, children, and slaves to obey their husbands, parents, masters. Again, the requisite concern of the superior for the inferior is enjoined and provided with Christian motivations; but the subordination of the wife to the husband, etc., remains in place.

Wives, give way to your husbands, as you should in the Lord. Husbands, love your wives and treat them with gentleness. Children, be obedient to your parents always, because that is what will please the Lord. Parents, never drive your children to resentment or you will make them feel frustrated.

Slaves, be obedient to the men who are called your masters in this world; not only when you are under their eye, as if you had only to please men, but wholeheartedly, out of respect for the Master. Whatever your work is, put your heart into it as if it were for the Lord and not for men, knowing that the Lord will repay you by making them his heirs. It is Christ the Lord that you are serving; anyone who does wrong will be repaid in kind and he does not favour one person more than another. Masters, make sure that your slaves are given what is just and fair, knowing that you too have a Master in heaven. (Col 3:18 to 4:1)

c. Titus 2:3–9

The author adopts the Stoic household tables and applies them not only to the typical family but also to the "household of God." The subordination of wives again stands clear.

Similarly, the older women should behave as though they were religious, with no scandalmongering and no habitual wine-drinking—they are to be the teachers of the right behaviour and show the younger women how they should love their husbands and love their children, how they are to be sensible and chaste, and how to work in their homes, and be gentle, and do as their husbands tell them, so that the message of God is never disgraced. In the same way, you have got to persuade the younger men to be moderate and in everything you do make yourself an example to them of working for good: when you are teaching, be an example to them in your sincerity and earnestness and in keeping all that you say so wholesome that nobody can make objections to it; and then any opponent will be at a loss, with no accusation to make against us. Tell the slaves that they are to be obedient to their masters and always do what they want without any argument; and there must be no petty thieving—they must show complete honesty at all times, so that they are in every way a credit to the teaching of God our saviour. (Tit 2:3–9)

d. 1 Peter 3:1–7

The author enjoins obedience to civil authority (1 Pet 2:13–17), to slave masters (1 Pet 2:18–20), and to husbands, thus also following the Stoic "household tables." The wife is urged to obey partly to convert her husband to Christianity. An asceticism in dress is urged on the wives (apparently seeing feminine, though not masculine, physical beauty as evil), much as is also in 1 Tim 2:9–10; nothing parallel is urged on the husbands. Again, along with slaves, wives are held to be subordinate.

For the sake of the Lord, accept the authority of every social institution: the emperor, as the supreme authority, and the governors as commissioned by him. . . .

Slaves must be respectful and obedient to their masters, not only when they are kind and gentle but also when they are unfair. . . .

In the same way, wives should be obedient to their husbands. Then, if there are some husbands who have not yet obeyed the word, they may find themselves won over, without a word spoken, by the way their wives behave, when they see how faithful and conscientious they are. Do not dress up for show: doing up your hair, wearing gold bracelets and fine clothes; all this should be inside, in a person's heart, imperishable: the ornament of a sweet and gentle disposition—this is what is precious in the sight of God. That was how the holy women of the past dressed themselves attractively —they hoped in God and were tender and obedient to their husbands; like Sarah, who was obedient to Abraham, and called him her lord. You are now her children, as long as you live good lives and do not give way to fear or worry.

In the same way, husbands must always treat their wives with consideration in their life together, respecting a woman as one who, though she may be the weaker partner, is equally an heir to the life of grace. This will stop anything from coming in the way of your prayers. (1 Pet 2:13, 18; 3:1–7)

§334. 1 Timothy

The deutero-Pauline First Letter to Timothy contains three sections dealing with women, one positive, one negative, and one ambivalent. For the positive statement, see above, p. 315.

The author has a lengthy statement about widows which is really three-layered. He speaks first of women whose husbands have died but who have relatives who can care for them. Secondly, he mentions those widows who have no one to support them—here the church should step in. Thirdly, he describes the widows who become members of the ecclesial order of widows (see §298). A downgrading of sex and marriage is apparent here: a second marriage makes a woman unfit to become an "ecclesial widow"; an opposition is set up between a legitimate desire for marriage and "dedication to Christ" (literally, "for when they may have grown wanton against Christ they wish to marry"). This seems to be an echo of Paul's plea for sexual continence over against marriage in 1 Corinthians 7, though the author of 1

Timothy reluctantly concludes it is actually better that young widows marry again.

> Be considerate to widows; I mean those who are truly widows. If a widow has children or grandchildren, they are to learn first of all to do their duty to their own families and repay their debt to their parents, because this is what pleases God. But a woman who is really widowed and left without anybody can give herself up to God and consecrate all her days and nights to petitions and prayer. The one who thinks only of pleasure is already dead while she is still alive: remind them of all this, too, so that their lives may be blameless. Anyone who does not look after his own relations, especially if they are living with him, has rejected the faith and is worse than an unbeliever.
>
> Enrolment as a widow is permissible only for a woman at least sixty years old who has had only one husband. She must be a woman known for her good works and for the way in which she has brought up her children, shown hospitality to strangers and washed the saints' feet, helped people who are in trouble and been active in all kinds of good work. Do not accept young widows because if their natural desires get stronger than their dedication to Christ, they want to marry again, and then people condemn them for being unfaithful to their original promise. Besides, they learn how to be idle and go round from house to house; and then, not merely idle, they learn to be gossips and meddlers in other people's affairs, and to chatter when they would be better keeping quiet. I think it is best for young widows to marry again and have children and a home to look after, and not give the enemy any chance to raise a scandal about them; there are already some who have left us to follow Satan. If a Christian woman has widowed relatives, she should support them and not make the Church bear the expense but enable it to support those who are genuinely widows. (1 Tim 5:3–16)

The third passage of 1 Timothy dealing with women is perhaps the most negative of the New Testament in its attitude toward women. Like 1 Pet 3:2–4, it expresses a hostile attitude toward women's physical beauty, though again nothing is said about men's. Women, apparently in general, are told they do not have this author's permission to teach or exercise authority over men; they are told to keep silence. Recalling Paul's reference to women "praying and prophesying" in the Corinthian church (1 Cor 11:5), Klaus Thraede remarked: "Apparently at the beginning of the second century [when 1 Timothy is thought to have been written] there were still communities in which Christian women collaborated in the worship service, although we could not say whether in 'prayer and prophecy,' or even in scriptural preaching. In any case, what could be learned about the Pauline communities from 1 Cor was confirmed a posteriori. Now, about a half century later, in the name of Paul, this custom was disallowed." (Klaus Thraede, "Frauen im Leben frühchristlichen Gemeinden," *Una Sancta,* 1977, pp. 292f.) The basis for this order is the Jewish apocalyptic interpretation of the Fall which lays the blame at Eve's feet (rather than Adam's, as is done in the undisputed Pauline letters—see §326), and they are relegated to pius mother-hood to gain salvation—all of which flew in the face of earlier state-ments and actions of Paul as recorded in the Acts of the Apostles and his undisputed letters.

Women should adorn themselves modestly and sensibly in seemly apparel, not with braided hair or gold or pearls or costly attire but by good deeds, as befits women who profess religion. Let a woman learn in silence with all submissiveness. I permit no woman to teach or to have authority over men; she is to keep silent. For Adam was formed first, then Eve; and Adam was not deceived, but the woman was deceived and became a transgressor. Yet woman will be saved through bearing children, if she continues in faith and love and holiness, with modesty. (1 Tim 2:9–15)

§335. 1 Corinthians 14:33b–35

As noted in §327, 1 Cor 14:33b–35 is almost certainly an interpola-tion inserted into the authentic Pauline letter to the Corinthians. It bears an extraordinary resemblance to 1 Tim 2:9–15, just quoted. There is one difference, however. The 1 Timothy passage restricts all women to silence in church, whereas this 1 Corinthians passage appears to refer specifically to married women, for the women are told to ask their husbands for information. Thus it treats at least married women as perforce unlettered inferiors, a puzzling attitude in a Hellenistic world where there were so many women readers and writers; perhaps the author thought of the women as all converts from Judaism, where women for the most part were kept illiterate.

As in all the churches of the saints, the women should keep silence in the churches. For they are not permitted to speak, but should be subordinate, as even the law says. If there is anything they desire to know, let them ask their husbands at home. For it is shameful for a woman to speak in church. (1 Cor 14:33b–35)

§336. 2 Timothy 1:5

In 1 Timothy the deutero-Pauline author stated that women would gain salvation by childbearing and child-rearing. This notion is similar to the rabbinic saying that a woman merits by sending her husband and sons off to synagogue to study Torah and waiting for them (Talmud bSotah 21a), and finds concrete fulfillment in 2 Tim 1:5, where the author subtly praises Timothy's grandmother and mother for having embraced the Christian faith and passed it on to him who, as an ordained man, will exercise church leadership.

How different from the earlier authentic Pauline situation where Phoebe, Lydia, Priscilla, Junia, and many other women were mentioned for themselves and their own accomplishments and leadership and not simply because they mothered a Christian son. The womanly model held up in the two letters to Timothy, and their probable interpolation into 1 Cor 14:33b–35, and 1 Peter is dramatically distinct from that presented in Luke's Acts of the Apostles and the undisputed Pauline letters. In the early materials the women are respected, vigorous, assertive co-workers; in the later writings they are silenced, subordinated, passive followers.

> Then I am reminded of the sincere faith which you have; it came first to live in your grandmother Lois, and your mother Eunice, and I have no doubt that it is the same faith in you as well. (2 Tim 1:5)

§337. Revelation

This last book of the New Testament—often called the Apocalypse, a transliteration of the Greek word *apocalypsis,* meaning "revelation"—was most probably written in its several parts by several unknown writers sometime during the latter part of the first century. The section attacking the woman prophet in the Christian church in Thyatira (Rev 2:20–29) is analyzed above, §290. The bulk of the book is full of visions and images, centrally including three images of women. The first is Israel (Rev 12:1–17), who gives birth to the Messiah. The second is the state of Rome, which is depicted in quite lurid terms as a great whore (chs. 17; 18; 19). The third is the Christian church, the New Jerusalem, descending from God in heaven (ch. 21). The impression given is that women are either the best or the worst; they never seem to be truly, equally human with men. But (one of) the author(s) reflects his basically negative attitude toward women in Rev 14:4, where he speaks of the one hundred and forty-four thousand who are *undefiled* by women, that is, they have no sexual intercourse with them. There is no talk of women being defiled by men: sex defiles, but only sex by women.

> There in front of the throne they were singing a new hymn in the presence of the four animals and the elders, a hymn that could only be learnt by the hundred and forty-four thousand who had been redeemed from the world. These are the ones who have kept their virginity and not been defiled with women. (Rev 14:3–4)

X. Negative Elements in Christian Tradition

A. WOMEN AND THE CHRISTIAN FATHERS

The Christians who wrote about things Christian after the close of the New Testament, from the beginning of the second century A.D. until the end of the eighth century, are referred to as the fathers *(patres)* of the church. For the most part they wrote in Greek and Latin, and to a much lesser extent in Syriac and other languages. Along with the decrees of the first seven universal, or ecumenical, councils of about the same period, their writings constitute a most important body of Christian religious literature reflecting on and applying the Bible message, Hebrew Bible and New Testament. In many ways the importance of this literature in Christianity is like that of rabbinic literature in Judaism.

As with rabbinic literature, with which it is basically contemporaneous, patristic literature reflects a largely negative, nonegalitarian attitude toward women. A number of positive statements concerning women from this patristic writing have been presented above. For the sake of a semblance of balance an extremely brief survey of the negative attitudes toward women expressed by the Christian fathers will be presented here.

§338. Christian Mothers

To begin with, there is no talk of "Christian mothers," no "mothers of the church," as there is of Christian fathers and fathers of the church, even though, for example, a significant number of the writings in the volumes of Migne's *Patrologia Latina* devoted to Jerome are in fact written by Christian women (e.g., Paula; see §320 for a discussion of female authorship of other Christian writings of early

Christianity). There is much written about the early Christian monastics of the third and subsequent centuries who founded monasticism in the deserts of Egypt and elsewhere. But practically all of it is about the Desert Fathers. There is not even a term "Desert Mothers," even though Christian women

took their part in every phase of the monastic movement in Egypt, and some lived the eremitical life as recluses in the desert, while communities of women came into existence earlier than those of men, and in Egypt were to be found as early as the middle of the third century. (Margaret Smith, *Studies in Early Mysticism in the Near and Middle East,* p. 35; London: Sheldon Press, 1931; repr. Amsterdam: Philo Press, 1973)

Anthony of Egypt (A.D. 251–356) is usually reckoned as the founder of Christian monasticism. And yet:

We are told that St. Anthony, when he renounced the world, placed his sister, for whom he was responsible, in a "house of virgins," a nunnery, when as yet there were no similar institutions for men. (Smith, *Studies in Early Mysticism,* p. 36)

One of Anthony's younger contemporaries, Pachomius, also of Egypt (A.D. 290–346), was the first to write a "rule" which monastics followed and hence is said to be the founder of communal monasticism (Anthony and his followers were hermits; they lived singly). It is recorded of Pachomius that he

built a convent for his sister Mary, on the bank of the Nile opposite to Tabennisi, where his own monastery was, and there *she established a nunnery, of which she was the abbess.* (Smith, *Studies in Early Mysticism,* p. 36; italics added)

Women continued to flock to the monastic life in great numbers. A dozen women's monasteries were founded shortly after the one by Mary the sister of Pachomius, and they continued to multiply, for in the city of Antinoë alone, Palladius (A.D. 365–425), who visited Egypt before A.D. 400, reported that there were twelve women's monasteries and that one of them was ruled by a woman, Amma Talis, who had already spent eighty years in asceticism (Palladius, *Historia Lausiaca,* Eng. tr. by W. K. L. Clarke, lix; London, 1918).

Around the same time the Egyptian abbot Shenoudi (A.D. 333–450) founded two monasteries, one with 2,200 men and one with 1,800 women. And in the same period it is reported by Palladius that in the city of Oxyrhynchus, twelve miles south of Cairo, there were as many as 20,000 nuns! (Palladius, *Paradise of the Fathers* i. 337, tr. by E. A. Budge; London, 1907).

Even earlier, in Syria, where perhaps several of the Gospels were composed, as well as the Didascalia (early third century), which spoke at length of deaconesses,

we find women ascetics also to the fore . . . and in the Christian Church of the third century we find "Daughters of the Covenant" *(B'nāth Q'yāmā)* alongside of the Sons. In the *Martyrdom of Shamōna and Guria* . . . is an account of the persecution of Diocletian against the Churches in which the *B'nāth Q'yāmā* and the cloistered nuns are described as standing in bitter exposure. (Smith, *Studies in Early Mysticism,* p. 44)

Thus there were thousands of Christian women ascetics and monastics along with and even before the Desert Fathers, but outside of rare places hardly a word is read of them—and they are never called Desert Mothers. In fact, the greatest recognition given them by their male contemporaries, and indeed by themselves—so low had the self-esteem of Christian women fallen—is that they had become "manly." One such "Desert Mother," Sara, once said to the male monks: "It is I who am the man and ye who are the women!" (Palladius, *Paradise of the Fathers* ii. 257).

1. The Greek Fathers

As mentioned above, the Christian fathers for the most part wrote either in Greek or Latin. The Greek fathers came from the eastern part of the Roman empire, while the Latin fathers came from the West. Quotations will be presented from six of the most outstanding Greek fathers from the second to the fifth century, providing a synoptic overview that is typical of the largely, though not exclusively, negative attitude toward women held by the Greek fathers—of course if Christian women de-sexed themselves and became "manly" they were treated as quasi equals (see Rosemary Ruether, "Misogynism and Virginal Feminism in the Fathers of the Church," in Ruether, *Religion and Sexism,* pp. 150–183).

§339. Clement of Alexandria (A.D. 150–215)

Clement of Alexandria was probably born in Athens, but after having studied philosophy and Christianity, he became a Christian and eventually became the head of the Catechetical School of Alexandria, Egypt. In general, Clement had a rather balanced and positive attitude toward life in a period that was marked by extremes, of which the Egyptian gnostics and ascetics are examples. He seems to have allowed women into his lectures and spoke occasionally of their equality of nature and capacity for wisdom (*Stromateis* 4, 8 and 9). But much oftener he treated women far more restrictively than men, which treatment is typified by his paean of praise for that symbol of manliness, the beard: man is strong, active, uncastrated, mature; woman is weak, passive, castrated, immature:

> His beard, then, is the badge of a man and shows him unmistakably to be a man. It is older than Eve and is the symbol of the stronger nature. By God's decree, hairiness is one of man's conspicuous qualities, and, at that, is distributed over his whole body. Whatever smoothness or softness there was in him God took from him when he fashioned the delicate Eve from his side to be the receptacle of his seed, his helpmate both in procreation and in the management of the home. What was left (remember, he had lost all traces of hairlessness) was manhood and reveals that manhood. His characteristic is action; hers, passivity. For what is hairy is by nature drier and warmer than what is bare; therefore, the male is hairier and more warm-blooded than the female; the uncastrated, than the castrated; the mature, than the immature. Thus it is a sacrilege to trifle with the symbol of manhood [the beard]. (Clement of Alexandria, *Paedagogus* 3.3)

§340. Origen (A.D. 185–254)

Origen, raised as a Christian in Alexandria, was a brilliant student of Clement of Alexandria and became his successor as head of the Catechetical School. Origen was an extraordinary intellectual who was also endowed with a certain impetuosity; at one point he was prevented from seeking martyrdom only by his mother's hiding of his clothes; at another point, in a literal application of Mt 19:12 ("There are eunuchs who have made themselves that way for the sake of the reign of heaven. Let anyone accept this who can"), he castrated himself. Not unexpectedly his attitude toward women is rather negative. Woman is antithetic to the divine, she is fleshly:

> What is seen with the eyes of the creator is masculine, and not feminine, for God does not stoop to look upon what is feminine and of the flesh. (Origen, *Selecta in Exodus* XVIII.17, Migne, *Patrologia Graeca*, Vol. 12, cols. 296f.)

> It is not proper to a woman to speak in church, however admirable or holy what she says may be, merely because it comes from female lips. (Origen, quoted in Tavard, *Woman in Christian Tradition*, p. 68)

§341. Dionysius the Great (A.D. 190–264)

Dionysius of Alexandria was Origen's successor as head of the Catechetical School of Alexandria and became bishop of Alexandria in A.D. 247. Holding to the Hebraic laws of ritual impurity (see §103) which Jesus rejected (see §131), Dionysius forbade Christian women from entering a church during their menstruation, implying of course a spiritual as well as a bodily impurity; naturally such women were cut off from receiving communion—they were literally excommunicated:

The one who is not entirely pure in soul and body must be stopped from entering the Holy of Holies. (Dionysius of Alexandria, Canonical Epistle, ch. 2, Migne, *Patrologia Graeca*, Vol. 10, col. 1282)

§342. Epiphanius (A.D. 315–403)

Epiphanius was a native of Palestine who became the bishop of Cyprus and later of Salamis. He was a very vigorous advocate of monasticism and of orthodoxy as he understood it, and was quick to believe evil of others. Thus he attacked one group he accused of according to Mary, Jesus' mother, divine honor (see above, p. 28, concerning the echo of Goddess worship in Mariology) and, assuming that women were responsible for that action, revealed clearly his male supremacist attitude:

For the female sex is easily seduced, weak, and without much understanding. The devil seeks to vomit out this disorder through women. . . . We wish to apply masculine reasoning and destroy the folly of these women. (Epiphanius, Adversus Collyridianos, Migne, *Patrologia Graeca*, Vol. 42, cols. 740f.)

§343. John Chrysostom (A.D. 347–407)

John Chrysostom was such an extraordinary preacher (especially in Antioch) that he was called "golden mouthed," *chrysostomos.* He was made Patriarch of Constantinople in A.D. 398. Despite his unusually deep and tender relationship late in his life with the deaconess Olympia, he often expressed an extremely low opinion of marriage and women in general. In writing to a monk who was thinking about the possibility of marriage, Chrysostom used rather savage language, indicating that he thought women, especially beautiful ones, were, if not evil, "at least" filthy:

Should you reflect about what is contained in beautiful eyes, in a straight nose, in a mouth, in cheeks, you will see that bodily beauty is only a whitewashed tombstone, for inside it is full of filth. (John Chrysostom, Letter to Theodora, Ch. 14, *Sources chrétiennes,* Vol. 117, p. 167)

After denigrating marriage as good only to keep men from "becoming members of a prostitute" (On Virginity, Ch. 25, *Sources chré-*

tiennes, Vol. 125, p. 175), Chrysostom violently attacked remarriage after widowhood. His language indicated a male supremacist, ownership attitude toward women that in the golden mouth of a sainted Patriarch of Constantinople is rather breathtaking:

> We are thus made, we men: through jealousy, vainglory or whatnot, we like above all what nobody has owned and used before us and of which we are the first and only master. (John Chrysostom, On the One Marriage, *Sources chrétiennes,* Vol. 138, p. 191)

Chrysostom did not see women as completely useless in marriage outside of satisfying male libido. Women had their function, but it was no more than that of a supportive servant, enabling the man to do active, creative things. The tone of paternalism and condescension is almost overpowering:

> Since private affairs are part of the human condition, as well as public ones, God has doled them out: all that takes place outside, he has trusted to man, all that is within the house, to woman. . . . This is an aspect of the divine providence and wisdom, that the one who can conduct great affairs is inadequate or inept in small things, so that the function of woman becomes necessary. For if he had made man able to fulfill the two functions, the feminine sex would have been contemptible. And if he had entrusted the important questions to woman, he would have filled women with mad pride. So, he gave the two functions, neither to the one, to avoid humiliating the other as being useless, nor to both in equal part, lest the two sexes, placed on the same level, should compete and fight, women refusing authority to men. (John Chrysostom, On the One Marriage, *Sources chrétiennes,* Vol. 138, p. 183; Homily *Quales ducendae sint uxores,* in *Opera,* Vol. 3, pp. 260f.)

§344. Cyril of Alexandria (A.D. 376–444)

Cyril, bishop of Alexandria, was a very clear, precise, orthodox dogmatic theologian, but at the same time a violent, self-righteous, unscrupulous protagonist of his own views. He militarily attacked the Jews of Alexandria, driving thousands of them from their synagogues and homes. As might be expected from a hostile ideologue, he also held a very low estimate of women. In a country with a long tradition of literate women (see pp. 14f.) he nevertheless held that women were uneducated and not able to understand difficult matters easily (Migne, *Patrologia Graeca,* Vol. 74, col. 692). In explaining why Mary Magdalene did not immediately recognize Jesus after his resurrection (Jn 20:14), Cyril put down women in general:

> Somehow the woman [Mary Magdalene], or rather, the female sex as a whole, is slow in comprehension. (Cyril of Alexandria, Migne, *Patrologia Graeca,* Vol. 74, col. 689)

In a way, this attitude is especially puzzling, since, when Cyril became bishop at Alexandria, the most celebrated non-Christian mathematician and philosopher of the Neoplatonic school in Alexandria was a woman, Hypatia. But in a neurotic sort of way the two elements fit together, for Hypatia, known for her "great eloquence, rare modesty, and beauty," attracted many students and naturally opposed much of what the authoritarian, violent Cyril stood for. Her existence as a proof of the falsity of Cyril's image of woman's uncomprehending nature was swiftly cut off by Christian monks who dragged her from her chariot into a Christian church, stripped her naked, cut her throat, and burned her piecemeal; Cyril was deeply complicit, indirectly if not directly (Socrates, *Historia ecclesiastica*, Vol. 7, 15).

2. THE LATIN FATHERS

Farther to the west in the Roman empire the predominant language was Latin. Hence the early Christian writers there are referred to as Latin fathers. The attitude toward women follows the same pattern as among the Greek fathers, namely, quite negative, although not totally so. For example, if a woman "gave up" her sex by remaining a virgin or a widow and embraced an ascetical life, Jerome had strong praise for her:

> As long as woman is for birth and children, she is different from man as body from soul. But when she wishes to serve Christ more than the world, then she will cease to be a woman and will be called man *(vir)*. (Jerome, *Comm. in epist. ad Ephes.* III.5, Migne, *Patrologia Latina*, Vol. 26, col. 567)

Again, only a selection of typical quotations of the negative attitude of several of the important Latin fathers, including the four "Doctors of the Church" par excellence (Ambrose, Jerome, Augustine, Gregory the Great), from the second through the sixth century will be presented here.

§345. Tertullian (A.D. 160–225)

Tertullian lived in Carthage, in North Africa, was a prolific, vigorous, even polemical writer who had such a pervasive influence that he has been called the father of Latin Theology. His polemical approach in thought as well as style led him into an extreme anti-Judaism in theology and such a rigorism in morality that he eventually left the Catholic Church and joined the rigorist Montanist movement. His polemicism and moral rigorism also found expression in extremely anti-woman treatises and statements in which he tended to see "materialism" as the basic evil in the world, sex as the most central dimension of that basically evil "matter," and woman as the personification of fundamentally evil sex. Men of course were innocent victims of the wiles of women.

The following quotation from Tertullian's Catholic period, like the deutero-Pauline first letter to Timothy and the Jewish pseudepigraphical and rabbinical writings, blamed woman for bringing sin and death into the world, and adds to that guilt the responsibility for the death of the Son of God! He writes to Christian woman that surely she would not wear cheerful clothes, but rather, somber ones,

walking about as Eve mourning and repentant, in order that by every garb of penitence she might the more fully expiate that which she derives from Eve—the ignominy, I mean, of the first sin, and the odium (attaching to her as the cause) of human perdition. "In pains and anxieties dost thou bear (children), woman; and toward thine husband (is) thy inclination, and he lords it over thee." And do you not know that you are (each) an Eve? The sentence of God on this sex of yours lives in this age: the guilt must of necessity live too. You are the devil's gateway; you are the unsealer of that (forbidden) tree: you are the first deserter of the divine law: you are she who persuaded him whom the devil was not valiant enough to attack. You destroyed so easily God's image, man. On account of your desert—that is, death —even the Son of God had to die. (Tertullian, *De cultu feminarum* 1.1, *The Fathers of the Church,* Vol. 40, pp. 117f.)

§346. Ambrose (A.D. 339–397)

Ambrose, "Doctor of the Church," was chosen by the Catholic laity of Milan to be their bishop even though he was not yet baptized. His many accomplishments include playing a major role in the conversion of Augustine to Christianity. His attitude toward women clearly was that they were inferior to men:

Whoever does not believe is a woman, and she is still addressed with her physical sexual designation; for the woman who believes is elevated to male completeness and to a measure of the stature of the fullness of Christ; then she no longer bears the worldly name of her physical sex, and is free from the frivolity of youth and the talkativeness of old age. (Ambrose, *Expositio evangelii secondum Lucam,* liber X, n161, Migne, *Patrologia Latina,* Vol. 15, col. 1844)

§347. Ambrosiaster

Commentaries on the thirteen Pauline epistles were attributed to Ambrose until the time of Erasmus in the sixteenth century, who recognized them as spurious and therefore named their unknown author Ambrosiaster. In these commentaries the same Ambrosian attitude toward women—that they are inferior to men—is expressed. In commenting on 1 Corinthians 11, Ambrosiaster wrote:

Although man and woman are of the same essence, nevertheless the man, because he is the head of the woman, should be given priority, for he is greater because of his causal nature and his reason, not because of his essence. Thus the woman is inferior to man, for she is part of him, because the man is the origin of woman; from that and on account of that the woman is subject to the man, in that she is under his command. . . . The man is created in the image of God, but not the woman. . . . Because sin began with her, she must wear this sign [the veil]. (Ambrosiaster, Migne, *Patrologia Latina*, Vol. 17, col. 253)

§348. Jerome (A.D. 342–420)

Jerome, born in Aquileia in northeastern Italy, studied in Rome, embraced an ascetical life, and spent much of his life in the Holy Land. He became a giant of a scholar in Sacred Scripture. He had a number of women disciples, but they all had to adopt a life of extreme asceticism, so as to "become a man *(vir).*"

Jerome obviously had grave difficulties with his own sexuality; in the midst of the most extreme ascetic life in the desert Jerome was filled with wild sexual fantasies:

Although in my fear of hell I had consigned myself to this prison where I had no companions but scorpions and wild beasts, I often found myself amid bevies of girls. My face was pale and my frame chilled with fasting, yet my mind was burning with desire and the fires of lust kept bubbling up before me when my flesh was as good as dead. (Jerome, Epistle 22.7)

At times he gratuitously projected debaucheries on women whom he did not even know and about whom he had no information, as, for example, in his letter to a Christian ascetic woman in Gaul in which he describes in lurid detail her imagined behavior, such as her mincing gait, pretended ascetic dress, carefully ripped to display the white flesh beneath, her shawl which she allows to slip and quickly replaces to reveal her curving neck (Jerome, Epistle 117). Professor Rosemary Ruether remarks on this letter:

All this is pure fantasy, since Jerome has never met the woman. Descriptions such as these, which fill Jerome's letters, leave the reader with a dilemma as to how to understand such ascetic enthusiasm that compels such remarkable pruriency toward women, known and unknown alike. This most probably should be taken as the by-product of violent libidinal repression that generates its own opposite in vivid sensual fantasizing under the guise of

antisensual polemics. In this his views and psychology do not differ essentially
from those of the other Church Fathers, although he was more skilled than
most in rhetorical expression. (Ruether, *Religion and Sexism,* p. 172)

Most Christian fathers thought of marriage as having two ends,
namely, to produce Christian offspring and to "allay concupiscence,"
so as to avoid fornication. Under the influence of a pervasive dualism
which thought of spirit alone as good and of matter as evil, all sense
pleasure, especially that most intense one, the sexual, was thought of
as evil at least to some degree. Hence, the second end of marriage,
the satisfaction of the sexual appetite, was only a concession to
human weakness—really not a good, but a necessary evil. In the
context of such a discussion Jerome draws the logical conclusion of
this position and in the process reveals again his fear and hatred of
women:

If it is good not to touch a woman, then it is bad to touch a woman always
and in every case. (Jerome, Epistle 48.14)

Although Jerome encouraged women to embrace the Christian
"religious" life, that is, the ascetic life, he in no way allowed them
to take any leadership roles in religion, or anywhere else, for that
matter. Following the "Pauline" stance, Jerome insisted that "it is
against the order of nature or law for women to speak in an assembly
of men" (Migne, *Patrologia Latina,* Vol. 30, col. 732). But in another
place he became much more vicious in his misogynistic hatred of
women who would play a leading role in religion:

What do these wretched sin-laden hussies want! . . . Simon Magus
founded a heretical sect with the support of the harlot Helena. Nicholas of
Antioch, the contriver of everything filthy, directed women's groups. Marcion sent on to Rome before him a woman to infatuate the people for him.
Apelles had Philomena as companion for his teaching. Montanus, the pro-
claimer of the spirit of impurity, first used Prisca and Maximilla, noble and
rich women, to seduce many communities by gold, and then disgraced them
with heresy. . . . Even now the mystery of sin takes effect. The two-timing
sex trips everyone up. (Jerome, Migne, *Patrologia Latina,* Vol. 22, cols.
1152f.)

§349. Augustine (A.D. 354–430)

Augustine was without question the greatest of the Latin fathers
and the most influential of the Doctors of the Church. He was born
in North Africa, eventually became a Christian and the bishop of
Hippo in North Africa. Before his conversion to Christianity, Augustine became a devotee of Manicheism, an explicitly dualistic philoso-

phy-religion, which greatly stressed the essential evil of matter, which notion Augustine largely carried over with him into Christianity, and, through his massive influence, into the rest of Western Christianity.

Augustine also had severe difficulties with his sexuality, which is reflected in his Christian writings about sex and about women. Augustine took a common-law wife, to whom he remained faithful for fifteen years and whom he obviously loved deeply. At his mother's insistence he drove away his common-law wife (whose name, tellingly, we never learn), though she also loved him intensely, so Augustine could take a legal wife with a more suitable social background; instead, he took another mistress, probably in some kind of quasi-covert revenge against his mother, Monica, with whom he had a love-hate relationship, and who played a dominant, even domineering, role in his life.

The basic dualism that Augustine had absorbed from his years as a Manichee turns up in his problem of what to do with his sexuality. When teetering on the edge of embracing Christianity, Augustine was plagued by what appeared to him as an obvious either-or choice: either choose Christ or choose sexual satisfaction. For Augustine the two were mutually exclusive; sexual desire was a disorder engendered by sin (see Tavard, *Woman in Christian Tradition,* p. 115):

> I feel that nothing so casts down the manly mind from its height as the fondling of woman and those bodily contacts which belong to the married state. (Augustine, *Soliloquies* 1.10)

Against this background it is not surprising to find Augustine going far beyond Paul (1 Cor 11:2–12—see §332) and directly contradicting Gen 1:27 (see §68) in saying that woman is not made in the image of God, only man is!

> How then did the apostle tell us the man is the image of God and therefore he is forbidden to cover his head, but that the woman is not so, and therefore she is commanded to cover hers? Unless according to that which I have said already, when I was treating of the nature of the human mind, that the woman, together with her own husband, is the image of God, so that the whole substance may be one image, but when she is referred to separately in her quality as a helpmeet, which regards the woman alone, then she is not the image of God, but, as regards the man alone, he is the image of God as fully and completely as when the woman too is joined with him in one. (Augustine, *De Trinitate,* 7.7, 10)

Augustine's dualism, his fixation on sex, and his consequent abhorrence of women find expression in the following:

A good Christian is found in one and the same woman: to love the creature of God *(quod homo est)* whom he desires to be transformed and renewed, but to hate in her the corruptible and mortal conjugal connection, sexual intercourse, and all that pertains to her as a wife *(quod uxor est).* (Augustine, *De sermone Domini in Monte* 1.15, Migne, *Patrologia Latina,* Vol. 34, col. 1250)

In another place Augustine likens men to the superior portion of the soul and women to the inferior—on what grounds we are not told; it is simply assumed to be obviously true—with the consequence that a woman leader is said to be a perversion of nature:

Just as the spirit *(mens interior),* like the masculine understanding, holds subject the appetites of the soul through which we command the members of the body, and justly imposes moderation on its helper, in the same way the man must guide the woman and not let her rule over the man; where that indeed happens, the household is miserable and perverse. (Augustine, Migne, *Patrologia Latina,* Vol. 34, col. 205)

Elsewhere Augustine makes the same point about women necessarily being followers and subordinate to men, but in so doing likens women now not even to the inferior part of the soul but to flesh, that epitome of dualistic evil:

Flesh stands for woman, because she was made out of a rib. . . . The apostle has said: Who loves his woman loves himself; for no one hates his own flesh. Flesh thus stands for the wife, as sometimes also spirit for the husband. Why? Because the latter rules, the former is ruled; the latter should govern, the former serve. For where the flesh governs and the spirit serves, the house is upside down. What is worse than a house where the woman has governance over the man? But that house is proper where the man commands, the woman obeys. So also is that person rightly ordered where the spirit governs and flesh serves. (Augustine, Migne, *Patrologia Latina,* Vol. 35, col. 1395)

§350. (Pseudo)Augustine and Canon Law

Just as Ambrose's negative writings on women fostered the attribution to him of the additional writings negative toward women which were written by a writer Erasmus named Ambrosiaster, so also were other writings negative toward women incorrectly attributed to Augustine. This Pseudo-Augustine we now know is the same person as Ambrosiaster. The reason for reproducing a Pseudo-Augustine quotation here is not to exemplify this historical curiosity, but rather because it typifies the massive influence these anti-woman writings of Augustine, authentic or pseudonymous, had not only on all subsequent theology but also on church law (for a thorough analysis of the whole problematic, see Ida Raming, *The Exclusion of Women from the Priesthood;* Scarecrow Press, 1976). Thus, the following statement attributed, incorrectly, to Augustine was used by Gratian in his twelfth-century collection of church law, which became so fundamental for subsequent canon law. Partly because of it and Augustine's authority, women were severely restricted:

> Woman certainly stands under the lordship of man and possesses no authority; she can neither teach nor be a witness, neither take an oath nor be the judge. [(Pseudo)Augustine, Migne, *Patrologia Latina*, Vol. 35, col. 2244]
>
> [For Gratian, see *Corpus Iuris Canonici* c. 14, C 33, q 5; ed. by A. Friedberg, 2 vols., Leipzig, 1879–1881; repr. Graz, 1955, Vol. 1, p. 1254.]

§351. Gregory the Great (A.D. 540–604)

Gregory was an upper-class Roman who sold his property, gave the proceeds to the poor, and became a Benedictine monk. In 590 he was made pope, and because of his extraordinary administrative abilities he laid the foundation for the medieval papacy. He was also a prolific writer, receiving in posterity the title of the fourth Latin Doctor of the Church. His religious writings were nonspeculative in nature, being given over mostly to moral lessons and allegorical interpretations of the Scriptures. His attitude toward women basically continued that negative pattern which was largely established by the Christian fathers before him. One example will suffice to exhibit the continuation of that anti-woman pattern. In commenting on Job 14:1, where it is written, "Man born of woman is short of life and full of woe," Gregory finds misogynist meanings that most would not have suspected were intended by the writer of Job:

> In Holy Scripture [the word] "woman" stands either for the female sex (Gal 4:4) or for weakness, as it is said: A man's spite is preferable to a woman's kindness (Sir 42:14). For every man is called strong and clear of thought, but woman is looked upon as a weak or muddled spirit. . . . What then is designated in this passage by the word "woman" but weakness, when it says: Man born of woman? Just as when it is said even more clearly: What measure of strength can he bear in himself who is born from weakness? (Gregory, Migne, *Patrologia Latina*, Vol. 75, cols. 982f.)

XI. Summary:
Woman in Christian Tradition

In summarizing the Christian section of this book, it should first of all be noted that Jesus was not a Christian—he was a Jew, indeed an observant, Torah-true Jew, a rabbi (see Hans Küng and Pinchas Lapide, "Is Jesus a Bond or Barrier? A Jewish-Christian Dialogue," *Journal of Ecumenical Studies,* Vol. 14, 1977, pp. 466-483). Jesus stood very much in the Jewish, Pharisaic, Rabbinic tradition of his day (see Robert Aron, *The Jewish Jesus,* Orbis Books, 1971, and Eugene Fisher, *Faith Without Prejudice,* Paulist Press, 1977). But in matters of attitude toward women Jesus was very different from his peers. He took an egalitarian, feminist position on women. He was not a social activist organizer like Saul Alinsky; he was not like Betty Friedan, the founder of the National Organization for Women. Jesus was much more personalist in his approach. It was his disciples who came after him who developed the organization, the *ecclesia,* the church. Hence, it is personal attitudes and actions that can be looked for in Jesus, regarding the place of women, as well as all other human issues of import—not organized actions and systematic social implementation of principles. This latter came, to the extent it came, later, with the church, with Christianity.

It was carefully noted that it is very difficult to discern precisely what in the Gospels is to be attributed to Jesus and what to the first believing communities or the evangelists, who are our only sources of information about Jesus. Nevertheless, it was also pointed out that the extraordinarily positive attitude toward women (especially in the Palestinian Jewish context of that time) depicted in the Gospels as that of Jesus ultimately must indeed be attributable to him, though the form, exact wording, etc., of many of the specific statements attributed to Jesus doubtless were reshaped by the evangelists and

352

their sources. The fact that the Gospels—whether written by Jews (probably Mark, Matthew, and John) or a Greek (Luke), whether for a Greco-Roman audience (Mark) or a Jewish one (Matthew)—all depict Jesus as egalitarian toward women argues that this feminism was not dictated by either a Greek or a Jewish author or audience. The fact that Matthew's Gospel, the most Jewish of all the Gospels, was quantitatively much more positive toward women than Mark's (in many ways the least Jewish of the Gospels) and almost as much so as Luke's Gospel (probably the only one written by a Greek) eliminates the possibility that the Gospel feminism was projected onto Jesus either by a Greek (Luke) influenced by the feminist movement in the contemporary Hellenist world or by an evangelist (Mark) writing to impress favorably a Gentile audience. If either of those assumptions were true, then the Jewish Matthew and his Jewish audience, and indeed his Jewish sources, should never have produced the feminist image of Jesus they in fact did produce. Further, the fact that most of the strongest pro-woman sections of Luke's Gospel are found in the "most Jewish" section of his Gospel reinforces that argument. In the end, the strongly pro-woman, feminist image of Jesus projected in the Gospels must find its source in Jesus. And in this matter Jesus profoundly differed from his peers—another, technically persuasive argument that Jesus and not the community was the source of that attitude and action.

The positive attitude of Jesus toward women clearly affected the early followers of Jesus, though patriarchal social structures by no means immediately all fell away. Nevertheless, women did play leading roles in the earliest Christian communities, from Lydia the first European convert, to the various women evangelists, deacons, and rulers, to the apostle Junia.

Paul, who never met Jesus, had an ambivalent attitude toward women, partly positive and partly on the borderline between positive and negative. The deutero-Pauline materials and the other later New Testament writings became progressively more negative toward women, veering toward the misogynist. The woman deacon *(diakonos)* of Paul's day became the deaconess *(diakonissa)* of the fourth-century Apostolic Constitutions, a holy order lesser in status than that of the male deacon. As Christianity moved into the age of the fathers the status of Christian women became ever more restricted. The fathers took a uniformly male superior attitude that often was misogynist. The trend continued into the Middle Ages and up to the most recent times.

What is puzzling here is that, although a strong anti-Jewish and pro-Greek trend quickly developed in Christianity as it spread throughout the Gentile world, unfortunately leading to a rejection of much of Jesus' and Christianity's Jewish heritage, on the subject of women it was the Hellenistic stance which was rejected. Why, with such a clear difference in attitude expressed by Jesus and by some of the Pauline writings, did Christianity's choice go not to Jesus but to the negative Pauline and deutero-Pauline writings? Apparently the rigid patriarchal system, which Jesus did his best to dismantle (cf. Mt 10:37–39; Lk 14:26), was so pervasive in the lives of the majority of Christians that they were blind to this choice; they automatically gravitated toward the most restrictive, subordinationist passages of the New Testament. Christianity early became so intent on identifying itself by differentiating itself from the world around it that it often vigorously rejected the pagan world—or at least part of it—and that pagan world included a relatively high status for women.

One additional partial answer to this puzzle is suggested by Johannes Leipoldt, *Die Frau in der antiken Welt und im Urchristentum,* p. 127: after the destruction of Jerusalem in A.D. 70 many Hellenistic Jews became Christian because they felt repelled by the intensified observation of the rabbinic prescriptions that developed in the attempt to preserve Jewish identity. These Hellenistic Jews, being used to a less rigorous observance, found in Christianity an environment which was familiar and receptive. They of course brought with them the strongly subordinating attitudes toward women that were then prevalent in Judaism, even Hellenistic Judaism.

Whether or not, or to whatever degree, that may be true, the receding *eschaton,* the "final days," imminently awaited by Paul and the other early Christians doubtless played a major role in the early decline in the status of women in Christianity. As long as the *parousia,* the Second Coming of Christ, was expected at any moment, the need to develop organized structures in the community of believers was felt very little. But as that expectation faded, the need for structured patterns of community life was increasingly sensed. In an almost inevitable development these "second generation" Christians naturally turned to the structures of the societies in which they lived for models to apply to the newly forming church structures. In the Greco-Roman society of the Roman empire, despite the advances women made in family life, economics, law, etc., women were almost entirely excluded from political life. Hence, in following this Greco-

Roman model (e.g., "diocese" and "parish" are originally Roman civil administrative terms) the church set up authority structures that almost entirely excluded women.

To this was added the pervasive Greek notion of dualism (matter and spirit, the former evil, the latter good, personified by woman and man, respectively) and its offshoot, asceticism. Of course dualism was not exclusively Greek (e.g., Persian Zoroastrianism, Manicheism), nor was asceticism (e.g., Essenes, Therapeutae), but they became extremely and increasingly widespread throughout the Roman empire. Paradoxically these aspects of pagan society, far from being rejected by the newly forming church, were embraced by it—again putting women at a serious disadvantage vis-à-vis men.

Thus, three attitudes characteristic of Jesus: (1) a service rather than authority orientation; (2) a full-life affirming stance (eating, wine-drinking, wedding-celebrating, etc.); and (3) an egalitarian perception of women, were all significantly reversed by the early Christian church.

Furthermore, a restrictive attitude toward women was also fostered in Christianity by the fact that early Christians in the Greco-Roman world faced the worship of the Goddess in strong resurgence, from the worship of the Phrygian Mater Magna or Kybele throughout Asia Minor and even in Rome, to the cult of Isis and her veneration under many other names—Demeter, Athena, Venus, Ceres, Ma Bellona, etc. The worship of Mater Magna or Kybele in Asia Minor was not only extremely influential but also often included ecstatic passion, self-mutilation, even self-castration by male devotees so as to attain complete identity with the Goddess (see James, *Cult of the Mother Goddess*, pp. 21f.). Although in fact the most pervasive Goddess worship at the beginning of the Christian era, the Isis cult, did not promote sexual excesses of promiscuity (see Sharon K. Heyon, *The Cult of Isis Among Women in the Graeco-Roman World*, pp. 111ff.; Leiden: E. J. Brill, 1975), it was widely rumored to do so, and thus the effect of seeing women priests of Isis on the early Christians was just as negative as if it were true. Edwin O. James notes that "her cultus was the most effective rival to Christianity from the second century onwards, and during the temporary revival of classical paganism in Rome in A.D. 394, it was her festival that was celebrated with great magnificence" (James, *Cult of the Mother Goddess*, p. 180). He further notes that "the unprecedented victory of the cultus [the cult of Isis] over official opposition and its persistence during the first three centuries of the Christian era are a testimony to the deep and genuine religious emotion aroused in the initiates by the ritual" (ibid., p. 177). In fact, her public worship was brought to an end only by Emperor Justinian in A.D. 560.

Thus the in-group/out-group mechanism that was at work within Judaism, intensifying its restrictions of Jewish women, also was at work in the early centuries of Christianity with a similar result. With Christian history, however, there is a special irony in that by turning toward the subordination of women Christianity turned away from its Jewish founder Jesus and his feminist attitude.*

*As this book was in press there appeared *Women of Spirit: Female Leadership in the Jewish and Christian Traditions,* ed. by Rosemary Ruether and Eleanor McLaughlin (Simon & Schuster, 1979). Although too late to make use of here, the two chapters, "Word, Spirit and Power: Women in Early Christian Communities," by Elizabeth Schüssler Fiorenza, and "Mothers of the Church: Ascetic Women in the Late Patristic Age," by Rosemary Ruether, both corroborate and supplement the corresponding sections above, especially pp. 289ff.

Structural Index

B. DIVINE LADY WISDOM

C. THE FEMININE DIVINE SPIRIT

II. FEMININE IMAGERY OF GOD—POSTBIBLICAL
    PERIOD

A. JEWISH FEMININE IMAGERY OF THE DIVINE

III. SUMMARY: FEMININE IMAGERY OF GOD

§67 Feminine and Masculine Divine Personifications
    Co-Identified

PART TWO: WOMAN IN HEBREW-JEWISH TRADITION

IV. POSITIVE ELEMENTS IN HEBREW-JEWISH
    TRADITION

A. THE STATUS OF WOMAN—BIBLICAL PERIOD

1. THE FIRST WOMAN AND MAN

§68 God Created Humanity: Genesis 1
§69 God Created Humanity: Genesis 2
§70 Ishshah and Ish — I
§71 Ishshah and Ish — II
§72 Humanity and the Fall
§73 Woman and Man After the Fall
§74 The Shifting Meanings of *ha adam*
§75 Eve the Seducer
§76 Female Superiority
§77 Mutuality Repeated: Genesis 5

2. HEBREW WOMEN LEADERS

§78 Women Prophets
        a. Daughters Prophesy
        b. Miriam the Prophet
        c. Deborah, Prophet and Judge
        d. Huldah the Prophet
        e. Huldah the Founder of Biblical Studies
        f. Noadiah a False Woman Prophet
§79 The Wise Women of Tekoa and Abel
§80 Hebrew Queens

3. BIBLICAL LOVE POETRY BY WOMEN

B. THE STATUS OF WOMAN—POSTBIBLICAL PERIOD

1. JEWISH WOMEN OF ELEPHANTINE

§81 No Polygyny
§82 Hebrew Women Divorce Their Husbands
§83 Jewish Women of Elephantine Receive and Exchange Property
§84 Women: Taxes and Military Service

2. POSITIVE MODELS OF WOMEN IN RABBINIC JUDAISM

§85 Beruria the Unordained Rabbi
§86 The Anonymous Maidservant of Rabbi Judah the Prince

V. AMBIVALENT ELEMENTS IN HEBREW-JEWISH TRADITION

A. AMBIVALENT MODELS OF WOMEN— HEBREW BIBLE AND APOCRYPHA

§87 Jael the Deadly Hostess
§88 Judith, a Femme Fatale
§89 Esther the Beauty Queen
§90 Ruth: Subservient to Men, but Loyal to a Woman
§91 Good Wives and Mothers
§92 Bad Wives
§93 Misogynism
§94 Great Women Behind Great Men

B. AMBIVALENT MODELS OF WOMEN— POSTBIBLICAL WRITINGS

§95 Therapeutae: Jewish Women and Men Contemplatives
§96 Ambivalent Rabbinic Attitudes Toward Women

VI. NEGATIVE IMAGES OF AND ATTITUDES TOWARD WOMEN IN HEBREW-JEWISH TRADITION

A. NEGATIVE IMAGES AND ATTITUDES— HEBREW BIBLE

§182 Women in Jesus' Passion and Resurrection
   a. Women at the Foot of the Cross
   b. Women First Witnesses to the Empty Tomb
   c. Women Testify to Male Disciples About Jesus' Resurrection
   d. The Risen Jesus Appears to Women
§183 Conclusion

b. The Gospel According to Mark

§184 Jesus' First Cures: Men and Women
   a. Jesus Teaches in Capernaum and Cures a Demoniac
   b. Cure of Simon's Mother-in-law
§185 Jesus' Mother, Brothers, and Sisters
§186 Lamp on a Lampstand
§187 Jairus' Daughter and the Woman with a Flow of Blood
   a. The Gerasene Demoniac
   b. Cure of the Woman with a Hemorrhage. The Daughter of Jairus Raised to Life
§188 Jesus' Problems with His Family
§189 Herodias, Salome, John the Baptist
§190 Jesus Affirms Parents
§191 Jesus' Mission to Non-Jews Through a Woman
§192 Marriage and the Dignity of Women — I
§193 Jesus Dismantles Restrictive Family Bonds
§194 Marriage and the Dignity of Women — II
§195 The Oppression of Widows
§196 The Widow's Mite
§197 Jesus' Concern for Women's Welfare
§198 Anointment of Jesus at Bethany
§199 Women in Jesus' Passion and Resurrection
§200 Conclusion

c. The Gospel According to Matthew

(1) Passages Common to Matthew and Mark

§201 Women Included in the Reign of God
§202 Jairus' Daughter and the Woman with a Flow of Blood
§203 Jesus' Mother, Brothers, and Sisters

B. DEUTERO-PAULINE (AND OTHER) AMBIVALENT (AND SOME NEGATIVE) ATTITUDES TOWARD WOMEN

§333 Household Tables
    a. Ephesians 5:21–33
    b. Colossians 3:18 to 4:1
    c. Titus 2:3–9
    d. 1 Peter 3:1–7
§334 1 Timothy
§335 1 Corinthians 14:33b–35
§336 2 Timothy 1:5
§337 Revelation

X. NEGATIVE ELEMENTS IN CHRISTIAN TRADITION

A. WOMEN AND THE CHRISTIAN FATHERS

§338 Christian Mothers

1. THE GREEK FATHERS

§339 Clement of Alexandria (A.D. 150–215)
§340 Origen (A.D. 185–254)
§341 Dionysius the Great (A.D. 190–264)
§342 Epiphanius (A.D. 315–403)
§343 John Chrysostom (A.D. 347–407)
§344 Cyril of Alexandria (A.D. 376–444)

2. THE LATIN FATHERS

§345 Tertullian (A.D. 160–225)
§346 Ambrose (A.D. 339–397)
§347 Ambrosiaster
§348 Jerome (A.D. 342–420)
§349 Augustine (A.D. 354–430)
§350 (Pseudo)Augustine and Canon Law
§351 Gregory the Great (A.D. 540–604)

XI. SUMMARY: WOMAN IN CHRISTIAN TRADITION

Index of References